D1233642

AMERICANS FROM WALES

AMERICANS
FROM
WALES

By

E D W A R D   G E O R G E   H A R T M A N N, Ph. D.

Member of the Welsh Society of Philadelphia
and the St. David's Society
of the State of New York

THE CHRISTOPHER PUBLISHING HOUSE
BOSTON, U.S.A.

PRINTED IN
THE UNITED STATES OF AMERICA

To

My parents, Louis and Catherine Jones-Davis Hartmann,
My grandparents, Edward R. Jones *(Penhernwenfach)*
and Jane Davies *(Tynllwyn)*, and
My aunt, Miss Harriet Jones

TABLE OF CONTENTS

PREFACE

From the earliest days of colonial settlement, the United States has been the mecca for the people of many lands. They came to escape religious or political intolerance, sometimes for the love of adventure, most often with the hope of bettering themselves economically. English, Dutch, Swedes, French, Germans, Scotch-Irish, Negroes, and others came over during the colonial period to join the Indians already here. More of the same, plus South Irish and Scandinavians, came in the early and middle portions of the nineteenth century, as well as numbers of Chinese. Then, starting in the 1880's, came the greatest influx of all when the overcrowded and comparatively impoverished lands of southern and eastern Europe answered the growing industrial needs of America by furnishing her with a much needed labor supply. Italians, Poles, Slovaks, Lithuanians, Czechs, Magyars, Greeks, Syrians, and scores of others crossed the Atlantic, took their places alongside the descendants of their predecessors, and did their bit to make America the great country which it has become today.

Coming over from early colonial days, too, and continuing throughout the entire period was a trickle of immigrants of yet another ethnic group. Not so strong in numbers as any of the others, not so well-known because of association with powerful rulers or mighty empires, not chauvinistic over past wrongs or vengeance-minded over former illtreatment, they came over quietly, modestly, willing to accept what opportunities the new environment might have to offer. Yet they were rightfully proud of their own peculiar past and ever conscious of their own cultural achievements. These people were the Welsh, the old Keltic-speaking inhabitants of Wales, the rugged mountainous peninsula of western Britain. Once politically independent, fate and superior arms had forced them within the political jurisdiction of the British Empire. Yet despite conquest, occupation, political amalgamation, and the great pressure of Anglicization, they remained loyal to their own language and distinctive culture throughout the centuries, and when members of this group began to emigrate to America, they came as another distinctive European ethnic group to add to the heterogeneous make-up of the American people.

Much has been written about the coming and achievements of many

9

of the other ethnic groups, particularly those numerically strong. The story of most of the smaller groups, however, remains to be written. Their story—the establishment of their settlements, their trials and difficulties with a new environment, their achievements and contributions—must also be told if a true picture of the evolution and amalgamation of the American people is to be achieved. It is in the hope that this latter goal may be partially realized that the author has attempted to gather together what data he could find concerning the story of one such smaller group in America—the Welsh; and to narrate the very striking achievements of this ethnic group and their very solid contribution to and support of what we now generally recognize as the great "American heritage."

Studies of this sort in the past have been marred through bias and exaggeration. The author has attempted to avoid this by maintaining a standard of objectivity throughout the narrative. In all fairness, however, it should be noted that he is the son of a Welsh immigrant mother, and quite naturally takes pride in the achievements of the group about which he writes.

After some fifteen years of research, it is virtually impossible for the author to express adequately his great indebtedness to the many people who cooperated with him in the preparation of this book. He wishes to express his appreciation, in particular, to the librarians and staff of Weidner Library, Harvard University, without whose cooperation this book could not have been written; to Yale University Library for permission to examine the Blackwell collection of Welsh-Americana; to the Brigham Young University Library, Provo, Utah, for permission to examine the files of *The Druid;* to Charles A. Andrews of the Presbyterian Historical Society, Philadelphia, for data on the Calvinistic-Methodists; to Edwin C. Starr of the American Baptist Historical Society, Rochester, New York, for data on the Welsh Baptists; to the Congregational Library, Boston, Massachusetts, for data on the Welsh Congregationalists; and to Howard H. Williams of the Friends' Historical Library and Swarthmore College Library, Swarthmore, Pennsylvania, for data on the Welsh Friends or Quakers. He also wishes to thank David E. Nichols of Pittsburgh for permitting him to examine the minutes of the American Gorsedd; George Bundy, the long-time secretary of the National Gymanfa Ganu Association of the United States and Canada, for his many suggestions and stimulating support; John T. Richards and Thomas E. Rees of Philadelphia, Albert Foulkes of Bangor, Pennsylvania, Arthur M. Roberts, former editor of *Y Drych,* and Sam Ellis of Utica, New York, the Reverend R. J. Williams of Scranton, Pennsylvania, and the Honorable Arthur H. James of Wilkes-Barre, Pennsylvania, for their guidance in interpreting various aspects of Welsh-American culture; his brother, Louis J. Hartmann, for helping with the statistics; his brother-in-law and sister, Anthony and Kathryn Hartmann Germann, for their editorial help; and the many other Welsh-Americans (from virtually every Welsh-American settlement) for their kindness in answering his questionnaires and furnishing him data on the various churches and societies. Finally to John Hughson Jones, M.B.E., of New York City, and to my loyal family, who never lost faith that this book would be published eventually, the author wishes to express his appreciation.

St. David's Day
March 1, 1967

Edward George Hartmann
Professor of History
Suffolk University
Boston, Massachusetts

Americans From Wales

CHAPTER I

THEY CAME HERE FIRST?—THE STORY
OF THE WELSH INDIAN LEGEND

On January 13, 1804, an American President of Welsh ancestry, Thomas Jefferson, dispatched a letter to another Welsh-American, Meriwether Lewis, containing a map of the upper Missouri River valley. The map had been prepared by a third Welsh-American, one John Evans, an immigrant from Wales, who had explored the upper reaches of the Missouri some nine years earlier and had been one of the first white men to penetrate into that area. Jefferson, in his letter to Lewis, wrote that the map should prove helpful in the forthcoming Lewis and Clark expedition, in as much as it was considered to be very accurate and had been prepared under the auspices of the Spanish authorities then in control of the area. The map proved to be accurate and was unquestionably of aid to the two explorers and their expedition as they worked their way up the Missouri to its source.

How did it happen that an obscure Welsh immigrant, fresh from his homeland, should be exploring the upper waters of the Missouri towards the end of the eighteenth century and rendering thereby a valuable service to his more distinguished followers, Meriwether Lewis and William Clark? We have the answer thanks to the excellent research of Professor David Williams of the University of Wales. In his very interesting article in the *American Historical Review* Professor Williams relates the romantic story.[1]

It begins with one of the most fabulous and romantic legends that had grown up concerning the mysterious lands and inhabitants of the new world. It was in pursuit of this romantic legend and its relationship to his own people, the Welsh, that John Evans penetrated into the wilds of the northern Louisiana country only to fail in his quest and to die disappointed on the banks of the Mississippi. Evans was a member of a valiant little nation, Wales, which had begun to send emigrants to America from the earliest days of British settlement. They were to establish them-

13

selves in sizable colonies in sections of Massachusetts, Pennsylvania, Delaware, and South Carolina. Wales was to continue to send a total of some 100,000 more to the new Republic in the nineteenth and twentieth centuries. Evans' compatriots and their descendants were to play vital roles in the opening up and settlement of the great American West, in the development of the American coal, steel, and slate industries, in the development of business, labor, and the professions, and were to furnish an array of distinguished American leaders, in proportion to their numbers unexcelled by any other ethnic group in the United States. It seems only fitting that Evans and his search for what he hoped might prove to be the first settlers from his homeland in America should be the point of departure of any study of the Welsh element in America.

The romantic legend that motivated Evans' actions concerned the activities of a medieval Welsh prince by the name of Madoc ab Owain Gwynedd, presumably the son of the ruler of North Wales, who became tired of the constant warfare and petty quarreling then current in his homeland. He sailed with a body of followers out into the Atlantic around 1170 A.D. to find a more satisfactory environment. Prince Madoc, according to the legend, discovered a new land across the seas to the west which he found very satisfactory for settlement. He returned to Wales to spread the good news of his discovery and induced more Welshmen to accompany him on his return to the new land. Nothing more was ever heard of the Prince or his followers. Presumably they settled down in the new area and made it their home.[2]

The origins of the legend are obscured in the mist of the Welsh medieval past, but the legend was to reappear time and time again with interesting repercussions. It appears, for example, in the *Historie of Cambria* written by the noted Humphrey Lloyd, one of the leading geographers of Elizabethan times. Lloyd identified the land which Madoc had supposedly discovered as Florida, and pointed out that the Madoc discovery gave England a prior claim to America that preceded the discovery of Columbus by some three hundred and twenty-two years, an important point when both Spain and England were strengthening their respective claims to North America. Another Briton, David Ingram, a companion of Sir John Hawkins, the noted sea-dog, in apparent support of the Madoc legend, claimed that he had heard stories of Indians who used Welsh words. Still another Briton, Sir George Peckham, writing in support of Queen Elizabeth's legal claims to North America, repeated the legend of Madoc and quoted Ingram's tales. The legend also appeared in a new edition of Lloyd's work in 1584 and thereafter at various times in the seventeenth century with little if any modifications.[3]

The Madoc legend acquired its fabulous corollary towards the end of the seventeenth century thanks to the utterances of the Reverend

Morgan Jones, a Welsh Presbyterian minister, who served as the rector of the church of Newton, Long Island, around 1680. Jones signed a formal statement in 1686 which stated that some seventeen years previously, while serving as a missionary in the Carolinas, he had been captured by the hostile Tuscarora Indians. They were about to put him to death. Jones relapsed into his native Welsh tongue and began to pray aloud. To his amazement and relief, two visiting Indians from the Doeg tribe, who happened to be present, understood his prayer and interceded on his behalf. They arranged for Jones' ransom and then took him home to their own tribe. According to Morgan Jones, these people claimed to be descendants of white men who had come across the seas many moons before and had retained their love for the language of their ancestors. They were still familiar with Welsh, so much so, that Jones remained with them for some four months preaching to them in that tongue no less than three times per week![4]

Upon his release by the Doegs, Morgan Jones returned to the Atlantic coast and made his way northwards to Philadelphia and New York. He told the story of his adventures to a fellow Welshman, Thomas Lloyd, the noted Quaker leader of Philadelphia, and signed the above mentioned formal statement in regard to his experiences for the official record. Morgan Jones' account then became the basis for all subsequent theories concerning a mysterious Welsh-speaking Indian tribe, presumably the descendants of Madoc and his followers, and dwelling somewhere on the mainland of the North American continent.[5]

A stream of stories concerning "Welsh-speaking" Indians continued to crop up during the eighteenth century. One Stedman, a Welshman from Brecknockshire, was said to have landed in Carolina in 1570 and to have spoken to them in their native language. They were supposed to have told him that their ancestors had come from Gwenedd in "Great Britain" (although this title was not adopted nor widely used until after 1603!). Then there was the story of Binion, a Welshman, who saw them west of the Mississippi in 1750, while a Colonel George Cochran wrote to Governor Dinwiddie of Virginia in 1753 concerning three young French priests who had returned from an expedition among the Indians and had brought back some Welsh Bibles. One Captain Stewart saw Welsh-speaking Indians along the Red River in 1776; another saw them on the Ohio. Even General Morgan Lewis of Revolutionary War fame claimed that his father, Francis Lewis, a signer of the Declaration of Independence, when he had been taken prisoner by the French at Oswego was assigned to the care of Indians who spoke to Lewis in the Welsh language. Finally there was the story of Maurice Griffiths which paralleled the Morgan Jones story. Griffiths, who had left Wales at the age of sixteen and had gone to the Virginia frontier, was captured by a party of Shawnees somewhere around the headwaters of the Roanoke River in Virginia. He remained with them for five years, and then accompanied a party of five braves to explore the Missouri country. While there he was taken prisoner by hostile Indians and condemned to death. Griffiths overheard them speaking in "pure Welsh." Because he was able to converse with them in that tongue he and his companions were spared and released. These were just a few of the stories that became current in regard to the existence of a real tribe of "Welsh-speaking" Indians somewhere out in the western frontier region.[6]

It was the Morgan Jones story, however, that received the greatest publicity both in America and Great Britain and had the most noteworthy ramifications. It was written up by Theophilus Evans under the title "The Crown of England's Title to America Prior to that of Spain" and made its appearance in the *Gentleman's Magazine* in 1740 at a time when both countries were at war, and was read with great interest by patriotic Britishers. The article was later reprinted in Rovington's *New York Gazette* in 1770, in N. Owen's *British Remains* in 1777, and in George Burder's *The Welsh Indians* in 1797, as well as in later collections in the nineteenth century.[7]

The strange stories concerning the Welsh Indians in time aroused both the interest of the Protestant churches which were about to embark upon a new phase of missionary activity, as well as the literati then just beginning to feel the first stirrings of the great Romantic movement in literature. The churchmen felt that the Gospel should certainly be brought again to the descendants of once Christians; the literati, ever on the alert for the strange and the esoteric, saw in the legend a theme which might be pursued properly in the romantic vein. Whatever their origin, as Professor David Williams has pointed out, the stories "exercised a fascination on the minds of a generation brought up on tales of exploration in strange lands, while the growth of national sentiment, which was related to the same romantic movement in literature, led the Welsh, as it did other peoples, to take pride in the legendary glories of their past. It was to be expected that sooner or later someone would go in search of the Welsh Indians."[8]

The movement that led up to the sending of such a mission was started in 1791 when Dr. John Williams published his *Enquiry into the Truth of the Tradition Concerning the Discovery of America by Prince Madog ab Owen Gwenedd about the Year 1170*. It reviewed all the data on the subject and aroused great interest among the little group of Welshmen then resident in London.[9] They had founded a social and literary society called the Gweneddigion in 1771. The society proved quite a success and was at the height of its influence around 1791. It numbered among its members some of the leading Welsh intellectuals of the time including William Owen-Pughe, the Welsh lexicographer, David Samwell, former surgeon in the Royal Navy and a poet of note, Owen Jones, a prosperous furrier, who was the chief patron of the London group, and the fabulous Edward Williams, more familiarly known to Welshmen as "Iolo Morganwg," a poet of some literary reputation in both Welsh and English. The Gweneddigion was intensely liberal in its political and religious views, and championed the cause of freedom of speech, of equality of all men, and of freedom of religious belief. It is believed to have championed the cause of Morgan John Rhees, a noteworthy Welshman, who issued the first Welsh periodical and later emigrated to America. It was largely instrumental in re-establishing the Welsh Eisteddfod.[10]

The facts presented by Dr. Williams were accepted eagerly as accurate by the Society's members, especially when they seemed to be corroborated later the same year by a mysterious visitor to Britain—one William Bowles, supposedly a Cherokee chieftain. David Samwell and Owen-Pughe sought his opinion on two occasions and were assured by Bowles that the legend was correct. The latter claimed that he knew a Welshman who had escaped from Mexico and had actually passed through the territory occupied by the Welsh Indians. Bowles further identified the Indians with the Padoucas, a name which lexicographer Owen-Pughe felt to be a corruption of Madogwys, the people of Madoc. Accordingly, the two men reported back favorably to the Society and the movement was on to send a mission to find the Welsh Indians.[11]

The Society's members debated the issue thoroughly, looked over maps attempting to locate the area of the Padoucas, and then made plans to raise funds to send out the explorers. They felt encouraged to continue when correspondence with the learned Dr. Samuel Jones, Welsh pastor of the Pennepek Baptist Church in Pennsylvania, indicated that he was a firm believer in the legend. Iolo Morganwg became one of the stoutest defenders of the legend while Dr. Williams issued a supplement to his book in 1792 entitled, *Further Observations on the Discovery of America by Prince Madog ab Owen Gwenedd about the Year 1170.* Iolo became enthusiastic to head the mission himself.[12].

Interest in the Welsh Indians had also developed in Wales, the homeland of the Society's members. One William Jones of Llangadfan, a radical bard and follower of Voltaire, and a champion of the oppressed Welsh peasantry, went about the country speaking against the oppressive landlords and recommended emigration to America where settlement near the Welsh Indians might result in the possibilities of trade and better living conditions. He even sought the aid of Thomas Pinckney, American Minister to England, in this respect. Jones is known to have spoken at Llanrwst, a town near the home of John Evans, the future seeker of the

Welsh Indians. Evans heard the story of the legend and was stimulated to attempt to join the expedition. As early as May, 1792, his name appeared along with Iolo's for consideration by the Gweneddigion Society. [13]

In time, Iolo Morganwg, as well as certain other members of the Society, began to have doubts about the authenticity of the Indians with the result that the whole issue was debated anew with many indicating skepticism. David Samwell even wrote a satirical poem dealing with the comic albeit fierce arguments that arose among the members of the Gweneddigion over what he called "the Padouca Hunt."[14] Iolo withdrew from the venture, but not without receiving unkind taunts from his enemies which hinted at his lack of courage when the chips were down. John Evans, however, indicated his willingness to embark upon the mission, and in due time received the blessings of the Society, a sum of money to cover his expenses, and then departed for America sometime in September, 1792.[15]

John Thomas Evans, the seeker of the Welsh Indians, was born in the small villlage of Wawnfawr near Caernarvon, North Wales, in 1770. He was the son of a Calvinistic-Methodist lay preacher of great influence in the Caernarvon district. An older brother, Evan, was also a lay preacher. It follows that John was reared in a traditionally pious Welsh home. He received the usual education offered to a lad of his circumstances, and may have been taught by David Thomas, a poet of some note at the time. It is felt by some that Thomas may have been responsible for bringing the young man to the attention of the London Society as a possible companion to Iolo on the impending quest. Evans must have impressed the Society's members favorably otherwise they would not have backed his mission. [16]

John Evans eventually reached Baltimore on October 10, 1792. He set off at once to visit Dr. Samuel Jones at Pennepek and the other Welsh settlements of Pennsylvania. He received a warm welcome from his Welsh compatriots although Dr. Jones, by this time skeptical of the Indian legend, advised him against making the trip to the west. Evans, however, a youth of twenty-two, had abundant confidence in himself, and stuck to his goal of making the westward trek. For the time being, he sought to round out his funds by working in the counting house of two Baltimore merchants. He made such a favorable impression upon his employers that they tried to persuade him not to make the trip, and if Evans can be believed, even offered to set up the young man in business if he would stay.[17]

Despite further efforts of Dr. Jones and others to have him abandon his plans, Evans left Baltimore for the west by way of Philadelphia in March, 1793. A two-weeks journey took him into the interior of Pennsylvania, across the Susquehanna, and on to Fort Pitt. He then went down the Ohio by flatboat and arrived eventually at Spanish St. Louis in the late spring of 1793. Evans arrived at an inopportune time for that city was then a center of the Spanish administration, of the fur trade with the western Indians, and a bulwark against possible American penetration beyond the Mississippi. The Spanish had become worried over the threat of American conquest, as well as over rumors of penetration of their territory in the north by British fur-traders and the expansion of the Russians down the Pacific Coast from their bases in Alaska.[18]

The Spanish authorities therefore viewed Evans with suspicion when he arrived in St. Louis. They thought him a possible British agent and his mission a British scheme. The young Welshman was therefore promptly clapped into jail where he remained for some two years. He was finally released when a fellow Welshman by the name of Jones, who resided in St. Louis, was able to intercede upon Evans' behalf with the Spanish governor, Don Zenon Trudeau. Evans was released and supplied with necessary papers by Trudeau. For the time being, he bided his time until he could join up with an expedition which would ascend the Missouri River to the Padouca country.[19]

The new Spanish governor, the Baron de Carondelet, decided to take steps to defend the Spanish possessions of the upper Missouri from British encroachments. A program was worked out to explore this area, cross the Rockies, and establish a series of forts along the entire Spanish frontier from the Missouri to California. The Spanish Missouri Company was founded the same year, 1793, and given exclusive trading rights along the upper Missouri. It was ordered to build a series of protective forts in this area.[20]

The Company sent out two expeditions to accomplish this aim in 1794 and 1795 with negative results. Then in July, 1795, a third expedition consisting of some thirty men and four vessels and with merchandise to trade with the Indians was sent out under the command of James Mackay, a Scotsman, who had had abundant experience as a fur trader in Canada. While on his way from Canada to St. Louis, Mackay stopped off at Cincinnati and there met Morgan John Rhees, the liberal Welsh intellectual, then on a tour of the United States. Rhees had been informed of Evans' presence in St. Louis and the nature of his mission. He passed this information on to Mackay and gave the latter a Welsh vocabulary for his use if he met the Welsh Indians. When Mackay arrived in St. Louis, he contacted Evans and offered the young Welshman the position of lieutenant on the impending expedition up the Missouri. Evans accepted gladly and made preparations for the trip.[21]

Mackay, Evans, and their party of thirty men set forth in mid-August, 1795, well armed and with plenty of supplies and funds. They proceeded up the swift river in their four boats, encountered bad weather, had trouble with leaks in their boats that delayed them some six weeks, and did not reach the mouth of the Platte River until October 14. They then pushed on to the junction of the Dakota with the Missouri where they spent the winter at a camp of the Mahas Indians some distance away. Mackay sent Evans and a party of men to hunt game in order to replenish their food supply. The little party spent some twenty-five days among the Indians hunting buffalo amid all the hardships of winter on the open prairies.[22]

The forced winter delay among the Mahas caused Mackay great concern because news had reached him that the British Northwest Fur Company had established a fort among the Mandan Indians farther up the river. He, therefore, ordered Evans to head a party to serve as a scouting element for the expedition, to push into the Mandan territory and beyond, to note the features of geography and varieties of Indians, and to mark his route each day with precise accuracy. Evans was instructed to avoid Indians on the warpath, and when he reached the sources of the Missouri to inquire of the Indians for information concerning the rivers that ran westward from that point. Wherever possible he was to mark certain trees in the name of the King of Spain. Evans was then to return down the Missouri and rejoin Mackay, who hoped by that time to have reached the Mandan country. If he found Mackay dead or was unable to locate him, Evans was to return to St. Louis and report his information to the Spanish authorities.[23]

Evans and his party, armed with a warning issued by Mackay in the name of the King of Spain ordering all interlopers to withdraw or have their property confiscated, departed in February, 1796, but had not progressed very far before they met hostile Indians on the warpath and were forced to return. They did not set out again until June 8. They went well armed and supplied. Evans immediately began keeping a journal which noted valuable information on the Indians that they met and the physical features of the land through which they passed. He also charted his route and drew up the map of the region which subsequently found its way into Jefferson's hands. The party advanced up the Missouri through the badlands of Dakota. After nine weeks of difficulty fighting the swollen waters of the river, Evans and his party eventually reached the territory of the Arikara Indians. The latter caused trouble by demanding all his supplies. The young Welshman used his best diplomacy to talk them into letting his party continue on intact. They finally arrived in the country of the Mandans (North Dakota) on September 23.[24]

Evans and his party were welcomed by the Mandans and, in return, the explorer distributed flags, medals, and other gifts on behalf of the King of Spain. He moved quickly against the British traders whom he found in the Mandan territory, and had ousted them within five days of his arrival. The little party spent the next six months among the Mandans, and Evans had abundant opportunity to study these so-called "White Indians" and to question them about the sources of the Missouri. From their accounts he deduced that the latter were much farther to the west than was then generally believed by the white settlers at St. Louis.[25]

Evans soon found himself in the midst of a quarrel with the British traders of both the Northwest and the Hudson's Bay Companies then expanding their activities into that territory. Superior in numbers and with greater abundance of trading materials, the British were able to incite the Mandans against Evans and his men to such an extent that his position soon became untenable. He waited as long as he could for the arrival of Mackay, and when the latter did not show up, and with his supplies virtually exhausted and the Indians threatening to take his life, Evans headed back down the Missouri in May of 1797. He learned on the way back that Mackay, too, had been forced to turn back when his supplies had run out and when anticipated reinforcements from the Missouri Company failed to materialize. The company was in a precarious condition financially and could not get the necessary aid from the Spanish authorities to strengthen the Mackay-Evans expedition.[26]

The intrepid Welsh explorer reached St. Louis on July 15, 1797, after having been away nearly two years. He rendered an account of his experiences to the Spanish authorities, and then wrote to Dr. Samuel Jones back in Pennepek, Pennsylvania, informing him to pass word along to his friends that he had found nothing in regard to the Welsh Indians and that they probably did not exist.[27] The data that he collected eventually passed from the Spanish authorities into the hands of Daniel Clark of New Orleans who sent it to Jefferson who, in turn, passed it on to Meriwether Lewis. Lewis and William Clark took Evans' map with them on their great expedition to the Pacific and found it so accurate that only minor corrections were made on it.[28]

The young explorer may have planned to return to Philadelphia, but he was induced to stay on at St. Louis when the Spanish authorities offered to employ him. He was engaged by them as a land surveyor at Cape Girandeau south of St. Louis at the juncture of the Ohio and Mississippi rivers. Evans was anticipating a gift of land from them when he died suddenly towards the end of May, 1799.[29] "It is evident," wrote Professor David Williams, "that with his courage and perseverence, his accurate observations and cartographical skill, Evans had in him the makings of a really great explorer. . . . Evans had had to live in the most primitive conditions through a winter in a region, the present day North Dakota, where the climate is as severe as in any habitable part of the globe. This may well have undermined his health and contributed to his early death."[30]

Thus ended the Evans saga in quest of the Welsh Indians, but not the interest in the subject by any means. The London Welsh still believed in their existence. So, too, did the little Welsh-American colony then expanding in Oneida County, New York. The Oneida Welsh decided to conduct a search of their own. They collected money to pay the expenses of a searching party, and selected John T. Roberts, a contractor on the Erie Canal, for the job. He was to take Willliam Parry, a young Welshman, along as his companion.[31]

Roberts and Parry left Utica on April 14, 1819, and went west by way of Pittsburgh. At the latter place they met Major Stephen H. Long, the noted explorer, who informed them that in the opinion of William Clark, then governor of Missouri Territory, the Welsh Indians lived near the Rocky Mountains. Encouraged, the two explorers reached St. Louis on May 28, 1819, and began an inquiry among the Indian traders concerning the whereabouts of the Welsh Indians. They met and discussed the subject with many people who had travelled thousands of miles in the Missouri country and were familiar with the languages of the Indians not only of that area but with those of the Columbia River territory beyond. All denied ever having seen either White or Welsh-speaking Indians. Roberts and Parry also questioned Indians of various tribes that appeared at St. Louis, again with negative results. Parry, still optimistic, travelled up the Missouri for seven hundred miles in search of them only to return disappointed. An account of their experiences was later written up by Roberts and appeared in the Welsh-American journal, *Seren Gomer*.[32]

John T. Roberts eventually wound up in California feeling that the Welsh Indians might still be discovered. As late as 1857, he wrote to *Y Cenhadwr,* another Welsh-American periodical, that a certain Mr. Gilman had met up with a Welsh-speaking White Indian with two children in Utah.[33] Other stories concerning the Welsh Indians continued to circulate from time to time. So strong was the belief in the legend that the noted artist of the American Indians, George Catlin, writing about the Mandans in the 1830's, referred to them as the "Welsh Indians" and devoted considerable space in his commentary to the marked similarity of certain Mandan and Welsh words.[34]

The legend about the "first" Americans from Wales thus remained alive for many years as a romantic part of the mysterious American West. Evidently, the similarity of certain Indian words to Welsh ones accounted for the various reports that kept the legend alive in the nineteenth century. Significantly, most of these reports were made by non-Welsh speakers.

The legend also remains alive in the South. An Alabama chapter of the Daughters of the American Revolution erected a commemorative marker in 1953 "in memory of Prince Madoc, who landed on the shores of Mobile Bay in 1170 and left behind, with the Indians, the Welsh language." It stands along a road not far from Mobile.[35]

That Prince Madoc and his followers could have reached America no one would deny in light of all the recent evidence that indicates that the Vikings had touched American shores even earlier. That the good prince actually *did* land in America is yet to be proved. What really happened to Prince Madoc and his followers will probably always remain a mystery.[36]

FOOTNOTES ON CHAPTER I

1. The author is greatly indebted for his information concerning the John Evans saga to the excellent scholarly article by Professor David Williams of the University of Wales entitled "John Evans' Strange Journey," *American Historical Review,* LIV (January, 1949), pp. 277-95; (April, 1949), pp. 508-29. Professor Williams is also an authority on the history of modern Wales.

2. Benjamin F. Lewis, "The Madog Tradition," *Cambrian,* XIV, pp. 165-67.

3. Williams, *op. cit.,* p. 282.

4. *Ibid.,* p. 283.

5. *Ibid.,* pp. 283-84.

6. Lewis, *op. cit.,* pp. 165-67.

7. Williams, *op. cit.,* p. 284.

8. *Ibid.,* p. 285.

9. *Ibid.,* p. 286.

10. *Ibid.,* p. 280; also see chapter IV of this book, pp. 64, 66-7.

11. *Ibid.,* pp. 286-87.

12. *Ibid.,* pp. 288-89; also see chapter III of this book, pp. 47, 48.

13. *Ibid.,* pp. 291-92.

14. W. Ll. Davies, "David Samwell's Poem—'The Padouca Hunt'," *The National Library of Wales Journal,* II (Summer, 1942), pp. 142-52.

15. Williams, *op. cit.,* p. 292.

16. *Ibid.,* pp. 278-80.

17. *Ibid.,* pp. 293-94.

18. *Ibid.,* pp. 508-10.

19. *Ibid.,* pp. 512-13.

20. *Ibid.,* pp. 511-12.

21. *Ibid.,* pp. 511-13.

22. *Ibid.,* pp. 515-17.

23. *Ibid.,* pp. 517-19.

24. *Ibid.,* pp. 519-20.

25. *Ibid.,* pp. 520-21.

26. *Ibid.,* pp. 521-25.

27. *Ibid.,* pp. 525-26.

28. *Ibid.,* pp. 528-29.

29. *Ibid.,* pp. 527-28.

30. *Ibid.,* pp. 521, 525. For additional data on Evans see Bernard de Voto, *The Course of Empire,* pp. 68-73, 373-79; see also A. P. Nasatir, "John Evans, Explorer and Surveyor," *Missouri Historical Review,* XXV (January, 1931), pp. 219-39; (April, 1931), pp. 432-60; (July, 1931), pp. 585-608.

31.   Lewis, *op. cit.,* pp. 194-95.

32.   *Ibid.,* p. 195.

33.   *Ibid.*

34.   George Catlin, *North American Indians* . . . , Edinburgh (John Grant), 1926, I, p. 231; II, pp. 295-98.

35.   Geoffrey A. Wolff, "Case Built for Welsh Columbus," *Boston Sunday Globe,* February 5, 1967, p. 2.

36.   For a recent interesting treatment of the Welsh Indian legend, see Charles Michael Boland, *They All Discovered America,* New York (Doubleday & Co.), 1961, chapter 16.

CHAPTER II

THE WELSH BACKGROUND IN THE HOMELAND

John Evans, in pursuit of his strange quest, was in the vanguard of a large-scale migration of people from Wales to the United States during the nineteenth and early twentieth century. They had been preceded by scores of Welsh immigrants during the colonial period, most of whom came over as the result of religious persecution in the homeland. As in the case of the great bulk of European immigration to the United States during the same period, however, Welsh immigration during the last two centuries was primarily economic in motive: most of the immigrants who came desired to better themselves economically. It would be unfair, however, to ignore the fact that the political and religious idealism of the new Republic appealed in no small measure to the democratic Welsh and was an additional stimulus which encouraged emigration. In order to understand this attraction of America upon the Welsh and because few people are familiar with Wales and its historical development, a brief consideration of the past history of the Welsh in their homeland is of value in laying the foundations for a study of the Welsh element in the United States.

The story of the valiant and successful struggle of the Welsh to maintain themselves as a separate people in the face of the constant pressure exerted upon them by the English, one of the most vigorous of the western European nations, is truly a romantic and heroic saga. Comparatively few in numbers, divided by regional loyalties, dwelling in a fairly stark and largely infertile environment, they, nevertheless, held invaders from England at bay for over six hundred years, until the superior strength of the consolidated kingdom of England during the reign of Edward I brought their land within its political jurisdiction in the thirteenth century.

The Welsh, however, continued to maintain their own cultural and linguistic independence for another two centuries until they had the pleasure of seeing one of their own nationality ascend the throne of England in the person of Henry VII. The beginnings of Anglicization can be said to have set in with the coming to power of this, the first of the House of Tudor. This movement together with the union of Wales with England which took place during the reign of another Tudor,

Henry VIII, weakened the position of the Welsh as a separate nationality, but not sufficiently so to cause it irreparable harm. The succeeding centuries saw the rise of new movements, non-conformity in religion in the seventeenth and eighteenth and resurgent nationalism in the nineteenth and twentieth, both of which arrested the inroads of Anglicization and the complete absorption of Wales into England. The result, of course, was such that the majority of the inhabitants of Wales continued to consider themselves a separate people with a distinctive culture quite different from their English neighbors to the east. Those who immigrated to the United States arrived with these conceptions strongly intrenched. And they seldom forgot their indebtedness to their distinctive cultural heritage.

The Welsh are the historic and present day inhabitants of the western, mountainous peninsula of the island of Britain called after them, Wales. It has an area of 8,012 square miles (approximately the size of Massachusetts) and a population of some 2,651,340. Wales consists of the thirteen shires or counties of Anglesey, Denbighshire, Flintshire, Caernarvonshire, Merionethshire, and Montgomeryshire in the north, and Radnorshire, Brecknockshire, Caermarthenshire, Cardiganshire, Pembrokeshire, Glamorganshire, and Monmouthshire in the south. The name Welsh comes from the Anglo-Saxon word for foreigner, *Waelisc*. The Welsh call themselves *Cymry* (companions or comrades), their land *Cymru*, and their language *Cymraeg*. They speak a Keltic language closely related to Breton, the language of Brittany, to Highland Scots Gaelic, and to Irish Gaelic. Modern Welsh developed from the language spoken by the ancient Britons found by Caesar when he invaded Britain in 54 B.C. The present day Welsh are for the most part descendants of tribes closely related to the people Caesar fought at that time. They all spoke a common Keltic language, Briton, and Welsh is the only example of that language still spoken in Great Britain today. It has been estimated that if the Welsh colonies in England, America, the Dominions, and Patagonia are included approximately 1,000,000 people speak Welsh today.

Wales, the homeland of the Welsh, is a mountainous peninsula lying to the west of the English plain. It rises some places in height to 2,000 and occasionally 3,000 feet. Because of its location well out in the Atlantic, it receives a very heavy rainfall. The interior of the country is largely moorland with a rocky, clayey soil. Large sections of the higher regions are marshy swamps with an atmosphere of dampness and frequent fog. In such a highland, wet, and infertile area, agriculture is virtually impossible in an important way. Therefore pastoral occupations have been the traditional means of economic sustenance throughout the greater part of Welsh history. Cattle raising and the making of butter and cheese have been the dominant economic activities in the lower regions while sheep raising has dominated in the higher regions because of the poorer pastures. A certain amount of agriculture is possible along the coastal plains and in the river valleys. Here oats, barley, and wheat can be grown. In the south of Wales and in certain areas of the north, vast fields of iron ore and coal existed. These began to be worked with the coming of the Industrial Revolution. Not until these rich mineral deposits began to be exploited could any area of Wales be called rich or prosperous.[1]

Because of its mountainous nature, Wales was a difficult area to conquer during the Middle Ages, and divided as it is into numerous valleys isolated from each other an equally difficult area to unite. The mountains unquestionably saved Wales from complete conquest on many occasions, but they were also responsible for stimulating local and regional loyalties which prevented political unity from being achieved and maintained for any great length of time. It was to this mountainous refuge in the west of Britain that scores of peoples from farther east fled in the face of invasion and conquest by hostile tribes from the European mainland during the prehistoric and historic periods. And it was here in mountainous Wales that comparatively simple defense tactics could be employed to prevent complete conquest by an invader. The Welsh had only to collect their flocks during such times and move to the safe retreat of the mountain fastnesses and remain there until the invaders had exhausted their food supplies and were forced to retire in the face of threatened starvation. It was not until the coming of the Norman-French (who took the precaution to erect strong fortresses or castles as they penetrated the country which could serve as supply depots for further penetration) that a systematic and permanent conquest of Wales became a possibility.[2]

The Welsh, as is true of most European peoples, are not of pure racial strain. Rather they are the descendants of a blend of peoples who descended upon Britain at various times during the prehistoric and early historic periods. Of these peoples, the one that left its strongest imprint were the Kelts, a people who first appeared in Britain around the fifth century B.C. The Brythonic branch of this family had become masters of southern Britain and Wales by the second century B.C. and it is from their language that present day Welsh is descended. A people well along the way to civilized status, the Kelts of Wales became divided into four tribal groups, defended themselves from crude hill forts, fought among themselves and with invaders from Ireland, and worshipped a variety of Keltic deities according to rites associated with nature. A special class of leaders, the Druids, dominated the field of religion and formed the moral factor around which the tribes rallied in defense of their territories.

Roman conquest of Britain began in 43 A.D. Despite frenzied

opposition, the Romans succeeded in over-running most of the island. Eventually they controlled mountainous Wales through military garrisons and then began the process of introducing Roman civilization. Wales, however, was always a frontier area of the Empire, and remained scarcely changed throughout the Roman period of occupation. The same kind of pastoral existence continued as before the conquest and the Keltic language remained the basic speech of its inhabitants. One late Roman institution, however, Christianity, did get introduced successfully into Wales during the period of Roman occupation. It spread rapidly and was fortified in the fifth century by the introduction of monasticism. A number of Welsh monkish saints made their appearance—Illtud, Dyfrig, Samson, Teilo and Deiniol among others—to aid in spreading the gospel message and to establish monasteries. Dewi (David), the best known of the Welsh saints, was the son of a Welsh chieftain born about 520. He founded the monastery of Mynyw in southwest Wales and organized a system of monastic regulations for his abbey and its later daughter foundations which became the awe of Christian Britain because of its severity of discipline. So famous did Dewi become as a model of saintly behavior among the Welsh, that they accepted him as their patron saint. March 1, the day of his death, has been celebrated as a national holiday by them ever since. The custom of observing "St. David's Day" was brought with them by the Welsh when they later emigrated to other lands. In America, "the day" became the occasion for the annual rallying of Welsh consciousness and a perennial reminder of the cultural heritage of the little motherland.

Thus by the time of the Anglo-Saxon invasions of the fifth century, Wales and the Welsh people had become Christianized. Everyone is familiar with the story of these invasions and how despite bitter opposition the pagan German invaders were able to over-run the eastern lowland areas of Britain. Although details of the conquest are vague, it is from this bloody period that the Keltic tradition of a marvelous hero among them grew up. The hero, Arthur, stemmed the tide of invasion for a time at least. Around this heroic figure a cycle of myths and legends sprang up during the Middle Ages which stimulated the writing of some of the best literature of the medieval period. Despite the efforts of Arthur and other leaders, the Anglo-Saxons had became by 600 strongly intrenched in present-day England thus isolating the Kelts in mountainous Wales. A series of petty Anglo-Saxon states became established. These warred among themselves and against their Welsh neighbors. In due time, the Welsh took the offensive to invade the border territories of their pagan neighbors. So serious did this menace become that Offa, the Anglo-Saxon king of Mercia (757-796), found it necessary to erect a defensive fortification in the form of an earthen dike along his entire western border to protect his lands from Welsh incursions. Offa's Dike served as a frontier barrier between the Welsh and the Anglo-Saxons throughout the rest of the Anglo-Saxon period. It tended to become a defining medium marking the eastern extent of the area which the Welsh were to consider their homeland. The series of earthworks still follows rather closely the present confines of Wales on the east.

During the greater part of the Middle Ages, Wales was divided into a number of small kingdoms each hostile to the others. The political story of Wales during this period was one of semi-constant rivalry between the princes of the respective kingdoms as they sought to conquer one another or annex adjacent territory to their realms. The influence of geography upon the history of the country was such that organization into a united country proved difficult to achieve. The many mountains and isolated valleys bred intense local loyalties. It was only the exceptionally strong princes who succeeded in achieving any degree of unity at any given time, and then only temporarily for the country immediately fell back again into division upon the passing of such strong princes from the scene.

One such family of strong rulers was that of Rhodri Mawr, 844-878, of Gwynedd, who succeeded in uniting the greater portion of Wales under his rule. For almost a century, he and his successors held power. Perhaps the best known monarch of this medieval Welsh royal house was the great Hywel Dda (Howell the Good) who was responsible for codifying the Welsh laws around 925. The Welsh until this time had been in a tribal stage of civilization. A uniform system of law did not exist. It was Howell who created such by reducing many different and contradictory legal practices into a single legal code which was then enforced throughout the whole of Wales. His code is considered by medieval specialists to have been one of the earliest and best endeavors of this sort made during the Middle Ages. It was Howell's Laws along with the continued existence of the Welsh language that kept Welsh recognition of themselves as a people alive during this hectic period.

Other strong rulers, Gruffydd ap Cynon, Owain Gwynedd, Llewelyn the Great, sprang up from time to time to keep the tradition of a unified Wales alive, an important factor to be considered in the face of the new Norman-French menace which endangered Wales with the coming of William the Conqueror. As long as the new Norman kings of England were busily occupied with the problem of keeping their extensive holdings in both England and France, Welsh independence maintained itself. But with the coming to power of Edward I the fate of Wales was sealed. That powerful monarch determined to control the western peninsula and brought the full power of the consolidated English kingdom to bear upon the issue. With the aid of superior man-power, Edward invaded Wales, built fortresses at convenient key points as centers for supplies and defense against guerilla attacks, and then proceeded to destroy the best that the Welsh could muster against him. Jealousy among the Welsh chieftains played its part in making the conquest easier. After a valiant effort to maintain Welsh independence, Llewelyn the Last was slain in mid-Wales in 1282. Within a short period of time all opposition to Edward I had been eliminated.

From 1282 until the present, the history of Wales had been associated with the political fortunes of England. Only once after 1282 did the Welsh attempt serious rebellion. This was the famous movement led by Owain Glyn Dwr (Owen Glendower) in the first decade of the fourteenth century. Owen took advantage of the division of the English during the Wars of the Roses to raise the Welsh dragon standard of revolt on behalf of Welsh independence. He was overwhelmingly successful in the early years of the revolt, ousted the English conquerors, and declared himself legitimate ruler of Wales. He inaugurated a progressive rule, held parliaments at various places, and made plans for the creation of Welsh universities.

Unfortunately for the cause of Welsh independence, Owen failed to take full advantage of the military situation in England, and was disastrously defeated by the capable Henry IV. Owen was forced to go into hiding. Nothing more was ever heard of him thereafter—his disappearance being one of the mysteries of Welsh history. Once again Wales became a conquered land. Even if Owen had not been defeated, it is unlikely that Wales could have remained independent for any great length of time. The superior resources of the united English regime and its determination to control the western portion of the island would have been more than a match for the impoverished Welsh opposition. The possibility of any future successful revolt through military means alone became out of the question. Owen, however, because of his valiant efforts, his patriotism, and his progressive statesmanship has remained a great national hero of the Welsh, perhaps their greatest. He goes down into history as the last "Welsh" Prince of Wales.

Although Wales had lost its independence, the centuries of warfare with the English, the heroic sagas of their great leaders, and the isolation of their homeland from the English centers of influence, kept consciousness of themselves as a distinct ethnic group alive among the Welsh. They faced the coming of modern times deprived of their political independence, but still living very much the same sort of pastoral existence, still aware of their separateness from their English neighbors and still speaking the language of their ancestors. They had developed a distinctive cultural heritage of their own consisting of a great body of music, folk dancing, an intricate legal code, and a very rich body of literature. Songs such as

"All through the Night," "The Bells of Aberdovey," and "Deck the Halls with Boughs of Holly" became in time part of the great store of popular songs dear to the hearts of the Anglo-Saxon world. Coming down from pagan times and the struggle with the Anglo-Saxons was a considerable amount of heroic poetry of unknown composition. Later, a number of great poets, Taliesin, Aneirin, Myrddin, and Llywarch Hen, made their appearance. These and others formed a special class in Wales during the Middle Ages, the so-called bards, who sang the praises of Wales and her heroes in the courts of the Welsh princes and were honored wherever they went in the principality.[3]

From this medieval period in Welsh history, too, dates the famous classic of Welsh literature, *the Mabinogion,* a series of prose tales of unknown authorship dealing with the legend of Arthur and his knights but revealing many evidences of former pagan beliefs and practices. Still later appeared the father of modern Welsh poetry and the greatest poet Wales ever produced, the renowned Dafydd ab Gwilym, who composed lyric poetry of exceptional beauty. These outstanding figures and their fellows enriched the Welsh language and helped to build up a body of literature to which the Welsh could point with pride. They played no small part in keeping the Welsh language alive and vigorous, and served to stimulate further literary creativity in that language. The Welsh had achieved a high state of civilization by the time the English conquest occurred, and they could fall back upon a type of cultural nationalism when their political independence disappeared. Significant movements in the future were to strengthen this cultural nationalism, prevent the Welsh from becoming Anglicized, and account for their arrival in America as a distinctive self-conscious ethnic group far different from their British neighbors.

The Welsh had been very loyal and devout members of the Roman Catholic Church for the greater part of the Middle Ages, but when Henry VIII led his people out of that church, the Protestant Reformation was introduced into Wales. Most of the Welsh clergy accepted Henry's changes and those of his successors. The reign of Elizabeth I, however, witnessed an event of great importance in the struggle to keep Welsh nationality alive. This was the translation of the *Bible* from the original tongues into Welsh. One William Salesbury produced such a translation of the *New Testament.* This was revised by the Reverend Dr. William Morgan to which he added his own translation of the *Old Testament* and published the complete *Bible* in 1588. Morgan's *Bible* is substantially the Welsh *Bible* of today, and to Morgan goes the credit of standardizing the Welsh language. Through his translation, he gave the Welsh the important instrument which was to later play such a vital part in the spiritual and secular education of the great masses of the people, and to assure that this spiritual and secular education should take place by means of the Welsh language.

Although the great majority of the Welsh people remained loyal to the established Church of England, it was only natural that Wales should be influenced by the contemporary religious developments then taking place in England. Dissatisfaction with aspects of Catholicism still retained by the official faith bred the famous Puritan movement in that country. Dissatisfaction with the nature of the administration of the same church and the feeling that religion should be divorced from its association with government, bred the movement called Separatism. These and other radical ideas in religion that filtered in from the continent soon created a religious ferment and revolt that effected England for at least a century.

The new beliefs also penetrated into Wales. Soon a number of distinctive religious sects claimed adherents within the Principality. Baptists, Presbyterians, Quakers, and the Congregationalists or Independents were the chief of these. All suffered severe persecution under the new Stuart kings as the Anglican hierarchy with the blessings of the monarchs took vigorous steps to stamp out such heresies. A period of respite occurred during the Commonwealth and Protectorate periods of the seventeenth century when elements sympathetic to the dissenting groups were in command of the English government, but further persecution occurred with the restoration of the Stuarts in 1660. This was the period when most of the Welsh Quakers and certain of the Welsh Baptists and Welsh Presbyterians emigrated to America to escape religious persecution. The arrival of the first substantial numbers of Welsh in America was therefore wedded to the cause of religious freedom.

The ousting of King James II through the so-called "Glorious Revolution" of 1688, and the passage of the famous Toleration Act the following year ended persecution of the dissenting groups. Henceforth they could worship freely. Although only a very small minority of the Welsh people had accepted the beliefs of the dissenting groups of this time, the latter remained an active group within Wales from that time henceforth always on the alert to convert when the opportunity presented itself.

That opportunity occurred later in the eighteenth century thanks to the ineptitude, incompetence, and indifference of the established church to the religious needs of the Welsh people. The continued practice of appointing non-Welshmen to the Welsh bishoprics (most of whom viewed the appointment as a mere stepping stone to a more lucrative bishopric in England), the generally low educational level and ignorance of the Welsh clergy, the prevalent immorality of the same, the poverty of the parishes deprived of their just tithes by grasping landlords—all tended to cause thinking religious elements to view reform as necessary.

The reform movement came from within the church and received its great stimulus from the pietistic evangelism introduced by the great John Wesley and his co-worker, George Whitfield. Soon these men and Welshmen of similar beliefs were emphasizing the necessity of abundant preaching within the church and the need for experiencing a rebirth in religious conviction as a necessary part in the salvation of the individual. The Methodist movement, so-called, was frowned upon by the hierarchy of the established church, but it succeeded in making great inroads among the masses of the Welsh people. The Welsh Methodist leadership followed the ideas of Whitfield when he broke with Wesley because of the latter's failure to accept the fundamental beliefs of Calvinism. The Welsh movement was therefore overwhelmingly influenced by Calvinism in contrast to English Methodism.

The Welsh Methodists strove seriously to remain within the Anglican fold during the early years of the movement, but eventually and reluctantly severed their connection towards the end of the eighteenth century. They thereupon organized themselves into a new religious sect called the Calvinistic-Methodists to distinguish themselves from the followers of Wesley who had rejected Calvinism. The withdrawal of the Calvinistic-Methodists from the Anglican Church was of tremendous significance in the history of the Welsh people. It stimulated their missionary fervor and the missionary fervor of the other older dissenting sects of Wales as well. Within a few decades, the Calvinistic-Methodists, the Congregationalists, and the Baptists had won over the great majority of the masses of Wales from the established church, and had converted them into enthusiastic supporters of extreme evangelistic varieties of Christianity. Wales became covered with an abundance of small chapels full to overflowing with worshippers, while the old church edifices in the same neighborhoods remained practically deserted.

The dissenting sects placed great emphasis upon a knowledge of the *Bible* as a fundamental part of their faith and salvation. Accordingly, they took proper steps to see to it that Welshmen became literate enough to read the sacred text. Educational opportunities were few indeed in the Wales of the period, and it became necessary for the invention of an institution that would provide this desired end. This was discovered in the form of the Sunday School made famous by the great Calvinistic-Methodist leader, Thomas Charles of Bala. In the Sunday School both old and young were instructed in reading Welsh and in interpreting the *Bible* when they had become literate. Thanks to the Sunday School movement, the mass of the Welsh people became literate in their own language—an event of great significance in the story of the struggle of the Welsh language to maintain itself and with it a separate Welsh nationality. The great revival of the eighteenth century also encouraged hymn singing as a fundamental part of the religious services. Many composers of hymns and hymn-tunes made their appearance, of whom the greatest was the renowned William Williams, Pantecelyn. His many hymns of great excellence, piety, and fitted to every emotional need rate him as one of the greatest hymn writers of all time. Thus to the overwhelming evangelistic expression of their faith was added the love of hymn-singing, a combination of religious emphasis which the Welsh of the nineteenth century were to bring with them to America and to color the life of the little settlements that they organized in the new Republic.

Until the last part of the eighteenth century the old economic ways of life in Wales continued. The Welsh carried on their pastoral activities throughout the great part of the country, engaged in fishing and coastal shipping in the maritime sections, and raised a certain amount of agriculture in the river valleys. However, towards the end of the eighteenth century the Industrial Revolution was introduced into the Principality to cause great changes in the life of the people, particularly in the area called South Wales. Here rich deposits of coal and iron ore were discovered in a vast belt of territory.[4]

The great demands for munitions and other implements of war caused by Britain's struggle with France during the French Revolutionary and Napoleonic periods, and still later ever increasing demands for coal and iron, led to the exploitation of these fields and the creation of a great industrial region in South Wales. Demands for labor were great and thousands of Welsh from elsewhere in Wales flocked to this region to meet this need. By the end of the nineteenth century over half the population of Wales was concentrated in the new urban industrialized areas of Glamorganshire and Monmouthshire. Merthyr-Tydfil became the first Welsh city of any considerable size. The growth of the export trade in coal and iron provided the still larger port cities of Cardiff, Swansea, and Newport.

The social problems that were associated with the change in character of South Wales were tremendous and involved housing, sanitation, strikes, and other manifestations of labor unrest as the result of exceedingly bad working conditions. When in time America also began to exploit its vast stores of iron, coal, and steel, it began to woo the skilled Welsh workers in these fields. Dissatisfaction with economic conditions at home and attracted by the lure of higher wages and other economic opportunities to be found in the newly developing industrial United States led thousands of Welsh industrial workers to emigrate to America. They were joined by hundreds of Welshmen from other parts of Wales as well.

Also of significance during this period of the nineteenth century was the coming into South Wales of thousands of English and Irish workmen and business people. In some areas they even outnumbered the native

Welsh. Since these people did not speak Welsh they had the effect of Anglicizing these hitherto exclusively Welsh-speaking areas. They and their descendants still form a large block of people unassimilated to Welsh culture. The visitor to Wales today will find such places as Cardiff and Newport as well as many of the smaller urban places overwhelmingly English in speech and generally speaking English in outlook. The general effect of the industrial revolution on Wales therefore was to divide its inhabitants into a rural Welsh-speaking section and an urban English-speaking one. This change, together with the knitting of Wales to the rest of the island through the development of better means of communication with accompanying encouragement of Anglicization, constituted the most serious challenge to the continued existence of the Welsh language and a distinctive Welsh culture. Still later in the century when the first system of free elementary schools was established in Wales, pressure from the central educational authorities in London led to the prohibition of teaching in Welsh and concentration on English as the language of education. Fortunately for the continued existence of the Welsh language, the presence of the by this time traditional Sunday School assured that the younger generation of the Welsh-speaking sections would be fluent in their own language.

Throughout the nineteenth century, therefore, and well into the twentieth, the continuance of the Welsh as a separate people faced a serious crisis. Consciousness of Welshness emerged successfully and even in a more aggressive form thanks to the effects of the romantic movement in literature and the growth of nationalism elsewhere in Europe. The romantic movement led Welsh intellectuals and others to re-examine their country's past, re-discover its great body of literature and other cultural contributions, and to stimulate studies and movements that had the effect of stemming the tide towards Anglicization. The medieval Welsh literary manuscripts were collected and published, the ancient institution, the Eisteddfod, was revived with its emphasis upon stimulating literary production in the Welsh language, and a body of Welsh scholars and educators was created constantly active in the defense of Welsh culture. The growth of nationalism elsewhere in Europe and the influence of such leaders as Kossuth and Mazzini stimulated these same intellectuals to even greater efforts. Despite many disappointments and frequently an indifferent Welsh public, their efforts to preserve Welsh culture were ultimately successful and led to the creation of the three great institutions which were to become the strongholds of Welsh nationality in the future: the University of Wales and its constituent colleges, the National Museum of Wales at Cardiff, and the National Library of Wales at Aberystwyth. Nineteenth century Welsh immigrants to America reflected these trends. They came to America more alertly Welsh conscious than their colonial predecessors. They quickly introduced the Eisteddfod and certain of them made valiant efforts to compose literature in the Welsh language.

The twentieth century witnessed a continuance of the movement in this same direction. Because the great majority of the Welsh were dissenters in religion, pressure was on for the disestablishment of the Anglican Church in Wales. After a bitter battle this was accomplished and went into effect in 1920. The heretofore official church was disestablished and made a separate entity, the Church in Wales, under the leadership of a newly created Archbishop of Wales, an elective position which circulated among the respective bishops. Two new dioceses were created, Swansea-Brecon and Monmouth, to join the four ancient sees of St. David's, St. Asaph's, Bangor, and Llandaff.

Continuous agitation led to the authorization of the use of Welsh as a medium of instruction in the free schools, the repeal of the legislation prohibiting the use of the Welsh language in the courts of law, and with the arrival of radio and television, the setting up of broadcasting beams and other facilities in the Welsh language.

For the most part Welsh nationalism in modern times had been primarily of a cultural variety divorced from any political implications or any desires for outright independence from the United Kingdom. However, the economic dislocation that occurred in Britain as an aftermath of World War I and the particularly severe unemployment that hit the Welsh coal fields during the greater part of this period led to the growth of a feeling that Wales would be better off if she could have more independence in solving the difficulties of her people. Although never held by the great majority of the Welsh people this feeling led to the formation of a Welsh Nationalist Party (which took for its end-goal dominion status for Wales) as well as other extremist groups. Although never numerous, this little group of people kept up a constant agitation on behalf of their program and kept alive among the Welsh the belief that Wales deserved special consideration from the central government as an area with institutions and problems quite different from the rest of the United Kingdom. Because of their continued pressure, all three major political parties were forced to consider the question. To the gratification of Welshmen generally, the newly elected Churchill government of 1951 immediately created a new cabinet post, the Minister for Welsh Affairs, as a move in that direction. Continued pressure led the newly elected Labour government of 1964 to create an even more important cabinet post, a special Secretary of State for Wales (with similar responsibilities to that of the Secretary of State for Scotland, a position which had existed for over a century). These moves are only considered a partial solution to the problem of Wales from the standpoint of the extreme nationalists. They will undoubtedly continue to agitate for dominion status or complete independence, but whether they will be able to win the majority of the Welsh people to their beliefs remains to be seen.

Today, the Welsh University is educating a professional class of leaders conscious of its Welsh heritage, the Welsh National Library has become the mecca for Welsh scholars in the pursuit of research in the arts and sciences, the Welsh National Museum through its holdings and exhibits (including a new Folk Museum which presents a complete picture of Welsh rural life in the past) is serving to keep knowledge of the distinctiveness of Wales alive, and the National Eisteddfod (held alternately in North and South Wales) is stimulating productivity in the writing of Welsh literature and achievements in native Welsh arts and crafts. The teaching of Welsh in the free schools, the continued existence of the Sunday Schools with their emphasis upon Welsh, and the radio and television programs in Welsh are all doing their part in supporting the struggle for the survival of the Welsh language.

Despite these efforts, the decline of the Welsh language continues. Whereas some 714,486 people spoke Welsh in 1951, the number had dropped to 652,002 in 1961. At the present time most of those who speak Welsh are also bi-lingual. The natural tendency to prefer fluency in a language of world-wide significance (English) may ultimately sound the death-knell for the Welsh language even in those areas of Wales where it is still strongly entrenched, unless vigorous governmental action is taken and taken promptly.[5] That the death of the Welsh language would be a tragedy, nearly everyone agrees.

Be that as it may, the end results of the movements that set in during the nineteenth century were such that the Welsh people, speaking their ancient language and maintaining their own distinctive culture, form a strong and separate nationality existing in the Europe of the contemporary period. Their kinsmen who emigrated to the United States proudly shared this heritage. Their ties to the homeland (particularly the first and second generations) were close. Many still retain contact with the old homeland and follow developments there with a great deal of interest.

FOOTNOTES ON CHAPTER II

1. A. H. Williams, *An Introduction to the History of Wales,* 2 Vols., Cardiff (University of Wales Press), 1948, Vol I., pp. 1-10. This is the best short treatment of the history of Wales prior to the English conquest.

2. *Ibid.,* p. 10.

3. For an interesting treatment of the Welsh and their culture see Eiluned and Peter Lewis, *The Land of Wales,* New York (Scribner's), 1937.

4. The best treatment of modern Wales and its problems is that of David Williams, *A History of Modern Wales,* London (John Murray), 1950.

5. For further details on the decline of the Welsh language see E. G. Bowen, ed., *Wales, a Physical, Historical and Regional Geography,* London (Methuen & Co., Ltd.), 1965, pp. 247-63. This volume is a mine of information on many topics of interest concerning Wales.

CHAPTER III

THE WELSH COLONIAL SETTLEMENTS

Safely relegating the story of the coming of Prince Madoc and his followers to the realm of myth and unproven legend, the first evidence of an active interest in the settlement of Welsh people in America can be credited to Sir William Vaughan, a large landholder of Carmarthenshire, Wales. The good baronet had become greatly concerned with the generally impoverished conditions of the people then living in southwestern Wales. In an attempt to improve their economic condition and also with the hope of making a profit through the enterprise, he selected the island of Newfoundland as a likely place for a Welsh settlement. Although earlier efforts to settle Newfoundland had failed, Vaughan remained optimistic. The area was the nearest part of the new world to Wales, and the existence of the recently discovered rich fishing banks of the vicinity might prove a substantial source of livelihood for the proposed Welsh settlers.

Sir William received a patent from King James I and set about planning his settlement. He called it "Cambriol" in honor of Wales and divided the territory into townships with distinctive Welsh names. Actual settlement began in 1616. The Welsh faced a difficult task in making the enterprise a success in this bleak area. Extremes of cold in the winter period, a rocky and barren soil, and the existence of lawlessness among the fishermen of the Newfoundland banks all combined to make it virtually impossible for the Welsh settlers to establish a permanent settlement. They continued their efforts, nevertheless. After twenty years of futile effort they gave up and returned to their native Wales. The Newfoundland venture of Sir William Vaughan was the first historical effort on the part of a group of Welsh to settle in the new world. It failed, but more successful group projects were to follow later in the century.[1]

We have ample data concerning these successful group projects of which more subsequently, but know very little concerning the steady trickle of Welsh individuals who joined the emigrant tide to the new colonies of America during the colonial period. That there were many such scattered among the English settlers of the period one can safely assume from the presence of many Welsh surnames among the settlers of these colonies. A tremendous job of genealogical research, examination of ship lists, port records, and the like would be necessary to determine just how extensive and how numerous this type of individual Welsh migration was, but from the author's mere superficial findings in this field it can be assumed that individual Welshmen could be found in all the colonies from their earliest beginnings. For examples of this type of immigrant see below.[2]

Probably all of these people merged quickly into the great body of their English-speaking neighbors so that only the existence of Welsh surnames gives a clue to their proper identity.[3] In most cases, too, they probably came over during this period in quest of bettering themselves economically as was the case with the great majority of the other newcomers among whom they settled.

The great group migrations of the Welsh to America during the first century of existence of the colonies, on the other hand, were stimulated primarily by the critical religious situation then present in the homeland which resulted in periodic outbursts of intense persecution of those not firm believers in the established Anglican church. We have already noted in chapter II that dissatisfaction with the continuance within the Anglican church of dogmas and practices retained from Roman Catholicism had bred the great Puritan movement which would have reformed the official church from within by cleansing it of these features of the old religion. Likewise there grew up in time the belief in certain quarters that church organization and control should be completely divorced from association with political government. People who held these latter views were called Separatists. They believed each congregation had the right to control itself, select its ministers, and worship according to practices of its own choice. Both Puritans and Separatists met vigorous opposition from the leaders of the Anglican church backed by the early Stuart kings. The resulting persecutions were a potent factor in the founding of the colonies of New Plymouth by the Separatists, and Massachusetts Bay by the Puritans during this period.[4]

In time new religious ideas and conceptions penetrated England during the seventeenth century and eventually found their way to Wales. These new beliefs had their greatest influence among the Separatists. Growing out of the new interpretations of religion, yet associated with Separatism in attitude toward the relationship of church and state evolved two distinctly new sects, the Baptists and the Quakers, both of which were soon introduced into Wales and won converts to their peculiar beliefs.[5] It was adherents of these two religious groups who were to be responsible for the group settlements of Welshmen made during the first century of existence of the American colonies. They were joined in time by fellow countrymen of the Anglican and Presbyterian faiths.

The Baptists were the first of the two to attempt settlement because

of religious persecution. They were Separatists in their church organization and attitude towards the relationship of church and state, but differed
from the great majority of the other Separatists in their emphasis upon
adult baptism rather than infant baptism as a necessary process in the
salvation of the individual.

To John Myles goes the honor of being called the father of the
Welsh Baptist movement as well as the father of the Welsh Baptist sect
in America.[6] Myles was born at Newton in what was then a Welsh-
speaking area of Herefordshire. He attended Brasenose College, Oxford,
and matriculated in 1636. He settled in the vicinity of Swansea, South
Wales, and became converted to Baptist beliefs after a trip to London.
Myles was baptized in the London church of the denomination, and
returned to Swansea to preach the new doctrines. He is credited with
founding the first Baptist church in Wales in 1649 when he gathered
together a group of his converts at Ilston in the Gower peninsula not far
from Swansea. Myles labored and preached with such zeal that soon a
number of daughter Baptist churches had been established at Llanharon,
Hay, Carmarthen, and Abergavenny—all in South Wales. Myles supervised all these during the remainder of his stay in Wales although he
served officially only as pastor of the church at Ilston.[7]

These were the years of the Commonwealth and Protectorate periods
in English history when dissenters generally were afforded full liberty of
religious expression hence the rapid spread of the Baptist movement.
With the restoration of the Stuarts in 1660, however, all dissenting groups
were once again persecuted severely. The pressure became so great that
Myles and certain of his followers decided to flee to America and to re-
constitute the little church they had founded in the New World. They
did so in 1663 and settled at Rehoboth in Plymouth Colony.[8]

The little group soon came into conflict with the Plymouth religious
authorities who viewed their lack of orthodoxy at first with disapproval.
Myles and his followers, who had been worshipping in Baptist fashion at
the home of one of the group, were fined five pounds for setting up a
public meeting without the knowledge or the approval of the authorities
as well as being accused of disturbing the peace. They were ordered to
desist and then advised to remove their meeting elsewhere where there
would be no conflict with a church already in existence (which seems to
have been the cause of all the controversy). The group thereupon moved
its place of meeting to Kelly's Bridge at the upper end of Warren in the
township of Barrington. They later removed it to its present site about
three miles from Warren and about ten miles from Providence, Rhode
Island.[9]

Apparently in this then sparsely settled section they aroused no great
jealousy from the official Congregationalism of the colony, for in 1667 the

General Court of Plymouth gave them an ample grant of land which included the territory upon which they had settled. They called their new grant, Swanzey (later spelled Swansea) in honor of the largest town in that part of Wales from which they had come. This original grant was later divided into the towns of Swansea, Warren, and Barrington, the latter two passing to Rhode Island upon the adjustment of the boundary of the latter colony with Massachusetts in 1741.[10]

Myles remained the pastor of the Swansea church until his death in 1683. By the end of the century four daughter Baptist churches had been founded, and the Swansea church had become one of the strong centers of the Baptist faith in America. To Myles and his fellow immigrants goes the credit of founding the first successful Welsh group settlement in America. The settlement prospered, most of the group becoming eventually prosperous farmers. Their descendants are still numerous in the vicinity and the church is still active. Perhaps the best known descendant of Myles was the late General Nelson Appleton Miles (1839-1925), chief of staff of the U.S. Army during World War I.[11]

The Welsh members of the Society of Friends, commonly known as Quakers, were responsible for the founding of the second and much larger Welsh group settlement in America toward the latter part of the seventeenth century. The Quakers were a religious group founded by the famous George Fox earlier in the same century. In contrast to the religious views then prevalent they held extremely radical ones. They placed reliance upon direct inspiration of the individual by God through the agency of conscience (or as they called it the "inner voice") as the prime guide to human behavior rather than upon the *Bible* and its inconsistencies. For the Friends there was no need of an organized ministry nor for an intricate ecclesiastical organization. They were pacifists and extreme equalitarians refusing to bow to any superior and insisting upon wearing their hats in court and even in the presence of the king to emphasize their views in this respect. That such extreme views should not result in persecution of the Quakers would have been exceptional indeed in a time of great religious intolerance. Almost from their first appearance they were subjected to the cruelest of inflictions by the civil authorities of England.

Ideas similar to those held by Fox had already been expressed in Wales by the Reverend Morgan Llwyd (or Lloyd), a leader of the dissenting groups. He taught that Christ dwelt mysteriously in the hearts of man and expressed these and other views in a book, *Llyfr y Tri Aderyn,* which was published in 1653. The same year he heard of George Fox and his ideas. He thereupon sent one of his followers, John ap John of Ruabon, to visit Fox and to sound out the latter on his religious beliefs. John ap John was converted after meeting Fox and then returned to

Wales as its first Quaker missionary. Fox, himself, made a great missionary tour of Wales in 1657 and had marked success in Radnorshire, Montgomeryshire, and Pembrokeshire where converts joined the movement after hearing him preach. Later Quaker missionary efforts led by John ap John and Richard Davis, a Welsh convert, won over large numbers of the Welsh in the vicinity of Dolgelly in Merionethshire to the new beliefs. It was Davis who converted Charles Lloyd, a great landed squire of Dolobran near Llanfyllin, whose celebrated kinsmen, Thomas and David Lloyd, were to play a very important part in the early political history of Pennsylvania.[12]

The Friends made their greatest conquest when they converted the noted William Penn to their beliefs, for it was the latter who furnished them a refuge in America where they might propagate their religion in peace. Penn, so tradition held, was the grandson of a Welshman, John Tudor, who was called Pen-mynydd (of the hill-top) and who took the name Penn when he removed from Wales to Ireland. William's father had been a noted admiral in the English Navy and had loaned King Charles II a considerable sum of money while the latter had been in exile.

William Penn became the apologist for the Quakers in the upper circles of English society and at court itself. Abandoning hope that his co-religionists could ever receive religious toleration at home, Penn and other Quaker leaders began to consider settlement in America as an alternative. Penn hit upon a scheme whereby he could liquidate the king's debt to him as heir to his father, the Admiral. He requested the grant of a large tract of land in America in exchange. King Charles was only too willing, and granted Penn the confines of the future colony of Pennsylvania in 1681. Penn then set to work planning his new colony in America.

Penn's plans for a Quaker refuge became known to the Welsh Friends. They viewed them with enthusiasm as a means of escaping the then current persecution. Furthermore they believed that in the new colony they could purchase a large tract of land and to settle there in a body so that they could maintain a community of their own with their distinctive Welsh language and institutions. Many of them were gentry of considerable means and could meet the liberal terms of purchase offered by Penn. Then, too, the fact that Penn was both a Quaker and a Welshman (so they believed) made the plan even more attractive. Accordingly, the Welsh Quakers were among the first to take advantage of Penn's liberal terms. A group of prominence among them, led by John ap John, went to London in 1681 to start negotiations with Penn for the proposed purchase. An agreement was later worked out with Penn whereby 40,000 acres in the new colony were purchased by the Welsh Quakers with the *oral* understanding that the plot would be set aside as a separate "barony" within which the Welsh would have full rights of self-government in order to protect their distinctive language and institutions. Unfortunately, this latter part of the agreement was verbal on Penn's part and was never put into writing. It was to become a cause of controversy between Penn and the Welsh later on.[13]

A special committee of the Welsh Quakers had consummated the purchase, but since considerable time might elapse before the land could be disposed of to settlers, leaders of the enterprise were made trustees for 30,000 acres of the tract and took out patents in their own names with the understanding that they would sell their holdings to other Welsh Quakers. The leaders formed self-constituted heads of seven companies for the division and sale of the land.

The so-called "Welsh Barony" was eventually located on the west side of the Schuylkill River to the northwest of Philadelphia. It included what became the townships of Upper Merion, Lower Merion, Haverford, Radnor, Tredyffrin, East Whiteland, West Whiteland, East Goshen, West Goshen, Willistown, East Town, and part of West Town, in the present counties of Montgomery, Chester, and Delaware. It was situated in a magnificently fertile territory and was admirably suited to meet the desires of the Welsh. The "Barony" was not surveyed until 1684, and its exact boundaries were not determined until 1687.

The Welsh did not wait for Penn to precede them, but started out at once to take up lands in the "Barony." Many arrived in the colony before him, and others came on the same ship that brought the great entrepreneur. The party of Dr. Edward Jones is believed to have been the first Welsh settlers to arrive. They came aboard the ship, *Lion,* in 1682, a group of some forty people. The group reached Upland, August 13, 1682, and were assigned the Merion district of the present county of Montgomery by Thomas Holme, Penn's surveyor. They became the founders of Merion in the "Barony." Dr. Jones, a "Chyrurgeon" or physician, later became a justice of the peace and one of Merion's representatives in the Pennsylvania Assembly. Most of the other members of the party became settlers of prominence.[14]

Between 1682 and 1700, authorities agree that the Welsh were the most numerous body of immigrants arriving in Pennsylvania. They made their initial settlements in Merion and Haverford townships in 1682, and then as later immigrants arrived spread over Radnor and Goshen townships, then Tredyffrin and Uwchlan townships, and eventually occupied the remaining townships of the "Barony." Most of the Welsh Quakers were either members of the gentry or yeoman farm classes. Some were wealthy enough to bring along their servants. They represented a rather high type of immigrant. All the 30,000 acres assigned to the original patentees were eventually occupied, but not the remaining 10,000 acres set aside for the Welsh Quakers. Apparently, the leaders of the venture were unwilling or unable to furnish the money necessary to purchase this acreage. Penn and his agents therefore sold these 10,000 acres later on to individuals, some non-Quaker Welsh, others not Welsh at all. As a result, a certain proportion of non-Welshmen found its way into the "Barony," but not in such numbers as to undermine the Welsh character of the area at least not during these early years.[15]

The Welsh Quakers took seriously Penn's verbal promise that they could rule the Barony in their own manner. They immediately put into effect a government of their own. Being pacifistically inclined they needed very little civil authority, and such that existed was exercised through their Quaker meetings where all land disputes and other problems were handled in democratic fashion. Interference on the part of Penn's administration soon occurred in 1685. In that year the provincial authorities ran a line between Philadelphia and Chester counties thereby dividing the Welsh Barony into two parts. Later in 1690 the colonial government abolished the civil authority of the Welsh Quaker meetings and set up instead regular township government within the Barony. The Welsh fought these actions claiming that they constituted a violation of their original agreement with Penn. They were willing to adopt the township form of government providing the entire Barony should constitute a single unit and providing the Welsh were allowed to decide among themselves who the officials should be and who should collect taxes. The Welsh proposal apparently did not seem feasible to either Penn or his representatives. Probably, the latter feared continuance of the Welsh arrangement might result in the creation of a separate colony within Pennsylvania with potential possibilities for serious political differences. For some five years the Welsh continued to protest to Penn, reminding him that he had broken his word, but by 1690, they realized the hopelessness of their position. Penn was their final court of appeal. He refused to sustain the legality of their position. Begrudgingly they gave in to the new administrative arrangements not feeling too kindly towards the great colonist. Thereafter, Penn was scarcely a popular person within the confines of the Barony.[16]

The Welsh Friends played a vital role in Quaker affairs of the Pennsylvania colony. They furnished a high percentage of both religious leaders and prominent laymen for this sect, and exerted a strong influence in determining Quaker policy. They worshipped at first under the trees if the weather permitted, or within the homes of the settlers—a pattern of religious behavior typical of Welsh immigrants generally during their first days of settlement in America. They built their first meeting houses in 1684 when three log edifices were erected at Merion, Haverford, and Radnor. The first two meeting houses were replaced by stone structures between 1695 and 1700, and the latter by a stone structure in 1717. The

Merion old stone meeting house, the only one still standing, is one of the historic buildings of Pennsylvania. All three meeting houses had libraries of books in both Welsh and English. Although chiefly religious in their content, they furnished reading matter in the native language at a time when such was very rare in America. One John Humphrey, realizing this need, left ten pounds for the printing of literature in Welsh.[17]

Quaint, indeed, were the means taken by the Welsh Quakers to preserve peace and order among themselves. If a delinquent did not reform, his offense was written down and nailed to the door of the meeting house for all to see. Every effort was made to see to it that members and their families living far away from the meeting house conducted themselves in accordance with good Quaker ethical concepts. Such would be visited each quarter by various of the religious leaders and encouraged to maintain their religious convictions.[18]

Penn's decision ended their hopes of maintaining a Barony of their own wherein they could enjoy the right of governing themselves. Otherwise they could continue with their own institutions and language without hindrance from the provincial authorities. For almost a century the Welsh language was the predominant speech among the settlers of the Barony. Not only was Welsh spoken in the Barony and the other Welsh settlements, but so numerous were the Welsh in the city of Philadelphia that Welsh was a tongue commonly heard on the streets of that municipality well into the eighteenth century.[19]

A second Welsh settlement was founded during the early years of the Pennsylvania colony. It was located in what was subsequently named Gwynedd Township in Montgomery County to the north of Philadelphia. It owed its origins to the favorable reports sent home to North Wales by the Welsh Quakers who had emigrated from that section of the Principality. Interest was also aroused by Hugh Roberts, an influential Quaker religious leader, who returned from Pennsylvania to visit Wales in 1697. The result was the organization of a group of Welsh who planned to emigrate to America. They sent over two advance agents the same year to make arrangements for their arrival. The latter, William John and Thomas ap Evan, purchased a tract of some 7,820 acres in Montgomery County well suited for their purposes. When the rest of the party arrived in Philadelphia in 1698 they resold it in small tracts to their fellow countrymen. Prompt occupation of the tract followed. The Welsh called it Gwynedd in honor of the ancient kingdom of North Wales. They were soon joined by others from the homeland.[20]

Although most of these Welsh settlers were Anglicans, all joined in building a Friends' log meeting house in 1700. This original edifice was replaced by a stone building in 1712 and this in turn by the present meeting house which dates from 1823. Gwynedd Monthly meeting was established in 1714 to form the fourth and last of the Welsh Quaker meetings to be established in America. Gwynedd became one of the most prosperous agricultural areas of Pennsylvania.[21]

The news of Penn's experiment in the new world as reported in letters from Welsh Quakers to their friends in the homeland soon became well-known in Wales. Additional Quakers continued to migrate and were soon joined by others—Baptists, Anglicans, and Presbyterians. The bulk of these people settled in the so-called "Barony" among the earlier Quaker Welsh; others took up lands elsewhere in the Philadelphia vicinity, while still others settled in the city itself.

The Baptists were perhaps the most numerous of these non-Quaker Welsh immigrants, and it was in connection with this denomination that the Welsh were to exert their most significant influence during the colonial period. From the very beginning, Welsh ministers and laymen played a vital part in aiding in the formation or serving as ministers of many of the early Baptist churches established in the middle colonies during the eighteenth century. In fact, the historians of the Philadelphia Baptist Association (which when it was formed in 1707 constituted the mother Baptist group for all America from Virginia to New York) give full credit to the Welsh Baptists by stating that "the Philadelphia Association originated with churches planted by members from Wales."[22] Some seven early Baptist churches in the Philadelphia area were founded by Welsh immigrants. Another five were organized in New Jersey with the aid of Welsh ministers and probably included Welshmen among their congregations.

Of the Baptist churches founded by Welsh immigrants, the best known was unquestionably historic Pennepek Church, mother church of the Baptist denomination in the middle colonies. It dates from 1683 when a group of Welsh arrived from Llanddewi, Radnorshire, and settled in Lower Dublin Township (now the 23rd ward of northeast Philadelphia). They joined with others to found the church in January of 1688. Two of the group, Samuel Jones and Evan Morgan, served as co-pastors while the old Welsh *Bible* brought from the homeland was used for services well into the eighteenth century. The other churches founded by the Welsh Baptists included the Tredyffrin or Great Valley Church organized in 1711, the Brandywine Church organized in 1715, the Montgomery Church organized in 1719, the Tulpohoken Church organized in 1738, and the Iron Hill Church near Newark, Delaware, organized in 1703. Then, too, there had always been a strong Welsh membership among the city parishioners of the Pennepek Church. When the Philadelphia branch separated to become an independent church (the First Baptist Church of Philadelphia) in 1746, they took with them as their first pastor the Reverend Jenkin Jones, an immigrant Welsh minister.[23]

An array of Welsh ministers did valiant work in promoting the Baptist cause during these early days. Such men as Evan Morgan, Samuel Jones, Nathaniel Jenkins, Thomas Griffiths, Elisha Thomas, and Hugh Davis not only ministered to their own congregations, but made frequent missionary tours, aided in setting up new churches, wrote and disseminated tracts and other types of religious literature, and played the role generally of Baptist patriarchs in the Philadelphia and surrounding area. Among these were included men who rose to such eminence that they rate among America's great religious leaders of the colonial period: Benjamin Griffith, native of Cardiganshire, scholar, author of numerous religious tracts and first official historian of the denomination in America; Abel Morgan, also of Cardiganshire, profound scholar and author of the first concordance of the *Bible* in the Welsh language (first printed in Philadelphia in 1730); Morgan Edwards of Monmouthshire, classical scholar, pastor of Pennepek Church for many years, and chief founder of Brown University.[24]

The Welsh Anglicans were perhaps as numerous as the Baptists. Some were present in Philadelphia as early as 1695. They joined with others to found historic Christ Church the same year. Others continued to emigrate in succeeding years, some settling in Philadelphia, others in the rapidly expanding surrounding country.[25]

The coming of the Reverend Evan Evans, a Welsh preacher, in 1700, to serve as pastor of Christ Church was of great significance to the future of the Welsh Anglicans and the Anglican church generally. Thanks to the efforts of this pioneer Anglican priest not only were the Welsh of this faith retained in loyalty to the church, but numerous others, Welsh and English, were converted from the Quaker faith and became members of the Anglican fold. Evans was able to take advantage of the heresy engendered by George Keith, which split the Quakers, to win converts by the score. Within two years time Evans' congregation numbered over five hundred of which a significant number were Welsh.[26]

Reverend Evans not only ministered to Christ Church, he also attempted to meet the needs of Welsh Anglicans elsewhere in Pennsylvania and Delaware. Most of the Welsh of the Gwynedd settlement were Anglicans. Encouraged by Evans, they built neat little Trinity Church at Oxford in 1711. Over in the Welsh "Barony" at Radnor enough Welsh Anglicans had settled by 1700 to allow Evans to establish a mission. From this mission evolved historic St. David's congregation. In time other distinctly Welsh Anglican churches were founded: St. James', Perkiomen in 1715, and St. Peter's in the Great Valley (Tredyffrin) to the west of Radnor in 1720. Two others, Bangor in Churchtown, Lancaster County, organized in 1733, and St. Thomas' in Morgantown,

Berks County, organized in 1756, were founded by the second generation of Welsh Anglicans along the then advancing frontier.[27]

As in the case of the Baptists, Welsh Anglican ministers played important parts in establishing their denomination in the middle colonies. Such men as John Chubb, Robert Wayman, and Griffith Hughes carried on the good work started by the Reverend Evan Evans; others, such as John Miles, Junior (son of the Baptist pioneer of Swansea), served as pastors of non-Welsh congregations, in this case historic King's Chapel, Boston. As one authority has stated his evaluation of the influence of the Welsh in the pioneer Anglican church: "An inclination to consider the Episcopal Church in colonial Pennsylvania and Delaware as 'English' is soon corrected by the documents, which reveal the startling fact that to a large extent it was Welsh."[28]

All six churches founded by Welsh Anglicans during the colonial period are still flourishing. One, St. David's, Radnor, still has the old stone edifice built in 1715. It had no paved floor until 1765. A vestry house was built in 1767. A gallery was built the same year, access to which was provided by an outside staircase, an arrangement believed to be unique in the story of colonial architecture in America. Today, a small, simple chapel of rough field stone, it stands as a monument to the faith of the little band of devout Anglican Welshmen who were the pioneer settlers of the region.

In time, the Welsh in Pennsylvania began to expand beyond the confines of their original settlements. From Gwynedd numbers of Welsh penetrated into the adjoining townships of Montgomery and Bucks counties. In similar fashion, the Welsh of the "Barony" overflowed into southwestern Bucks county. Still later in the eighteenth century, beginning around 1718 and continuing for some fifty years, groups of Welsh moved beyond what they called the "Welsh Mountains" west of Radnor into the Conestoga Valley then the Pennsylvania frontier. By 1720, several thousands of acres in the Morgantown area of Berks County and the Churchtown area of Lancaster County had been assigned to Welshmen. More Welsh settlers took up some 20,000 acres along the Wyomissing and Cacoosing Creeks in Berks County. Thus another extensive Welsh settlement grew up in southern Berks County and adjacent Lancaster County.[29] The two villages of Morgantown and Churchtown marked the centers of the settlement with most of the Welsh settlers occupying farms in the surrounding areas. Most of these Welsh settlers (many of the second generation) were Baptists and Anglicans, and ever mindful of their religious duties soon began to organize churches. The Baptists founded a congregation along Tulpohoken Creek, Caernarvon Township, Berks County, in 1738. It moved subsequently to Reading in 1828.[30] The Welsh Anglicans founded a church which they called Bangor in 1733.

It became the nucleus of the village of Churchtown in Lancaster County. The Anglicans also organized St. Thomas' Church on the banks of Conestoga Creek in Caernarvon Township, Berks County, in 1756. The church was subsequently moved to the village of Morgantown in 1786.[31]

Welsh immigrants were also responsible for the settlement of a large stretch of territory in northwestern Delaware. The settlement, called the Delaware Welsh Tract, dates from the boundary dispute between Lord Baltimore and William Penn, both of whom claimed the area. Baltimore's fiery governor, George Talbot, had driven the first white settlers out of the area. Penn, in retaliation, determined to settle it en mass. As proprietor of the Delaware area, he granted a tract of some 30,000 acres to three Welsh immigrant settlers of the Great Valley (Tredyffrin) in Pennsylvania, David Evans, William Davies, and William Willis in 1701. Under the stimulus of the original grantees, Welsh immigrants from Pennsylvania and from Wales flocked into the Tract and soon had taken up most of the land. The present-day Pencader Hundred, the new settlement soon became a prosperous community and the site of two noted colonial American congregations, the Iron Hill Welsh Baptist and the Pencader Welsh Presbyterian churches.[32]

The first of these, the Iron Hill Church, was known as the emigrating church and had its origins in Wales itself. In the spring of 1701, several Welsh Baptists from Pembrokeshire and Caermarthenshire resolved to emigrate to America. They were advised to organize themselves into a church before emigrating. This they did and came to America as a church-emigrant in 1701. Upon arriving in Philadelphia they were advised to settle in the Pennepek area where they were received courteously by their Baptist fellow countrymen. They remained in the area for about a year when religious dissention between them and the Pennepek group arose over the question of the laying on of hands in the process of the ritual of Baptism. This as well as general dissatisfaction with the Pennepek area led to the group's migration in 1703 to the newly established Welsh Tract in Delaware. They settled in the vicinity of Iron Hill near Newark and built a small church edifice at the foot of the hill the same year. The discovery of iron ore led to the mining and smelting of this raw material and brought considerable wealth to a number of the settlers. The others became successful farmers. The Iron Hill Baptist Church became the mother church to eight new congregations in Delaware and adjacent Pennsylvania as well as to the equally well-known Welsh Neck Baptist Church on the Peedee River in South Carolina. For over a period of seventy years the pastors of the little church were native Welshmen while Welsh continued to be used in preaching and keeping church records until the beginning of the nineteenth century. Among the famous sons of this church were Able Morgan, Jr., founder of Fogg's Manor Academy, the first Baptist educational institution in America, and Oliver Evans, one of America's prominent early inventors.[33]

The other religious congregation, Pencader Welsh Presbyterian Church, enjoyed according to some authorities the honor of having been the chief center of Presbyterianism in America for a number of years.[34] Presbyterianism (not to be confused with Calvinistic-Methodism introduced into America by the nineteenth century Welsh immigrants and also referred to as Welsh Presbyterianism) had never been strong as a dissenting religion in Wales. A number of congregations made their appearance in Caermarthenshire and elsewhere in Wales during the early part of the seventeenth century, and a presbytery was established in Caermarthenshire. With the restoration of the Stuarts and the renewal of persecution of dissenters, people from Caermarthenshire were responsible for the appearance of this faith among the Welsh of colonial America. A Welsh preacher, Malachi Jones, organized a Presbyterian church at Abington, Pennsylvania, in 1714. Undoubtedly some Welshmen were among the members of his congregation. Others of this religious persuasion settled in the Great Valley and founded what became the Pencader congregation sometime in the first decade of the eighteenth century. David Evans and William Davies, two of the original grantees of the Delaware Welsh Tract, were members of this congregation, and because of their influence the vast majority of the little congregation eventually settled in Delaware. The little church was flourishing there (now the village of Glasgow) by 1711 and had taken the name of the Welsh Tract Presbyterian Church.[35] David Evans, a young layman, was its first religious leader. Censured at first for preaching without having been properly licensed, Evans attended Yale for proper religious training and then returned to Delaware to be ordained as pastor of the church. The latter continued to include the Welsh who had remained back in the Great Valley until 1714 when the Pennsylvania settlers formed themselves into a distinct congregation and named their church the Great Valley Presbyterian Church. It shares with the Pencader congregation the distinction of having been one of the two Presbyterian churches founded in colonial America by Welsh immigrants.[36]

Two of Pencader's pastors became outstanding leaders of the Presbyterian denomination in America. David Evans was chosen first clerk of the newly created New Castle Presbytery upon its formation in 1717. The new presbytery embraced all the territory in the colonies south of Philadelphia. His election made the Welsh Tract Church, of which he was pastor, the seat of the chief administrative officer of the denomination for this area and probably accounts for the change of its name to "Pencader" which means "high chair" in Welsh and interpreted as chief center of the faith. The name maintained its significance when Evans was succeeded in this office by his cousin, Thomas Evans, the second pastor of the church.

The latter was later elevated to the position of clerk of the entire Presbyterian Synod of the colonies, then the highest Presbyterian body in America. The intimate association of the little congregation with two of the chief officers of early Presbyterianism in America during these years has been held responsible for the belief that it was the accepted center of the faith for many years. The church gave its name, Pencader, to the hundred or township which was soon set up for the region by the Delaware Assembly.[37]

David and Thomas Evans both wrote religious tracts of importance and contributed greatly to the organization of early Presbyterianism in the middle colonies. Thomas Evans established an academy at Pencader, believed to have been the first school established by the Presbyterians in America. Timothy Griffiths, the third pastor, played an active role as captain of a regiment of Delaware troops in the defense of New York Colony against the French in 1744.[38] Other Welsh Presbyterian ministers held pastorates of various churches in Pennsylvania, New Jersey, and Delaware. Here again the Welsh furnished important religious leaders to another religious denomination in organizing churches and carrying on missionary activities. Perhaps the most distinguished son of the Pencader Church was the noted Samuel Davies, Presbyterian missionary to Virginia, one of the founders of Princeton University, and subsequently that institution's second president.[39]

Both the Welsh Baptist and Presbyterian churches figured in the events of the American Revolution. During the Battle of Cooch's Bridge in September, 1777, the Baptist Church was used as a last stand by the American forces in an abortive attempt to halt the advance of Lord Howe's troops. The Presbyterian Church was used as a hospital by the British and Hessian troops during the same engagement. The present Baptist edifice, built in 1746, rates as one of Delaware's historic monuments.

There was also a strong Anglican element among the Welsh who settled in Delaware. The Welsh Anglicans were especially strong at Apoquinimink in the southern part of Newcastle County. They helped to form a church at that place in 1705. Welsh Anglicans were also to be found among the congregations of Emmanuel Church, Newcastle, and Whiteclay Church some ten miles to the west.[40]

The Welsh were responsible for establishing two colonies in the deep South, the last of their group efforts during the colonial period. A small group settled in New Hanover County, North Carolina, and in adjacent Dauphine and Sampson counties along Burgaw Creek and the Black River in the 1730's. Unfortunately, not much is known of the background and history of this little colony.[41]

Quite the opposite is the case of the Welsh colony along the Peedee

River in South Carolina concerning which we have detailed information. Interest in South Carolina among the Welsh resulted from the propaganda efforts of the authorities of that colony to induce settlements within its limits. Propaganda of this sort reached the Delaware Welsh Tract and aroused sufficient interest to lead to the sending by that group of two representatives to South Carolina in 1735. They were shown the Peedee River area which they found to their liking, but insisted that the colonial authorities permit Welsh settlement in a body with ample land and exclusive privileges of ownership of the soil. They therefore petitioned that an extensive tract be appropriated for them according to these terms. The South Carolina Assembly agreed and granted to them in 1736 a tract of land consisting of some 173,000 acres in Queensboro Township, Craven County, on both sides of the Peedee River for exclusive Welsh settlement. Subsequently in 1737, the tract was extended up the Peedee to the juncture of its two main branches.[42]

The terms were generous and the Welsh were not slow to migrate. Beginning in the spring of 1736, a company of Welsh, among them Jenkin and Owen David, ancestors of the prominent South Carolina family of that name, arrived at the Peedee. Evidently the lands bordering the river at one of its bends attracted their fancy most. Here, opposite the present village of Society Hill, they settled in such numbers that the region has been known ever since as the Welsh Neck. The Neck or bend of the river extended a distance of six miles and embraced rich agricultural land several miles in width on both sides of the Peedee. Between 1736 and 1746 almost all the lands of the tract were taken up by Welsh families (chiefly Baptist) from Delaware, Pennsylvania, and the homeland. The little colony soon assumed a permanent character thanks to the leadership of James James who held large stretches of land on both sides of the river. Since many of the first settlers had been members of the Iron Hill Baptist Church back in Delaware, they organized the Welsh Neck Baptist Church in 1738 and selected Phillip James, the son of James James, as their first pastor.[43]

The South Carolina authorities offered bounties in the form of free food supplies and farm implements to attract more Welsh settlers. Their efforts were so successful that the Welsh Neck settlement became so exclusively Welsh that all efforts of immigrants of other nationality to settle in the region were successfully opposed until the older generation of Welsh settlers had passed away. Conditions in the Peedee settlement were difficult in the beginning, but obstacles were overcome rapidly. The Neck became a prosperous plantation area by the time of the American Revolution.[44] Negro slavery was introduced quite early with the result that the South Carolina Welsh colony became (the North Carolina settlement may have had slaves also) the only Welsh settlement in America where slavery was championed by the freedom-loving Welsh as a necessary institution. Elsewhere, the Welsh, because of their democratic and equalitarian background, were to be found in the forefront of the critics of the "unique" institution. The Welsh Neck settlement was strong enough to muster thirty-nine men for service with the American Revolutionary forces. As for the Welsh Neck Baptist Church, it became the mother of thirty-eight Baptist churches in South Carolina.[45]

Thus by the end of the colonial period, Welsh immigrants and their descendants were to be found not only scattered throughout the thirteen colonies, but also in compact numbers in various key areas. In the north was the smallest of these Welsh settlements, that of Swansea, Massachusetts, consisting of some two hundred settlers. Farther to the south were the extensive Pennsylvania settlements, comprising the so-called Welsh Barony and adjacent Great Valley settlements to the west of the Schuylkill River, the Gwynedd settlement to the north of the city of Philadelphia, the small Lancaster and Berks counties settlements, and a considerable proportion of the inhabitants of the Pennsylvania metropolis itself. It has been estimated that the number of Welsh settlers in these areas amounted to some 6,000.[46] Over the provincial line lay the Delaware Welsh Tract in Newcastle County with a Welsh population estimated around 1,000. Then far to the south were to be found the North Carolina Black River colony of unknown strength and the Welsh Neck settlement of South Carolina with an estimated Welsh population of some 500.[47]

As one might expect, it was in Philadelphia and Pennsylvania that the Welsh exerted a very strong influence socially and politically for here they were most numerous. For over a century, men of Welsh blood occupied prominent positions in the life of the city, and in as much as the city and its surrounding counties dominated the life of the province, the Welsh played an equally prominent part in the life of the Pennsylvania province itself. A large proportion of the early city fathers, including mayors, Edward Roberts and Robert Wharton, were Welsh. Such, too, was the case in respect to the fields of justice, the arts, science, business and commerce. For the first quarter of the century, 1682-1730, almost all the physicians were Welshmen including Dr. Thomas Wynne, who attended William Penn during his first voyage to America. Many of the eminent religious leaders, too, as we have seen were Welshmen.[48]

Here in early Philadelphia were published two monumental books in the Welsh language. The first, *Annerch i'r Cymru* (Salutation to the Welsh), was the pietistic work of Ellis Pugh, a humble stonemason and Quaker preacher, who willed the manuscript to the Gwynedd Quaker Meeting. The latter had it printed by Andrew Bradford in 1721. It was subsequently translated and issued in an English version. The other, *Cyd-gordiad Egwyddorawl o'r Scrythurau* (Alphabetical Concordance of the Scriptures), was the work of Abel Morgan, the noted Baptist divine, and was the first real Welsh concordance of the *Bible*. It was published in 1730 by Samuel Keimer and Dafydd Harry, a Welshman, eight years after Morgan's death. Both books rate among the rarest of Americana.[49]

Two other works in Welsh were also published in Philadelphia during these early years. The firm of Benjamin Franklin and Hugh Meredydd published a Welsh translation of an English book by Benjamin Wallin *Y Dull a Fedyddio a Dwfr* (The Manner of Baptizing with Water) in 1730. Meredydd, a Welshman, later aided Franklin in publishing the noted Pennsylvania *Gazette*. The other work in Welsh entitled simply, *A Welsh Pamphlet,* was a reprint of a British original printed by Andrew Bradford in 1735. It dealt with moral reflections on death, judgment, Heaven and Hell.[50]

It was in Philadelphia that the oldest Welsh-American society was founded in 1729 for the purpose of honoring St. David, the patron saint of Wales. It developed eventually into a benevolent society aiding newly arrived immigrants from Wales, dispensing charity when necessary, and sponsoring interest in Welsh culture. The Welsh Society of Philadelphia is still in existence today, a monument to the durability of self-consciousness of the little ethnic group that made its weight felt so strongly in the early life of the city. It claims the honor of being the oldest existing society of Philadelphia.[51]

Throughout the thirteen colonies, Welsh immigrants and those of Welsh stock rose to eminence in various fields of leadership, adding their skill and talent to the development of the new country. Among the outstanding Welsh immigrants of the colonial period in statecraft were the father and son combination, Nicholas and John Easton, both governors of Rhode Island; John Evans, friend of William Penn and governor of Pennsylvania; and David Lloyd, foe of arbitrary government, who served as chief justice of Pennsylvania. Another immigrant, Thomas Lloyd, headed the liberal party in Pennsylvania, forced constitutional concessions from the Penn family, and served as governor of the colony and speaker of the assembly for many years. Joseph Jenckes, the son of an immigrant, served as governor of Rhode Island. Two members of the noted Morris family, Lewis and Robert Hunter Morris, occupied the two highest governmental positions that existed during the colonial period. The former, the son of an immigrant, served as governor of New Jersey and later as chief justice of New York, while the latter, his son, played a similar role as governor of Pennsylvania and chief justice of New Jersey. Another son of Welsh immigrant parents, Gabriel Jones, occupied the high position of King's Attorney for the colony of Virginia.[52]

Other distinguished Welsh colonial immigrants included Price

Hughes, Indian agent and leader in the effort to oust the French from their control of the trans-Appalachian southwest; the Leonard brothers, pioneer ironmasters of Massachusetts; and Joseph Jenks, inventor, ironmaster, and minter of the famous Pine Tree shilling. Another immigrant, Lewis Evans, became America's most distinguished geographer whose maps of the middle colonies were unsurpassed. As one would expect from a highly religious people, the Welsh furnished a constellation of famous religious leaders. Ellis Pugh, the Quaker mystic; Evan Evans, the Anglican divine; Benjamin Griffith, the first historian of the Baptists; Abel Morgan, the Baptist divine; Morgan Edwards, Baptist scholar and founder of Brown University; the Evans cousins, David and Thomas, pioneer Presbyterian leaders; all were Welsh immigrants and leaders of their denominations. Leaders, too, were Able Morgan, Jr., the Baptist educator, and Dr. Samuel Davies, Presbyterian missionary to Virginia and president of Princeton University, both sons of Welsh immigrant parents.[53]

Three Welsh-Americans acquired eminence as pioneers in American medicine. Thomas Cadwallader, first to inoculate against the smallpox and to make an autopsy, and John Morgan, medical scholar and Physician-in-Chief of the Revolutionary Army, were both sons of immigrants, while John Jones, the author of the first American surgical textbook, was the grandson of Welsh immigrants. Two sons of immigrants acquired international reputations in vastly different fields. David Rittenhouse, son of a Welsh Quakeress, became renowned as a scientist and inventor; Elihu Yale, a native of Boston and the benefactor of Yale University, worked his way up in the service of the British East India Company and served as the governor of the Company for many years.[54]

Welsh-Americans played their part, too, in the great struggle for American independence. Each of the little settlements sent its quota of volunteers to fight with the revolutionary forces. Five of the famous signers of the Declaration of Independence were definitely of Welsh stock: Francis Lewis, wealthy merchant of New York, was born in Wales. Lewis Morris of New York was a grandson of Welsh immigrants. Thomas Jefferson, the author of the noted document, and William Floyd of New York were descendants of early seventeenth century Welsh immigrants. Button Gwinnett, the last of the quintet, revolutionary governor of Georgia and general in the patriot cause, was born in England, the son of Welsh parents.[55]

Other patriotic leaders included John Nicholson, Comptroller-General of Pennsylvania, a Welsh immigrant; Robert Morris, the "financier of the Revolution," born in Liverpool of Welsh parents; Samuel Meredith, Treasurer of Pennsylvania, a son of Welsh immigrants; Lambert Cadwallader, Philadelphia leader, and Abner Nash, revolutionary governor of North Carolina, both grandsons of Welsh immigrants; and the brothers, Allen and Willie Jones of North Carolina, Joseph Jones and Fielding Lewis of Virginia, and Edward Lloyd of Maryland—all of Welsh stock.[56]

In the military field, a number of Welsh-Americans occupied important positions. Evan Shelby, an immigrant, played a vital role as a frontiersman and general in charge of frontier operations in Virginia and Tennessee; Frederick Watts, another immigrant, played a similar role as general in charge of the Pennsylvania frontier; Otho Holland Williams, the son of immigrant parents, played an active role in the southern campaigns and rose to the rank of general. Three grandsons of immigrants, Francis Nash, John Cadwallader, and the renowned Daniel Morgan, all served as generals in the Revolutionary Army. The Reverend David Jones, Baptist minister and son of immigrants, became perhaps the most famous chaplain of the American forces.[57]

Welsh-Americans were represented on the Loyalist side as well. Two of the descendants of the Leonard Brothers, pioneer iron-masters, chose the side of the king. Daniel Leonard, later chief-justice of Bermuda, and his brother, George, led the fight for king and crown in Massachusetts, and were forced to flee to Halifax when the British vacated Boston.[58]

Welsh blood and Welsh talent thus contributed its modest share to the development of America both during the colonial and revolutionary periods. Thousands of small farmers, tradesmen, merchants, and businessmen toiled in their own humble way for America's betterment, while an array of distinguished individuals of their ethnic stock rose to eminence among the leaders of the evolving nation and contributed their talents for the common good. An example had been set for subsequent Welsh immigrants and their children to emulate. The stage was set for the coming of the nineteenth century when thousands of Welsh immigrants were to flock to America and to add their bit to the development of the new Republic in virtually every field of endeavor.

FOOTNOTES ON CHAPTER III

1. David Williams, *Cymru ac America, Wales and America,* Cardiff (University of Wales Press), 1946, p. 19.

2. The following data on individual Welsh immigrants was obtained from biographical sketches of certain of their distinguished descendants in the *Dictionary of American Biography.* To New England in the seventeenth century came Griffith Bowen and his son Henry, the first settlers of Woodstock, Conn.; Alexander Evans, who settled in Springfield, Mass. in 1640; Thomas ap Jones to Weymouth, Mass. in 1651; James and Myles Morgan to Boston in 1636; Rev. John Jones to Concord, Mass. in the 1630's; one Moody, the father of Rev. Joshua Moody, a Harvard College benefactor, to Roxbury, Mass. in 1635; John Thompson to Mass. before 1623; Evan Thomas to Boston in 1640; David Yale, father of Elihu Yale, to Boston with his mother and step-father, Theophilus Eaton, in 1637; Nicholas Easton and his son John to Mass. in 1634 (both later served as governors of Rhode Island); Thomas

Flint to Salem, Mass. in 1642; Captain Nathaniel Jarrett to Boston in 1668; Nathaniel Oates to Mass. in 1660; John Russell to Raynham, Mass. in 1652; William Buell to Windsor, Conn. in 1639; Thomas Merrick to Springfield, Mass. around 1635; Richard Rhys Morgan to Boston in 1660; Solomon and James Leonard to Plymouth, Mass. in 1630.

To the Middle Colonies came Jaspar Griffing to Southeld, Long Island in 1675; Richard Floyd to Setauket, Long Island in 1655; the controversial Rev. Morgan Jones to Newton, Long Island in 1660; Lewis Morris to New York in the 1660's; and John Condit to Newark, N. J. in 1678.

To the Southern Colonies came Robert Lewis to Gloucester County, Va. in 1635; Thomas Owen to Henrici County, Va. in the seventeenth century; Rhys ap Thomas to Maryland in the seventeenth century; John Price to Henrici County, Va. in 1620; Philip Thomas to Va. in 1651; John Jones to Va. in the seventeenth century; Anthony Hardy to North Carolina in 1695; Robert Jones to Va. in the seventeenth century; and the ancestors of Thomas Jefferson, Fielding Lewis, Edward Lloyd, John Marshall, and Thomas ap Catesby Jones to Va. in the seventeenth century.

3.   The Welsh surnames present numerous difficulties to the student of local Welsh history, genealogy, and Welsh settlements throughout the world. Some thirty-nine surnames and their variant spellings include about ninety-five percent of the Welsh wherever found. Surnames are of three sorts: Anglicanized patronomic possessives; their Welsh equivalents, and those of pure Keltic derivation. The first are the most numerous and in order of their numerical strength follow: Jones, Williams, Thomas, Edwards, Richards, Owens, Davies or Davis, Hughes, Roberts, Lewis, Evans, Howell or Howells, James, Humphreys, Morris, Harris, Daniels, Jenkins, Walters, Hopkins. The second group, corresponding to the Mac's and Mc's of the Irish and Scots, are the result of the incorporation of the Welsh word for son, *mab* before vowels and *map* before consonants, with the patronomic. Thus mab Owen (son of Owen) eventually became ab Owen, and then Bowen; map Richard, ap Richard, then Pritchard; map Hugh, ap Hugh, and dropping the h, Pugh. The most numerous of such names include Powell, Pugh, Price, Parry, Probert, Pritchard, Bowen, and Bevan. To the third class belong such names as Lloyd, Morgan, Gwynne, Griffith, Vaughan, Meredith, and Llewelyn.

With such a paucity of surnames even the Welsh found it difficult to distinguish their fellows accurately for identification purposes. It became the custom to tack onto the person's name some further identification. Virtually every Welsh colony had its John Jones the Shop, John Jones the Deacon, John Jones Peg-leg, and the like. Very amusing examples of such further identification exist, including that of the prairie community of Powell, South Dakota, where there was a Hugh Roberts Religious, a Hugh Roberts Ungodly, and a Hugh Roberts Inbetween!

4. For the story of nonconformity in Wales, see Thomas Rees, *History of Protestant Nonconformity in Wales,* London (John Snow), 1861; also David Williams, *A History of Modern Wales, op. cit.,* pp. 110-26, 139-57.

5. *Ibid.*

6. Generally accepted among the American Welsh is the belief that the great Roger Williams, the founder of Rhode Island and a leader of the Baptists, was born in Wales. It is now known that Williams was born in London. He may have been of Welsh extraction.

7. For the story of John Myles, see J. Davis, *History of the Welsh Baptists from the Year Sixty Three to the Year One Thousand Seven Hundred and Seventy,* Pittsburgh (D. M. Hogan), 1835, pp. 38-40; also Thomas Armitage, *A History of the Baptists Traced by Their Vital Principles from the Time of Our Lord and Savior Jesus Christ to the Year 1886,* New York (Bryan, Taylor & Co.), 1887, pp. 678-81.

8. *Ibid.*

9. *Ibid.*

10. *Ibid.*

11. Otis Olney Wright, *History of Swansea, Massachusetts, 1667-1917,* Swansea, Mass., 1917, pp. 101-7.

12. For the background of the Quakers in Wales, see T. Mardy Rees, *A History of the Quakers in Wales and Their Emigration to North America,* Carmarthen (W. Spurrell), 1925, pp. 1-178.

13. For a detailed analysis of the early Welsh Quaker settlement of Pennsylvania, see Charles H. Browning, *Welsh Settlement of Pensylvania,* Philadelphia (W. J. Campbell), 1912, *passim;* also Wayland F. Dunaway, "Early Welsh Settlers of Pennsylvania," *Pennsylvania History,* XII (Oct., 1945), pp. 251-69.

14. Dunaway, *op. cit.,* p. 255.

15. *Ibid.,* p. 258.

16. *Ibid.,* pp. 258-60.

17. Browning, *op. cit.,* pp. 505, 525.

18. *Ibid.,* pp. 519-21.

19. Hartmann, Edward George, "The Welsh Society of Philadelphia," *Y Drych,* CII (Feb. 15, 1953), pp. 12-13.

20. Howard M. Jenkins, *Historical Collections Relating to Gwynedd, a Township of Montgomery County, Pennsylvania, Settled 1689 by Welsh Immigrants, with Some Data Referring to the Adjoining Township of Montgomery, also a Welsh Settlement,* Philadelphia (Ferris Bros.), 1884, pp. 1-76.

21. *Ibid.*

22. A. D. Gillette, ed., *Minutes of the Philadelphia Baptist Association from A.D. 1707 to A.D. 1807; Being the First One Hundred Years of Its Existence,* Philadelphia (American Baptist Publication Society), 1851, p. 3.

23. For data on the early Welsh Baptist churches of Pennsylvania, see Gillette, *ibid.,* pp. 11-24.

24. See biographical sketches in the *Dictionary of American Biography.*

25. Nelson R. Burr, "The Welsh Episcopalians of Colonial Pennsylvania and Delaware," *Historical Magazine of the Protestant Episcopal Church,* VIII (June, 1939), pp. 101-5.

26. *Ibid.*

27. *Ibid.,* pp. 107-16.

28. *Ibid.,* p. 120.

29. Dunaway, *op. cit.,* p. 262. For additional data on these Welsh frontier settlements, see H. Frank Eschelman, "Two Centuries of Caernarvon History," Lancaster County Historical Society, *Proceedings,* XXVI (June, 1922), pp. 145-51; John J. McKenna, "Early Welsh in Berks County," *Historical Review of Berks County,* Reading, Pa., Jan., 1950; Benjamin F. Owen, *The Welsh of Cumru Township, an Address Delivered before the Historical Society of Berks County, Pa.,* Sept. 12, 1899, Reading, Pa., 1899.

30. Gillette, *op. cit.,* p. 24.

31. Burr, *op. cit.,* pp. 113-16.

32. Edward W. Cooch, "Pencader—Chief Chair of Presbyterianism," *Delaware Historic Events,* pp. 85-8; "Welsh Tract Baptist Meeting House," *Delaware Historic Events,* pp. 79-84.

33. Gillette, *op. cit.,* p. 15; Richard B. Cook, *The Early and Later Delaware Baptists,* Philadelphia (American Baptist Publication Society), 1880, pp. 13-20.

34. Cooch, "Pencader—Chief Chair of Presbyterianism," *op. cit.,* pp. 85-8.

35. W. T. Skinner, "History of Pencader Presbyterian Church of Glascow, Delaware," in *History of Pencader Presbyterian Church, Historical Addresses,* Wilmington, Del. (John M. Rogers), 1899, pp. 31-51.

36. Robert M. Patterson, *History of the Presbyterian Church of the Great (Chester) Valley,* Philadelphia (Alfred Martin), 1869, *passim.*

37. Cooch, "Pencader—Chief Chair of Presbyterianism," *op. cit.,* pp. 85-8.

38. Skinner, *op. cit.,* p. 35.

39. See biographical sketch in the *American Dictionary of Biography.*

40. Burr, *op. cit.,* pp. 117-18.

41. S. A. Ashe, *History of North Carolina,* I, p. 254 and note; see also William H. Foote, *Sketches of North Carolina,* New York (Robert Carter), 1846, p. 159.

42. Alexander Gregg, *History of the Old Cheraws,* New York (Richardson & Co.), 1867, pp. 47-50.

43. *Ibid.,* pp. 52-4.

44. *Ibid.,* pp. 55-62.

45. *Ibid.,* p. 405; also Armitage, *op. cit.,* p. 713.

46. Wayland F. Dunaway, *A History of Pennsylvania,* New York (Prentice Hall), 1948, p. 75.

47. Robert L. Meriwether, *The Expansion of South Carolina, 1729-1765,* Kingsport, Tenn. (Southern Publishers, Inc.), 1940, p. 160.

48. Dunaway, "Early Welsh Settlers of Pennsylvania," *op. cit.,* p. 261.

49. See William Williams, "The First Three Welsh Books Printed in America," *National Library of Wales Journal,* II (Summer, 1942), pp. 109-20; also his "More About the First Three Books Printed in America," *National Library of Wales Journal,* III (Summer, 1943), pp. 19-22.

50. *Ibid.*

51. Hartmann, *op. cit.,* pp. 12-13.

52. See biographical sketches of these important Welsh-Americans in the *Dictionary of American Biography, passim.*

53. *Ibid.*

54. *Ibid.*

55. *Ibid.*

56. *Ibid.*

57. *Ibid.*

58. *Ibid.*

CHAPTER IV

THE STORY OF NINETEENTH CENTURY
WELSH IMMIGRATION TO AMERICA

During the greater part of the eighteenth century Welsh emigration to America was confined to isolated individuals. Pressure on dissenting religious groups had ceased and the strong economic influences which encouraged later emigration had not as yet set in. Towards the end of the eighteenth century, however, the Welsh began again to emigrate in numbers to America. From 1795 onwards, a stream of Welshmen and their families left their homeland for the new Republic across the sea—a movement that was to continue with little let-up for over a century. In certain cases, the Welsh came because they were attracted by the idealism and democracy of the new nation and felt that America was the home of political and religious freedom. In most cases, however, they came as the result of bad economic conditions at home and in the hope of bettering themselves economically in the new world.[1]

The bulk of the Welsh immigrants of the nineteenth century fell into two main classes, those primarily interested in agriculture and those having a skilled labor background. In addition, a minority of immigrants representing the various professions, the trades, business and commerce, and preachers, singers, and musicians accompanied the larger groups. These latter people either settled among their countrymen in the compact Welsh settlements or struck out on their own wherever they thought opportunities seemed brightest.

For the first quarter of the new century, Welsh farmers were unquestionably the most numerous of the immigrants. They were joined by skilled industrial workers in the late 1820's. Thereafter immigrants of both groups poured in a continuous stream into the new nation for the rest of the century.

Post-medieval Wales was primarily a region of great landlords and was to remain such. The country-gentry owned most of the land but rented a considerable portion of it to tenant farmers on a lease arrangement. A small percentage of free farmers eked out a miserable existence. Welsh custom, governed by the paucity of acreage holding or renting, saw either the oldest or the youngest son inherit the farm or the father's tenant rights upon the death or retirement of the latter. Other sons, and since Welsh families were large there were many of these, were forced either to seek work as farm laborers or leave their native environment. Many of these flocked in time to the new industrial areas of South Wales to find work in the coal mines and iron manufacturing plants. Others desiring to continue as farmers were forced to leave Wales. It was these sons and their families who were to form the chief reservoir for future emigration.

Unfortunately for Wales, an unbroken succession of bad harvests had plagued that country during the years 1798 to 1802, and this factor together with the rising cost of living engendered by the war with France brought about depressed conditions among the Welsh farming population and reduced many to the status of destitution. The repressive measures taken by the Pitt government to curb free speech during this period discouraged many of the Welsh intellectuals, imbued with the idealism of the American and French revolutions. News of inexpensive, fertile land easily obtainable in the frontier regions of the new Republic and of the Ohio Country in particular soon became widely known in Wales. The combination of bad economic conditions at home, repressive governmental policies, plus this rosy information, proved good enough to convince many Welsh farmers of the wisdom of emigrating to the United States. A movement set in which, before it had ceased with the outbreak of war between Britain and America in 1812, resulted in the establishment of five new Welsh-American pioneer agricultural communities, one in Pennsylvania, one in New York, and three in the Ohio country.

The beginnings of the new Welsh immigration date from the coming of a small party of some eighteen Welsh people to New York in March, 1795, after a fourteen weeks ocean voyage. They came in search of good agricultural land. Learning that the lands granted to Baron von Steuben of Revolutionary War fame by the state of New York were being thrown open to settlement, they determined to take advantage of the cheap prices offered and to settle in up-state New York. Accordingly, they went up the Hudson by sloop to Albany, thence to Fort Schuyler, the present Utica, by flatboat, and then overland to the Steuben area where they arrived in September, 1795. The little group formed the nucleus of the future, strong, Oneida County Welsh settlement, destined to rate for over a half century as the area of greatest concentration of Welsh settlers in America.[2]

Another party of Welshmen, led by Ezekiel Hughes and Edward Bebb of Llanbrynmair, Montgomeryshire, and comprising some fifty Welsh immigrants, sailed for Philadelphia in August, 1795. Fortunately, we know much more concerning the adventures of this little party of Welsh pioneers. Hughes and Bebb, enthusiastic over the advantages of America, had persuaded the others to join them in emigrating to the new world. They arranged for the ship, *Maria,* sailing from Bristol, to pick up their little party at the small Welsh port of Caermarthen, and in July, 1795, started their trek to America by walking from inland Llanbrynmair to Caermarthen with their personal belongings following by cart. Arriving in July, they found that the *Maria* was much too large to dock at Caermarthen. Arrangements then had to made for a smaller ship to take them to Bristol where the *Maria* was docked.

Since the period was one of warfare between Britain and France, a policy of impressment of likely males into the British Navy prevailed. To the dismay of the little party, such an impressment group made its appearance at Caermarthen. The men, knowing that they would be impressed if caught, slipped away to walk overland to Bristol with the understanding that the women and personal belongings should follow aboard the small ship. The men completed the long walk in a week's time and boarded the *Maria.* To complicate matters, however, the small ship at Caermarthen was held up for three weeks for want of a suitable wind. The women, becoming impatient, decided to walk to Bristol also. Before they could arrive, the *Maria* had sailed with the men aboard. It met the small vessel from Caermarthen in Bristol channel only to find that the women were not aboard. Beset with fears for the worst, Hughes and Bebb induced the captain to return to Bristol to await the arrival of the women. Within a few days, the little party was united joyfully and the trip to America could begin its next lap.

Fifty immigrants (all but three were Welsh) were aboard. Crowded into the hold of the vessel with rations of stale food and water, the immigrants bore up under the filthy conditions as best they could. Hard luck seemed to plague them. Enroute, the *Maria* was intercepted by two warships flying the French flag. Fears for the worst were scarcely changed when the naval craft turned out to be British flying the French colors in disguise. Again the males ran the risk of being impressed into the British Navy. Fortunately, the vessel was allowed to continue on intact. Some twelve weeks after sailing, having survived a vicious storm and the long ordeal, the *Maria* docked in Philadelphia. Prophetic of the future experiences and hardships of the early nineteenth century Welsh immigrants was this journey of the Hughes-Bebb party.[3]

The new immigrants settled temporarily in the Great Valley to the west of Philadelphia, a region then still conscious of its Welsh origins. Here they spent the winter and spring of 1795-1796, while the menfolk investigated the possibilities for future settlement. Hughes and Bebb, with Ohio as their ultimate goal, remained until the spring of 1796, and then headed west. The others then began to separate, some to join their fellow countrymen in the Steuben, New York, settlement, most to throw in their fortunes with the plans of a distinguished Welsh intellectual for establishing a new settlement in western Pennsylvania.

Morgan John Rhees, their distinguished leader, was a religious and political rebel, who had been forced to flee Wales because of his republican sympathies and his opposition to the established church. An ordained Baptist minister, he had become well-known in Welsh religious circles, had written tracts attacking the evils of slavery, had gone to France to proselitize during the early years of the French Revolution, had returned to establish the first periodical in the Welsh language, and is credited by some as having been the founder of the Sunday School movement. Having earned the hatred of the Pitt government through his biting periodical articles, Rhees fled to America in 1794 imbued with the idea of founding a settlement to which his fellow Welshmen might come to enjoy religious and political freedom in the new American environment.[4]

Rhees made horseback tours to the South, the West, and New England in quest of a likely spot. He wrote a diary of his journeys in which he strongly condemned the way Americans were then treating Negro slaves in the South and the Indians in the frontier regions. He returned to the Philadelphia area, organized a union church for the Welsh of the Hughes-Bebb party in the Great Valley, petitioned the governments of both Pennsylvania and the United States for free land for his proposed settlement, and when these efforts failed formed with his fellow countrymen the Cambrian Land Company. Through it was purchased some 20,000 acres of land in western Pennsylvania in what is now Cambria County.[5]

The trek to the proposed settlement began in the fall of 1796 when the Reverend Rees Lloyd, a Congregational minister, led the first little band of sturdy pioneers to the Susquehanna, then through the primeval forests and across the various ranges of the Alleghenies, cutting a road as they went. They reached the Cambria County area towards the end of the year and selected the present site of Ebensburg as their place of settlement. Rhees followed with a group of his fellow Baptists in the following spring and settled his group some three miles to the west of Ebensburg. Thus a second Welsh center had been established in America to serve as a Mecca for future Welsh immigrants.[6]

Ezekiel Hughes and Edward Bebb had in the meantime reached the Ohio country, after having walked across Pennsylvania to Old Fort Redstone on the Monongehela, and after having floated by flatboat from that place down the Ohio to Fort Washington, present-day Cincinnati. They spent some time in search of desirable land, settled temporarily on a tract that they had purchased in the vicinity while awaiting the rich lands beyond the Great Maumee River to be thrown open to settlement. When this occurred in 1801, the two men were among the first to buy. They chose lands near the juncture of the Whitewater with the Maumee in what became Whitewater Township of Hamilton County and Morgan Township of Butler County. They were joined by two other Welshmen shortly thereafter and the nucleus of a third Welsh settlement in America had been established. Now called Shandon, it originally bore the less dignified name of "Paddy's Run," and it was by this latter title that it was to become best known to the emigration-minded Welsh.[7]

The newly arrived Welshmen of all three places set to work at once engaging in the typical pioneer activities of building log cabins, clearing enough land for the sowing of the first crops, and then continuing the process of clearing the forests until sufficient acreage had been provided for their sustenance. In time, provision was made for a schoolhouse, and of course dear to the hearts of the religious-minded Welsh, the inevitable chapel. Within the next decade they were joined by a substantial number of their kinsmen freshly arrived from the homeland. Depending upon where their ship happened to dock usually determined their first permanent place of residence. If it came to New York, they joined their fellows at the Oneida County settlement; if it arrived at Philadelphia, they headed for Cambria County, some to go on eventually to Paddy's Run in Ohio. Emigration during these early days was also encouraged by enthusiastic letters written by the pioneers of all three settlements to their friends and neighbors at home, a form of inducement to emigration which was to continue throughout the century. The return of Ezekiel Hughes to Wales in 1803 to marry his sweetheart and to bring her to America had interesting ramifications. Bubbling with enthusiasm for the Ohio country, he electrified the farmers of his native district. "Ohio Fever" began to stimulate the younger farmers and serious consideration of emigration to America gripped many. Hughes' visit was but the first of many to be made by successful Welsh immigrants to the homeland during the nineteenth century. The effect of such visits in stimulating emigration was far from insignificant.

The Welsh Oneida County settlement became concentrated in what became in time Steuben and Remsen townships, although practically from the beginning a small number remained in Fort Schuyler to become some of the first settlers of Utica as it was soon renamed. Some of these founded a Welsh Baptist church in 1801 which was the first church to be established in Utica. The surrounding Oneida County area reminded the Welsh of their old homeland with the Steuben Hills in the background to add atmosphere. The land was heavily forested and proved to be far from fertile. Summers were short; winters exceedingly harsh. With the fortitude of a people long used to hardships, however, the Welsh pioneered. It soon became evident that land and climatic conditions were not conducive to large-scale growing of grain. The Welsh therefore turned to dairying due to the abundance of good grazing land, and began to specialize in the by-products of this industry—butter and cheese-making. In certain areas of the settlement, an abundance of limestone formations encouraged quarrying—an activity with which the Welsh had been very familiar in their homeland.[8]

Certain of the later Welsh arrivals, attracted by the opening of new lands in neighboring Lewis County, carved out farms for themselves in this area to the north of Steuben, and thus extended the Welsh settlement into the neighboring county. The strength of the Welsh penetration of the two counties was revealed in a survey made in 1812 which indicated that within a distance fifteen miles long and ten miles wide with the village of Steuben as its center there were approximately seven hundred Welsh settlers. The area was well started on the way to becoming America's largest Welsh agricultural settlement.[9]

The Cambria County settlement of Pennsylvania also flourished. Under the leadership of the Reverend Rees Lloyd, the town of Ebensburg was laid out, forests were cleared, dwellings constructed, and farming commenced. Ebensburg soon became a thriving village and the center of a community of Welsh farmers. Morgan John Rhees' grandiose plans for his Beulah (Land of Freedom), which he called his settlement some three miles away, was to prove another story. In a burst of enthusiasm, he laid out his town on an exact model of Philadelphia, with streets inter-secting each other at right angles. Some sixty to seventy log buildings were soon erected including a church, a school containing a library of six hundred volumes, a mill, two inns, and various small shops for artisans. Rhees served as the first schoolmaster and founded a newspaper, the *Western Star*. All went well with Beulah until 1805, when it was decided to locate the seat of the newly created Cambria County (incidentally named after the Latin name for Wales) in nearby Ebensburg because of the latter's more central location. With this decision, Beulah began to decline; new turnpikes by-passed the village; most of the inhabitants moved to the new county seat. Within a few short years, Beulah had become an abandoned village. Today, only a few remnants of the founda-tions of the buildings indicate the former presence of the once thriving community. In a sense, Beulah became one of America's first ghost towns.

Morgan John Rhees served in various local governmental capacities, including that of county judge, but died suddenly in 1804 at the compara-tively young age of forty-four. His death ended the career of one of the most distinguished Americans from Wales. His humanitarianism as re-vealed in his championship of the enslaved Negro and the cause of the American Indian, his hatred of political and religious oppression, his love of democracy and faith in the common people, all marked him as a leading liberal of his time and an outstanding defender of all those ideals which the Welsh immigrants held dearly. Among his descendants was the late Nicholas Murray Butler, internationally known educator and president of Columbia University.[10]

Paddy's Run, the third Welsh settlement, also thrived. To it came a steady number of Welsh farmers in the years prior to the War of 1812. The land was rich and fertile, and with the opening of a public road from Cincinnati to the Maumee, a market was furnished for the farm produce of the Welsh settlers. In time many of them became well-to-do. Edward Bebb, the pioneer companion of Ezekiel Hughes, became the father of Ohio's first native-born governor, William Bebb, who served in this capacity from 1846 to 1848.

Growing pains had resulted in the enlargement of the Oneida settlement into Lewis County as we have seen. Similar growing pains soon afflicted the Cambria County settlement. The area, however, was much too close to the Ohio country to cause much serious consideration of possible farm sites in the comparatively less fertile Allegheny region surrounding Ebensburg. "Ohio Fever" turned attentions to the neighboring state where farming land was better. Two of the original Beulah settlers, Theophilus Rees and Thomas Phillips, imbued with the "Fever," went to Ohio to scout for land. They found such to their liking in Licking County and purchased some eighteen hundred acres in what became Granville Township. They moved to the area in 1802, soon to be followed by others from the Cambria County community. A new Welsh settlement, named Welsh Hills, became established as a magnet for future immigrants.[11]

Still another Welsh community made its appearance in the Ohio country during this early nineteenth century period. The founder of the new settlement, David Pugh, was a young Welshman from Radnorshire who had come to Baltimore in 1801. He purchased some four thousand acres in Delaware County, Ohio, from Dr. Samuel Jones of the Pennepek Church in Philadelphia. Located just east of the Scioto River some five miles north of present Delaware City, Pugh named his settlement Radnor after his native Welsh shire. He subdivided the tract into lots of one hundred acres each and sold these on attractive terms to a number of Welsh immigrants who had heard of his venture and soon arrived in the area. The Radnor settlement was the last of these new Welsh agricultural colonies to be established prior to the War of 1812. The outbreak of hostilities between Britain and the United States put an end temporarily to further Welsh immigration.[12]

With the cessation of hostilities in 1814, however, the movement began again. Conditions in Wales grew even worse in the post-Napoleonic period. The notorious "Corn Laws" kept the Welsh from obtaining necessary cheap food supplies from abroad while forcing up the price of food at home. A scarcity of food resulted which coupled with the high prices forced many of the Welsh farmers to the brink of starvation. During this same period the great enclosure movement which had had its beginnings in the eighteenth century was accelerated. Many of the tenant farmers were ejected from their holdings while those fortunate enough to retain their farms were plagued by a rise in rentals. Greedy and grasping landlords made the lot of the farm workers an exceedingly difficult one. Conditions such as these were to continue well into the century. Discouraged at their lot in the homeland, encouraged by glowing accounts of the great opportunities awaiting them in the new nation, many became brave enough to cut the ties with their loved ones, to risk the dreaded ocean voyage, and to chance their lot in the new world.[13]

Most of the newcomers flocked to the established Welsh farming communities where many had friends or relatives. Here they settled down or took up farms not too far away. Some, discouraged after the hectic ocean voyage or attracted by opportunities afforded, remained in the two main ports of entry, Philadelphia and New York, both of which had small Welsh immigrant colonies which dated from the turn of the century. In one case, accident played its part, prevented a party of Welsh from going on to their destination, the Paddy's Run settlement, and resulted in the creation of yet another distinctive Welsh settlement. The group, consisting of six families, set out from Baltimore in the summer of 1818 in two covered wagons. Arriving in Pittsburgh, they purchased a flatboat and floated down the Ohio. Not being experienced navigators, the trip was one of constant crisis with threats of drowning occurring with menacing frequency. Arriving in Gallipolis, they tied up to reprovision and to spend the night. Received with great hospitality by the French inhabitants of that village, they spent the night in the homes of the latter. In the morning they arose to find to their dismay that their flatboat had broken loose and had floated away (some claim that the French shrewdly set it adrift during the night to encourage the Welsh to stay). The incident was enough to convince the womenfolk, by this time more than fed up with adventures, to refuse to go farther. Remain they would and remain they did, the magic allure of Paddy's Run to the contrary notwithstanding. The usual search for cheap land in the neighborhood followed. They found it in nearby Gallia and Jackson counties where land was being offered at the cheap rate of $1.25 per acre. The usual log-cabin community soon made its appearance with the little village of Centerville in Jackson County aptly named as its nucleus. For the time being the settlement remained insignificant.[14]

The decade of the 1820's saw the yearly arrival of small groups of Welsh farmers from the homeland, most of whom settled among their kinsmen in the various established settlements. No new agricultural settlements were formed during this period, but in the following decade, the 1830's, a number of new ones made their appearance. One such grew up as a daughter colony of Paddy's Run where by this time the best agricultural land had been taken up. A group of Welshmen from that colony set out in search of good "Congress-land" (priced at $1.25 per acre) and found it in Allen County some one hundred and forty miles from the mother settlement and about ten miles from Lima in Ohio. Settlement began in 1833. Named Gomer after the Biblical figure generally accepted by the Welsh as their common ancestor (hence the frequent reference to themselves as Gomermen), the settlement prospered as it attracted more and more Welsh immigrants. With the village of Gomer as a nucleus, the Welsh spread out through Allen County.[15] Another early agricultural settlement also made its appearance in Ohio at approximately the same time. This was the Palmyra settlement in the Portage area. In this case, however, the Welsh farmers did not play the role of pioneers, but purchased farms already cleared and abandoned by Americans who had gone west in quest of new adventures.[16] Small Welsh agricultural settlements also grew up during this decade in Green Township, Indiana County, some twelve miles from Ebensburg, at Neath in Bradford County, at Spring Brook in Lackawanna County, and at Clifford near Dundaff in Susquehanna County, all in Pennsylvania.[17]

Illustrative of the strong role played by individuals in encouraging Welsh emigration at this time and determining its ultimate destination was that of the Reverend Benjamin Williams Chidlaw. The latter, a pioneer Welsh Congregational minister, had been brought to America as a child, had grown up in Ohio, had received his education at Miami University, and had then entered the ministry. He served as a missionary for the American Sunday School Union for over fifty-four years. Chidlaw was particularly interested in his fellow countrymen resident in America, and made frequent visits to all the Welsh settlements preaching and helping to organize churches. He also visited the homeland in 1836, spreading the good news of the many advantages afforded by the new Republic. In 1840, he published *Yr American, yr hwn sydd yn Cynnwys Nodau a'r Daith o Ddyffryn Ohio i Gymru* (The American, which Contains Notes on a Journey from the Ohio Valley to Wales), a pamphlet planned to furnish guidance to his compatriots who were planning on emigrating to America. In it he described the various settlements then in existence, analyzed the advantages and opportunities, stressed the qualities needed to succeed, gave instructions on how to travel, and a host of other informative details. Thanks to his pamphlet and its wide distribution in Wales, hundreds of Welsh immigrants were induced to come to America. Reverend Chidlaw enjoyed the role of a beloved elder patriarch of the Welsh people in America for the remainder of his life.[18]

Illustrative, too, of the strong role played by individuals in encouraging Welsh emigration and in this case determining its ultimate destination, was the later story of the Gallia-Jackson settlement. It had remained comparatively insignificant, attracting few additional Welsh settlers. Then the Reverend Edward Jones, a Calvinistic-Methodist minister, arrived to preach to the settlers. Impressed with the area, Jones later returned to his native Cardiganshire, and wrote a pamphlet extolling the virtues of the little settlement. The Welsh, always impressed by the writings of the clergy, read the pamphlet and soon Gallia-Jackson became a household word in Cardiganshire. Beginning in 1835, and continuing for some twenty-five years, the Welsh of that shire migrated to the little settlement in such numbers that the area was soon dubbed "Little Cardiganshire." They spread over various townships of the two counties. The result of the propaganda of the Reverend Jones was the turning of this comparatively insignificant settlement north of Gallipolis into the second strongest Welsh agricultural settlement in America (rivaling Oneida County) with its population numbering some six thousand Welsh settlers by the end of the emigration.[19]

The decade described in British history as the "hungry forties" did not improve matters among the agricultural population of Wales. Instead, conditions became more depressed than ever. The disgruntled Welsh farmer, oppressed by high rentals, harassed by new toll roads that taxed his produce on the way to market, living on the borderland of starvation, looked to America as a means of solving his dilemma. Letters from friends who had made the trek to America exuded optimism and satisfaction with their new lots. Visits by prominent Welsh-Americans who had prospered pointed out the moral. Lectures and pamphlets issued by clergymen who had been to America and had seen for themselves the advantages which the new country had to offer were received with enthusiasm. The fact that America offered an opportunity for the ambitious to own *land,* really *own it outright,* could not help but impress a people inclined to view landholding as a badge of social prestige. Welsh emigration to America, which heretofore had been on modest proportions, now mounted to flood stage and continued in this fashion until the outbreak of the Civil War.

Arriving in America, many settled in the older communities temporarily, and then pushed on to those parts of America then the popular meccas for settlement. Others joined with the second-generation Welsh and founded new settlements not too far from the mother nucleus. Thus groups of this sort left Oneida County to take up farms in the West Turin, Leyden, Greig, and Collinsville areas of Lewis County;[20] or to take up lands vacated by the westward movement at Freedom and Fairview in Cattaraugus County, at Newport in Herkimer County, at Nelson in

Madison County, and in other areas of New York State.[21] Others took advantage of the inducements offered by William Bebb, the Welsh-American governor of Ohio, to found a new Welsh colony in Van Wert County, Ohio. A group, led by his cousin of the same name, began settlement in 1848. Soon another extensive colony came into existence in the vicinity of Venedocia in that county.[22]

By far the great majority of the Welsh farmer immigrants of the 1840's and 1850's, however, were attracted to Wisconsin then being opened to settlement. Joined by members of the second generation from many of the older settlements, they again played the role of pioneers in removing forests, clearing land, and turning into agricultural areas large sections of that state. Five large new Welsh settlements made their appearance plus a number of smaller ones. All of the new settlements were made within a few years of each other in the 1840's.

The Welsh influx began with the coming of John Hughes and his family to Waukesha County in 1840. They settled in the town of Genesee, and finding the country to their liking wrote back home encouraging their friends and neighbors to join them. Within two years of Hughes' arrival the Genesee community numbered ninety-nine Welsh settlers. The general area where the Welsh settled came to be known as "Wales" in honor of the old homeland with the village of the same name as its nucleus. Others of the Welsh were attracted to the area around Racine. Here the first Welsh started arriving the same year and were joined by a group of some sixty-seven more the following year. More Welsh settlers trooped in as the decade progressed. Most of these settled in the areas of Mt. Pleasant and Pike Grove not far from Racine.[23]

Columbia County, Wisconsin, became the site of another extensive Welsh settlement when the first Welsh settlers began arriving in 1845. They called their settlement "Welsh Prairie," a community which in time embraced the village of Cambria and the surrounding farming region for some ten or twelve miles.[24] Another large Welsh settlement grew up in Winnebago County not far from the city of Oshkosh. Settlement dated from 1847 when the Welsh began taking up lands in Eldorado, Nekimi, and Utica townships. Arrival of more immigrants enlarged the settlement into the Rosendale area of Fond du Lac County. A number of minor settlements were also established in Wisconsin in the 1840's. These included the Baraboo-Caledonia colony in Sauk County, 1846, the Ixonia colony in Jefferson County, 1845, the Blaenydyffryn, Fish Creek, and Bangor settlements in LaCrosse County, 1849, and the Union colony in Rock County, 1845. Small settlements sprang up, too, at Spring Green in Sauk County, 1850, and at Cataract, 1854.[25] The former enjoys the honor of having been the hometown of Frank Lloyd

Wright, the distinguished American architect, the grandson of Welsh immigrants.

Although the great majority of Welsh who settled in Wisconsin were farmers or took up agricultural pursuits, in certain cases the finding of lead and zinc deposits and the development of the industries associated with these minerals led to an influx of Welsh who were familiar with these occupations. Iowa County, in particular, attracted this type of Welsh immigrant. Such places as Dodgeville and Picatonica in that county attracted both Welsh lead and zinc workers as well as Welsh farmers in the early 1840's. Nearby Barneveld and Ridgeway shared in this influx. Iowa County soon rated a Welsh population which compared in numbers with the purely Welsh agricultural settlements farther to the east.[26]

The newly organized state of Iowa shared with Wisconsin in receiving large numbers of Welsh immigrant and second generation farmers. As early as 1838, Welsh pioneers from the Ebensburg colony had settled in the Old Man's Creek (now Iowa City) district of Iowa County in that state. They were soon joined by others from the homeland and another small Welsh colony soon developed. Other such small settlements were made at Long Creek in Louisa County, 1842, and at Williamsburg in Iowa County, 1844. Still later, in 1858, was founded the extensive Welsh colony of Howard County which expanded in time across the Iowa River to include a large section of neighboring Fillmore County in Minnesota.[27]

The organization of the territory of Minnesota in 1849 and news that the "Blue Earth" country along the Minnesota River to the southwest of St. Paul comprised some of the richest soil in America led to large-scale Welsh settlement in that area. A small group settled in present LaSueur County in 1853. Others were encouraged to come to the general area due to the propaganda efforts of two Welshmen, David C. Evans and the Reverend Richard Davies, who had visions of building a thriving city at South Bend in the heart of the Blue Earth country. Although their ambitions for South Bend failed to materialize, scores of Welsh, chiefly from the Wisconsin settlements, but many from Wales as well, trooped into what became organized as Blue Earth County, Minnesota, in the years immediately preceding the Civil War.[28]

Located as it was on the Indian frontier, the Blue Earth Welsh community not only faced the pioneering difficulties heretofore experienced by most of the earlier Welsh settlements, but had the unusual distinction of having been the only Welsh settlement that became involved in Indian difficulties. Branches of the powerful Sioux nation maintained reservations not too far from the Welsh settlements. On two occasions the Indians went on the warpath. In 1857, a minor outbreak occurred; then in 1862 the much more serious Sioux War occurred due to frauds perpetrated by Indian agents and the failure of the American government to furnish necessary supplies to the Indians. The latter took to the warpath and began to massacre the settlers in the outlying farms of the Minnesota River valley. Many of the isolated Welsh settlers were killed during the early days of the outbreak. The Welsh immigrants played an active part in defending the military post of Fort Ridgely and the nearby German settlement of New Ulm against powerful Indian attacks. The Welsh and other settlements of the area were particularly vulnerable because many of their able-bodied men had enlisted in the Union Army. The Sioux uprising was stamped out in the spring of 1864. The Blue Earth settlement and its nearby LaSueur associate soon ranked among the larger Welsh-American agricultural communities.[29]

The years immediately preceding the Civil War also saw the beginnings of Welsh settlement in Kansas, where a group of some twenty families had settled in the neighborhood of Emporia during the years 1856-58. They were joined by others in later years.[30] Other Welsh, attracted by the land inducements offered by the land company affiliated with the Hannibal and St. Joseph Railroad, chose Missouri as their goal. In the decade of the 1860's, a number of small Welsh settlements became established along the main line of the railroad from Hannibal to the west. Of these, the most important were Bevier and New Cambria in Macon County, and Dawn in Livingston County.[31]

Occupying a special place in the Welsh migration of the 1840's and 1850's was a large and substantial group which came to America for peculiar religious reasons, although aided of course by the sorry state of economic conditions at home. These were the Mormon converts, first of the foreign-language speaking groups to join their co-religionists in the New Zion on the banks of Great Salt Lake in Utah.

Looming large in the saga of Welsh Mormon immigration was Captain Dan Jones of Flintshire, who emigrated to America in 1840, went west to the Illinois country, and settled at Nauvoo. Jones became the owner of a small river schooner, the *Maid of Iowa,* and plied the Ohio and Mississippi rivers transporting settlers to the west. On one such occasion, in 1843, he carried a company of English converts to Mormonism from St. Louis to Nauvoo. Upon their arrival, Jones met the renowned Joseph Smith, the founder of the new sect. Smith converted the little captain and Jones soon assumed an important place in the affairs of the growing sect. He attended meetings of the important "Quarum of Twelve" which included both Smith and the second great Mormon leader, Brigham Young. At one such meeting, Captain Dan was informed by Smith that he had been selected to head a mission to Wales and had best prepare himself for departure to the homeland. Jones' departure was delayed, however, due to the series of events that led to the martyrdom of the great prophet. The Captain was one of the group that accompanied Smith on his last journey to Carthage in June, 1844, and spent the night preceding the martyrdom in jail with the prophet. The next day, Jones was sent on an errand by Smith and was prevented from reentering the jail by the mob. He thus escaped the same fate as that of the prophet.[32]

Captain Dan Jones' Welsh mission was again delayed due to the unsettled conditions existing among the Mormons following Smith's death. In 1845, however, accompanied by his wife and other Mormon missionaries, he left for the homeland. Arriving there he made his headquarters at Merthyr-Tydfil, then the largest city of Wales, and organized a Welsh district of the Mormon church. Jones labored with fervor and diligence, preaching, proselytizing, and writing and publishing pamphlets in Welsh on the Mormon faith. By March, 1847, he reported some nine hundred converts. Extensive preaching tours of Wales resulted in many more. By the close of 1848, the Mormon movement in Wales had grown to some twelve conferences and a total membership of 4,654, all thanks to the enthusiastic work of the little captain. The great majority of these converts eventually made the trip across the Atlantic and settled in Utah.[33]

Captain Jones returned to America in February, 1849, accompanied by a party of two hundred and forty-nine Welsh Mormon converts. Under his leadership, the group made its way to Iowa and then took the long trek across the Great Plains and Rockies to Utah. Arriving in Salt Lake City, they were assigned the so-called Welsh Settlement on the west side of the Jordan River, now around 48th Street in that city. Subsequently many Welsh became residents of the 15th and 16th wards; others went on to found the small settlement of Wales in San Pete County, Utah. The little Welsh party was the first foreign-speaking group to settle in Utah.[34]

Jones played important roles in the social and political life of the Mormon colony before returning to Wales on a second missionary tour in 1852. Four years more he labored converting his countrymen by the score. He returned to Utah to reside at Provo until his death in 1861. An eloquent and magnetic speaker in both Welsh and English, Jones was the instrument which converted thousands of his countrymen. Because of his success, he is known among his co-religionists as the father of the Welsh Mormons.[35]

A great influx of Welsh converts set in for Utah from 1849 onwards. Eventually the Welsh predominated in the settlements of Wales, Spanish Fork, Williard, and the 15th and 16th Wards of Salt Lake City. Certain of them founded the Mormon settlements of Malad and Samaria in Idaho. Others became numerous in the coal-mining areas of Carbon County at Winter Quarters, at Ophir, and in other mining areas of Utah.

So great was the Welsh influx that the official historian of the Mormon church estimated their numbers as some 25,000.[36] The Welsh played a prominent part in the affairs of the Mormon church and contributed their talents and culture to the developing community of the Latter Day Saints. Many of the leaders of the church boast of their Welsh ancestry. Much that is cherished in Mormon music came from Wales. John Parry, a Welsh immigrant, formed the little song group in 1850 which became the nucleus of the world-famous Tabernacle Choir. Another Welsh immigrant, Evan Stephens, became one of America's foremost composers of religious music, and under his guidance, the Tabernacle Choir became one of the most famous in America.[37]

The coming of the Civil War put an end to Welsh emigration to America temporarily, but the movement set in again soon after hostilities had ceased. An additional factor encouraging emigration during this period was the political persecution that resulted in 1868 and the years following when many Welsh farmers were forced from their farms because of their strong stand for disestablishment of the Anglican church in Wales. To be considered, too, was the hold which America had always exerted upon the democratic and idealistic Welsh. The type of democratic society which they read about in America formed a marked contrast to caste-ridden Britain. The great war which had been fought for the liberation of the Negroes fired the Welshman's imagination. No wonder that the Welsh became enthusiastic Americans and enjoyed for years the highest percentage among the various immigrant ethnic groups in numbers acquiring citizenship. They retained a love for Wales, their homeland, but for the most part they had no strong love for or loyalty to what they considered alien English rule of their country.

Thanks to a Congregational minister, the Reverend Robert D. Thomas, the Welsh of the post-Civil War period had a convenient guidebook in their own language concerning the opportunities afforded by America. Reverend Thomas had made an extensive tour of all the American Welsh settlements in 1851-52. He later settled in America and brought out his monumental *Hanes Cymry America* (History of the Welsh in America) in 1872. It not only included a history and description of the various settlements, their economic advantages, their merits and demerits, but also included useful data on every section of the United States, plus railroad data, fares, transportation difficulties, and other helpful hints for the immigrants. Thomas' book became very popular in Wales and unquestionably played its part in encouraging further emigration.[38]

Most of the immigrant farmers of the post-Civil War period settled in the mid-west among their fellow countrymen in the various settlements of Wisconsin, Iowa, Minnesota, and Missouri. Others, however, founded new settlements in the new state of Nebraska at Prairie Union, Richardson County, 1867, at Blue Springs and Wymore in Gage County, at Postville in Platte County, at Norden in Keyapaha County, at Carroll in Wayne County, and elsewhere in the 1870's. Others settled in neighboring Kansas, chiefly in Osage and Lyon counties where they formed a significant part of the pioneer population of Osage City, Burlington, and Reading. The little Welsh colony of Arvonia near Lebo was founded around 1866.[39]

Small Welsh agricultural settlements also were established in South Dakota after the subjection of the Sioux Indians in the 1880's. Most of those that came to this state did so as the result of the influence of W. E. Powell of Milwaukee, the Welsh-American general agent for the Chicago, Milwaukee, St. Paul and Pacific Railroad. A Welsh poet of note, Powell, because of his wide acquaintance in Welsh circles, became a strong personal influence in the settling of Welshmen in the new state. Under his leadership, hundreds of Welsh settled in South Dakota during the decade 1880-1890. The largest of these settlements, named Powell in his honor, was established by a party of some three hundred Welsh people some nine miles south of Ipswich in Edmunds County in 1883. Other Welsh settlers located at Plana, Canova, Plankinton, Spain, and Ipswich, all in South Dakota.[40]

Also dating from the period of the 1880's was the growth of the distinctly Welsh agricultural settlement of Beaver Creek, Oregon, some twenty-five miles southeast of Portland. One David Thomas, an enterprising Welsh immigrant, had acquired considerable timber land in the vicinity and offered it for sale at a reasonable price to Welsh settlers. He inserted an advertisement in *Y Drych*, the Welsh-American newspaper, in 1884. Many Welsh in America and in the homeland saw the ad and went west to take advantage of his offer. They were instrumental in helping to develop the area into one of the most attractive gardening spots in the far west with fruit-growing as the chief specialty.[41]

By 1890, the Welsh agricultural migration to America drew to a halt. Conditions in the agricultural districts of Wales had improved during the decade of the 1890's, most of the excess farming population had been drawn off, new areas of the British Empire—Canada, Australia, and New Zealand replaced America as centers of possible emigration. The result of all these factors was the practical cessation of Welsh farmer emigration to the United States. Although some continued to come over during the twentieth century to join friends or relatives, emigration of this sort was relatively insignificant.

Until the decade of the 1830's, Welsh immigration to America had been overwhelmingly agricultural in its background and ambitions. With the opening up and development of the great iron and coal districts of

Pennsylvania and Ohio from the 1830's onwards, however, a new type of Welsh immigrant made his appearance, the skilled industrial worker. The Welsh of South Wales had pioneered in the development of the iron and steel industries and in the extraction of coal, for South Wales with its large stores of both coal and iron rapidly became Britain's chief area of production of these important commodities. When news of the opening of the Pennsylvania iron and coal holdings reached Wales, it was only natural that an influx of immigrants should follow. Here in America, the Welsh reasoned, would be better possibilities for more rapid promotion and accumulation of wealth than existed in the homeland, especially since they were the specialists in these fields and could anticipate assuming leading places in these industries in growing industrial America. To America they began to come and soon were playing a vital role in the pioneering work concerned with both industries.

Welsh miners and steel workers began to emigrate in significant numbers about the same time in the 1830's. Movement was slow at first, but soon gained momentum in the pre-Civil War decades. It then boomed after hostilities had ceased and the new nation entered upon its most rapid period of industrial expansion. Immigration of such industrial workers fluctuated according to economic conditions both in America and in the homeland. When working conditions were good at home, emigration slackened; depressed conditions in turn resulted in increased emigration. Likewise, depending upon conditions in America, immigration tended to boom or to slacken.

The coming of the new type of immigrant from Wales had its romantic side. While Captain Dan Jones was leading his party of Welsh Mormons to Utah in 1849, news of the discovery of gold in California shook the Western world and had profound ramifications upon Wales itself and upon the Welsh settlements in America. Lured by glowing tales of riches easily obtained for the seeking and reports that no capital was necessary only pick, shovel, and pan, and that gold could be frequently picked out of the crevices, many Welshmen yielded to the call and started out on the long, tedious, and expensive trip to California. Although Welshmen representing all pursuits of life came, the overwhelming majority were Welsh miners. Most felt that they would get rich quickly and then be able to retire in comfort. Most were doomed to be disappointed.[42]

Although many of the Welsh travelled across the Great Plains to California, the great majority made the trip by way of Panama by means of slow steamers at a cost of some $600. The entire trip from New Orleans to Panama, across the isthmus, and then to San Francisco, took from twenty to twenty-five days. Certain of the Welsh made the much longer all-water trip via Cape Horn. Having arrived in San Francisco, they travelled inland to the gold fields. Many combed the California hills and mountains as lonely prospectors for years. Others tended to congregate in key centers of the gold fields with the result that a number of small Welsh settlements soon sprang into existence.[43]

Most of the Welsh who came to California in the first years after the discovery of gold located at Placerville, the area of the first strikes. Soon new finds at Camptonville in Yuba County and at North San Juan in Nevada County, some ten miles apart, led to the migration of most Welsh miners to these places. For nearly two decades the immediate area of these towns contained large numbers of the sons of Cambria. Other gold centers that attracted the Welsh were Port Wine, Holldan Flat, Scala Diggings, Brandy City, La Porte, Monte Cristo, Forest City, Pike City, and Whiskey Diggings in Sierra County, Empire Flat and Burchville in Nevada County, and Yorktown in Touloume County. As late as 1871, fifteen large gold mining projects were being operated by Welshmen. Of these, the Snowdon Hill Mine was perhaps most successful. It had been located by a party of eighteen Welshmen and had been operated by them for some years. In time it was purchased by Jeremiah Watts, one of the leading members of the California Welsh settlements, who continued to operate it for years.[44]

As the Welsh population in the gold fields increased during the 1850's, it was inevitable that churches should be established to meet the needs of these fundamentally religious people (in many ways forming a contrast to the average prospector). Such were organized through the contributions of the Welsh prospectors at the Camptonville, Brandy City, and Yorktown settlements. Love of music and poetry led to the introduction of the eisteddfod in these frontier communities. Three were held at various times prior to the Civil War.[45]

Certain of the Welsh miners made fortunes through their gold strikes. One such was "January Jones," a colorful character prominent in the early days of California and Nevada. Born John Jones in Aberystwyth, he worked in the lead mines of Wales before joining the gold rush. He prospected in several states, founded the town of Molsom, Washington, and eventually started prospecting at Goldfield, a few miles south of Tonopah in Nevada. He used the name "January" to distinguish his claim which turned out to be one of the richest strikes in the area. Jones eventually became the heaviest individual operator in the Goldfield area working eleven leases and employing over two hundred men.[46]

Some of the Welsh miners, after having made fortunes, returned to their homes in the East or in Wales. Others, broke, did the same. Many of them, however, found California to their liking and decided to remain permanently. As soon as possible, they had their families brought to

California.   Just how strong the Welsh were in numbers in the gold fields at the height of the "rush" is impossible to estimate. Suffice it to say that with the playing out of the finds, the great majority of the Welsh moved elsewhere. As late as 1872, however, long after the peak of the gold rush, the Welsh population of the gold fields was estimated to number around five hundred. [47]

Elsewhere throughout the mountain region of the far West, Welsh miners and prospectors were active from the days of the great gold and silver discoveries. A sprinkling of Welshmen could be found in virtually every county of the Rocky Mountain area. The opening of bituminous coal mines and copper and lead mines attracted other Welsh miners during the post-Civil War period. Colorado became the mecca for most of the coal miners. At such centers as Russell Gulch, Erie, and Lafayette, small settlements grew up as well as at Denver, the capital city.[48] At Butte, Montana, copper mining attracted Welsh miners in the 1880's.[49] Other areas where small Welsh settlements grew up in the far West during the last decades of the nineteenth century were Spokane, Almira, Big Bend and Seattle in Washington; Twin Falls, Idaho; and in the coal fields of Utah and California.[50]

The California and prospector fever had resulted in a romantic chapter in the story of Welsh industrial migration to the United States. At most, however, the lure of the west attracted but a small fraction of the new type of Welsh immigrant. The great majority, sober-minded, conservative, and cautious by nature, chose instead those areas of the industrial East where their skill and labor would be most appreciated and the financial returns guaranteed.

As one might expect, the Pittsburgh area, where the industries had received their earliest impetus, became the focal point for the first Welsh immigration of this sort. Enough had arrived by 1824 to allow for the founding of a Welsh church. Then with the coming of the 1830's, a steady stream of Welsh iron workers descended upon the city, a movement that continued throughout the rest of the century until Welsh immigrants in the city ranked fifth in number in the 1870's, fourth in the 1880's, and fifth in the 1890's among the five strongest ethnic groups to settle in the city.[51]

The old Welsh settlement of Ebensburg also became an important iron and coal center when the surrounding region began to produce coal and iron ore. It became a strong center for Welsh immigration of the new type during the decade of the 1840's and 1850's.[52] Elsewhere in Cambria County, the great coal and iron industries of the Johnstown area became a strong mecca for Welsh immigrants in the 1850's and succeeding years, and the small Welsh farming community of Green Township in Indiana County, not far from Ebensburg, became converted into an industrial area when coal and iron deposits were discovered on the farms of the Welsh settlers.[53] Throughout western Pennsylvania, the coal and iron industries attracted Welsh immigrants as new mines were opened and new steel mills were placed in operation. In some cases the Welsh only stayed temporarily; in others they founded little nuclei to add to the growing list of small Welsh-American communities. Included among such latter places were Brady's Bend and Sugar Creek in Armstrong County in the 1840's, Brisbin in Clearfield County and Irwin in Westmoreland County in the 1870's, Houtsdale in Clearfield County and Homestead in Allegheny County in the 1880's, and Lindsey and Punxsutawney in Jefferson County in the 1890's.[54]

The Welsh were also attracted to the bituminous coal fields of the Blossburg basin of Tioga County in north-central Pennsylvania. Blossburg, the center of this mining area, received its first quota as early as 1840. Further expansion of mining facilities in the post-Civil War period saw a new influx of miners to the Antrim and Arnot coalfields nearby.[55]

In Ohio, the opening of bituminous mines attracted Welsh immigrants to Pomeroy in 1843, to Minersville in 1853, and to Syracuse in 1858, all in Meigs County; to Ironton in Lawrence County in 1853; to Thomaston and Sherman in Summit County in 1847; to Shawnee in Perry County in 1873; to New Straitsville in Hocking County in 1879; to Paris in Portage County in 1850; and to Gloucester in Athens County in 1870. In each case small Welsh cultural communities developed.[56]

Rich finds of iron ore were discovered in the 1850's in parts of the old Gallia-Jackson Welsh agricultural community. Blast furnaces were soon erected for the manufacture of pig-iron. Two of these, Jefferson and Cambrian Furnaces, erected in 1854, were owned exclusively by Welshmen and continued in operation for many years. In keeping with Welsh sensibilities in respect to Sabbath observance, they never allowed their employees to work on Sundays. The development of the iron industry led to an influx of Welsh iron workers and the partial transformation of the Gallia-Jackson Welsh settlement into an industrial region. Some of the original Welsh settlers, who became associated with the iron industry, became some of the wealthiest citizens of southern Ohio.[57]

In the post-Civil War period, the great industrial area which embraces Trumbull and Mahoning Counties, Ohio, and Mercer and Lawrence Counties, Pennsylvania, attracted a great influx of Welsh immigrants. The bituminous coal mines and great steel factories then being opened up were the magnets. As early as 1847, enough Welsh had settled in Youngstown, soon to become the metropolis of the area, to organize a church. Scores of others joined to make this nucleus one of the strongest Welsh urban settlements in America. To the north of the city lie the industrial communities of Trumbull County. Here the coal fields of

Brookfield, Coalburgh, and Mineral Ridge, and the steel mills of Niles, Girard, Hubbard, Churchill, Vienna, and Weathersfield attracted so many Welsh immigrants beginning in the late 1860's that a total of nineteen churches were organized. Across the Pennsylvania boundary, the steel towns of Farrell, Sharon, and Wheatland in Mercer County attracted their share of Welsh industrial workers in the 1870's. The Welsh element in this important four-county area was greatly strengthened in the 1890's when large-scale immigration of tin-plate workers occurred and New Castle in Lawrence County became one of the main producers of this type of industrial enterprise.[58]

Elsewhere in America, the bituminous coal industry and its allied steel industries attracted Welsh immigrants in the mid and later nineteenth century. Such bituminous coal centers as Mason City and Hartford City, West Virginia, in the 1850's; Frostburg, Maryland, in 1860's; Soddy, Tennessee, Flint Creek, Given, Georgetown, Excelsior, Cleveland, and Lucas County, Iowa, in the 1870's; and the Kansas centers of Osage City, Pittsburg, Shenandoah, and Scranton; Bevier in Missouri; Erie and Lafayette in Colorado—all in the 1880's, attracted their share of Welsh miners. In many of these places the Welsh remained only so long as the mines flourished, then left to find employment elsewhere when the coal fields had become exhausted or the mines had ceased operating. In such places as Soddy, Bevier, Frostburg, Flint Creek, and Given, however, the Welsh established permanent settlements.[59]

Welsh miners and steel workers formed the specialized personnel that pioneered in the development of both industries in the United States. Many of them advanced to occupy important supervisory positions with the various native American companies then engaged in these activities. In time some of them rose to head these large-scale enterprises. Others among them became enterpreneurs and organized small mining and steel companies in their own right. Such, for instance, was the case of the brothers David I. and John Jones, who founded the Cleveland Rolling Mill Company in the Newburg district of Cleveland in 1853, the brothers, David, Joseph, and William Richards, who founded the Knoxville Iron Works of Knoxville, Tennessee, in 1867, Giles Edwards, who pioneered in the growing industrialization of the Chattanooga area and subsequently established the Shelby Iron Works at Birmingham, Alabama, in 1862, and the little group of Welshmen who founded Cambria and Jefferson furnaces in Jackson County, Ohio, in the 1850's. Others became operators of bituminous coal mines such as Daniel H. Davis at Knightsville, Indiana, in 1867, Anthony Howells at Massillon, Ohio, in 1865, Evan Morris at Girard, Ohio, in 1854, Richard Thomas, inventor of the Thomas Coke Oven, at Birmingham, Alabama, in 1886, James

F. Pierce in Jefferson County, Alabama, in the 1870's, and Abram Lloyd at Soddy, Tennessee, in 1866, to mention just a few.[60]

As for developments in the anthracite coal industries, here, too, the Welsh made valuable contributions. Looming large as a figure in the story of the iron and anthracite coal industries of America was David Thomas, frequently referred to as "the iron-master of America." Thomas had had a brilliant career in the growing iron manufacturing of South Wales. He became manager of the Yniscedwyn Anthracite Iron Works in the Swansea Valley. After patient years of study, Thomas perfected a technique whereby anthracite coal could be used as a smelting fuel. The technique consisted of heating the blast prior to its introduction into the furnaces. News of Thomas' process soon reached the coal operators of Pennsylvania by way of the *Mining Journal.* They bargained with him to come to America and to introduce his new method. He did so in 1839, and built a blast furnace for the Philadelphia Coal and Navigation Company at Catasauqua on the Lehigh River, some three miles above present-day Allentown. The opening of the furnace marked the beginning in America of the use of anthracite as a fuel for iron and steel manufacturing. Thomas remained at Catasauqua and became one of the leading iron-masters of America, and the acknowledged authority on all aspects of the industry for the remainder of his lifetime.[61]

The Catasauqua plant attracted Welsh iron workers and soon another small Welsh community came into existence. Likewise at Danville, Pennsylvania, to the west on the Susquehanna River where new iron plants were erected to utilize the Thomas technique, a small Welsh settlement grew up which became noted for its great interest in Welsh culture. Danville was the place where Joseph Parry, later one of Wales' outstanding composers, was discovered working in the iron mills. Thanks to the generosity of his fellow Welsh workers here and elsewhere in the anthracite region, Parry's musical education was underwritten, and this musical genius was given his opportunity to start on his distinguished career.[62]

The introduction of the Thomas technique led to a boom in the extraction of anthracite coal, for thanks to it this valuable product became definitely linked up with the industrial development of America. The boom was aided in later years by the full utilization of anthracite as a heating fuel in the homes of America. Since the Welsh of South Wales had pioneered in anthracite mining, they soon began to infiltrate into the anthracite fields of eastern Pennsylvania, the only area in America containing this valuable product.

As early as 1830, a company of Welsh immigrants, some twenty families in all, arrived at Carbondale at the northern tip of the fields attracted by a small mine which had just been opened by the Delaware and Hudson Canal Company.[63] Others came to the Schuylkill County towns of Pottsville, Minersville, and St. Clair in the decade of the 1830's to pioneer in the extraction of anthracite.[64] Then thanks to the increasing popularity of anthracite and the establishment of railroad links with the seaboard, the anthracite coal industry began to expand in a serious way. New mines were opened in Schuylkill County and in the Lehigh River basin of Luzerne and Carbon counties in the 1840's. An influx of Welsh miners followed. Soon such places as Hazleton and Jeansville in Luzerne County, Tamaqua, and Beaver Meadows in Carbon County had substantial colonies of Welsh miners and their families. Further development of the anthracite industry led to the opening of more mines at the Lansford area of Carbon County in the 1850's, at Shenandoah, Mahanoy City and Mount Carmel in Schuylkill County, at Shamokin in Northumberland County, at Wiconisco in Dauphin County, and at Audenried in Carbon County, all in the 1860's, and elsewhere in the lower anthracite fields in the 1870's.[65] Large-scale settlement of Welsh miners at these places set in immediately. Soon this area of east-central Pennsylvania rated as one of the strongest concentrations of Welsh population in America, a position which it continues to hold down to the present.

Large as was the influx of Welsh miners into Schuylkill County and adjacent anthracite areas, it was dwarfed, as were all the other large Welsh settlements in America, when the migration into the Wyoming and Lackawanna anthracite coal valleys gained full momentum. The opening up of the rich deposits in this area of northeastern Pennsylvania (Luzerne and Lackawanna counties) had been delayed due to the absence of proper railroad facilities to get the product to market. When the latter were constructed and completed in the 1850's, new shafts were sunk and the hidden wealth beneath the surface began to make its way to market. In came the Welsh to furnish the necessary skilled labor and supervisory techniques. Although Welsh miners were to be found throughout the mine workings of the two valleys, they tended to settle in compact groups at key places where certain of their leaders had obtained positions of supervisory importance and used their influence to attract Welsh miners to their own operations.

Scranton, soon to become the largest municipality of the area, had received its first Welsh settlers as early as 1845 when a blast furnace was opened at that place. Then in the later 1840's, mines were opened at the Hyde Park and Providence sections of the city and a great influx of Welsh miners commenced. By the beginning of the post-Civil War period, Scranton had the largest Welsh immigrant population of any city in America. In the surrounding area, new mining centers sprang up each in turn attracting Welsh miners. Thus the towns of Taylor, Olyphant, Old Forge, Moosic, and the early Welsh centers of Carbondale and Blakely, all received substantial quotas.[66]

Farther south in the Wyoming Valley proper, similar exploitation of the extensive anthracite coal deposits set in. Again the story of Welsh influx was repeated. Wilkes-Barre, the metropolis, received large numbers, while its suburbs, Pittston, Miners Mills, Parsons, Ashley, Sugar Notch, Warrior Run, Nanticoke, Plymouth, and Edwardsville contained enough Welsh immigrants to form large substantial Welsh settlements in time.[67]

So attractive did the Wyoming and Lackawanna Valleys become to Welsh anthracite workers that by 1890, the peak year of Welsh immigrant strength in America, approximately one-fifth of the entire Welsh population in America was concentrated in the above mentioned places. As of 1890, Wilkes-Barre and its suburbs rated as the area of greatest concentration of Welsh people in America with some 8,578 immigrants and a total Welsh stock numbering 21,552. As of the same year, Scranton and its suburbs, only eighteen miles away, numbered some 7,708 immigrants and a total Welsh stock of 19,358. Together, the Welsh population of the two areas embraced some 16,280 immigrants and some 40,910 first and second generation Welsh-Americans.[68]

Scranton, and the Hyde Park section of the city in particular, became one of the most active Welsh cultural centers. Here *Baner America,* one of the strongest of the Welsh-American newspapers, flourished for many years. Here the *Druid,* the only successful Welsh newspaper printed in English, was first published. The great interest of the Welsh people in music led to the formation of choirs which achieved a national reputation. Of these, the Cambro-American Choir, directed by Robert James, and the Scranton Choral Society, directed by William Evans, were outstanding during the latter part of the nineteenth century, and the Cymrodorion Choir, directed by the noted Daniel Protheroe, the Scranton Choral Union, under the leadership of Haydn Evans, and the Scranton Oratorical Society, directed by John T. Watkins, gained renown during the early twentieth century. The Scranton Welsh colony also organized the Welsh Philosophical Society, a discussion and debating group, which maintained a library and functioned from 1860 to 1905. The Scranton Welsh community is still of such strength that it maintains its own home for the aged. Of the thirty Welsh churches organized in the Scranton area, fourteen are still flourishing.[69]

The Wilkes-Barre Welsh community, supported by the many Welsh settlements in its suburbs, was also very active in a cultural way. A Philosophical Society was maintained for many years in the last decades of the nineteenth century. Various choirs were organized, of which the most famous was the Gwent Glee Club, directed by Evan Davis, of Edwardsville, which flourished well into the twentieth century. The Welsh colony of Plymouth was the home of the noted Gwilym Gwent (William Aubrey Williams), the "Mozart of the Coal Fields," a musical genius who composed hundreds of songs, hymns, and anthems. The Wilkes-Barre area is still the home of two well-known Welsh choirs, the Shawnee Welsh Chorus of Plymouth, and the nationally renowned Orpheus Glee Society of Wilkes-Barre. The latter, founded in 1919, by Gwilym Amos, quickly gained prominence under his direction and maintained it under his successors, John Jones Owen and William R. Reese. Today, it is perhaps the best known of the Welsh-American musical societies. So strong is the Welsh feeling of kinship in the Wilkes-Barre area today that twelve Welsh societies maintain themselves and were recently united to form a Wyoming Valley Federation of Welsh Societies. Of the forty-five Welsh churches organized in the Wilkes-Barre area, twenty-eight are still flourishing.[70]

Welsh leadership in anthracite mining existed throughout the entire earlier period of the history of the industry and well into the twentieth century. Mine superintendencies, foremanships, and other posts of supervisory importance were held by scores of Welshmen, who had advanced themselves through hard work and diligent application from their first jobs as miners and laborers. In some cases, Welsh immigrants were able to amass enough capital to conduct mining operations of their own. Among these outstanding successful enterpreneurs were William Jones, who operated during the early days at St. Clair and was widely known as the "coal king" of his day; W. Powell, an early operator in the Upper Lehigh Basin; Edward Jones, organizer of the important Jones, Simpson, and Company which operated extensively in upper Lackawanna County; Daniel Edwards, who founded the Kingston Coal Company with workings at Edwardsville in the Wilkes-Barre area; and Morgan B. Williams, founder of the Red Ash Coal Company of Wilkes-Barre, who subsequently served as a Congressman from Luzerne County.[71]

The end of the nineteenth century saw the influx of yet another type of Welsh industrial worker, the tin-plate specialist. Tin-plate had been one of the chief industries of South Wales and for many years that area enjoyed a virtual monopoly in the production of this commodity. Towards the end of the century, however, Americans began to manufacture this product in a serious way and to put the pressure on Congress to erect tariff barriers to protect their budding industry. The famous McKinley Tariff of 1890 brought about this desired end. Since America had been one of the chief markets for Welsh tin-plate, depressed conditions resulted in South Wales and many Welsh tin-plate workers determined to emigrate to America to find work in her new tin-plate works. They came in significant numbers throughout the decades of the 1890's and 1900's to flock to the centers where the new plants were making their appearance. They settled in greatest numbers at Philadelphia and New Castle, Pennsylvania, Wheeling and Weirton, West Virginia, Martin's Ferry and Steubenville, Ohio, and Gas City, Indiana.

This new type of Welsh industrial immigrant became the backbone of America's infant tin-plate business. Intensely clannish, they cherished their trade secrets at first, handing down the art of tin-plating from father to son, and doing their best to keep a monopoly of the industry. Many developed into the key men of the business, becoming executives and capitalists in their own right. In the forefront of such were F. R. Phillips, who formed the Welsh-American Tin Plate Company with a capital of over one million dollars. Its plant at Philadelphia became one of the leaders in the field. Another Welsh immigrant, John Charles Williams, organized the Phillips Sheet and Tin Plate Company in 1905. It later was renamed the Weirton Steel Company. Williams became a millionaire and headed the firm until his death in 1936.[72]

Welsh immigrant workers of yet another sort were responsible for the development of another type of American economic endeavor—the slate industry. The Welsh of North Wales had excelled for years in this field. Certain of them, feeling that America might offer even better opportunities, began to arrive as early as the 1830's to begin the search for slate producing areas in the new Republic. One such pioneer was John J. Roberts, whose search was rewarded when he found outcroppings of slate in York County, Pennsylvania, on the Maryland boundary just west of the Susquehanna River. Roberts opened the first quarry in this section around 1835. Other Welshmen hearing of his finds trooped into the area in the 1840's and succeeding years. One of these, John Humphrey, became a very successful operator and one of the leading slate producers in America. The little Welsh slate settlement that soon grew up in York County was first called Bangor, after the Welsh town of the same name, then Bangor West by which name it was best known to the nineteenth century Welsh immigrants, and finally Delta, the name it bears today.[73]

Other pioneer Welsh slate-producing entrepreneurs searched the Delaware River valley and its tributary, the Lehigh, for outcroppings of slate. One such pioneer, Owen Jones, discovered finds along the middle Lehigh in 1846. He returned to Wales and persuaded a number of Welsh quarrymen to go with him to develop the new fields. They did so and founded the Slatington Welsh settlement in Lehigh County. Jones and two others, William Roberts and David Williams, all established slate quarries and carried on large-scale operations in this district.[74]

Elsewhere in Pennsylvania Welsh slate entepreneurs were responsible for introducing the new industry. Robert Jones found extensive slate fields about fourteen miles north of Easton in Northampton County. He set up quarrying operations and an influx of slate workers from Wales soon arrived in the area. Jones named his settlement Bangor, too, after his hometown in Wales. He subsequently operated one of the largest slate quarries in the world. Bangor flourished as a distinctly Welsh town for many years and is still one of the strong centers of Welsh influence. Its "Welsh Day" celebration, held annually around Labor Day, attracts thousands of spectators from throughout the east. A smaller Welsh slate settlement grew up at Wind Gap, also in Northampton County, some seven miles from Bangor in the 1880's.[75]

The border region of Rutland County, Vermont, and Washington County, New York, also became a mecca for Welsh slate quarrymen in the 1850's. Various quarries began to operate in this region around 1850, and news of their activities attracted Welsh immigrant workers from the beginning of their operations. A strong movement of Welsh quarrymen into Rutland County set in which continued throughout the rest of the century. Soon a number of small Welsh slate settlements, Fair Haven, Blissville, Poultney, South Poultney, Pawlet, and West Pawlet, dotted the border area in Rutland County, while across the New York line in Washington County many more were attracted when William R. Williams, a Welsh immigrant, opened a quarry in 1852. Other quarries sprang up in the general vicinity of Granville and Middle Granville. Both places soon had substantial numbers of Welsh immigrant quarrymen and their families.[76]

The Rutland County-Washington County slate producing area thus became an important area of concentration of Welsh settlers. Certain of the Welsh quarrymen became entrepreneurs in their own right. Included among these, in addition to William R. Williams, were Benjamin Williams, a successful operator in the Middle Granville area, and Hugh W. Hughes, called the "Slate King of America," who operated some of the most extensive slate quarries in the United States.[77]

In the first decade of the twentieth century, depressed conditions in the slate producing areas of Wales led to large-scale migration of slate workers to America. Most settled in the New York-Vermont areas, thus strengthening the Welsh character of the region. Then as the twentieth century progressed, decline in the use of slate led to depression in the Vermont slate fields. Many of the Welsh settlers migrated elsewhere, particularly to the Utica area, and strengthened the Welsh character of that community thereby. [78] Consciousness of their Welsh origins still remains in these little communities, however. As late is 1939 the Poultney Welsh Male Chorus was organized. Directed by the capable Evan G. Williams, a Welsh immigrant, it quickly became one of America's out-

standing male choirs. It gave concerts in New York City, and filled en-
gagements in New England and New York.[79]

Welsh slate workers were to be found during the latter nineteenth
century in most areas where slate was being quarried. The Virginia slate
belt and the Rock Mart area of Georgia attracted many, while a sprinkling of others could be found elsewhere.

The great bulk of the Welsh of America settled either in concentrated agricultural settlements or in and around those regions which
because of their industrial specialization attracted the skilled Welsh iron,
tin-plate, slate-worker, or coal-miner. In addition, many Welsh immigrants were attracted to various of America's growing cities, there to find
employment in the new industries of such places, to serve as small tradesmen and business contractors, to carry on small businesses, or to engage
in other economic activities according to their background and inclina-
tions. A number of strong Welsh colonies located in the midst of certain
of the larger American municipalities eventually made their appearance.
To this class can be added the Welsh colonies of Scranton, Wilkes-Barre,
Pittsburgh, Youngstown, and New Castle, although as we have seen,
most of Welsh populace in these cases were specialists in either the coal
or steel industries. In other cases, however, such colonies grew up within
large municipalities not necessarily exclusively associated with these industries. For the most part, these latter places were in close proximity
to certain of the the Welsh agricultural settlements and drew their quotas
of Welsh settlers from the latter.

Ohio's three largest cities, Cleveland, Cincinnati, and Columbus,
fitted into this pattern. All received quotas of Welsh immigrants and
second-generation young people in the decades of the Civil War and
thereafter. Cincinnati, because of the close proximity of both the Paddy's
Run and Gallia-Jackson settlements, attracted the ambitious young Welsh
men and women of those areas. The girls found work as servants in
private homes; the men entered the shops and factories or learned various
trades. Letters to friends in Wales attracted many immigrants from the
homeland. A strong Welsh settlement grew up in time which dated from
the early 1830's.[80] Columbus, the Ohio capital city, likewise attracted
Welsh settlers from the nearby Radnor and Welsh Hills settlements.
Again a Welsh settlement arose which became the rallying point for
immigrants from the homeland. Beginning in the 1840's, immigrants
began to come directly to the city from Wales, a movement that continued for some years after the Civil War. Most found work in the
expanding factories of the city. Columbus became a stronghold of Welsh
settlement and has continued so down to the present.[81] Cleveland and its
industrial suburbs attracted substantial numbers of Welsh immigrants
as well as the younger elements of the older Welsh settlements of Ohio.

The Welsh were probably first attracted to the general area when two Welsh brothers, David I. and John Jones, founded the Cleveland Rolling Mill Company in the Newburg district in 1853. Others found employment in the growing factories of the city. Subsequent settling of Welsh industrial workers in the city continued on into the post-Civil War period. The Cleveland Welsh colony became quite extensive and active in cultural affairs.[82]

The story was similar in the case of Wisconsin's growing cities of Racine and Milwaukee, and Minnesota's Minneapolis-St. Paul. A substantial number of Welsh immigrants remained in or returned to the two former cities, the entrepots into Wisconsin of most of the immigrants. They found employment as tradesmen or in the growing industries of the towns. A number became businessmen. Some became sailors, and in the case of Racine, the majority of the sea captains that sailed from this port on the Great Lakes during these early days were Welshmen.[83] The close proximity of the Blue Earth Welsh colony to the Minneapolis-St. Paul area led many of the younger members of this community to move to the metropolitan area.[84] Important Welsh colonies in all three cities have maintained themselves down to the present.

New York, the great entrepot for the nineteenth century immigration, had its quota of Welsh settlers even in colonial times, but it was not until the beginning of the nineteenth century that the nucleus of a closely knit Welsh settlement was established in that city. From that period until the present, the New York Welsh colony has been large and influential in Welsh-American affairs. Five Welsh churches existed at one time of which only one, founded in 1826, is still functioning and offering preaching in Welsh as a feature of its services.[85] Philadelphia, the colonial site of a considerable Welsh population, continued to attract Welsh settlers during the nineteenth century, but it was not until the 1890's, when a great influx of tin-plate workers arrived, that the city recaptured its position as a prominent center of Welsh settlers. Its Welsh church likewise still offers preaching in Welsh. [86] Chicago, because of its close proximity to the Wisconsin Welsh settlements, served as an attraction for Welsh settlers from its earliest days of settlement. A constant stream of Welsh immigrants took up residence during the rest of the nineteenth century. So strong did the Welsh immigrants became in that city that its Welsh colony rivaled New York's in numbers. Only one of the five churches organized survives. It still offers services in Welsh.[87] Detroit, too, received a small quota of Welsh immigrants in the middle of the nineteenth century, then with the development of the automobile industry, a large influx of newly arrived immigrants strengthened the Welsh colony in that city in the twentieth century. A small Welsh church was established which is still in existence and, indicative of the first generation background of its membership, still offers preaching in Welsh.[88] Out on the west coast, San Francisco, entrepot for the gold rush crowd, had a Welsh settlement dating from the late 1840's. The golden city continued to attract Welsh immigrants throughout the rest of the century.[89] With the coming of the twentieth century and the development of California as a mecca for eastern migrants, many Welshmen from the eastern settlements moved to the west coast. Some settled in San Francisco, others in Oakland, and many in Los Angeles and San Diego. Welsh churches were established in the first three cities. Only the Oakland and Los Angeles churches survive. Both offer services in Welsh today.[90]

Practically every other city of significance in America attracted a few Welsh settlers at one time or another. In these cases, however, the number involved was comparatively insignificant, and in no case did a strong Welsh cultural nucleus arise. The same can be said of other areas of the United States not heretofore mentioned. Scarcely a county of any state existed which did not have at least one or two Welsh settlers if American census records can be believed. Thus, although the great bulk of the Welsh immigrants preferred to settle among their fellow countrymen in well-known agricultural, industrial, or municipal settlements, a small number of hardy individualists preferred to work out their fortunes elsewhere in the American environment far from the familiar sound of mother tongue and far from the nostalgic chapel life which they held so dear.

By the year 1900, Welsh immigration to America had reached its peak and the Welsh stock in America as officially determined by the United States Bureau of the Census had reached its all-time high of 267,160, of which 93,744 were immigrants and 173,416 children of Welsh immigrants. All in all, in the period from 1820, when a breakdown by nationality was first made by the Bureau, until 1919, a total of some 73,608 Welsh immigrated to the United States. The number of Welsh stock in the United States was estimated at 225,582 in 1890, 267,160 in 1900, 248,947 in 1910, and 230,380 in 1920, while the number of Welsh immigrants in the United States was cited as 29,868 in 1850, 45,763 in 1860, 74,533 in 1870, 83,302 in 1880, 100,079 in 1890, 93,744 in 1900, 82,488 in 1910, and 67,066 in 1920. As will be seen from these figures, the year 1890 represents the date when the greatest number of Welsh immigrants were present in the United States, while the date 1900 represents the date when the total Welsh stock (both immigrants and their children) was at its greatest numerical strength. We shall therefore take the year 1900 as the peak year in which to make an analysis of the distribution of the Welsh in America. With the exception of a large influx of Welsh tin-plate workers in the first decade of the twentieth century, the Welsh communities in the United States can be said to have stabilized themselves by that period.

Most of the Welsh were to be found in the traditional Welsh centers already discussed in this chapter, although a small number of Welshmen were to be found in most of the counties in every state of the union. As one might expect, the three states of Pennsylvania (100,143), Ohio (35,971), and New York (20,456) contained over one-third of the entire group, and Pennsylvania alone over one-third of the Welsh stock in America. Ranked in numerical importance thereafter were Illinois (11,878), Wisconsin (11,222), Iowa (9,510), Utah (6,174), Kansas (5,728), Colorado (5,385), Indiana (5,232), and California (5,173). Other states having more than 1,000 population of Welsh-stock were: Missouri (4,799), Minnesota (4,167), Washington (4,119), Massachusetts (3,396), Nebraska (2,899), New Jersey (2,857), Vermont (2,833), Montana (2,441), Idaho (2,333), Michigan (2,128), Maryland (2,018), South Dakota (1,794), Connecticut (1,507), West Virginia (1,384), Oregon (1,094), and Wyoming (1,061). Kentucky, Tennessee, Alabama, Texas, Oklahoma, Virginia, Maine, and Rhode Island each had over 500, while the remainder of the states all had less. Grouping the states by sections, the greatest percentage of Welsh stock was to be found in the Middle Atlantic States, followed by the East North Central, Pacific, Mountain, West North Central, New England, South Atlantic, West South Central, and East South Central states.

In Pennsylvania, as one might expect, the Welsh were to be found most numerous in the anthracite counties and in the Pittsburgh area. The breakdown of the Welsh stock by counties in the Census of 1900 revealed the chief distribution of the group as follows: Luzerne County (Wilkes-Barre and suburbs) 21,552; Lackawanna County (Scranton and suburbs) 19,358; Allegheny County (Pittsburgh and suburbs) 13,165; Schuylkill County (various anthracite communities) 5,280; Lawrence County (New Castle and vicinity) 4,240; Philadelphia City (tin-plate workers, business and industry) 2,593; Cambria County (Johnstown, Ebensburg and vicinity) 2,376; Northampton County (slate communities) 2,092; Westmoreland County (various coal and iron communities) 1,765; Lehigh County (slate communities) 1,737; Mercer County (various iron and coal communities) 1,535; Northumberland County (anthracite communities) 1,328; Carbon County (anthracite communities) 1,154; Clearfield County (various coal and iron communities) 1,129; Jefferson County (various coal and iron communities) 1,088. Dauphin County (Harrisburg and anthracite communities) 1,020. Other counties having less than 1,000 but more than 500 were Fayette, 990; Washington 864; Susquehanna, 734; Tioga, 697; and Montour, 536; all other counties had less than 500.

In Ohio, the Welsh immigrants were to be found chiefly in the great industrial areas and in the mining sections. The 1900 county distribution of the Welsh-stock was as follows: Mahoning (Youngstown and vicinity) 4,997; Cuyahoga (Cleveland and vicinity) 4,792; Trumbull (various iron and coal centers) 3,625; Franklin (various iron and coal centers) 1,957; Stark (iron and coal centers) 1,797; Tuscarawas (iron and coal centers) 1,598; Belmont (iron and coal centers) 1,598; Summit (coal and iron centers) 1,352; Perry (iron and coal centers) 1,000. Other counties having less than 1,000 but more than 500 were Hamilton, 883; Portage, 819; Columbiana, 750; Licking, 684; Van Wert, 683; Allen, 675, and Guernsey, 579. All others had less than 500.

In New York State, the Welsh immigrants were to be found chiefly in the urban areas of Utica and New York City, and in the rural areas of Oneida and Washington counties. The 1900 county distribution of the Welsh-stock was as follows: Oneida (Utica and vicinity) 6,676; New York City 4,436; Washington (slate settlements) 1,785; Madison 682; Herkimer, 524; and Cattaraugus, 490. All other counties had less.

In Illinois, the Welsh stock was most numerous in Chicago, 5,037, virtually one-half of the state's quota. Other counties having more than 500 were Will, 649; Kane, 587; and LaSalle, 521. All the rest had a sprinkling of Welsh stock. In Wisconsin, Columbia County ranked first in number of Welsh stock 1,365; it was followed by Racine, 1,124; Waukesha, 1,060; Milwaukee, 1,037; Iowa, 972; Winnebago, 806. All other counties had less than 500, with practically all having a sprinkling of Welsh-Americans. In Iowa, the 1900 county distribution of Welsh-stock was as follows: Mahaska, 1,219; Monroe, 980; and Polk, 608. All other counties had less than 500. Again there was a sprinkling of Welsh throughout the state, with sizable groups located in Howard, Wapello, Lucas, Montgomery, and Louisa counties. Kansas had two counties with a Welsh-stock population of over 500: Lyon, 1,346, and Osage, 987. A sprinkling of Welsh-Americans could be found elsewhere throughout the state and in Wyandotte County in particular.

Utah's Welsh population was concentrated chiefly in Salt Lake City, 2,205, with sizable quotas in the counties of Utah, 889; Carbon, 641; and Weber, 499. California's was most numerous in San Francisco, 1,024. Other counties having more than 500 were Alameda, 680, and Los Angeles, 587. Small settlements were to be found in Riverside and Contra Costa counties and a sprinkling elsewhere throughout the state. Missouri's Macon County (Bevier and New Cambria settlements) contained 1,583 persons of Welsh-stock. The counties of St. Louis, Randolph, Livingston, and Jackson had sizable quotas. Colorado had two counties with over 500: Arapahoe, 1,058, and Fremont, 767. Small groups were present in Teller, Pueblo, and Boulder counties.

Minnesota's old Blue Earth settlement contained 1,460 persons of Welsh-stock, while Hennepin County with 834 was the only other county with over 500. Washington's King County (Seattle) had 1,377 such residents. Pierce with 746 was the only other county having more than 500. A sprinkling could be found elsewhere throughout the state with a goodly number in the city of Spokane. Massachusetts' Berkshire County attracted many Welsh from adjoining Vermont and New York and contained 773 of Welsh-stock. Suffolk County (Boston) with 653, and Middlesex (Cambridge) with 515, were the only other counties with over 500. Nebraska's quota of Welsh stock was distributed throughout the state. No county had over 500, although the Welsh were most numerous in the counties of Platte and Wayne. New Jersey's Essex County (Newark and vicinity) contained most of the Welsh-stock with a sprinkling elsewhere. No county had over 500. The same was true of Michigan where most of the Welsh were to be found in Wayne County (Detroit and vicinity). Indiana had three counties with over 500: Madison with 1,352, Grant with 961 and Clay with 679. Vermont's slate settlements in Rutland County contained 1,939.

None of the other states had counties with a Welsh-stock of over 500 persons, although sizable colonies were to be found in Idaho's Oneida County, Maryland's Allegany and Baltimore counties; West Virginia's Ohio County; Connecticut's New Haven and Fairfield counties; Oregon's Multnomah and Clackamas counties; Maine's Piscataquis; Tennessee's Hamilton; Alabama's Jefferson; and Wyoming's Uinta and Sweetwater counties.

The 1900 Census is a fairly accurate gauge for estimating the strength of the Welsh in America of the first and second generations. Its figures scarcely give a true picture of the full strength of the Welsh element in America even in 1900, however, for they do not include figures for the grandchildren and great-grandchildren of the early nineteenth century Welsh immigrants nor for the descendants of the colonial Welsh immigrants. In this respect, too, the Census figures do not do justice to certain of the older areas of settlement where grandchildren and even great-grandchildren of Welsh settlers dwelt side by side with the newer immigrants and their children. Particularly is this true of the Ohio, Wisconsin, Minnesota, and Oneida County, New York, settlements, hence the comparatively low figures for Gallia-Jackson, Ohio, Blue Earth, Minnesota, Oneida County, New York, and the Wisconsin communities generally. Nor do the Census figures reflect the strength of Welsh consciousness. In the case of these communities and the agricultural communities, in particular, Welsh consciousness continued to exist among those of the third and fourth generations.

The same is true today. Census figures now record only immigrants from Wales. These figures have naturally declined as the immigrants pass out of the picture and because immigration from Wales has practically ceased. In practically every instance, however, the strength of the Welsh element has increased as more and more grandchildren and great-grandchildren make their appearance. These, of course, are not listed in the census records under the category of Welsh. Intermarriage with other American groups is increasing steadily, yet consciousness of Welshness still maintains itself, largely stimulated by the various Welsh-American societies and groups.

It is difficult to estimate accurately today the total number of Americans who have one or more Welsh ancestors. Taking the descendants of the colonial settlers into consideration, as well as the descendants of the nineteenth century Welsh immigrants, it is this author's guess that there must be at least 500,000 such. The percentage of those who are conscious of their Welshness is naturally much smaller. The latter are to be found primarily in those areas where the Welsh settled in significant numbers. Such interest among others is limited to those who are interested in antiquarian lore.

DISTRIBUTION OF WELSH-STOCK IN AMERICA BY STATES
(Census of 1900)

	Immigrants	American-Born Children	Total
Pennsylvania	35,453	64,690	100,143
Ohio	11,481	24,490	35,971
New York	7,304	13,152	20,456
Illinois	4,364	7,514	11,878
Wisconsin	3,356	7,866	11,222
Iowa	3,091	6,419	9,510
Utah	2,141	4,033	6,174
Kansas	2,005	3,723	5,728
Colorado	1,955	3,430	5,385
Indiana	2,083	3,149	5,232
California	1,949	3,224	5,173
Missouri	1,613	3,186	4,799
Minnesota	1,288	2,879	4,167
Washington	1,509	2,610	4,119
Massachusetts	1,680	1,716	3,396
Nebraska	922	1,977	2,899
New Jersey	1,195	1,662	2,857
Vermont	1,056	1,777	2,833
Montana	935	1,506	2,441
Idaho	732	1,601	2,333
Michigan	838	1,290	2,128
Maryland	674	1,344	2,018
South Dakota	549	1,245	1,794
Connecticut	650	857	1,507
West Virginia	482	903	1,384
Oregon	401	693	1,094
Wyoming	393	668	1,061
Kentucky	337	660	997
Tennessee	300	581	881

Alabama	306	526	832
Texas	313	461	774
Oklahoma	269	496	765
Virginia	267	406	673
Maine	199	331	530
Rhode Island	256	274	530
North Dakota	147	301	448
Arizona	136	237	373
Nevada	128	224	352
Louisiana	126	214	340
Arkansas	113	201	314
New Mexico	105	168	273
Florida	169	55	224
District of Columbia	82	133	215
Georgia	65	84	149
New Hampshire	68	67	135
Delaware	43	67	110
Alaska	41	57	98
Mississippi	30	58	88
Hawaii	21	22	43
North Carolina	20	23	43
South Carolina	8	12	20
Total:	93,744	173,416	267,160

County (with chief center)	Immigrants	Children	Total
Luzerne, Pa. (Wilkes-Barre)	8,578	12,974	21,552
Lackawanna, Pa. (Scranton)	7,708	11,650	19,358
Allegheny, Pa. (Pittsburgh)	5,245	7,920	13,165
Oneida, N. Y. (Utica)	2,536	4,140	6,676
Schuylkill, Pa. (Pottsville)	2,100	3,180	5,280
Cook, Ill. (Chicago)	1,917	3,120	5,037
Mahoning, O. (Youngstown)	1,627	3,370	4,997
Cuyahoga, O. (Cleveland)	1,592	3,200	4,792
New York City	1,686	2,750	4,436
Lawrence, Pa. (Newcastle)	1,690	2,550	4,240
Trumbull, O. (Warren)	1,205	2,420	3,625
Philadelphia, Pa.	1,033	1,560	2,593
Cambria, Pa. (Johnstown)	946	1,430	2,376
Salt Lake City, Utah	695	1,510	2,205
Northampton, Pa. (Bangor)	832	1,260	2,092
Franklin, O. (Brown Township)	649	1,308	1,957
Rutland, Vt. (Poultney)	979	960	1,939
Stark, O. (Alliance)	597	1,200	1,797
Washington, N. Y. (Granville)	675	1,110	1,785
Westmoreland, Pa. (New Kensington)	703	1,062	1,765
Lehigh, Pa. (Slatington)	692	1,045	1,737
Belmont, O. (Martin's Ferry)	530	1,068	1,598
Tuscarawas, O. (Sugar Creek)	530	1,068	1,598
Macon, Mo. (Bevier)	503	1,080	1,583
Mercer, Pa. (Sharon)	611	924	1,535
Blue Earth, Minn. (Mankato)	428	1,032	1,460
King, Wash. (Seattle)	567	810	1,377
Columbia, Wis. (Columbus City)	442	923	1,365
Madison, Ind. (Anderson)	590	762	1,352
Summit, O. (Akron)	448	904	1,352
Lyon, Kan. (Emporia)	451	895	1,346
Northumberland, Pa. (Shamokin)	568	860	1,328
Mahaska, Ia. (Beacon)	377	842	1,219

Allegany, Md. (Frostburg)	354	811	1,165
Carbon, Pa. (Lansford)	459	695	1,154
Clearfield, Pa. (Houtzdale)	449	680	1,129
Racine, Wis. (Racine)	364	760	1,124
Jefferson, Pa. (Horatio)	433	655	1,088
Waukesha, Wis. (Waukesha)	343	717	1,060
Arapahoe, Col. (Denver)	423	635	1,058
Milwaukee, Wis.	336	701	1,037
San Francisco, Cal.	386	638	1,024
Dauphin, Pa. (Wiconisco)	406	614	1,020
Perry, O. (Shawnee)	332	668	1,000
Fayette, Pa. (Connellsville)	394	596	990
Osage, Kan. (Osage City)	331	656	987
Monroe, Ia. (Hiteman)	303	677	980
Iowa, Wis. (Dodgeville)	315	657	972
Grant, Ind. (Gas City)	416	545	961
Utah, Utah (Spanish Fork)	280	609	889
Hamilton, O. (Cincinnati)	293	590	883
Washington, Pa. (Washington)	344	520	864
Hennepin, Minn. (Minneapolis)	244	590	834
New Haven, Ct. (New Haven)	383	441	824
Portage, O. (Palmyra)	272	547	819
Winnebaga, Wis. (Oshkosh)	261	545	806
Berkshire, Mass. (Pittsfield)	407	366	773
Fremont, Col. (Canyon City)	307	460	767
St. Louis, Mo.	238	518	756
Columbiana, O. (E. Liverpool)	249	501	750
Pierce, Wash. (Tacoma)	307	439	746
Susquehanna, Pa. (Welsh Hill)	292	442	734
Tioga, Pa. (Blossburg)	279	422	697
Licking, O. (Welsh Hills)	227	457	684
Van Wert, O. (Venedocia)	227	456	683
Madison, N. Y. (Nelson)	259	423	682
Alameda, Cal. (Oakland)	256	424	680
Clay, Ind. (Brazil)	294	385	679
Allen, O. (Gomer)	224	451	675
Suffolk, Mass. (Boston)	344	309	653
Will, Ill. (Joliet)	247	402	649
Carbon, Utah (Maxwell)	202	439	641
Polk, Ia. (Des Moines)	188	420	608
Kane, Ill. (Elgin)	223	364	587
Los Angeles, Cal.	221	366	587
Guernsey, O. (Cambridge)	192	387	579
Montour, Pa. (Danville)	134	402	536
Herkimer, N. Y. (Ilion)	199	325	524
LaSalle, Ill. (Ottawa)	198	323	521
Middlesex, Mass. (Cambridge)	271	244	515
Weber, Utah (Ogden)	157	342	499
Cattaraugus, N. Y. (Freedom)	186	304	490

FOOTNOTES ON CHAPTER IV

1. For background material on the causes of Welsh emigration to the United States, see David Williams, "Some Figures Relating to Emigration from Wales," *Bulletin of the Board of Celtic Studies,* VII (May, 1935), pp. 396-415; see also his *A History of Modern Wales,* pp. 177-269.

2. Iago ap Owain, "The Early Welsh Settlers of Steuben and Vicinity," *Cambrian*, VII (Nov., 1887), pp. 334-35.

3. William Harvey Jones, "Welsh Settlements in Ohio," *Ohio Archeological and Historical Quarterly*, XVI (April, 1907), pp. 20-23.

4. John T. Griffith, *Reverend Morgan John Rhys: the Welsh Baptist Hero of Civil and Religious Liberty in the Eighteenth Century*, Carmarthen, Wales (W. M. Evans & Son), 1910, pp. 9-36.

5. *Ibid.*

6. *Ibid.*

7. Jones, *op. cit.*, pp. 198-203; see also Daniel Jenkins Williams, *The Welsh of Columbus, Ohio; a Study in Adaptation and Assimilation*, Oshkosh, Wis., 1913, pp. 20-23, 35.

8. Howard Thomas, "The Welsh Came to Remsen," *New York History*, XXX (Jan., 1949), pp. 33-42; see also Sam Ellis, "The Background," *Moriah Presbyterian Church, 1830-1930*, Utica, N. Y., 1930, pp. 38-40; Erasmus W. Jones, "The Early Welsh Settlers of Oneida County, New York," *Cambrian*, IX (Feb., 1889), pp. 38-40; (Mar., 1889), pp. 78-80.

9. *Ibid.*

10. J. F. Barnes, "History of the City of Beulah; also of the Beulah Baptist Church," in Griffith, *op. cit.*, pp. 59-73.

11. Jones, *op. cit.*, "Welsh Settlements in Ohio," pp. 203-9; see also Ira M. Price, *Historical Sketch of One Hundred Years of the Welsh Hills Baptist Church*, Granville, Ohio, 1908, *passim*.

12. Jones, *Ibid.*, pp. 210-16; B. Harris, ed., *One Hundredth Anniversary of the Congregational Church, Radnor, Ohio, 1820-1920, passim*.

13. Williams, *History of Modern Wales, op. cit.*, pp. 197-212.

14. Jones, "Welsh Settlements in Ohio," *op. cit.*, pp. 216-19.

15. *Ibid.*, pp. 222-25; see also Clarence J. Bradbury, *Centennial Anniversary, 1839-1939, Gomer Congregational Church, Gomer, Ohio, 1939, passim*.

16. See Benjamin Chidlaw, "Translation of *Yr American, a Welsh Pamphlet*," *Quarterly Publications of the Historical and Philosophical Society of Ohio*, VI (Jan.-Mar., 1911), pp. 25-26.

17. Daniel Jenkins Williams, *One Hundred Years of Welsh Calvinistic Methodism in America*, Philadelphia (Westminster Press), 1937, pp. 160-61; Jones, "Welsh Settlements in Ohio," *op. cit.*, pp. 34-36, 58-61, 80-86.

18. Childlaw, *op. cit.*, pp. 1-41.

19. Jones, "Welsh Settlements in Ohio," *op. cit.*, p. 217; J. W. Evans, "The Founders of the Welsh Settlement in Gallia and Jackson Counties, Ohio," *Cambrian*, III (Nov.-Dec., 1883), pp. 286-87.

20. Williams, *One Hundred Years, op. cit.*, pp. 71-76; Lewis Williams, "Lewis County, New York," *Cambrian*, XXV (Sept., 1905), pp. 372-78.

21. Williams, *One Hundred Years, op. cit.*, pp. 69-70; D. L. Williams and E. Mayfield Spooner, *Illustrated History of the Congregational Churches of Richville, New York*, Utica (T. J. Griffith), 1915, pp. 100-16.

22. J. P. Morgan, "Early History of the Welsh Settlers in Van Wert County, Ohio," *Cambrian*, II (Jan.-Feb., 1882), pp. 1-5; Gerald B. Johnson, ed., *Centennial History of the Salem Presbyterian Church, Vendocia, Ohio, Sept. 3, 4, and 5, 1948*, Vendocia, Ohio, 1948, *passim*.

23. Sadie Rowlands Price, "The Welsh of Waukesha County," *Wisconsin Magazine of History*, XXVI (Mar., 1943), pp. 323-32; E. S. Roberts, ed., *Centennial Souvenir Program, Y Capel Log, the Present Jerusalem Church Society, Wales, Wisconsin*, Wales, 1942, *passim*.

24. Williams, *One Hundred Years, op. cit.*, pp. 169-84; Richard W. Evans, ed., *Our Ninety-Fifth Anniversary, 1853-1948, Olivet Welsh Presbyterian Church, Cambria, Wisconsin*, 1948, *passim*.

25. David Davies, ed., *Oshkosh, Wisconsin, Welsh Centennial, 1847-1947*, Oshkosh, Wis., 1947, *passim;* for data on other Wisconsin settlements, see Williams, *One Hundred Years, op. cit.*, pp. 167-204.

26. Williams, *One Hundred Years*, *ibid.*, p. 168; Donald W. Vanderwerp, *Plymouth's Centennial, 1847-1947, Plymouth Congregational Church, Barneveld, Wisconsin,* Barneveld, 1947, *passim;* also, *Peniel Church Centennial, 1847-1947,* Barneveld, 1947, *passim.*

27. Williams, *One Hundred Years*, *ibid.*, pp. 222-25; R. N. Chord, ed., *Centennial Program of the Welsh Congregational Church, Columbus Junction, Iowa, 1846-1946,* Columbus, Iowa, 1946, *passim;* George Reichard, *The History of the Welsh Congregational Church Known as "Old Man's Creek," Iowa City, Iowa,* West Branch, Iowa, 1846, *passim;* Daniel Williams, "The Welsh Settlement of Lime Springs, Iowa," in *Hanes Cymru Minnesota, Foreston, and Lime Springs, Iowa,* Mankato, Minn., 1895, pp. 138-58.

28. Thomas E. Hughes, ed., *Hanes Cymru Minnesota, Foreston, and Lime Springs, Iowa,* Mankato, Minn., 1895, *passim.*

29. Williams, *One Hundred Years*, *op. cit.*, pp. 245-54; see also, *A Brief History of the Sardis Congregational Church, 1871-1949,* Emporia, Kansas, Emporia, 1949, *passim;* Paul L. Carpenter, ed., *Memorial Pipe Organ Dedication, Second Presbyterian Church, Emporia, Kansas,* Emporia, 1948, *passim.*

29. *Ibid.*

31. *Williams, One Hundred Years, op. cit.*, pp. 242-43; Edgar White, "A Noted Welsh Colony," *Cambrian,* XXXI (Aug. 15, 1911), pp. 4-5; Ohla Edsall Edwards, "The Welsh in Macon County, Missouri," *Y Drych,* CII (Sept. 15, 1953), pp. 14-15.

32. Richard L. Evans, *A Century of "Mormonism" in Great Britain,* Salt Lake City (Deseret News Press), 1937, pp. 184-96.

33. *Ibid.*

34. *Ibid.*, p. 196.

35. *Ibid.*

36. For excellent data on the Welsh in Utah, see Kate B. Carter, *The Welsh in Utah,* Salt Lake City (Daughters of Utah Pioneers, Lessons), Oct., 1949, 52 page pamphlet, *passim.*

37. *Ibid.*

38. Robert D. Thomas, *Hanes Cymry America,* Utica, N. Y. (T. J. Griffiths), 1872.

39. Williams, *One Hundred Years*, *op. cit.*, pp. 241-43, 251.

40. *Ibid.*, pp. 225-31; John T. Llewellyn, "The Welsh Colony of Powell, Edmunds County, South Dakota," *Cambrian,* XIV (April, 1894), pp. 103-6.

41. "Among the Raspberries and Strawberries, Festivities at Beaver Creek," *Yr Enfys,* No. 16 (Summer, 1952), p. 15.

42. David Hughes, *Welsh People of California, 1849-1906,* San Francisco, 1923, pp. 5-6.

43. *Ibid.*

44. *Ibid.*, pp. 23-25.

45. *Ibid.*, *passim.*

46. *Ibid.*

47. *Ibid.*

48. Williams, *One Hundred Years*, *op. cit.*, pp. 253-54; see also Evan Williams, *Traethawd ar Hanes Cymry Colorado,* Denver, 1889, *passim.*

49. E. R. Williams, "Butte, Its Welsh People and Welsh Church," *Cambrian,* XXIX (June 1, 1909), pp. 13-14.

50. Williams, *One Hundred Years*, *op. cit.*, p. 255.

51. *Ibid.*, pp. 159-60; David Jones, *Memorial Volume of the Welsh Congregationalists of Pennsylvania, U.S.A.,* Utica, N. Y. (Utica Printing Co.), 1934, pp. 69-74.

52. Williams, *One Hundred Years*, *op. cit.*, pp. 159-60.

53. *Ibid.*, pp. 160-62; Jones, *Memorial Volume*, *op. cit.*, pp. 45-50; see also Evan W. Jones, "Our Welsh Churches," *Johnstown Democrat,* April 3, 1897.

54. Williams, *One Hundred Years*, *op. cit.*, pp. 160-65; Jones, *Memorial Volume,* *op. cit.*, pp. 21-22, 45-46.

55. Jones, *Memorial Volume*, *op. cit.*, pp. 12-13, 21-23, 55-56.

56. Williams, *One Hundred Years*, *op. cit.*, pp. 157, 162-63.

57. *Ibid.*, pp. 144-53; see also Daniel M. Jones, "History of Jefferson Furnace," in *Celebration of the Ninety-Second Anniversary of the Founding of Jefferson Furnace Held on the Furnace Grounds, Labor Day, Monday, September 2, 1946*, pp. 8-13.

58. Williams, *One Hundred Years, op. cit.*, pp. 162-64.

59. *Ibid., passim.*

60. See biographical listings in Appendix.

61. Hobart S. Perry, "David Thomas," *Dictionary of American Biography*, XVIII, pp. 427-28.

62. Jones, *Memorial Volume, op. cit.*, pp. 32-33; Williams, *One Hundred Years, op. cit.*, pp. 119-20.

63. Jones, *Memorial Volume, op. cit.*, pp. 23-30; Williams, *One Hundred Years, op. cit.*, pp. 89-92.

64. Williams, *One Hundred Years, op. cit.*, pp. 116-18; Jones, *Memorial Volume, op. cit.*, pp. 31-32, 53-55, 78-80.

65. Williams, *One Hundred Years, op. cit.*, pp. 120-21; Jones, *Memorial Volume, op. cit.*, pp. 13, 19-21, 33-34, 50, 53-55, 99-100; see also bibliography for other sources on these places.

66. Jones, *Memorial Volume, op. cit.*, pp. 50-52, 64-66, 86-99, 105-7; Williams, *One Hundred Years, op. cit.*, pp. 101-5, 107-9; see bibliography for other sources.

67. Jones, *Memorial Volume, op. cit.*, pp. 37-44, 52-53, 58, 66-69, 74-78, 107-113; Williams, *One Hundred Years, op. cit.*, pp. 105-8, 109-13; Edward George Hartmann, ed., *Welsh Baptist Association of Northeastern Pennsylvania, 1855-1955*, Plymouth, Pa. (Payne Printery), 1955, pp. 10-14, 19-22; see bibliography for other sources.

68. Statistics compiled from the United States Census Reports for the year 1900.

69. Thomas Murphy, *Jubilee History, Commemorative of the Fiftieth Anniversary of the Creation of Lackawanna County, Pennsylvania*, Topeka-Indianapolis (Historical Publishing Co.), 1928, I, pp. 116, 182-84, 338-47.

70. "History of the Gwents," *Druid*, II, No. 1 (Jan. 2, 1908), p. 1; manuscript data on Orpheus Musical Society in possession of the author.

71. See biographical entries in Appendix.

72. Roy Rutherford, *Romancing in Tin Plate*, Warren, Ohio (Wean Engineering Co.), 1951, pp. 55-60.

73. Edward George Hartmann, "Background Notes on the Delta, Pa. Welsh Community," *Y Drych*, CII (Aug. 15, 1953), p. 7. Williams, *One Hundred Years, op. cit.*, p. 120; Jones, *Memorial Volume, op. cit.*, pp. 18-19.

74. Williams, *One Hundred Years, op. cit.*, pp. 118-19; Jones, *Memorial Volume, op. cit.*, pp. 100-1.

75. Bangor Welsh Day Association, *Sixth Annual Welsh Day Program*, Lutheran Grove, Bangor, Pa., September 5, 1936, *passim.*

76. Williams, *One Hundred Years, op. cit.*, pp. 81-88.

77. See biographical entries in Appendix.

78. Sam Ellis, "Conditions that Contributed to the Growth of the Church," *Moriah Presbyterian Church, op. cit.*, pp. 40-42.

79. Poultney Welsh Male Chorus, *Poultney Welsh Male Chorus*, Poultney, Vermont, 1948, *passim.*

80. Williams, *One Hundred Years, op. cit.*, pp. 129-32, 153; Vincent Jones, ed., *The Saga of the Welsh Congregational Church, Lawrence Street, Cincinnati, Ohio, 1840-1952*, Cincinnati, 1952, *passim.*

81. Williams, *The Welsh of Columbus, Ohio, a Study in Adaptation and Assimilation, op. cit., passim.*

82. Williams, *One Hundred Years, op. cit.*, pp. 163-64; see also Henry T. Jones, *Centennial Congregational Church*, Cleveland, 1896, *passim.*

83. Mary E. Pugh and John D. Roberts, *More Than a Century With the Welsh in Racine, 1840-1948*, Racine, 1948, *passim.*

84. Joshua T. Evans, "The Welsh of Minneapolis," in *Hanes Cymry Minnesota, Foreston a Lime Springs, Iowa, op. cit.*, pp. 112-16.

85. Williams, *One Hundred Years, op. cit.*, pp. 77-79; Jones, *Memorial Volume,*

op. cit., pp. 62-64; Henry Blackwell, "The Welsh in America," *Cambrian Gleanings*, I, (June, 1914), pp. 84-96; William R. Jones, *Welsh Presbyterian Church, New York, N. Y. 1828-1953, One Hundred and Twenty-Fifth Anniversary*, New York, 1953.

86. Williams, *One Hundred Years, op. cit.*, pp. 122-23.

87. Jay Monaghan, "The Welsh People in Chicago," *Illinois State Historical Society Journal*, XXXII, (Dec., 1939), pp. 498-516; William J. Griffith, ed., *One Hundredth Anniversary, 1848-1948, Hebron Welsh Presbyterian Church, Chicago, Illinois*, Chicago, 1948.

88. Daniel Hughes, "The History of the Welsh Church of Detroit," *Directory and Telephone Register, 1945, Welsh Presbyterian Church, Detroit, Michigan*, Detroit, 1945, pp. 13, 15, 17.

89. Ronald G. Smith, *History of St. David's Presbyterian Church, San Francisco, California, One Hundredth Anniversary, 1853-1953*, San Francisco, 1953, *passim;* Williams, *One Hundred Years, op. cit.*, pp. 254-55; Hughes, *Welsh People of California, op. cit., passim.*

90. Hughes, *Welsh People of California, op. cit.*, pp. 103-10.

CHAPTER V

THE WELSH-AMERICAN CULTURAL COMMUNITY
ITS RELIGIOUS EMPHASIS

Perhaps with no other ethnic group in America did religion govern the group's activities and so shape behavior patterns as it did the Welsh. The strong impact of non-conformity in the seventeenth century and the Methodist revival in the eighteenth changed the Welsh from a carefree, lighthearted, mountaineer people into a sober, death-fearing and puritanical folk, an impact which is only of late years beginning to lose its hold over the people of Wales. Religion and the institutions related to it therefore occupied the chief interests of the Welsh in the homeland. Those that came to America brought these same interests and ways of life with them, and wherever in America the Welsh settled in numbers small cultural nuclei based upon the old ways of life in the homeland made their appearance.

The Welsh immigrants who came to America were overwhelmingly non-conformist, and in this respect they reflected the general religious situation in the homeland where perhaps as many as eighty-five percent of the population were non-conformist during the latter part of the eighteenth century and during the entire nineteenth century. The three great faiths of the Welsh immigrants in America were Calvinistic-Methodism (often referred to as Welsh Presbyterianism), Congregationalism, and Antipaedo-Baptism. So far as the author has been able to determine, the first and second groups were about of equal strength in numbers among the immigrants of the nineteenth century and their children; the Baptists were less numerous.

Certain other religious groups were represented in the Welsh settlements. The so-called Wesleyan-Methodists, although today fairly strong in Wales, were never very numerous in America. Ten churches of this persuasion were organized at various of the Welsh settlements in contrast to the many organized by the other three denominations. These churches were all short-lived, and the group as a whole never played an important role in shaping or influencing the religious life of the Welsh communities of America.[1] Adherents of the Church of England also immigrated to America during the nineteenth century. Although churches of this denomination were founded by Welsh people during the colonial period, none were established by the later Welsh immigrants.[2] To the extent that these people were Anglicized in speech, to that extent they joined Episcopal churches of the areas wherein they settled. To the extent that they depended upon Welsh as the medium of their religious expression, to that extent they joined the local Welsh churches of non-conformist persuasion.

Both the Quakers and the Mormons were decided minorities among the Welsh. The former practically ceased to exist in Wales after the great seventeenth century migration to Pennsylvania. The Church of Latter Day Saints or Mormons, as well as its branch, the Reorganized Church, still have active missionaries in Wales. The former is responsible for a steady trickle of Welsh immigration to Utah even today.[3]

Since the great bulk of the Welsh people belonged to dissenting groups by the coming of the nineteenth century, it is not therefore strange that they should bring their various forms of dissent with them when they came to America. Three of the early dissenting groups, the Quakers, the Baptists, and the Presbyterians, were already represented in America by the time the eighteenth century opened, most concentrated overwhelmingly in Penn's new colony. All these groups eventually became Americanized in habits and English in speech, although certain of the Baptist churches continued to hold services in Welsh down to 1800. The Welsh Quaker meetings linked themselves with the neighboring Philadelphia English-speaking Quaker meetings right from the start. The Baptists and Presbyterians, although having distinctly Welsh congregations at first, eventually joined with their English-speaking Baptist and Presbyterian neighboring churches to form district organizations to consider problems of general denominational concern. In neither case was an attempt made to set up a distinctly Welsh-American denominational organization during colonial times.

The situation was much different in the nineteenth century. The Welsh settlements made in America from the 1790's onwards were self-conscious of their nationality and were led by Welsh-minded clergymen. They kept in touch with each other thanks to the frequent visitations made throughout these settlements by both Welsh clergymen and laymen from Wales and from other Welsh settlements. From the beginning of the nineteenth century onwards, all three main branches of Welsh dissent—Congregationalism, Calvinistic-Methodism, and Antipaedo-Baptism, were represented in America by numerous immigrants. Members of all three faiths were to be found among the little group that accompanied Morgan John Rhees to the Ebensburg area. All three faiths were also soon represented in the newly founded Welsh settlements of Oneida County, New York. With some exceptions, this pattern was followed in the case of the many other nineteenth century Welsh settlements.

At first the Welsh settlers agreed to worship together until they had become oriented to the new environment and their numbers had been augmented by further immigration. They therefore set up what they called "union churches." All groups were represented and had a voice in determining the policy of such a church. This situation continued until such time as increase in immigration of Welshmen into the area led to the strengthening of the various wings of dissent. When this stage had been reached, movements set in to establish separate congregations representing the branches of dissent in the homeland. Groups, therefore, withdrew to form separate congregations of their own denomination. In the great majority of cases, it was the Baptists and the Calvinistic-Methodists who did the withdrawing leaving the Congregationalists in control of the former "union" church. In certain instances, the strength of the two former groups did not become great enough to organize separate congregations. In these cases, love of worship in the Welsh language kept the Baptist and Calvinistic-Methodist groups within the "union" church. Since these "union" churches had been organized on the Congregational pattern, such congregations continued on the Congregational basis and later joined in the various gymanvas or associations founded in time by Welsh-Americans of this denominational persuasion. They became full-fledged Congregational churches. In most settlements, however, the inflow of Welsh immigrants was sufficiently strong in time to allow for the setting up of at least two and even three denominational churches.[4]

The Welsh settlers differed among themselves over the issues of church organization, Calvinism, and infant baptism. Accordingly, they established churches in conformance with their beliefs on these subjects. Those that favored a strong church organization, well-knit through district and regional bodies, formed Calvinistic-Methodist churches. Those that did not favor such strong organization but insisted on the utmost independence of the individual congregation divided over the question of infant or adult baptism. Those that favored adult baptism formed Baptist churches. Those that did not believe in this rite formed Congregational churches. In both cases the churches were governed on the same basic principle, utmost and complete independence of the individual congregation. Generally speaking, all three groups, Calvinistic-Methodists, Baptists, and Congregationalists accepted the fundamental tenets of Calvinism over those of Arminianism, although there were some exceptions among the Baptists and Congregationalists in this respect. All three groups were definitely what would be called "fundamentalist" in their attitudes towards the religious controversies of the America of the nineteenth century.

The Welsh immigrants took their religion seriously. They quarreled bitterly among themselves over the above mentioned religious differences. At times the quarreling became so intense that even the children took sides on the various issues. Whole settlements were rent with religious argument. Often hard feelings were developed that lasted for the lifetimes of the individuals concerned.

Despite these differences, there were many characteristics of the religious life of the Welsh settlers that were decidedly similar—so similar in fact that all three denominations conformed to a general pattern of religious expression (and since religion dominated the life of the Welsh immigrant) that can be described best as the Welsh way of life. It dominated the behavior pattern of the Welsh in Wales. It became transplanted to America and governed the lives of the Welsh settlers over here as well.

Religion in this case was emphatically Puritanical in its emphasis, demanding rigid observance of the sabbath, temperance if not total abstinence in respect to liquor, strict observance of the marriage vows and the discouragement of divorce, and an austere observance of conduct of life generally. The church was the acknowledged nucleus of the Welsh settlements. Its affairs and its activities were the dominating interests of the Welsh immigrants beyond the normal problems of earning a living. To the church they owed their allegiance. From it they obtained the spiritual sustenance necessary to meet the problems of their everyday existence. On the church and on religious activities associated with it the Welsh immigrants focused practically all their leisure time. A description of the "Welsh way of life" follows. With a few minor exceptions it applies to all Welsh-American settlements.

Sunday was the big day for the Welsh communities. In true Puritan fashion the Welsh observed it strictly. All food was prepared in advance the preceding day so that manual labor of any sort would not soil the Lord's Day. All activities of a worldly sort (to the extent that the Welsh indulged in these) were taboo. Even the reading of Sunday newspapers or secular literature was considered improper. It was accepted as the only true and proper Christian attitude to reserve Sunday strictly for religious activities. Activities of one sort of another took place in the church edifice from 9 A.M. until 8 P.M. A typical schedule of Sunday activities as outlined to the author by one of the older generation of Welsh Congregationalists ran somewhat as follows:

9 A.M.	Classes for adult beginners (converts) in the fundamentals of the faith.
10 A.M.	Preaching Session.
11:15 A.M.	Christian Endeavor (for ages 10-20).
2 P.M.	Sunday School (for both adults and children).
5 P.M.	Christian Endeavor (for ages 5-10).
6 P.M.	Preaching Session.
7:15 P.M.	Singing School (Choir Practice).

If one substituted for the Christian Endeavor sessions Baptist and Calvinistic-Methodist activities of a similar nature for the youth groups, a similar schedule of activities applied for these denominations as well.[5] For the adults, and therefore for the bulk of the Welsh immigrants, the preaching sessions were the all important highpoints of a Sunday. These were awaited with great expectancy all through the preceding week. These were to form the basis of conversation and argument during the week following. Heaven help the preacher who turned up with too many Biblical inconsistencies in his sermon! Former Governor Arthur H. James of Pennsylvania recalled to the author that on many an occasion in his youth he remembered his father and his fellow Welsh cronies debating the merits of the Sunday sermon, the ways in which the preacher's talk was inconsistent with the words of Luke, or those of Paul, yea, even those of Samuel, for the Welsh knew their *Bible,* many of them being capable of quoting large sections of it on occasion.

In delivering these sermons, the Welsh preachers used a technique that was unique in its enthusiasm and which captured their audiences and led the latter to the heights of religious emotionalism and fervor. This technique was called by the Welsh *hwyl,* a word that cannot be translated. Its significance can be obtained by reading the description of this gift as presented by Erasmus W. Jones in his article in the *Atlantic Monthly* on "The Welsh in America":

> The effect often produced by a popular Welsh preacher is wonderful. There is one peculiarity connected with their preaching which differs entirely from anything that I ever observed in English pulpits: it is usually marked by a great variety of intonations. I do not know the origin of this chanting style of preaching prevalent among the Welsh, though it probably was introduced by the founders of Calvinistic-Methodism. The judicious use of it is confined to the more passionate or pathetic parts of a sermon. It differs entirely from that monotonous tone that is heard in English churches, or the chromatic chanting of the mass before papal altars; it is a melody of the purest nature. It is not an easy matter to import to the English mind a clear idea of the genuine Welsh *hwyl,* or that musical style in which the minister pours forth his pathetic passages when under 'full canvas'. A clergyman who has not an ear for music can never charm his hearers with this melodic *hwyl,* and it would be exceedingly unfortunate for him to attempt it, for it embraces the tones and semitones of the scale. Occasionally, however, a Welsh minister wholly destitute of this talent will endeavor to practice it. The best description I can give of this peculiarity is this: it is the application of sentences in a chanting style to portions of the minor scale. The minister is never at a loss how to apply the words to the melody; they appear to run together as by mutual attraction. The sentence is started, for instance, on E minor. The minister has his own peculiar melody. It ranges here and there from the first to the fifth, often reaching the octave, and then descending and ending in sweet cadence on the key-note. I am sure that in the genuine *hwyl* the intonations are always in the minor mode. The introduction and the deliberative parts are in the major, and the voice continues thus until the emotional point is reached; then it glides triumphantly into a thrilling minor, which generally continues to the close.[6]

It follows, that to the extent that the preacher had this capacity of delivery, to that extent he was admired and respected by the congregation. *Hwyl*, however, was not the only thing that counted; the sermons had to be well thought out with plenty of Biblical references in order to be considered acceptable by the critical congregations.

Second only in importance to the sermons for the Welsh immigrants was the Sunday School. This venerable institution was a creation of the Welsh, and perhaps can be considered a Welsh contribution to Protestantism. Certainly the Welsh were holding Sunday School classes in their settlements long before such activities were introduced into the neighboring churches of the areas in which they settled. We have noted already that it was the Sunday Schools that made the Welsh a literate nation, for they were established at a time when there were no opportunities for elementary education of the masses in the homeland. But the Sunday School did more than create a literate people; it also created theologians and logicians as well. Reverend Llewelyn Jones of Utica, New York, stated that in the opinion of authorities on the subject the method used in conducting Welsh Sunday Schools was closely allied to the Socratic method, considered by many as the most perfect medium for teaching. It avoided the evil of doling out facts by the teacher and their being docilely received by the students without any questioning on their part. "The teacher was not always better trained than his pupils but both teacher and pupils participated in a common search for knowledge and truth".[7]

Classes were divided on the basis of age, but always included the adult members of the congregation as well. The usual topics of Protestant Christianity were taught in the children's classes. The adult classes, however, dealt with far more complicated theological topics, and as in the case of the sermons, formed the basis of a great deal of discussion during the week that followed. One knew in advance the topic to be discussed. One studied the Welsh *Bible* and the commentaries thoroughly in advance during the week so that one could be properly prepared for Sunday School. And then one argued and discussed the merits of the topic both in the class and on the way home, or at the home of a crony if the topic proved stimulating enough—and with the Welsh this was usually the case.

Reverend Llewelyn Jones cites the following incident to illustrate the excellent theological background of an average Welsh adult Sunday School class in Wales. Sir Henry Jones, professor of philosophy at Glasgow University, was asked to take over the class upon the occasion of his return to his native village:

> He began, well knowing how to captivate the interest of those rural theologians: "Do you believe in the existence of Hell?" Without undue haste, answers in the affirmative with verses facilely quoted to prove the

point, came from several quarters. Sir Henry proceeded: "Do you believe in the omnipresence of God?" Again answers in the affirmative, always of course, accompanied by proof-texts. "Then is God in Hell?" After some moments' pause several answers of "Yes" were forthcoming. Fixing upon a certain person, Sir Henry asked for the necessary proof. " 'If I ascend up into Heaven, Thou art there! If I make my bed in Hell, behold, Thou art there'." Then said Sir Henry: "If God is there, how can it be Hell?" How well he knew how to corner the old logicians! Had he endeavored to present to them the modern conception of Hell from the pulpit, he would have met with endless opposition, but using the traditional methods of the Sunday School he forced them to realize the inadequacy of their old conception.[8]

Reverend Jones then proceeded to note the comment made by Reverend Thomas Charles Williams, who preached in both England and Wales, that the great difference between preaching to an English congregation and to a Welsh one was that the preacher could take for granted that the Welsh congregation knew its *Bible* and that the English congregation did not. The difference was the result of the Welsh Sunday School.[9]

Most Welsh churches held two meetings during the week in addition to the Sunday services. These were held normally on Tuesday and Thursday nights. In both cases, lay members of the congregation ran the meetings themselves—the preacher remaining in the background and intruding only if requested to do so by the congregation. The Tuesday night meeting was usually devoted to prayers and the singing of hymns— with one of the Deacons or Elders of the church serving as chairman. The Thursday night meeting was devoted to what we would call today the experience meeting, a time when various individuals of the congregation stood up and related how a firm faith in Jesus and Christianity had made it possible for them to overcome their weaknesses or fortified them in the face of the many discouragements that faced them daily. The experience meeting had its origins in the old Calvinistic-Methodist *seiat*, a type of religious meeting gradually taken over in a modified form by other Welsh religious sects by the time that they came to America in the nineteenth century. The main purpose of the *seiat* was to provide a forum for the general discussion of some truth or profitable subject pertaining to the experiences, fears and doubts, or temptations of the attending audience. From the discussion often came advice, warning, or consolation that could be taken to heart by the listeners and aid in their spiritual uplifting. The *seiat* meetings generally lasted for about two hours and could be used as a sounding board for criticisms of all sorts concerning congregational affairs and even the sermons of the pastor.[10]

The *seiat* meetings often comprised all communicant members of the church together with their children. The latter were given their opportunity to testify first and were then excused while the meeting continued. "It was a sort of minature democracy. Its power resided in the elders and other communicant members—not in the minister. The latter while usually present was not essential to the workings of the system. . . . It was in this institution of the church that the Welsh people of two centuries ago learned the art of self-government, for here it was that the laity learned to manage their organizations with remarkable skill and success."[11]

Second only to the sermon and the Sunday School, and indeed, probably ranking first in the hearts of most of the Welsh immigrants as a part of their religious life (and since religion was so intimately intertwined with their everyday existence, with their daily living as well) was the congregational singing, a characteristic feature of the Welsh way of life wherever it established itself. Congregational singing was a natural means of expressing his emotions for the Welshman. As one authority on the Welsh expressed it: "Whenever or wherever the Welsh people are gathered in masses there must be singing. It is the Cymric way of giving expression to an intensely religious and an innate musical feeling, and for that reason they choose to sing hymns in preference to any other form of music."[12] And abundant singing there was at every religious service or any other social activity of the Welsh in America.

A unique feature of the congregational singing of the Welsh was the natural use of four-part harmony—an ability which seems to be inherent in the Welsh nature, and, if contemporary accounts can be believed, was characteristic of the Welsh people from the earliest days of their historical past. Abundant use of four-part harmony—aided in time by hymnals using the tonic-solfa musical notation—and a rich storehouse of hymns to choose from made the congregation of even the smallest Welsh chapel a massed choir of magnitude and excellence. Reverend Llewelyn Jones makes this interesting analysis of Welsh congregational singing:

> If one were asked what are the inherent characteristics of Welsh congregational singing, one would be tempted to say, thought and emotion. The singing itself cannot be considered apart from words of the hymns. We find in the hymns every kind of emotion expressed: fear, joy, despondency, hope, delight, anticipation, and love. These experiences, when they are thoughtfully sung, produce a religious fervor. This fervor, which is characteristic of Welsh congregational singing, is undoubtedly born of the words of the hymns and not the music. When a congregation is moved by this fervor it develops a complete self-abandonment and from this abandonment are born the warmth and the volume. From it also, we dare say, is born harmony which is so peculiarly characteristic of Welsh congregational singing. A person that has learned the rudiments of music will naturally when he is moved to fervor, want to express himself as fully as possible. Thus a man is moved to sing the bass or the tenor part of a tune, not the air, and a woman to sing the soprano or the alto, whichever it is that suits her best. Here we believe, lies the reason for the predominancy of part-singing in Welsh congregational singing. Good singing produces an atmosphere. It arouses our deepest emotions. It makes members of the congregation receptive and the task of the preacher easier.[13]

Hymns as a medium of Welsh religious expression probably antedate the great Methodist revival of the eighteenth century, but few scholars will dissent from the belief that it was this great movement which expressed itself in song and gave to the world one of the great hymn writers of all time—William Williams of Pantycelyn, who wrote over a thousand hymns—that made hymn-singing so fundamentally a part of the Welsh way of life. "New tunes had to be found for the new hymns and musical talent was consecrated to this purpose. Ever since those days Welsh composers have devoted their talent to the production of hymn tunes."[14] Verifying the above analysis, Dr. David E. Jones, the noted musical critic wrote: "In the Welsh hymnology they have a rich literature to draw upon; these cover every phase of human experience, sunshine or shadow; and they arouse stronger emotions in an already superlative emotional nature."[15] One has only to hear a Welsh congregation going full steam ahead on such numbers as *Cwm Rhondda, Diadem, Ton y Botl,* or *Aberystwyth* to realize the full significance of these accurate observations.

Next in importance to the Sunday and weekly services of the various churches in the religious and social life of the Welsh-American settlements were the great preaching festivals or gymanvas as the Welsh called them. They are still a prominant religious feature of Wales today, but have gradually died out in America as the Welsh ethnic group became Americanized. The gymanvas were held by all the denominations in those areas strong enough to sustain a yearly meeting. As one Welsh-American expressed it "the *Cwrdd Mawr* (great meeting) was regarded by the Welsh with as much veneration as the Jew regarded the Passover."[16] The meetings were largely attended with Welshmen coming from miles around to listen to the great preachers and to take part in the inevitable hymn singing. "The great object of the preaching gymanva was to seek the outpouring of the Holy Spirit and the saving of souls. Very little business was transacted at these (early) annual gatherings, but for three or more days three and even four sessions would be held with two or three preachers at each session, especially on Sunday."[17]

From these religious beginnings evolved the business gymanva; that is, the gymanva was made the occasion for a district conference of clergymen and leading laymen at which time important issues of the day were discussed. Slavery, itinerant preachers from Wales, temperance, the missions, and the like, were perhaps the chief of these. As we shall see later in this chapter, the preaching gymanva and its later modification, the combined preaching and business gymanva, became the sole basis of a type of unity for the Welsh Baptist and Congregational churches, and an integral functioning subdivision of church government of the Calvinistic-Methodist denomination. Dr. Daniel J. Williams has described the gymanva, in this case the Ohio gathering of the Calvinistic-Methodists, as follows:

> The gymanva when it convened in regular session was a great gathering in the historic days of Welsh settlements in Ohio. It was the great institution of the Church, and the Church was in control socially as well as religiously in Welsh communities. It was anticipated for weeks beforehand, and the churches held special prayer services for its success, and for the outpouring of spiritual blessings upon the community by reason of its presence. Many details had to be attended to. Ministers and elders from every church were expected to be present and a great docket was arranged when the outstanding preachers of the gymanva proclaimed the gospel message. Local choirs and congregations rehearsed special hymns selected for the gymanva services. These hymns were frequently printed in pamphlet form for distribution at the services. Generally a delegate or invited preacher from Wales was present and the guest was given an honored and prominent place on the preaching schedule.
> The gymanva came to the Jackson Presbytery every two years in the month of May. Moriah, the mother church, was host as the largest church in the community for many years although the entire community shared in the entertainment. Since the church edifice was far too small to accommodate the multitude the gymanva preaching services had to be held in a nearby grove. A platform and pulpit were built for the occasion. Seats made of planks were provided for several hundred people. Estimates of crowds ranging from 3000 to 6000 were made upon occasion. The Welsh *hwyl* pervaded the multitude as the divines swayed the multitude with Welsh eloquence. Congregational singing at such times was an experience never to be forgotten.[18]

Similar gatherings were held yearly by the Baptists and the Congregationalists in various sections of America.

Very few of the early Welsh-American preachers of any of the three denominations were college-trained men. This condition remained pretty general throughout the nineteenth century. Most of the preachers were well-informed men, having obtained their knowledge through self-discipline, diligent application, and from the school of experience generally. Upon obtaining sufficient background in theology and a knowledge of the Welsh *Bible* and the Welsh commentaries, they presented themselves to their respective denominations for acceptance as candidates for ordination. If accepted, they then served a period of apprenticeship—going about the country as itinerant preachers. In due time they were examined carefully by special committees of their denomination, composed of both lay and clerical representatives. If found worthy, they were then ordained as ministers of the gospel in accordance with the procedure laid down by the denomination concerned. In practically every case, these clergymen had some other speciality of occupation to help support themselves, for very few of the churches were large enough to be able to support a clergyman completely. Numerous cases of Welsh clergymen who worked during the week as farmers or miners existed in the American settlements of the nineteenth century, and some of them still do so today.

Many of them acquired large libraries of select books which were bought after scrupulous saving of their hard-earned money. The money came, not from compensations made by churches for preaching the gospel, but from the daily toil of the ministers themselves in manual labor of one form or another. Many of the ministers were farmers; others were skilled artisans who pursued their trade; while still others were unskilled laborers. By dint of hard labor during the day and study at night, chiefly of theological books, many of these men became preachers of high rank and of superior attainments, and some indeed masters of assemblies. These men, thus diligent on week days and week nights, preached twice or three times on Sundays, for little or no compensation from the churches for a period of years. In time the churches felt able to furnish a modest stipend.[19]

In time a general awareness of the need for more formally trained clergymen was felt by all three denominations. Interest in collecting funds to support students for the ministry became greater. Most of the larger congregations insisted on having college-trained pastors. To the extent that they could attract such formally trained persons, the smaller churches did likewise. By the coming of the twentieth century, college trained clergymen were numerous among the Welsh-American preachers, although many of the smaller churches relied, and some still do, upon the old-fashioned preacher, self-educated in theology and religion, but well-informed in the problems of human nature and human relationships.

There are many examples of the zeal of the early pioneer Welsh preachers, laboring among their far-flung flocks, and sacrificing health and comfort in order to bolster up the faith of their countrymen—faced as they were with the numerous difficulties of life in a new environment. The Reverends E. B. Evans and Lewis Williams were men of this sort. Williams travelled on foot over the mountains in the 1850's from the Carbondale, Pennsylvania, settlement to the settlements at Wilkes-Barre, Hazleton, and Pottsville. He walked fifteen to twenty miles on Sundays to preach to three, four, and five congregations. Evans, later Congregational pastor at the Hyde Park (Scranton) settlement, travelled on one occasion on foot all the way from Pittsburgh to Pottsville, a distance of 350 miles. He left Pittsburgh on a Monday evening and arrived at his destination on the following Friday evening![20]

Reverend Edward Jones, a Calvinistic-Methodist minister, travelled thousands of miles on foot to organize churches and to strengthen weak ones in Ohio.

On one such tour in 1835 he walked from Cincinnati to Palmyra, Portage County, in the northeast corner of the state to organize Palmyra Church. On this trip he was overtaken by a severe storm of rain and wind. Houses on the trail were few and far apart. The roads were mere tracks through the woods. During the storm he had to remove his shoes, for he feared to lose them as he walked in the sticky clay. He trudged along barefoot through the evening hours, almost blinded by the rain and nothing but frequent flashes of lightning to show the way. Tired and almost exhausted, at last he saw a light from a window. Encouraged by this, he continued to trudge to the humble farmhouse, where he was kindly received and given quarters

for the night. Weary and with bleeding feet, he retired for the night, grate-
ful for the kind hospitality. Not until three days later could he wear his
shoes and continue his journey in the interest of the churches. After organizing the church at Palmyra he went to Pittsburgh and then down the Ohio
on a flatboat to his home in Cincinnati.[21]

Thanks to the efforts of these pioneer preachers and a score of others
like them, the three denominations struck strong roots into American
soil. Thanks to their earnest efforts the Welsh-American immigrants
remained faithful to the Christian ways of life of the homeland. Thanks
to these leaders of the Welsh-American settlements, pride in the ac-
complishments of their homeland, its culture, and its ideals tended to
check the demoralizing tendencies which beset all immigrants facing a
new and hostile environment. The Welsh-American clergy of the nineteenth century therefore performed a very important service in bridging
the gap until such time as the Welsh immigrant could get his bearings
and the best features of the Americanization process could become effective.

By the 1830's, the Welsh churches of all three denominations had
become numerous enough in America to warrant organization of some
sort on a larger scale. To the extent that church polity would permit,
this was done. The Calvinistic-Methodists went ahead and organized a
distinct denomination or church in America, governed by district presbyteries, state gymanvas or synods, and an all-over national convention.
The Baptists and Congregationalists, because of their stress on the independence of the individual congregation, organized regional associations
where business of general interest to the various churches might be discussed and recommended for the consideration of the member churches.
Beyond this latter step, the Baptists and the Congregationalists never
advanced. On the contrary, they affiliated very early with their fellow
American churches of the same denomination in supporting the Northern
Baptist Convention and the American Congregational Union. Even so,
they insisted on maintaining their separate gymanvas or associations
and it was through these latter organizations that they met with their
fellow American co-religionists to discuss problems and topics of general
interest to the denomination as a whole.

The steady influx of Welsh immigrants after the Civil War, a movement which continued until World War I, greatly strengthened the
churches and organizations of the three Welsh groups. New churches
sprang up in the Pennsylvania coal fields, in the industrial centers of
western Pennsylvania and Ohio, and in a score of small agricultural communities in Wisconsin, Iowa, Minnesota, Kansas, Nebraska, Missouri,
South Dakota, in the far West, and elsewhere. All three groups as distinctly Welsh organizations reached their peak strength in the 1880's.
Decline set in thereafter.

Turning our attention to the three denominations themselves, the author must confess that the amount and variety of materials on the Calvinistic-Methodists is much more numerous than on the Congregationalists or Baptists. This was due to the very nature of the three denominations. The Baptists and the Congregationalists, because of their emphasis upon the utmost complete independence of the individual congregation, avoided strong organization on a large scale. It is true that they had their gymanvas or regional associations, but these were purely advisory bodies with no control over the individual congregations other than that of moral prestige. Then quite early, as noted above, these groups entered into close association with the American churches of these denominations. The Welsh churches in both cases contributed to the general programs sponsored by these American bodies and did not attempt to carry on special programs of their own.

The Welsh Calvinistic-Methodists, on the other hand, formed a separate denomination, closely integrated and unified through local presbyteries, regional gymanvas or synods, and finally in a national governing body, the general assembly, at the top. As a separate denomination, the Calvinistic-Methodists had to meet all the problems faced by other denominations and to make decisions accordingly. Excellent and complete records were kept by this religious group during the lifetime of its denomination in America. They had the foresight, also, to provide for the preparation of a history of their church upon the occasion of its merger with the Presbyterians in 1919.[22] Would that the Baptists and Congregationalists had done likewise! The Welsh Congregational Gymanva of northeastern Pennsylvania did bring forth such a history upon the occasion of its dissolution in 1934.[23] The author is happy to add, with the aid of the Pennsylvania Welsh Baptists, he was able to bring out a little history of the last surviving Welsh Baptist gymanva upon the occasion of its one hundredth anniversary in 1955.[24] It is because of these factors that the data on the Calvinistic-Methodists in America is much more complete than is that on the other two denominations.

The Three Denominations

THE BAPTISTS

The Baptists were the least numerous of the three denominations in membership and in churches organized. In this respect they reflected the situation in Wales itself where their position is a similar one. As we have seen, Welsh Baptists came to America during the colonial period when the Reverend John Myles established his church at Swansea, Mass., and Baptist congregations were founded in Pennsylvania, Delaware, and South Carolina. In no case during the colonial period did these early

Welsh Baptists organize a Welsh conference of their own. Instead, they joined the local American conferences as these were organized. As we have noted, Welsh Baptists and their clergymen played a leading role in the early history of the Philadelphia Baptist Conference.

An influx of Welsh Baptists set in with the coming of the noted Morgan John Rhees in the 1790's and the founding of his Beulah, Pennsylvania, settlement. Then as Welsh immigration picked up momentum in the nineteenth century the number of Welsh Baptists increased. In those settlements where numbers were sufficient, churches of this faith were organized. Some of these early Welsh Baptist churches were:

1. Swansea, Mass., 1663
2. Pennepek, Pa., 1688
3. Iron Hill, Del., 1703
4. Tredyffrin or Great Valley, Pa., 1711
5. Brandywine, Pa., 1715
6. Montgomery, Pa., 1719
7. Welsh Neck, S. C., 1738
8. Tulpehoken, Pa., (now in Reading), 1738
9. First Baptist, Philadelphia, 1746
10. Beulah, Pa., (now in Ebensburg), 1797
11. Utica, N. Y., 1801
12. New York City, 1807
13. Welsh Hills, Ohio, 1808
14. Bordville, N. Y., 1810
15. Carbondale, Pa., 1830
16. Remsen, N. Y., 1831
17. Pittsburgh, Pa., 1831
18. Pottsville, Pa., 1832
19. Welsh Baptist Tabernacle, New York City, 1833
20. Minersville, Pa., 1835
21. Ebenezer, Centerville, Ohio, 1838

From the 1840's onwards, the Welsh Baptist element had become strong enough in America to organize a total of 117 churches distributed throughout the various Welsh settlements. Some of these lasted only a decade or two. Others are still going strong today in the anthracite regions of Pennsylvania in particular. As one might expect, the Baptist churches were most numerous in the heavily populated settlements of Pennsylvania and Ohio; less numerous in the settlements of the west.[25]

Preaching gymanvas were established by the Baptists in the 1840's which were later modified into business gymanvas as well. As noted above, the gymanvas were merely advisory bodies to the churches of the districts. They rotated annually among the member churches serving the purpose of reinvigorating Baptist Christian enthusiasm within the district where the meetings were held, as well as serving as a convenient arena where problems of general interest to all the congregations could be thrashed out and recommendations made to the respective churches. Strong stands in support of abolition and temperance were taken by these gymanvas; recommendations that careful screening be given the numerous preachers, who came over from Wales, to weed out charlatans were made; enthusiastic support of the home and foreign missionary activities of the Northern Baptist Convention was given; and a host of problems concerning ways of increasing church attendance, adding new members, and the like were considered at these gymanva meetings. Beyond this point the gymanvas never went—leaving the individual congregations complete freedom to follow the recommendations or not.

Five such gymanvas or conferences of the Welsh Baptist churches were formed eventually in America: New York, Eastern Pennsylvania, Ohio and Western Pennsylvania, Wisconsin, and the Gymanva of the Trans-Mississippi West. The oldest of these started under the name of the Gymanva of Oneida County, New York, and Eastern Pennsylvania. In 1835, however, the Eastern Pennsylvania churches withdrew to form a separate gymanva of their own—the Eastern Pennsylvania Gymanva. The Oneida County churches then took the name of the New York Gymanva. Difficulties of communication and transportation undoubtedly led to the new arrangement.[26] The Ohio Gymanva was formed in 1839 and included in its membership the Welsh churches of Western Pennsylvania. The latter had belonged for a time to the Eastern Pennsylvania body but chose to join the new organization, again because of transportation difficulties. In this respect, it should be noted that the Welsh churches of Western Pennsylvania of all denominations formed closer associations with their Ohio neighbors rather than with their Eastern Pennsylvania fellows largely because of the difficulties of transportation across the Alleghenies during the nineteenth century.[27]

The Wisconsin Baptist Gymanva was formed in 1860 and the Trans-Mississippi Gymanva sometime in the 1870's. Records concerning these groups are incomplete, but the *Wawr Americanaidd,* the journal of the Welsh Baptists, lists both of them as functioning in the 1880's.[28]

In time, as the full effects of Americanization became felt and immigration from Wales slackened, the Baptist gymanvas began to disintegrate. We hear nothing more of the Trans-Mississippi after 1888; of the Wisconsin after 1890; of the New York after 1897. The Ohio disbanded in 1922.[29] Only the Eastern Pennsylvania (now called the Welsh Baptist Association of Northeastern Pennsylvania) is still functioning today, now in its 112th year with a total membership of twelve churches. Disbandment and merger with the local American Baptist

Association has been considered at various times and can be expected as an eventuality within the near future.[30]

Seven periodicals were established for the benefit of the Welsh Baptists of America. All except one were in Welsh, and all were published and printed in America. Some of these were of very brief existence; others had fairly long careers. Of the latter publications, the following were most important: *Y Seren Orllewinol* (1844-1867), a monthly edited by the Reverend W. T. Phillips and later by the Reverend John T. Harries; *Y Glorian* (1872-1894), a monthly, published at Youngstown, O., and edited by D. J. Nichols and J. Aubrey; and *Y Wawr Americanaidd* (1876-1896), a monthly, edited and published by Owen Griffith. All are mines of information on Welsh Baptist activities in America. These and other Baptist periodicals will be considered in detail in the chapter on Printing and Journalism.

THE CONGREGATIONALISTS

The Welsh Congregationalists were much more numerous than the Welsh Baptists and organized a total of 229 churches in America. Some of these were short-lived and existed about a decade; others are still going strong today. Unlike the Welsh Baptists, the Welsh Congregationalists never established churches in America during the colonial period.

As we have noted earlier in this chapter, it became the custom of the Welsh settlers upon their arrival at a new settlement to form "union" churches where all worshipped jointly. By the very nature of the arrangement, these "union" churches were Congregational in polity. Then as more and more Welsh immigrants arrived in the settlement, denominational strength became sufficiently strong to form separate churches. The Baptists and Calvinistic-Methodists usually withdrew leaving the former "union" church in the hands of the Congregationalists. It is for this reason that the Welsh Congregational churches frequently antedate their Baptist and Calvinistic-Methodist neighbors in a given community.

Among the early Welsh Congregational churches founded in America were the following:

1. Ebensburg, Pa., 1797
2. New York City, 1801
3. Bethesda, Utica, N. Y., 1802
4. Paddy's Run (Shandon), Ohio, 1803
5. Capel Ucha, Steuben, N. Y., 1804
6. Radnor, Ohio, 1820
7. Carbondale, Pa., 1831
8. Deerfield, N. Y., 1831
9. Penymynydd, East Steuben, N. Y., 1832

10. Neath, Bradford County, Pa., 1833
11. Minersville, Pa., 1833
12. Palmyra, Ohio, 1834
13. Gomer, Ohio, 1835
14. Welsh Hill, Susquehanna County, Pa., 1835
15. Coleraine (Junedale), Pa., 1837
16. Troedrhiwdalar, South Radnor, Ohio, 1839
17. Spring Brook, Lackawanna County, Pa., 1839

As in the case of the Welsh Baptists, the Congregationalists established preaching gymanvas. These in time developed into business gymanvas as well. As in the case of the Baptists, too, these gymanvas served the purpose of reinvigorating Congregational enthusiasm within the district where the gymanva was held as well as serving as a convenient arena for consideration of problems of general interest to the churches and the denomination as a whole. Strong stands in favor of abolition and temperance were taken. Recommendations in regard to screening itinerant preachers from Wales were given. Vigorous support to the home and foreign mission programs of the American Congregational Union was recommended. A host of other problems concerning better church attendance, the recruiting of new members, education of youth, and the like, were considered and action recommended. In every case, however, as in the case of the Baptists, the decisions of the gymanvas were strictly recommendatory, for the individual congregations were left perfectly free to follow the advice of the gymanvas or not.

Six such gymanvas or associations were formed by the Welsh Congregationalists in America: New York, the oldest, was founded in 1837; Pennsylvania, organized in 1838, later divided into two separate gymanvas in 1873, Eastern Pennsylvania and Western Pennsylvania; Ohio, organized in 1840, also divided into two separate gymanvas in 1871, Ohio Eastern and Ohio Central South; Wisconsin was organized in 1850. Lastly Iowa founded in 1884 soon divided into two separate organizations, Iowa East and Iowa West, then in 1896 the latter disbanded and a single Iowa Gymanva was formed again.[31]

As in the case of the Baptists, so too in that of the Congregationalists, the effects of gradual Americanization were felt and forces set in which led to the dissolution of the gymanvas. No data exists on Wisconsin after 1916. Iowa disbanded in 1921; New York in 1930; Western Pennsylvania in 1910; Eastern Pennsylvania in 1931, and Ohio Eastern in 1956. Only Ohio Central South is still in existence today with four member churches. Dissolution will undoubtedly occur in the near future.[32]

The Welsh Congregationalists also had their periodicals but not so many as the Baptists. Their one main publication, *Y Cenhadwr Ameri-*

canaidd (The American Messenger), (1840-1901), an excellent periodical, waxed so strong that it lasted for sixty-one years. It was edited
by Reverend Robert Everett of Steuben, New York, one of the leading
Welsh Congregational clergymen in America. This and the other periodicals of the Congregationalists will be considered in the chapter on
Printing and Journalism.

THE CALVINISTIC-METHODISTS OR WELSH PRESBYTERIANS

The Calvinistic-Methodists or as they sometimes called themselves
Welsh Presbyterians (to distinguish themselves from other Methodist
bodies) were, perhaps, the most numerous of the three Welsh religious
groups in America. They organized a total of 236 churches, all of which
belonged to the denomination officially, but in addition founded a number
of churches on the Pacific coast which never affiliated with the official
bodies of this denomination, but rather joined the Presbyterian Church,
U.S.A., because they were too far away from the nearest gymanva of the
Calvinistic-Methodist Church.[33]

Although Calvinistic-Methodists were among the early settlers of
Ebensburg, Pa., and Steuben, New York, the first *bona fide* congregation to be founded by this denomination was the Penycaerau Church
of Remsen Township, Oneida County, New York, in 1824. Other
churches sprang up in the various Welsh settlements, some of brief existence, others still going strong today. Among the early Calvinistic-Methodist churches were:

1. Penycaerau, Remsen, N. Y., 1824
2. New York City, 1826
3. Penygraig, Remsen, N. Y., 1827
4. Hebron, French Road, Remsen, N. Y., 1828
5. Nant, French Road, Remsen, N. Y., 1828
6. Moriah, Utica, N. Y., 1830.
7. Capel Ceryg, Remsen, N. Y., 1831
8. Cincinnati, Ohio, 1832
9. Carbondale, Pa., 1832
10. Minersville, Pa., 1832
11. Pottsville, Pa., 1832
12. Pittsburgh, Pa., 1833
13. Palmyra, Ohio, 1835
14. Moriah, Jackson County, Ohio, 1835
15. Welsh Hills, Ohio, 1835
16. Horeb, Jackson County, Ohio, 1836
17. Granville, Ohio, 1838
18. Zoar, Jackson County, Ohio, 1838

19. St. Clair, Pa., 1838
20. Bethel, Jackson County, Ohio, 1839

With the founding of the Penycaerau church, the Calvinistic-Methodist denomination became established in America. The little church was accepted as legitimate by the mother church of Wales and this undoubtedly led to an influx of Calvinistic-Methodists into Oneida County, New York, for by the year 1828, four other churches of this denomination had been established and in that year the first gymanva of the Calvinistic-Methodists took place at the Penycaerau church. Other such gymanvas were held in the Ohio and Pennsylvania settlements soon thereafter.

As in the case of the Baptists and Congregationalists, the early gymanvas of this group were nothing more than preaching festivals of one or two days. In time one of the days was devoted to business matters when both clergy and elders of the churches discussed religious and doctrinal subjects as well as the welfare and outlook of the churches. Such official matters became increasingly important until the gymanva was extended into a state body having a permanent organization. The old name, gymanva, was retained because the characteristics of the true gymanva—the great preaching sessions, six to eight per gymanva with two sermons delivered at each—were retained.

Unlike the Congregational and Baptist gymanvas which were purely advisory, these state gymanvas became the controlling institutions of the Calvinistic-Methodist Church, and their authority was final concerning all matters. Even the General Assembly of this denomination, which was later set up, could only advise and counsel the gymanvas. In time, local presbyteries were established as sub-divisions of the gymanvas when feeling arose that the Gymanva covered too large an area to carry on certain types of local business. The presbyteries, with the permission of the gymanvas, were allowed to exercise certain types of ecclesiastical authority, but always the gymanva exercised ultimate authority.

Six gymanvas of the Calvinistic-Methodist Church were organized: New York and Vermont, 1828; Ohio and Western Pennsylvania, 1838; Pennsylvania (East), 1845; Wisconsin and Northern Illinois, 1844; Minnesota, 1858; and the Gymanva of the West, 1882.[34] The rapid increase of Welsh immigrants, however, and the steady founding of new settlements in the west, led to a feeling among the Calvinistic-Methodists that some all-over organization was needed to unite the various churches throughout America. Two things led to serious consideration of this proposal, the safeguarding of the doctrines of the Church and the necessity of maintaining high standards of church discipline. All three existing gymanvas, New York, Pennsylvania, and Ohio, went on record in 1842 as being in favor of such an all-over organization, and formed that same year the Organized Assembly (Y Gymanfa Gorphoredig) of the Calvinistic-Methodist Church in America. It was to have the same powers as the Quarterly Assembly of the mother church in Wales. It met annually thereafter until 1853 when it was forced to disband. The project was too ambitious for the times. Communications were too difficult between the various areas and too costly for the various groups to cooperate.[35]

Within a dozen years, however, talk of an all-over organization arose again. The leaders of the denomination felt that since the gymanvas tended to act independently and not always uniformly on important questions that this constituted a serious weakness. Closer unity would eliminate this and assure uniformity. The time had come, too, for a unified program for planning missions and organizing educational projects. This could best be undertaken by a General Assembly which could simplify such work and prevent overlapping. One after another the gymanvas (by this time increased to five) went on record as favoring the organization of such a supervisory body.[36]

In 1869, representatives of the five gymanvas met at Columbus, Ohio, and organized the General Assembly of the Welsh Calvinistic-Methodist Church of America. Members were to consist of two ministers and two laymen from each gymanva, plus such people as former moderators, clerks, the editor of the denominational journal, the statistician, various clerks, and those appointed to read important papers. The General Assembly proved to be very successful. It met annually for the first three meetings, then biennially until 1877, then every three years until the merger of the denomination with the Presbyterian Church of the U.S.A. occurred in 1919. [37] The Assembly could only recommend measures to the gymanvas, each of which could take independent action as it saw fit. Despite this seeming weakness, the Assembly rendered genuine usefulness to the denomination through its guidance and coordinating efforts.

The Calvinistic-Methodists also carried on a missionary program, modest in the beginning but evolving into full-scale independent activity. At first the churches and gymanvas contributed to the missionary activities of the mother church in Wales. Then, in addition, they aided the work of the American Missionary Association, an interdenominational group, which in turn helped support Calvinistic-Methodist efforts to establish churches in the new Welsh settlements. With the founding of the General Assembly, however, a Home and Foreign Missionary Society was established to support denominational activities in these fields. The Home Mission field received the chief interest during the early years of the existence of the Society as efforts were made to establish churches in the new western settlements and in the anthracite areas. The Reverend William Hughes, the Society's first secretary, made a tour of the West in

1872. On the basis of his recommendations, a program was drawn up to assure the furnishing of preachers and the establishing of churches for the Welsh settlers of the trans-Mississippi west.[38]

From the 1880's onwards, the Calvinistic-Methodists devoted more and more of their attention to the foreign missionary field. They supported the efforts of the mother church of Wales in India, an area then as now of great interest to the Welsh Church. In time, the American Church felt ambitious enough to seek a district of its own in India in support of which it could carry on activities. The mother church thereupon turned over to its American daughter the district of Habiganj in South Sylhet with a population of one-half million for its own missionary efforts. Reverend Thomas John Jones, Ph.D., a Welsh immigrant preacher of the Wisconsin Gymanva, and his wife were sent over to become the first American missionaries for the denomination abroad. They labored for some ten years in this district making missionary tours, preaching in the market places, and eventually organizing the first Christian church at Silchar in 1894. Two schools for boys and one for girls were also established in this city. A day school and a night school were started at Rampoon and a combination school at Sahuai Basai. Church edifices were built at Rampoon in 1901 and schoolhouses there and elsewhere within the district.[39]

Reverend Jones and his wife were joined by Miss Harriet Davies, M.D., of Oshkosh, Wisconsin, in 1906. Through her efforts a hospital and dispensary were built at Habiganj over which she had complete supervision. A total of ten native assistants aided the missionaries. Jones died in India in 1912 and his place was taken by Reverend Charles Ernest Powell, also a Welsh immigrant clergyman, and his wife. In 1914, a Welsh immigrant lay missionary, Lewis Evans, of Hebron Church, Chicago, and his wife, joined the little group in India. Evans was a bricklayer and stonemason. He supervised the construction of various buildings erected by the missionaries. He also preached as well and became so successful in this respect that he was ordained by the Church in 1927.[40]

When the Calvinistic-Methodist Church of America merged with the Presbyterian Church in 1919, the latter agreed to take over its mission field in India. The Habiganj Mission, however, was too far afield from the other Presbyterian fields in India for practical supervision. Arrangements were therefore worked out with the Calvinistic-Methodist Church of Wales to return the area to its guidance in 1924. The Welsh-American missionaries were given their choice of staying or being assigned elsewhere. Reverend and Mrs. Evans decided to stay and continue serving under the Welsh Church. Dr. Harriet Davies and her assistant, Miss Ann Gwen Jones, were transferred to other fields in India. Reverend Powell had resigned his position in the meantime.[41] The foreign missionary effort of the American Calvinistic-Methodists, although modest in scope, was overwhelmingly successful and illustrates only too well the enthusiasm of the Welsh-Americans of this denomination to bring the Gospel message to the attention of non-Christians.

The Calvinistic-Methodists also had their periodicals. Of these, *Y Cyfaill* (the Friend), 1838-1933, was by far the most important. It was founded, edited, and published by the Reverend William Rowlands in 1838, and had a distinguished career for ninety-six years. This periodical, a monthly, was purchased by the denomination in 1869 and was owned by it until the dissolution of the journal in 1933. The story of *Y Cyfaill* and the other publications of the denomination will be told in the chapter on Printing and Journalism.

As the Americanization of the Welsh groups in America took place, the question of merger of the Calvinistic-Methodist Church with the Presbyterians cropped up frequently. On theological issues the two churches held the same basic tenets. On organizational matters there was a great deal upon which they both agreed. From 1892 onwards, elements among the Welsh pushed for such a merger in line with the growing tendency among Protestant groups to favor denominational merger. Conservative elements among the Calvinistic-Methodists, however, opposed this step, although the Presbyterians went on record as favoring the move. It took some three decades of further discussion among the Welsh gymanvas and a further Americanization of the churches before a majority of the Welsh Church in favor of the merger could be obtained. By 1919 this had become a possibility. Accordingly, the General Assembly of the Calvinistic-Methodist Church appointed representatives to meet with those of the Presbyterians to work out the details of the merger. This was done and merger became effective in 1919. Under the merger, the Welsh gymanvas were allowed to continue as synods of the Presbyterian Church, U.S.A.[42]

The effects of continued Americanization eventually led to the dissolution of the Welsh gymanvas. Trans-Mississippi West disbanded in 1921, its churches joining the presbyteries of the area in which they were located. Ohio did likewise in 1933. Minnesota disbanded in 1935, its churches forming a new presbytery of Blue Earth instead. New York-Vermont followed suit in 1936. Pennsylvania disbanded in 1935, but formed its churches into a new Welsh Presbytery of the Pennsylvania synod. This Welsh presbytery lasted until 1947 when it, too, was disbanded and its churches joined their area presbyteries.[43] Wisconsin disbanded in 1934 to form instead the Welsh Presbytery of Wisconsin. Until 1954 it was the only distinctly Welsh organization left of the old

Calvinistic-Methodist Church. In that year it disbanded with the member churches joining their area presbyteries.[44]

The story of the Welsh churches and the respective denominations in America is one paralleled by other immigrant groups in America, that of modest beginnings, then waxing of strength as the peak period of immigration arrived, then that of gradual decline. The peak period for the Welsh churches was the post-Civil War era until the opening of the twentieth century. This was the time when all three faiths flourished as never before. Then decline set in brought about by two main factors— the Americanization of the children of the immigrants and the cessation of immigration from Wales.

As early as the 1880's the Welsh churches had to face the language problem. Not only were the children of the immigrants often lacking in enthusiasm for worship and preaching in the Welsh language, but a considerable body of non-Welsh-speaking Welsh immigrants from Angli- cized South Wales began to make their appearance at the various Welsh settlements. Pressure mounted in favor of the use of more and more English in religious services. The oldsters, who usually dominated the various congregations, would have none of it. Although most of the latter were bi-lingual by this time, they would not hear of worship other than in their mother tongue because all their religious traditions were asso- ciated with the Welsh language. A battle royal raged over this issue in many of the Welsh settlements during the decade of the 1880's. It led in many cases to the secession of the pro-English wing and the setting up of all-English speaking congregations, sometimes with the blessings of the mother church, sometimes only after vicious quarreling and the crea- tion of great enmity. In most of the Welsh settlements, and in the anthra- cite communities in particular, such churches were organized and are flourishing today along side the old mother churches.

The Baptists and the Congregationalists were the chief sufferers from this secessionist movement. The Calvinistic-Methodists were able to meet the challenge better. No new churches could be formed without the approval of the gymanva concerned. To do so meant leaving the denomination and espousing some other faith. This tended to stem the pro-English movement among this denomination, although undoubtedly many individuals left the group to affiliate with English-speaking churches.

In time, as the twentieth century advanced, the Americanization of the Welsh-speaking churches of all denominations continued. The pressure for services in English continued and as the older generation passed away the forces of opposition weakened. One by one concessions were made to the vigorous crop of American-born youngsters. First the morning services were given in English with services in Welsh continuing at night. Then both services were held in English with a Welsh service being held every other week. As the years advanced, Welsh services were relegated to once a month, and finally in most cases were dropped completely. Depending upon the age of the settlement and whether or not it had received a considerable body of recent immigrants, the Welsh churches bowed to the inevitable, the earlier settlements becoming English in speech by the turn of the century, the later ones in the 1920's and 1930's. Only in places having a strong attraction for continued immigration did services in Welsh continue: New York City, Chicago, Detroit, Oakland, Los Angeles, Philadelphia, and Utica (reinforced by immigrants from the Vermont slate areas). These are the only places where regular services in Welsh are carried on today. On special occasions, however, such as St. David's Day, commemorative services are held in Welsh in various of the settlements.

The Americanization of the Welsh churches was also reflected in the process which set in to disband their various gymanvas and to affiliate their churches with the American organizations of their respective denominations within whose geographical jurisdiction they lay. Traditions and the older generation spragged this movement, but as the Americanization of the individual churches continued and the Welsh language became weaker, the continued need for such distinctly Welsh organizations ceased to exist. Demands for closer unity with American churches of similar polity became increasingly stronger. One by one the Welsh religious organizations surrendered.

Dissolution appeared earliest and fastest in those areas where the Welsh settlements were widely dispersed and weakest. The Congregational and Baptist gymanvas of the trans-Mississippi western settlements went first. Among the Calvinistic-Methodists, the Trans-Mississippi Gymanva which covered the same general area was also the first to disband. Then the dissolution movement hit the stronger eastern areas with consequent disbandment of the respective gymanvas of all three denominations. Today, only two distinctly Welsh organizations above the church level remain of the many that were flourishing in the nineteenth century: The Welsh Baptist Association of Northeastern Pennsylvania (now in its 112th year) and the Welsh Congregational Association of Ohio Central South (now in its 127th year).

Of the 606 odd churches founded by the Welsh immigrants, 177 survive as well. All have become completely Americanized. They have not forgotten their Welsh heritage, however, for in many cases the old Welsh hymns are still sung in Welsh by the second and third generations, who have been taught to pronounce the words but do not understand their meaning. How long this situation will continue is only a matter of time. It is probable that the Welsh hymns will continue to be sung but to English words, as very little effort is being made to orient the coming generation to singing in Welsh. As the old bilingual hymnals wear out and are replaced by the official hymnals of the respective American denominations—displacement of the Welsh hymn tunes may also occur.

As for the fate of the Welsh churches themselves, this will probably depend upon the nature of the environment within which they are located. Where no serious competition from American churches exists the Welsh churches will continue to function and to serve (as many of them do now) the needs of whole communities irrespective of ethnic origin. They will become American congregations serving a definite area. In other cases, where there is vigorous competition from American churches or where because of economic changes the original Welsh population has moved elsewhere, one can expect the Welsh churches to decline, to merge with some larger American neighbor, or to disband completely. This has happened in many cases as a check of the list of churches will show. Whatever the fate in store for them, the Welsh churches played an important part in American history by serving the spiritual needs of the Welsh immigrants and their children, and by helping to shape them into law-abiding, highly moral, and intelligent Americans.

FOOTNOTES ON CHAPTER V

1. Welsh Wesleyan-Methodist churches were established at New York City and Remsen, N. Y., Johnstown, Bangor, Delta, and Wilkes-Barre, Pa., Chicago, Ill., Oshkosh, Wis., and South Bend, Minn.
2. See Appendix for list of Welsh colonial churches.
3. See chapter IV for the story of the Welsh Mormons in America.
4. Daniel Jenkins Williams, *One Hundred Years of Welsh Calvinistic Methodism in America*, Philadelphia (Westminster Press), 1937, pp. 39-40.
5. Conversation of the author with Mrs. John M. Thomas, daughter of the Reverend Dr. T. C. Edwards (Cynonfardd), of Kingston, Pa., summer of 1952.
6. Erasmus W. Jones, "The Welsh in America," *Atlantic Monthly*, XXXVII (Mar., 1876), pp. 305-13.
7. Llewelyn Jones, ed., *Moriah Presbyterian Church, 1830-1930*, pp. 51-2.
8. *Ibid.*
9. *Ibid.*
10. *Ibid.*, p. 53.
11. Williams, *op. cit.*, p. 9.
12. David E. Jones, "Music Just Natural When Cymry Meet," *Scrantonian*, July 24, 1938.
13. Jones, *Moriah Presbyterian Church, op. cit.*, p. 57.
14. *Ibid.*
15. Jones, "Music Just Natural," *op. cit.*
16. Jones, "Welsh in America," *op. cit.*, p. 309.
17. R. S. Jones, "Congregationalism in Pennsylvania during the Early Years of the Nineteenth Century," in *One Half Century of Work, History of the Providence Welsh Congregational Church of Scranton, Pennsylvania*, pp. 9-10.
18. Williams, *op. cit.*, pp. 137-38.
19. *Ibid.*, p. 291.

20. David Jones, *Memorial Volume of the Welsh Congregationalists in Pennsylvania*, p. 24.

21. Williams, *op. cit.*, pp. 130-31.

22. This impressive history was written by the Reverend Daniel Jenkins Williams, Ph.D., a leading member of the denomination from Ohio. Entitled *One Hundred Years of Welsh Calvinistic Methodism in America*, it constitutes one of the chief sources on the Welsh in America. Although stress is placed upon the Calvinistic-Methodists, the book contains a mine of information on the Welsh settlements generally. The author cannot express enough his indebtedness to Dr. Williams for the information contained in this book, which he has cited so frequently.

23. This work, *Memorial Volume of Welsh Congregationalists in Pennsylvania, U.S.A.*, was published in 1934, and was written by the Reverend David Jones, D.D., a leading member of the denomination from Scranton, Pa. It, too, is a main source on the Welsh in America, in this case the important Pennsylvania communities.

24. See Edward George Hartmann, ed., *Welsh Baptist Association of Northeastern Pennsylvania, 1855-1955,* 1955.

25. "The Welsh Baptists in America—an Evaluation," *ibid.*, pp. 25-31; this article also appears in *The Chronicle*, XIX (April, 1956), pp. 90-96.

26. Hartmann, *op. cit.*, pp. 3-4.

27. See *Annual Reports of the Welsh Baptist Association of Ohio and Western Pennsylvania*, 1895-1922, *passim*.

28. For data on the Wisconsin, New York, and Trans-Mississippi gymanvas, see files of *Y Wawr Americanaidd*, *passim*.

29. *Ibid.*

30. See *Annual Reports of the Welsh Baptist Association of Northeastern Pennsylvania*, 1885 to date.

31. For data on the various Welsh Congregational gymanvas, see the *Minutes* of the Congregational Association of Iowa, Kansas, New York, Ohio, Pennsylvania, and Wisconsin, *passim*; also the *Congregational Yearbooks*, *passim*; *One Hundredth Anniversary of the Welsh Gymanfa of Ohio*, 1930, *passim*.

32. *Ibid., passim.*

33. The western Calvinistic-Methodist churches that did not affiliate with the mother denomination were those of Oakland, San Francisco, Los Angeles, Seattle, and five short-lived Churches in the California mining districts.

34. Williams, *op. cit., passim.*

35. *Ibid.*, pp. 257-65.

36. *Ibid.*, p. 266.

37. *Ibid.*, pp. 268-89.

38. *Ibid.*, pp. 343-94.

39. *Ibid.*

40. *Ibid.*

41. *Ibid.*, p. 383.

42. *Ibid.*, pp. 395-412; see also *Minutes of the General Assembly of the Presbyterian Church in the United States*, New Series, XX, August, 1920.

43. *Minutes of the General Assembly of the Presbyterian Church in the United States*, 1921, 1933, 1935, 1936, 1947.

44. *Ibid.*, 1955.

CHAPTER VI

WELSH-AMERICAN JOURNALISM AND PRINTING

Within a short time after the coming of the Welsh to America in significant numbers, ambitious individuals among them began to issue newspapers and periodicals in the Welsh language to cater to the literary, social, and religious needs of their fellow immigrants. When one considers the paucity of their numbers in comparison to other ethnic groups that emigrated to America and their rather wide dispersion geographically, the record of the Welsh in the field of journalism is rather remarkable and indicative of the tremendously important hold which their native tongue had upon them. A total of some sixty-five journals made their appearance during the nineteenth century to serve the Welsh-American communities. Most of these were short-lived (of less than five years duration), but certain of them flourished for decades, and one of them, *Y Drych* (the Mirror), is still going strong today in its one hundred and sixteenth year!

The story of Welsh-American journalistic efforts was one of constant struggle to keep "the wolf from the door." Ambitious individuals with the noblest of intentions would start these little periodicals in the Welsh language, often print them themselves, try to work up enough of a circulation to make the periodicals self-supporting, and usually fail—with the result that the journal ceased to be published. Depending upon their content and emphasis, these periodicals perished quickly or survived for various lengths of time. As one might expect—those of religious emphasis and of general news content were most successful and had the longest careers. Those of a specialized or literary emphasis were short-lived.

Thanks to the painstaking efforts of two Welsh scholars, Bob Owen and Idwal Lewis, the difficult tracing of these various journalistic efforts on the part of Welsh-Americans has been revealed. The summary which follows is largely based upon their findings which appeared in two articles in the *National Library of Wales Journal*.[1]

Newspapers

The pioneer Welsh-American newspaper and the first journal in Welsh to be published in America was *Cymro-America* (Welsh America), a fortnightly which made its appearance early in 1832. It was published and edited by J. A. Williams (Ioan Glan Towy) in New York City at a cost of two dollars per year. It featured information of general interest to the American Welsh including obituaries, marriages and births, and contained a poetry column. Only twelve numbers were issued for the paper was forced to suspend publication during the cholera epidemic of that year. It never appeared again due to lack of funds.[2]

Not until sixteen years later was a second attempt made to establish another Welsh-American newspaper. This was *Haul Gomer* (The Welsh Sun), a fortnightly which made its first appearance January 1, 1848. It was published at Utica, New York, by Evan E. Roberts (Iewan o Geredigion). A journal of general news coverage, it also contained a special poetry column edited by "Eos Glan Twrch," a noted Welsh poet. The newspaper failed after nine numbers had been issued.[3]

Three years later, in 1851, the most successful of the Welsh-American newspapers made its appearance. This was the famous *Y Drych* (the Mirror) which is still going strong today. It made its first appearance January 2, 1851 in Utica, New York, under the longer title of *Y Drych Americanaidd* (the American Mirror). A weekly, it was owned and edited by John W. Jones, a native of Llanaelhaiarn, Caernarvonshire.[4] *Y Drych* succeeded where most other Welsh periodicals failed —in tiding over the grim pioneering period during which time a periodical must continue in the face of great financial risk while it builds up its circulation. *Y Drych,* because of its general informatory nature and its news coverage of the various Welsh communities, became more and more popular as the years passed. It soon became a full fledged Welsh institution and could be found in the homes of most Welsh immigrants. So strong did *Drych* become eventually that it was able to meet the challenge of vigorous new rivals for the affections of the Welsh-American communities, hold its own circulation, and in various cases buy out its rivals. *Drych* had to face its strongest test during the first decades of the twentieth century when a new all-English language Welsh-American rival, *The Druid,* ran it a merry race. The "old lady of Utica" weathered the crisis safely and eventually had the satisfaction of witnessing the folding up of its rival in 1937.[5]

Y Drych has had a career that has seen changes of management and a changeover from a weekly to a monthly. As was true of most Welsh institutions in America, it too had to face the question of a switchover to the use of the English language. Despite the competition of the English-language *Druid,* the newspaper held on to its all-Welsh policy which was supported by the older generation of Welshmen. Not until the 1930's did *Drych* begin to publish some news in English. Then followed a period when more and more English appeared in its columns. Today the newspaper is chiefly English although some columns appear occasionally in Welsh. *Y Drych* continues today to perform the same purpose that it did at its first appearance—to keep the Welsh-Americans informed of activities occurring in the respective Welsh communities: marriages, deaths, eisteddfods, gymanfa ganus, and general news concerning the homeland.[6]

Among the later names associated with *Drych* are Thomas J. Griffiths who published the periodical for over fifty years, John C. Roberts, its editor for over forty-five years and the man most influential in building it up as the strongest Welsh-American newspaper, and Arthur M. Roberts, who owned and edited the newspaper during most of the twentieth century.[7] *Y Drych* was purchased by Horace Breece Powell of Milwaukee, Wisconsin, in 1962. The newspaper was moved to Milwaukee where it is still going strong.

The year 1852 saw the brief appearance of *Haul Gorllewinol* (Western Sun), a fortnightly published in Milwaukee under the editorship of Robert Emrys Jones. It failed probably due to lack of financial support. In 1854, another short-lived newspaper made its appearance. This was *Y Gwylieddydd Americanaidd* (The American Sentinel), edited by Reverend Robert Littler and printed by E. E. Roberts of Utica, New York. It was later edited by Reverend Morgan A. Ellis. The newspaper survived only one year and then merged with *Y Drych,* the first rival to be bought out by that enterprising newspaper.[8]

From 1855 to 1860 a new vigorous weekly newspaper became popular with Welsh-Americans. This was *Y Cymro Americanaidd* (The American Welshman), edited, printed, and published by John M. Jones in New York City. In addition to its general Welsh news coverage, it featured a column edited for a time by John Frost, the renowned Chartist of Wales, then temporarily in America. It featured the literary efforts of Welsh-Americans. The reasons for its demise are unknown.[9]

It was not until 1868 that another vigorous newspaper made its appearance. This was the well-known *Baner America* (Banner of America), the first newspaper effort of the rapidly growing Welsh mining communities of Eastern Pennsylvania. *Baner* was published at Hyde Park now a part of Scranton, Pennsylvania, by a company of Welsh Americans headed by Henry M. Edwards, then a prominent attorney and subsequently a distinguished jurist. Among its editors were Reverend Morgan A. Ellis, the leading Calvinistic-Methodist divine, Frederick Evans, David Parry, and Thomas B. Morris (Gwyneddfardd). *Baner America* furnished strong competition to *Y Drych* and was well respected both in America and Wales. It merged with *Drych* in 1877 after a distinguished career of eleven years.[10]

Sharing honors with *Drych* and *Baner* during the decade of the 1870's and furnishing stiff competition to the consolidated paper until

1890, was *Y Wasg* (The Press), a new weekly newspaper published at Pittsburgh. It made its first appearance in May of 1871. It was edited by Reverend T. C. Davies, L. H. Lewis, and H. E. Thomas. It was later purchased in 1883 by D. J. Edwards, R. T. Daniels, and W. J. Davies. *Y Wasg* continued to appear until 1890 when it, too, merged with *Y Drych*.[11]

Still another newspaper made its appearance in 1883, the first to have its headquarters in the west since the demise of *Haul Gorllewinol*. This was *Colomen Columbia* (Columbia Dove), first published in Emporia, Kansas, by Edwin C. Jones, later a prominent printer for the Government Printing Office and in charge of the government printing office in Manila for many years. Jones later moved the newspaper to Chicago and changed its title to *Y Columbia* (The Columbia). It was the first bi-lingual Welsh-American newspaper, and the first to recognize the increasingly important place English was assuming in the life of the Welsh-American communities. It helped to sponsor the World's Fair Eisteddfod in Chicago in 1893. It merged with the powerful *Drych* in 1894.[12]

It was not until well into the twentieth century, 1907, that the last of the important Welsh-American newspapers made its appearance. *Y Drych* had absorbed all the others and enjoyed a monopoly of the field. There were those who felt, however, that an all-English language newspaper for the Welsh communities would prove successful. Accordingly, T. Owen Charles and others of the Scranton Welsh community formed a company to publish *The Druid,* the first issue of which appeared June 6, 1907. Charles served as its first editor. The new newspaper became immensely popular and soon became firmly established. It was published at Scranton, Pennsylvania, until 1912, when a group from the Pittsburgh Welsh community headed by James J. Davis, subsequently Secretary of Labor and United States Senator from Pennsylvania, purchased the newspaper and switched its publication place to Pittsburgh. *Druid* was published as a weekly until 1913, then bi-weekly until 1934, and finally monthly until its demise in 1937. A paper of from 8 to 12 pages, *Druid* resembled *Drych* in its contents furnishing in English the same type of information that the latter furnished in Welsh. *The Druid,* as noted above, furnished *Y Drych* its stiffest competition. For a brief period, 1917-1918, it bore the title of *The Welsh-American.* The Americanization of the Welsh communities and a lagging interest in things Welsh led to its demise.[13]

A number of short-lived Welsh-American newspapers also appeared from time to time. *Baner y Bobl* (Banner of the People) was printed at Hyde Park (Scranton) in the 1860's. *Y Negesydd* (The Messenger) appeared at Pittsburgh around 1869. *Y Bardd* (The Bard) (not to be confused with the magazine of the same name) appeared in 1856-57. *Llais y Gan* appeared in 1883. *Y Brython, Cyfaill yr Aeswyd,* and *Tarian y Bobl,* were three others about which data is nil.[14]

Four political newspapers of short duration also made their appearance, all in support of the Democratic Party. The first of these, *Seren Oneida* (The Oneida Star), appeared in the early part of 1845 and lasted until the end of the year. *Y Gwron Democrataidd* (The Worthy Democrat), appeared during 1856-57 as an organ for the Welsh-American Democrats. It was published in New York City and carried on a political feud with *Y Drych* accusing the latter of being pro-slave. It was an enthusiastic supporter of James Buchanan in the presidential election of 1856. Thomas Jones was its editor and owner. *Cyfaill yr Undeb* (Friend of the Union) appeared during the 1860 presidential campaign on behalf of the Democrats. It was published in Utica, New York. *Yr Amserau* (The Times) appeared briefly at Utica during the campaign of 1862.[15]

A total of 21 newspapers thus served the Welsh-American communities at one time or another from the early decades of the nineteenth century until the present day. During the peak years of Welsh immigration, 1860-1880, at least three competed with one another. Thereafter at least two right down to the decade of the 1930's. Today, only *Y Drych* survives.

Magazines

Turning to the field of magazines and journals, one finds an interesting array of journalistic efforts of varied success among the Welsh-Americans. The greatest number of these, as one might expect, dealt with religion as the chief field of interest. Others, with their emphasis on other things, appeared briefly.

The oldest of the Welsh-American religious magazines was *Cyfaill o'r Hen Wlad yn America* (Friend of the Old Country in America) founded by one of the great Welsh-American clergymen, Reverend William Rowlands, in New York City. It made its first appearance in January, 1838, as a monthly and played a great role in the life of the Welsh in America. Rowlands, although a Calvinistic-Methodist minister, tried to make *Y Cyfaill* a medium to serve all the Welsh denominations. It served this purpose for some years, but the appearance within a short time of similar magazines to serve the Congregationalists and the Baptists resulted in *Y Cyfaill's* becoming eventually the organ of the Calvinistic-Methodists in America. Rowlands served as the magazine's editor and owner until his death in 1866.[16]

The magazine was purchased from the widow of Dr. Rowlands in 1869 by the General Assembly of the Calvinistic-Methodist Church in

America and made the official organ of that denomination. The name
of the periodical was eventually shortened to *Y Cyfaill* (The Friend).
It contained sermons by prominent Calvinistic-Methodist preachers, com-
ments on Sunday School affairs, short articles on current events, reports on
the meetings of the respective presbyteries, gymanvas, and the General
Assembly, columns of marriages, deaths, and births, and a section for
poets and bards. Subsequent editors were Reverend Morgan A. Ellis of
Ebensburg, Pa., until 1874, Reverend William Roberts until 1886, Dr.
H. P. Howell of Columbus, Ohio, until 1899, T. Solomon Griffiths of
Utica until 1910, Dr. Joseph Roberts of New York City until 1920, Reverend John Hammond of Wales, Wis., until 1926, and various editors
thereafter until its demise in 1933.[17]

As the official organ of the largest of the Welsh-American denominations, *Y Cyfaill* had a long and distinguished career. It and *Y Drych*
were the only American journals in the Welsh language to survive well
into the twentieth century. The passing from the scene of the bulk of
the Welsh immigrants as the new century wore on, and the unfamiliarity
of their children with the Welsh language, led the Presbyterian Church,
U. S. A. (with which the Calvinistic-Methodists had merged in 1919)
to discontinue publication of the venerable old magazine in 1933 just five
years short of its centennial birthday.

The second religious magazine to appear in the Welsh language was
Y Cenhadwr Americanaidd (The American Missionary). It was founded
by another famous Welsh-American clergyman, Reverend Robert Everett of Steuben, New York, in 1840. The new magazine soon assumed the
position of unofficial organ of the Welsh Congregationalists in America.
Y Cenhadwr, unlike *Y Cyfaill* which was supported by the Calvinistic-
Methodist Church, had to depend upon subscriptions entirely for its
livelihood because of the independent nature of the Congregational
church set-up. That the magazine could prosper for some sixty-one years
without official subsidation is a tribute to the high qualities of the magazine
and to the loyalty shown toward it by the Welsh Congregationalists. For
some thirty-five years, Reverend Everett edited this excellent periodical,
thundering against the evils of slavery and praising the merits of temperance. Later editors included Reverends J. P. Williams, Thomas Cynonfardd Edwards of Edwardsville, Pa., and E. Davies of Waterville. *Cenhadwr* resembled *Cyfaill* in its contents, featuring such items as sermons
by prominent Welsh-American clergymen, Sunday School notes and news,
a section for children, items of special interest, notes on marriages, births,
and deaths, and news of the various gymanvas. It ceased publication in
1901.[18]

The Welsh Baptists soon followed the example of the other two
Welsh sects and established a magazine devoted to their religious interests.

However, they were not fortunate in having a magazine of the strength or longevity to match *Y Cyfaill* of the Calvinistic-Methodists or *Y Cenhadwr* of the Congregationalists. A number of Baptist magazines made their appearance, most short-lived but four having distinguished careers. The first to appear was *Y Beread* (The Berean), a fortnightly edited by Reverend D. Phillips of New York City. It appeared in 1842 but ceased publication the following year.[19] It was followed by a new monthly magazine, *Y Seren Orllewinol* (The Western Star), which made its first apperance in July of 1844. It was edited by Reverend W. T. Phillips of Utica, New York, and later by the Reverend John P. Harries (Iewan Ddu) of Minersville, Pennsylvania. The new magazine was first printed at Utica by Evan E. Roberts, then from 1854 until its demise by the *Miners' Journal* at Pottsville, Pennsylvania. It featured materials similar to those that appeared in *Cyfaill* and *Cenhadwr*. *Y Seren* continued to be published until 1867 when it ceased publication due to financial difficulties.[20] Another short-lived magazine attempted to take its place. This was *Y Wasg* (The Press), not to be confused with the newspaper of the same name mentioned above, which made its appearance in 1868. It was edited and published by the Reverend Richard Edwards of Pottsville, Pennsylvania. The magazine lasted only one year.[21]

It was not until 1872 that the Welsh Baptists again had a magazine devoted to their interests. The Welsh Baptists of Oneida County, New York, brought out *Y Ford Gron* (The Round Table), a magazine printed for them at Youngstown, Ohio, and edited by the Reverends W. L. Evans, D. J. Nichols (Iver Ebwy) and A. J. Aubrey (Cynval).[22] Its ultimate fate is not known but it may have merged with a new Baptist magazine that also made its appearance in 1872. This was *Y Glorian* (The Balance), a monthly edited by the same three men. It was printed at first at Pittsburgh, then in its second year and thereafter at Youngstown, Ohio. *Y Glorian* had a distinguished career of twenty-two years. It ended publication in 1894.[23]

The Welsh Baptists also enjoyed two other publications during this period. These were *Y Wawr Americanaidd* (The American Dawn) and *The Dawn*, both edited and printed by the Reverend Owen Griffith (Giraldus) at Utica, New York. A graduate of Crozer Theological Seminary, Griffith served as pastor of the Utica Welsh Baptist Church from 1870 until his death. He issued the first number of *Y Wawr* in April, 1876. In time it assumed the same importance for the Baptists that *Cyfaill* and *Cenhadwr* had for the Calvinistic-Methodists and the Congregationalists. Its standards and coverage of information was very similar. *Y Wawr* continued to be published until 1896 when Griffith died. Through it he exerted a powerful influence upon his fellow Welsh-Americans. Reverend Griffith also published *The Dawn* during much of this same period. It was a monthly in English which closely parallelled *Y Wawr* in form and content. Its last number appeared in 1890.[24]

Three other religious periodicals, all short-lived, also made their appearance in the nineteenth century. *Yr Arweinydd* (The Guide), a fortnightly, published by the Reverend Robert R. Meredith of Rome, New York, and edited by the Reverend Thomas T. Evans of Floyd, New York, appeared during the years, 1858-1861.[25] *Y Pwlpud Cymreig* (The Welsh Pulpit), a magazine for preachers published by T. R. Jones of Rome, New York, appeared only during 1864. *Y Pregethwr a'r Esbonwir* (The Preacher and the Public), a bi-monthly published by Thomas R. Jones of Randolph, Wisconsin, and printed at Utica, New York, appeared briefly during 1881.[26]

Two anti-slavery periodicals made their appearance at the height of the controversy. Both were edited by the Reverend Robert Everett, the distinguished Congregational minister. *Y Dyngarwr* (The Philanthropist), a monthly, advocated freedom for the slaves and other philanthropies. It first appeared in 1843. A liberal journal, it hit at all types of abuse including Russian serfdom. It was discontinued in 1844. Again in 1850, a new anti-slave journal made its appearance. This was *Y Detholydd* (The Chosen), an ardent defender of the northern position during the years 1850-1852.[27]

The Welsh were not forgetful of the needs of the children, both from the religious and the cultural standpoints. Although most of the more important of the aforementioned periodicals had their columns and sections for the children, several attempts were made to issue all-juvenile journals. The earliest of these was a monthly entitled *Yr Ysgol* (The School), published and edited by H. J. Hughes of New York City, which first appeared in 1869. It was meant to be a monthly for the young people of all denominations. It contained articles and illustrations to appeal to youngsters. It continued to be issued until 1870 when Hughes died. The magazine publication rights were evidently purchased in 1872, and it was reissued that year under the title of *Blodau'r Oes a'r Ysgol* (Flowers of the Age and School). The magazine was a small one which resembled one then being published in Wales *(Tysorfa'r Plant)*. It was published by William ap Madoc and T. Solomon Griffiths of Utica, New York. The magazine was later purchased by the Reverends M. A. Ellis and Thomas (Cynonfardd) Edwards. It ceased publication in 1875.[28]

The Welsh Calvinistic-Methodists of Wisconsin also published a juvenile magazine for a short time. This was *Y Lamp* (The Lamp), a small monthly magazine for the use of the Sunday Schools and edited by the Reverend D. Davies of Oshkosh, Wisconsin. It appeared during the years 1897-1903. The Calvinistic-Methodist General Assembly also published a monthly magazine for young people for a brief period. This was *Y Tresor* (The Treasury), a monthly printed at Columbus, Ohio, and edited by the Reverend John Hammond. It appeared only during 1906. Still another juvenile magazine to appear was *Ym Ymdrechydd* (The Endeavor), a monthly organ for the Christian Endeavor organizations published by P. M. Evans and Company of Chicago, and edited by the Reverends J. C. Jones of Chicago, and G. James Jones, Ph.D. of Oak Hill, Ohio. It appeared during the years 1894-1895.[29]

Three short-lived magazines devoted to music also made their appearance. *Y Detholydd Cerddorol* (The Musical Selection), a monthly edited by John Owen (Glan Marchlyn), and printed by S. E. Roberts of Utica, New York, appeared during the years 1867-1868. *Anthemydd Solffa* (Solfa Anthem), a monthly for the benefit of Welsh musicians and resembling a similar magazine of the homeland, appeared during the years 1868-1870. *Y Cor-Drysor* (The Choir's Treasury) was the third, a monthly concerning which the author has no data.[30]

Several efforts were made to bring out successful literary magazines. The first of these was *Yr Adolygydd Chwarterol* (The Quarterly Review), devoted to art and science and edited by John W. Jones of Utica, New York. It appeared only during 1852. Another, *Y Bardd* (The Bard), a journal devoted to Welsh poetry and literature as well as articles of general interest, made its appearance in 1858. It was published at Minersville, Pennsylvania and edited by Thomas Gwallter Price. Only five numbers were issued, all in 1858. Still another, *Y Traethodydd yn America* (The Essayist in America), was published by the Reverend William Roberts of New York City beginning in 1857. It reprinted the most important articles from *Y Traethodydd,* a distinguished journal of Wales, as well as articles by prominent American Welshmen. It was a literary magazine of high calibre, but was forced to discontinue in 1861. Another outstanding magazine was *Y Cylchgrawn Cenedlaethol* (The National Monthly), published by John M. Jones of New York City. It first appeared in 1853 and lasted for some three years.[31]

The Cambrian, the most important and only successful Welsh-American magazine of general content, made its first appearance in January of 1880. An excellent journal, published in English, *the Cambrian* was owned, edited, and published by the Reverend D. J. Jones at Cincinnati. At first bi-monthly, it later appeared in monthly form. It was later published in 1886 by the Reverend Edward C. Evans of Remsen, New York, and then printed at Utica by Thomas J. Griffiths. *Cambrian* had a long and distinguished career that lasted until 1919. It is one of the most important sources of information concerning the activities of the Welsh in America during the period 1880-1919.[32]

Other short-lived magazines that were issued by American Welshmen included: *Y Golygydd* (The Editor), edited by Reverend John

Jones of Cincinnati, in 1856; *Y Ford Gron* (The Round Table), edited by Thomas G. Price, William Aubrey Powell, and Aneurin Jones of Hyde Park (Scranton), in 1867; *Yr Ymwelydd* (The Visit), edited by Henry M. Edwards, in 1877; *The Welshman,* edited by D. J. Williams of Jackson, Ohio, in 1895; *Yr Adlais* (The Echo), published by P. M. Evans of Chicago, in 1894-1895; *Yr Eryr* (The Eagle), published by Ellis Roberts, in 1879-1880; *Llais y Gan* (Voice of Song), in 1883; *Yr Yspiydd* (The Spy), in 1871-1872; *The American Celt,* edited by John Griffiths of Scranton, in 1867; and *Yr Eginydd* (The Blade), at Hyde Park.[33]

The last two attempts to found Welsh-American magazines occurred in the twentieth century. *Cambrian Gleanings,* a monthly in English, privately printed by the well-known scholar, Henry Blackwell of New York City, appeared only during the year 1914.[34] *The Welsh American Magazine* was published by Cadwyn Jones of New York City. It was first issued in January of 1929. It contained articles in Welsh and English. Although designed as a monthly, it appeared irregularly. Its last number was printed in 1936.[35]

Books in Welsh

Books and pamphlets in Welsh were first published in Philadelphia during the eighteenth century, as we have seen, with the firms of Andrew Bradford, Samuel Keimer and Dafydd Harry, and Benjamin Franklin and Hugh Meredydd, issuing some of America's rarest printed items. So far as can be determined, the three books and one pamphlet produced at that time were the only such published in the Welsh language during colonial times.[36]

However, with the coming of the large influx of Welsh immigrants in the nineteenth century, various printing firms began to produce books in the Welsh language to meet the needs of these new arrivals. Fortunately, we have a fairly accurate knowledge of just how extensive this printing was thanks to the hard work and research skill of Henry Blackwell, a Welsh immigrant of New York City. Blackwell painstakingly collected copies of all books published in Welsh in America over the years. He then analysed the contents and listed the respective printers in an article which appeared in his own magazine, *Cambrian Gleanings,* in 1914.

We learn from Blackwell that a total of some sixty-two printing houses produced books in Welsh at one time or another during the nineteenth century. Among these were various of the Welsh-American newspapers including *Baner America, Y Wasg* and *Y Columbia.* Some of the Welsh immigrants were printers themselves. They soon set up printing plants which catered to the Welsh immigrants. Of these, Evan E. Roberts of Utica, Robert R. Meredith of Rome, New York, and later of Chicago, and Thomas J. Griffiths (called by Blackwell "the dean of Welsh printers in America") of Utica, were the leaders in the field. New York City and Utica shared honors in the number of publishers of Welsh books. Pottsville and Scranton, Pennsylvania, and Rome and Remsen, New York, were also important centers of Welsh printing.[37]

As could be expected, the books produced were overwhelmingly religious in content reflecting in this respect the chief interest of the Welsh immigrants. Sermons, Bibles, testaments, commentaries on the scriptures, and memoirs of leading clergymen were most numerous. Books on travel, poetry, essays, history, and guide-books were issued occasionally.[38]

Henry Blackwell donated this entire collection of Welsh books, together with an extensive bibliography in manuscript of all writings on the Welsh in America that he had compiled, to Yale University Library. Portions of this extensive bibliography were later published by the National Library of Wales.[39] This distinguished Welsh-American also compiled biographical data on most of the leading Welsh-Americans of the eighteenth and nineteenth centuries. He donated his extensive biographical notes (all neatly bound by him in leather) to the National Library of Wales in Aberystwyth.[40] Unfortunately, this pioneer "Dictionary of Welsh-American Biography" has never been published. Hopefully, some day it will appear in print.[41]

FOOTNOTES ON CHAPTER VI

1. See Bob Owen, "Welsh American Newspapers and Periodicals," *National Library of Wales Journal*, VI (Winter, 1950), pp. 373-84; also Idwal Lewis, "Welsh Newspapers and Journals in the United States," *National Library of Wales Journal*, II (Summer, 1942), pp. 124-25.
2. Owen, *op. cit.*, pp. 377-78.
3. *Ibid.*, p. 381.
4. *Ibid.*, p. 379.
5. Richard H. Costa, "Utica Is Home of Only Welsh Language Paper," *Y Drych*, CV (December 15, 1956), pp. 9 and 15. See biographical sketch of John C. Roberts, *Cambrian*, 1905, pp. 312-13.
6. *Ibid.*
7. *Ibid.*
8. Owen, *op. cit.*, p. 381.
9. *Ibid.*, p. 378.
10. *Ibid.*, p. 374; see biographical sketch of Morgan A. Ellis, *Cambrian*, 1880, pp. 9-11; Henry M. Edwards, *Cambrian*, 1889, pp. 129-30; 1884, p. 188.
11. Owen., *ibid.*, p. 383.
12. *Ibid.*, p. 376; see biographical sketch of Edwin C. Jones, *Cambrian*, 1908, pp. 183-84.
13. Data from author's notes taken from the masthead and elsewhere in the file of the *Druid* at the Brigham Young University Library in Provo, Utah.
14. Owen, *op. cit.*, *passim*.
15. *Ibid.*, *passim*.
16. Williams, *One Hundred Years of Welsh Calvinistic Methodism, op. cit.*, pp. 331-34. See biographical sketch of William Rolands in the *Dictionary of American Biography*.

17. *Williams, ibid.,* pp. 334-40.
18. Owen, *op. cit.,* p. 376; see biographical sketch of Robert Everett in the *Dictionary of American Biography.*
19. Owen, *ibid.,* p. 375.
20. *Ibid.,* p. 382.
21. *Ibid.,* p. 383.
22. *Ibid.,* p. 379.
23. Lewis, *op. cit.,* p. 128.
24. Owen, *op. cit.,* p. 283; see biographical sketch of Owen Griffith (Giraldus), *Cambrian,* 1896, pp. 193-95.
25. Owen, *ibid.,* p. 374.
26. Lewis, *op. cit.,* p. 128.
27. Owen, *op. cit.,* p. 379.
28. *Ibid.,* pp 375, 384.
29. *Ibid.,* pp. 381, 83, 84; Williams, *op. cit.,* pp. 341-42.
30. Owen, *ibid.,* pp. 379, 373, 376.
31. *Ibid.,* pp. 373, 374, 377, 382.
32. *Ibid.,* p. 376; see biographical sketch of Edward C. Evans, *Cambrian,* 1912, pp. 13-14.
33. Owen, *ibid., passim.*
34. Lewis, *op. cit.,* p. 126.
35. Owen, *op. cit.,* p. 384.
36. See Chapter III.
37. Henry Blackwell, "Printers of Books in Welsh in the United States," *Cambrian Gleanings,* I (May, 1914), pp. 65-69.
38. *Ibid.*
39. Henry Blackwell, "Bibliography of What Has Been Published in the United States Relating to Wales and the Welsh from the Earliest to the Present Time Together with the Productions of Welsh Authors on Miscellaneous Subjects Chronologically Arranged," manuscript, dated February 22, 1886, in Yale University Library; see also, Henry Blackwell, "A Bibliography of Welsh Americana," *National Library of Wales Journal,* Supplement Series III, No. 1, 1942.
40. See biographical sketch of Henry Blackwell in the *Dictionary of Welsh Biography.*
41. The reader may be interested to know that fairly complete files of *Y Cyfaill, Y Cenhadwr, Y Wawr Americanaidd, Y Drych,* and *the Cambrian* exist in Weidner Library of Harvard University, Cambridge, Mass. A complete file of *the Druid* exists in the Brigham Young University Library, Provo, Utah.

CHAPTER VII

THE EISTEDDFOD, THE GORSEDD,
AND THE GYMANFA GANU

The Welsh people enjoy the distinction of having created three unique institutions—the Eisteddfod, the Gorsedd, and the Gymanfa Ganu—all of which were later introduced into America by Welsh immigrants to become a part of the social activities of the Welsh-Americans. The oldest and best known of the three is the Eisteddfod, a great gathering or assembly of Welshmen at which competitors vie with each other for honors in singing, literature, and allied fields. A large gathering serves as audience, and a number of judges as abjudicators.

No one knows for certain just when the Welsh first began to hold eisteddfods (eisteddfodau in Welsh), but there is evidence to indicate that the holding of contests in the fields of music and poetry was a very ancient custom. Mr. Tom Parry of Wales gathered together the historical data on the eisteddfod, and under the auspicies of the National Eisteddfod Council issued a small pamphlet on the subject.[1] The gist of this historical background is as follows:

Chief bards at the courts of the Welsh princes are known to have existed as early as the days of Howell Dda (the Good), who died in 950 A.D., and historical authorities believe that the individuals that held such posts obtained them as the result of competition with other aspirants, perhaps in the manner of the eisteddfod of today. The first eisteddfod to bear the name of which we have record was held at Carmarthen in 1450 under the auspices of a Welsh nobleman, Gruffydd ap Nicholas, who bore the burden of its expense. It is said to have lasted for weeks! Another historic eisteddfod was held at Caerwys in Flintshire, in 1523, at which contests were held in the fields of music, poetry, and song, and prizes were awarded to the winners. Still another noteworthy eisteddfod was held at the same place in 1568. It was at this festival that Queen Elizabeth I ordered the leading Welsh noblemen of the region to examine all those claiming to be poets and musicians, and to license the real ones so as to distinguish these from the host of beggars then roaming at large and passing themselves off as legitimate bards and musicians.[2]

Various eisteddfods were held during the seventeenth century about which data is scanty. This was the period of low ebb in Welsh culture.

The gentry had become Anglicized and had lost interest in Welsh culture; they no longer sponsored Welsh poets and musicians as they once had. The language remained entrenched among the masses, but very little writing of true literary merit made its appearance. It was not until the great Romantic movement in literature and music swept over western Europe and with it Britain, beginning in the last quarter of the eighteenth century, that interest in the literature and early customs of the Welsh revived and with this interest in the eisteddfod as well.

Thanks to a progressive Welshman at home and to the little society of Welshmen in London, the Gwendeddigion Society (the same that had sponsored the mission of John Evans), a movement began which resulted in the successful revival of the Welsh eisteddfod. One Thomas Jones of Corwen, North Wales, after a great deal of labor aroused sufficient interest to hold an eisteddfod at Llangollen in January, 1789. Elated by the success of the venture, he planned an even larger one for the following May. It was held at Corwen and was likewise successful. In order to obtain the support of the London Society, Jones hit upon the idea of having members of the latter determine certain of the winners. Subsequent correspondence between Jones and the Gwendeddigion led to the sponsoring by the latter of still a third eisteddfod which was held at Bala in September, 1789. The holding of three such fetes all in the same year tended to publicize the institution with such success that interest in the eisteddfod remained high and led to the founding of district societies with the goal of sponsoring eisteddfods. From 1789 onwards and during the early part of the nineteenth century eisteddfods were held at St. Asaph, Llanwrst, Denbigh, and other places, all sponsored by such regional societies.[3]

It was not until 1858 that an effort was made to hold a great national eisteddfod at which competitors from all parts of the principality should take part. In that year a great national eisteddfod was held at Llangollen in North Wales, which proved so popular that a special committee was appointed to plan future national eisteddfods. Such another great festival was held at Denbigh in 1860, at which time it was decided to hold national eisteddfods annually thereafter, with the sites of the competitions to alternate between North and South Wales year by year. An eisteddfod council was set up to manage the events and to work out the necessary details. A period of partial success followed with certain eisteddfods being held despite numerous handicaps. A rather haphazard control of the national events lasted until 1880, when the leading Welsh scholars and others revamped the whole program and organized the National Eisteddfod Association to run the affairs in the future. It was this group that supervised the annual eisteddfods of the Welsh until 1927, when due to certain conflicts of jurisdiction among the groups comprising the Association, the latter was replaced by a new agency, the National Eisteddfod Council which now controls the Royal National Eisteddfod of Wales.[4]

Today, the eisteddfod is one of the greatest interests of the Welsh people. Hardly a district of Wales fails to hold a small eisteddfod of its own which serves in a sense as a preliminary test for the great national event held alternately in North and South Wales during the first week of August of each year. To this great gathering come Welshmen from all parts of Wales and from abroad to compete with each other for prizes in poetry, prose, music, arts and crafts, and to witness the competitions. It has been this author's great pleasure to attend such a National Eisteddfod and to take part in the special exercises reserved for the so-called "Welshmen in Exile"—those emigrants who have returned to attend the festival, their children, and anyone of Welsh ancestry. Such individuals are grouped together by country, marched into the great eisteddfod tent to the singing of the Welsh nostalgic hymn, "Unwaith Eto Yng Nghymru Annwyl" (Once Again in Dear Wales), and seated on the great platform to receive the welcoming cheers of the audience in attendance. It follows that the United States, having received the great bulk of Welsh immigrants, should always be well represented on such occasions, and usually has the largest delegation of "Welshmen in Exile." As Tom Parry put it: "During the first week in August, the eyes of all Wales are upon the town in which the National Eisteddfod is being held and that town is, for the time being, the 'capital' of Wales." So great is the interest of the Welsh in their unique institution.[5]

The Welsh National Eisteddfod competitions are of very high quality and are judged by the best talent that can be obtained in the respective fields. The abjudicators or judges are stern critics and brook no compromise with mediocrity. Frequently prizes are withheld (particularly in the literature fields) if all entries are considered substandard or unworthy of the highest honors that Wales can bestow. Although competition at first was reserved to the music and literature fields, the important place played by arts and crafts in the life of the Welsh people has now received recognition and prizes in these fields are also awarded. The chief competitions of the National Eisteddfod today are the following:

   1.   The competition for the Bardic Chair which is offered for the best *awdl* or poem written in the strict traditional meters of Welsh alliterative verse. The prize—an elaborately carved chair—is awarded to the successful candidate in a great solemn ceremony of recognition of his primacy as a poet of all Wales. The chair is usually a gift of one of the Welsh colonies abroad. Various of the American Welsh communities have donated such in the past.
   2.   The competition for the Bardic Crown which is offered usually for a *pryddest* or ode in free Welsh meters although the Eisteddfod authorities can substitute a heroic poem or a verse play in Welsh as the

subject of the competition if they so desire. Crowning the successful bard is another high point of the Eisteddfod.

3.   The competition for the chief essay. This may be written in either Welsh or English on a subject determined by the Eisteddfod committee.

4.   The competition for the prose medal which is offered for the best work in Welsh in one of the following fields—the novel, the short story, the essay, or literary criticism.

5.   The competition for the drama medal which is offered for the best full-length play in Welsh.

6.   The chief choral competition. A sum of money is awarded to the best mixed chorus.

7.   The chief male voice choral competition. A money prize is awarded to the best male choir. In addition, the winning choir has the honor of holding for one year the Memorial Cup presented to the Eisteddfod by the Royal Welch Fusiliers

8.   The second male choral voice competition. A money prize is given to the winning choir. In addition, the latter has the honor of holding for one year the Memorial Cup presented to the Eisteddfod by the Royal Welsh Guards.[6]

Many minor prizes complete the eisteddfod competitions. The whole program comprises a well thought out means of bringing out the best of Welsh talent and aims at keeping the Welsh language and the best features of Welsh culture alive. It follows that many subsidiary programs of cultural interest to the Welsh, including the inevitable singing sessions, form part of the festivities of the week.

A second great eisteddfod has been held annually in Wales for some years. This is the International Eisteddfod, a purely musical fete, held at Llangollen in North Wales each summer. As its name indicates, this eisteddfod is international in its scope. Choirs and orchestras, choral groups, and musicians, from both Wales and various foreign countries compete for prizes. The International Eisteddfod has grown in prestige over the years until it is now recognized as one of the great musical fetes of Great Britain.

Closely associated with the National Eisteddfod of Wales and represented on the latter's governing board is the Gorsedd of the Bards of the Isle of Britain (referred to simply as the Gorsedd), an institution that dates from the influence of the Romantic Movement in literature upon Great Britain. We have seen that this movement aroused great interest among the Welsh intellectuals and others in Welsh antiquities and Welsh medieval literature. It also aroused interest in the ancient druids, or priests and teachers, of the pagan Keltic peoples. These famous leaders, who helped organize the Welsh in opposition to Roman conquest, are believed by scholars to have carried on rites of magic and other ceremonies connected with nature worship. For many years they were believed to have been responsible for the erection of the monoliths and circles of standing stones to be found throughout Britain and elsewhere. We now know that these monuments date from an even earlier period, but their association with the druids was generally accepted during the nineteenth century.

One of the Welsh romanticists, and a poet of no mean ability, the well-known Iolo Morganwg, sought to prove that Welsh literary traditions had continued unbroken from the days of the druids, and tried to revive in his imagination the rites and practices of the same. Not finding sufficient evidence to bear out his whimsies on this subject, Iolo resorted to fabrication with such success that scholars even today find it difficult to tell authentic Welsh poetry and legend from Morganwg's creations.[7]

The poet elaborated a ritual, supposedly that practiced by the ancient druids, and sponsored the first Gorsedd or esoteric gathering of the bards on Primrose Hill in London in 1792. He also designed suitable costumes to be worn for the occasion, laid out the magic circle of standing stones within which the exercises were to be held, and invented rites and ceremonies to be performed. Morganwg's prestige was great enough, and the rites were interesting enough, to catch the imagination of the Romanticists. They were accepted as legitimate, became very popular, and were made an integral part of the Eisteddfod exercises in 1819.[8] They have retained this position ever since. Regardless of origin, they form one of the most interesting features of the activities during eisteddfod week, help to create an atmosphere of mysticism always associated with the Keltic spirit, and add color and ceremony to the great fete.

Today the Gorsedd of the Bards is an organization composed of the leading poets, musicians, and men of learning of Wales. Membership is obtained only through passing rigid examinations or through contributing in some outstanding way to the benefit of Wales. The organization, because of its high literary standards and taste and because of its representation on the Eisteddfod governing board, serves the useful purpose of keeping Welsh literary and other standards high and champions Welsh culture generally.

"Cynan," the former Archdruid of Wales, outlined the nature of the Gorsedd and a description of the Gorsedd ceremonies in a pamphlet issued by the National Eisteddfod Council.[9] The essence of his analysis is as follows:

The Gorsedd organization is governed by an Archdruid (generally an outstanding poet of Wales) elected for three years by the members. He is assisted by other officers: the past Archdruids, the attendant druid, the recorder, the herald poet, the swordbearer, the financial secretary, the organizer of examinations, the director of music, the mistress of the robes, and the Gorsedd Bard, all elected by the Gorsedd members.[10] There are three classes or orders of membership, each entitled to wear a distinctive colored robe. The Ovate Order (the disciples or beginners, hence ovate or egg from which the bard develops), the lowest of the three, wear robes of green, symbolic of the earth. Membership is given to those who pass comprehensive tests in the fields of Welsh literature and history or of music. In special cases, upon the recommendation of the Gorsedd board, honorary membership in this order is bestowed upon distinguished scholars and others who have rendered some special service for Wales. The Order of Bards (those whose genius has taken further flight), the next highest order, wear blue robes, the color of the heavens. Membership is bestowed upon those who have passed even more difficult examinations in the same subjects. The Druidic Order (those who have passed through the lower graces in the pursuit of truth), the highest of all, wear robes of white, the color of purity. Membership is restricted to those presented by the Druids themselves and recognized as having made substantial contributions of high national standards in the fields of literature, music, scholarship, or art. Because of its rigid standards and great prestige, membership in the Gorsedd is considered one of the greatest honors to which a Welshman can aspire, and is one of the goals of achievement of most young Welsh literati and intellectuals.[11]

Although Gorsedd ceremonies can be held at other times upon the determination of the Gorsedd Board, the most famous sessions take place in connection with the Royal National Eisteddfod. The latter may not be held without a ceremonial proclamation by the Gorsedd at least one year and a day in advance of the session. At this time, the first official list of subjects for competition is presented formally to the Archdruid. He then issues the official proclamation calling for the holding of the eisteddfod. Other Gorsedd ceremonies are held on two mornings during eisteddfod week. The first one opens the Eisteddfod officially. This as well as all sessions of the Gorsedd must be held in some open and conspicuous spot where they can be viewed by the public without payment. This is symbolic of the idea that everything done by the Gorsedd must bear the scrutiny of the light of day. A level green plot is selected somewhere near the town which is host to the Eisteddfod. A circle of standing stones, representing the points of the compass, is erected within which the ceremonies will be held. Outside the circle three other standing stones are erected. From the center of the circle the rising sun can be seen over their tops. The whole construction thus represents the supposed astronomical knowledge of the ancient Britons.[12]

Into this circle of stones the members of the Gorsedd, in procession according to order with the lowest in the lead and accompanied by important dignitaries of the district, proceed on the Tuesday morning of eisteddfod week. The Archdruid proceeds to the center of the circle where he stands upon the so-called flat Logan Stone, surrounded by the chief officers of the Gorsedd. At each of the twelve stones of the circle stand one or more of the bards. Among the group within the circle are the harpist, who plays the old Welsh triple stringed harp, the penillion singer, the keeper of the *hirlas* or drinking horn, the trumpeter, the recorder, the herald bard, the Gorsedd bard, and other officials including chaired and crowned bards of the past. The stones of the circle are usually draped with oak, ash, and birch foliage, and with grain and mistletoe, all plants associated with the ancient druids. The Archdruid is presented with a bouquet of these plants in a horn together with mead, meal, fruits, and vegetables. He then recites the chief Gorsedd prayer, and calls the roll of all the bards from the earliest times to the present. Then occurs the ceremony of the sword, symbolic of the medieval days when the bardic circle was not to be broken by armed men, a ceremony wherein the Archdruid brandishes the sword halfsheated in his hand and asks "A oes Heddwch?" (Is there Peace?) three times, and is answered "Heddwch!" (There is Peace!) three times by the accumulated group. The sword is then sheathed, various addresses are given, poems recited, music played, and then those who have passed their examinations for the Gorsedd orders are brought forward. The Archdruid decorates each with a ribbon of proper color on his arm and announces the person's bardic *non de plume*. The ceremony is then concluded and the procession marches from the circle back into the eisteddfod town and on to the eisteddfod platform to open the great competition. The Gorsedd group appears again on the platform in the afternoon and then on the following Thursday afternoon when the successful bards are chaired and crowned.[13]

The Gorsedd has been provided with official regalia for the administration of its ceremonies. These were made by Welsh artists around the turn of the twentieth century and presented to the Gorsedd by various patrons. When not in use, the regalia is kept in the Welsh National Museum in Cardiff. The regalia includes the Gorsedd Banner of elaborately embroidered silk which bears the mystic sign of the Gorsedd ╱ | ╲ and the legend in Welsh: "In the face of sun, the eye of light. The Truth against the World. Peace"; the Gorsedd Grand Sword, over six feet in length, which is borne before the Archdruid in procession and is used at the opening and closing of the Gorsedd and in the crowning and chairing of the bards; the Half Sword, a short sword divided lengthwise, the other half being kept in Brittany (it is used whenever a joint Gorsedd of the Bards of Wales and Brittany occurs, at which time the two halves are united to represent the spiritual unity of King Arthur's sword between the two nations); the Archdruid's Crown, a bronze chaplet of oak leaves enclosing a velvet covering; his breast-plate of silver-gilt wrought on an ancient Keltic pattern; his Sceptre which bears the clear crystal of his authority; the *Hirlas* Horn, guarded by the Red Dragon, the symbol of Wales, in which is offered the wine of welcome to the Archdruid; the Gorsedd Trumpet; the Jewels of Office worn by the Gorsedd officials, and the Proclamation Scroll bearing the illuminated traditional proclamation formula and decorated with the heraldic devices of the respective Welsh counties.[14]

Both the eisteddfod and the gorsedd eventually made their appearance in America. The revival of the eisteddfod in Wales after 1819, and the subsequent popularity of the institution among the Welsh people led to its introduction into America by the Welsh immigrants that came over to the United States in the 1830's. Just when the first eisteddfod was held in America is uncertain. Claims are made that one such was held in New York City as early as 1838. Probably other small ones were held elsewhere in the decade of the 1840's. Early eisteddfods, of which there is record, were held at Carbondale, Pa., on Christmas Day, 1850, at Pittston, Pa., during the 1850's, at Utica, N. Y., on January 1, 1858, at Hyde Park, Pa. (Scranton), on January 1, 1859, and those held by the Welsh gold miners in California at North San Juan on July 4, 1860, at Camptonville on the same day in 1861, and at Port Wine in 1862.

From the 1860's onwards, eisteddfods of various types and sizes were held in many of the Welsh-American settlements, generally around Christmas and New Year's Day. For the most part they were small in scale although in time considerably large ones took place in several of the larger communities. They tended to be of two sorts, those sponsored by the various churches and those having the backing of the whole Welsh community irrespective of creed. The number of such eisteddfods held annually increased rapidly as the flood of Welsh migration quickened in the post-Civil War years. The decades of the 1870's, 1880's, and 1890's saw as many as twenty and even twenty-five eisteddfods held in as many different places annually. Most of these were small community ventures. Prizes offered on such occasions amounted to several hundred dollars in most of the smaller endeavors, but often topped one thousand dollars in many of the larger ones.[15]

Although the eisteddfods came in time to be dominated by various musical competitions, in the early years prizes were given for recitations and the composition of essays and poems in the Welsh language. In the abjudication of the latter every effort was made to meet the high standards set by the contemporary eisteddfods of the homeland. Compositions both in the strict meters of Welsh classical poetry and in free verse, often submitted from Welsh poets in the homeland, poured forth for consideration. The judges, too, followed the example of their equivalents in Wales by often refusing to award prizes if the compositions submitted failed to meet acceptable standards. In time, the Americanization of the various communities and the paucity of individuals able to handle the Welsh language well enough to compose in Welsh saw the disappearance of competitions of this sort and the substitution of prizes for similar efforts in the English language. Provisions, however, were generally made for at least one prize for an original composition of some sort in the Welsh language.[16]

Competitions in the musical field began to dominate the American eisteddfod to such an extent that the contemporary American tended to think of the eisteddfod as primarily a musical phenomenon. Competitions in music included not only those between choirs, but between individual soloists, quartets, duos, and trios, as well as in the way of original musical compositions. It was unquestionably the great choir competitions, wherein the best of Bach, Handel, Mendelssohn, and other classical composers of sacred music were rendered with a skill unsurpassed by similar aggregations, native American or other, that won renown for the Welsh and tribute both from the American public and from American musical circles. Many of these Welsh-American choirs could hold their own with the best produced by the homeland. Occasionally, they made the trip to the homeland to compete in the great Welsh National Eisteddfod.

The Pennsylvania anthracite coal communities were particularly eisteddfod minded. Led by such eisteddfod enthusiasts as Judge Henry M. Edwards of Scranton and the Reverend T. C. (Cynonfardd) Edwards of Edwardsville, eisteddfods of one sort or another were held at Scranton, Wilkes-Barre, Pittston, Plymouth, Nanticoke, and Edwardsville in the northern anthracite field, and in Pottsville, Shenandoah, Shamokin, Mahanoy City, and Minersville in the southern field, as well as in numerous smaller anthracite communities.[17]

The Ohio settlements were also ardent eisteddfod enthusiasts. Various area events were held by the Venedocia, Gomer, Columbus, and Lima communities. A Central Ohio Eisteddfod Association was formed in 1886 to sponsor annual fetes in these settlements. It functioned well into the twentieth century. The numerically strong Gallia-Jackson colony and the Welsh center of Cincinnati were also eisteddfod conscious. Annual events took place in these settlements, and in 1922 a Southern Ohio Eisteddfod Association was formed. This was generally referred to as the Jackson Eisteddfod because the sessions were held in the town of Jackson. For many years it sponsored annual sessions. The extensive Welsh settlements of the Warren-Youngstown-New Castle area were likewise active in sponsoring eisteddfods from the 1860's well into the twentieth century. As late as 1930, interest in the unique Welsh institution was so strong that the Welsh societies of the area joined to form The Trumbull County Eisteddfod Association. For over a decade it sponsored under the leadership of George Bundy some of the most successful eisteddfods to be held in America in the twentieth century.[18] Elsewhere throughout the Welsh settlements of Wisconsin, Minnesota, Iowa, and other sections of the middle-west, various eisteddfods were held from time to time in the post-Civil War period. Eisteddfod spirit was especially strong in Iowa where an Iowa Eisteddfod Association was formed in 1889, and among the Mormon Welsh in Utah.[19]

In time large eisteddfods of national scope were held by the Welsh-Americans in key centers of the nation. At such large gatherings, an effort was made to match the standards and competitions set by the National Eisteddfod of Wales. Competitors from all over the United States and usually from Wales met to vie for prizes in singing and the composition of poetry. Large sums of money went to the successful choirs, and elaborately carved chairs to the successful bards. Among these larger eisteddfods which commanded the attention of the Welsh of America were the following: the Hyde Park (Scranton) Eisteddfod cf 1867, the occasion of the presentation of Dr. Joseph Parry's glee, *Ar Don o Flaen Gwentoedd*, written especially for the event; the Chicago International Eisteddfod of 1893 held in connection with the Columbian Exposition—one of the largest if not the largest eisteddfod ever held in America, with prizes amounting to over twelve thousand dollars; the Atlantic City Eisteddfod of 1900; the Scranton Eisteddfod of 1908; the Alaska-Yukon-Pacific Eisteddfod held at Seattle in 1909; the Pittsburgh International Eisteddfod of 1913, the occasion of the establishment of the American Gorsedd; and the International Exposition Eisteddfod held at San Francisco in 1915.[20]

Interest in the Eisteddfod during the twentieth century led to the establishment of the National Eisteddfod Association of America, Incorporated, in 1923 by a special grant from the governing authorities of the National Eisteddfod Association of Wales. From its headquarters at Utica, the new organization encouraged and promoted the holding of such national eisteddfods annually along the lines of the mother institution. It hoped thereby to develop and to stimulate interest in music, literature, art and science. It approved of the holding of national eisteddfods from 1923 until 1940. The first were held annually at Utica from 1923 until 1927, then at Wilkes-Barre in 1928, at Scranton in 1929, at Jackson, Ohio, in 1930, at Warren, Ohio, in 1938, at the Golden Gate International Exposition at San Francisco in 1939, and the last at Warren, Ohio, in 1940.[21]

By all odds the most famous eisteddfod in America today is the Utica Eisteddfod—the oldest continuous eisteddfod to be established in America. It held its first session on January 1, 1858, and has held annual sessions ever since. It was sponsored originally by the Utica Cymreigyddion Society and in later years by the allied Welsh societies and churches of this, perhaps, the most famous Welsh center in America. Now of modest scope, it keeps alive the competitive tradition of the Welsh immigrants of the nineteenth century in the field of music.[22] Second in renown and age is the eisteddfod sponsored by the Dr. Edwards Memorial Congregational Church of Edwardsville, Pa., a Wilkes-Barre suburb. Now called the "Cynonfardd Eisteddfod" in honor of Dr. T. C. Edwards (Cynonfardd), renowned pastor of this church and dean of Welsh-American clergymen, it held its first session in 1889, and has held annual sessions ever since on, ironically enough, St. Patrick's Day.[23] The third existing eisteddfod is that held by the Girard Avenue-Welsh Presbyterian Church of Philadelphia. It held its first session in 1903 and has held annual sessions in early January ever since. These latter two eisteddfods are probably the last survivors of many such once sponsored by various Welsh-American churches.[24]

So far as the author has been able to determine, the three eisteddfods of Utica, Edwardsville, and Philadelphia are the only ones still held annually in America. The cessation of Welsh immigration to the United States and the Americanization of the children of the Welsh immigrants sounded the doom of the eisteddfod in the United States. Although many such were held in the twentieth century, the effects of Americanization were revealed in the nature of the competitions. Originally Welsh in speech and emphasis, the eisteddfods became more and more English in emphasis with competitions predominating in the English language. Today, the Edwardsville Eisteddfod reveals the complete triumph of the American environment over the original Welsh character of the institution. Competitions are all in English except for one or two prizes reserved for the surviving oldsters. These, all over seventy, may compete for prizes in the singing of songs in Welsh of their choice. Usually, there are only one or two contestants and the result often ends diplomatically in a tie with both contestants sharing the prize—a nostalgic tribute to the indomitable oldsters![25]

The Gorsedd eventually made its appearance in America as a Welsh institution. Although a Gorsedd-type ceremony was held in connection with the Youngstown Eisteddfod of 1865, the first true Gorsedd conclave to be held in America occurred at the Chicago International Eisteddfod of 1893. The then Archdruid of Wales, Hwfa Mon, presided. The usual procedures and ceremonies took place, and candidates were initiated into the various orders. Continued pressure on the part of leading Welshmen in America led to the issuance of a special decree by the Welsh Gorsedd in convocation at the National Eisteddfod at Wrexham in 1912, authorizing the Archdruid to attend the Pittsburgh International Eisteddfod of 1913 and to establish an American Gorsedd. The Archdruid did so, and the American Gorsedd became the first daughter organization to be established. Other daughter Gorsedds were later established in Australia and Brittany. The Reverend Dr. T. C. Edwards

(Cynonfardd) was chosen first American Archdruid. Candidates from all over the United States were admitted to the various orders.[26]

The American Gorsedd held a conclave the following year at the International Eisteddfod at Golden Gate Park, San Francisco, and again at Pittsburgh in 1919 upon the dedication of its headquarters at that place. At the latter time, the possibility of widening the scope and usefulness of the new organization along the lines of creating a large national society of Welsh-Americans to support Welsh cultural activities was considered. It was decided that membership in the American Gorsedd should be thrown open to all Americans of Welsh extraction upon the payment of annual or life dues. A program of objectives was drawn up which included the unification of all Americans of Welsh origin in support of Welsh-American cultural activities and democracy as a whole, support of a national eisteddfod for America as a type of poor man's university, support for the Welsh Home for the Aged then newly established in Ohio, and support of the preaching of the gospel in Welsh for those areas in need of the same. A special agent for the organization was appointed to visit the various Welsh settlements in the hope of obtaining new members.[27]

Despite the efforts of its organizers, the American Gorsedd failed to gain members on a large scale. The total membership never numbered over three hundred and three and these came principally from the Pittsburgh area. An effort to establish a branch circle at Youngstown failed. Interest among the Welsh communities, by this time considerably Americanized, remained indifferent. As a consequence, the American Gorsedd became to a large extent a local Welsh society for the Pittsburgh area. In time it became the chief sponsor of the various St. David's Day banquets and Welsh days held annually in that area. Official Gorsedd conclaves continued to be held from time to time at which new members were admitted. Such colorful ceremonies were held at Schenley Park, Pittsburgh, in June of 1919 and 1920, at Wick Park, Youngstown, in June, 1922, at Mansfield, Ohio in June, 1923, and again at Youngstown in June, 1926. This latter conclave was the occasion of an eisteddfod in honor of Dr. John Reese, the well-known Welsh immigrant physician. Referred to affectionately as "Bonesetter Reese," the aged physician was honored by the Gorsedd by being elected to the highest degree or druid status of the Society, the only person so honored by the American Gorsedd. Other conclaves were held at the Warren Eisteddfod of 1938 when a chairing of the bard ceremony was held, and in 1940 at another Warren Eisteddfod when the Honorable James J. Davis, Welsh immigrant Senator from Pennsylvania and former Secretary of Labor, was installed as Archdruid. The last conclave of the American Gorsedd took place at Warren in 1941.[28]

The American Gorsedd had only three archdruids during its life-time: the Reverend Dr. T. C. Edwards (Cynonfardd) of Edwardsville, Pa., from 1913 to 1918; the Reverend Dr. William Survidal of Middle-point, Ohio, from 1918 to 1940; and Senator Davis, who served from 1940 until the demise of the Society in 1941. The American Gorsedd had the honor of receiving and entertaining the British Prime Minister and noted Welsh leader, David Lloyd George, upon the occasion of the latter's official visit to America in 1923. Special festivities were con-ducted by the Society in his honor at that time.[29]

The attempt to establish a Gorsedd along Welsh lines in America proved too ambitious a project for the American temperament and environment. The Gorsedd in Wales could and does take an active par-ticipation in art, music, literature, and other cultural affairs. In the much different atmosphere of America, such a Gorsedd could never have the wide appeal that it did in the homeland. The widespread nature of the Welsh settlements, the decline of Welsh immigration, the decline of inter-est in the Welsh language among the younger elements due to the process of Americanization, loyalties to local societies and groups—all contrib-uted to checking the ambitious aims of the American Gorsedd. Despite the valiant efforts of Robert H. Davies (Gomerian) of Pittsburgh, the recorder of the society, and others, the American Gorsedd in time had to be content to play the role of just another local Welsh-American society.

In time, as the Americanization of the Welsh-American commu-nities progressed, the Eisteddfod was replaced by the Gymanfa Ganu, or Welsh singing festival, as the popular institution of Welsh-Americans. Although by this time many of the latter could no longer handle Welsh as a living language, they still could sing in Welsh for they had been taught to do so from their early Sunday School days. Love of the old Welsh hymns and the singing of the same in Welsh lingers on in most of the Welsh-American communities. This nostalgia for the days of their youth and the remembrances associated with the same is the reason why the Gymanfa Ganu is still a strong institution in America today.

The Gymanfa Ganu, as a special independent festival, is compara-tively new. It dates from the lifetime of the Reverend John Roberts (Ieuan Gwyllt), a Calvinistic-Methodist minister and one of the great hymn-tune writers of all time. It was he who received credit for con-ducting the first Gymanfa Ganu at Aberdare in 1859. Similar singing sessions were led by him during the years 1860 to 1863 at Merthyr where he was then serving as pastor of Pantywyll Chapel. These sing-ing festivals are believed to have been the first Gymanfa Ganus. The festivals became popular and soon each of the three main denominations of Wales began to hold such gatherings: the Baptists in 1868, the Calvinistic-Methodists in 1875, and the Congregationalists in 1884. Since these dates, the Gymanfa Ganu or group singing festival has become a fundamental institution of the Welsh. The noted Dr. Joseph Parry conducted annual ones from 1889 until his death in 1903. In time all three faiths began to hold district Gymanfa Ganus with one of the larger churches serving as host church. Choirs from all the churches of the respective Associations were represented at such gatherings and representatives from all such choirs formed special committees to choose the music directors for the occasion, usually the best musical leaders that could be obtained. Three sessions were normally held (in the morning, afternoon and evening). Usually the hymns to be sung by the assembled gatherings were selected, printed, and circulated throughout the Association's area in advance of the meeting. From fifteen to twenty hymns or anthems were selected for that purpose. Reliance was often based upon the old sulfa notation so that the older generation could participate to the fullest.[30]

In America, the Gymanfa Ganu—as a separate gathering for congregational singing—is a twentieth century phenomenon. Influenced no doubt by the popularity of the institution in the homeland during the last decade of the nineteenth century, individual churches began to hold such gatherings. They caught on instantly with the music and song-loving Welsh, and the movement spread to the Welsh communities as a whole. Various of the churches of a given community would alternate yearly and sometimes semi-yearly in playing host to such gatherings. By the 1920's, whole areas, comprising a score of Welsh communities, were holding area Gymanfa Ganus in addition to the community or smaller gatherings, and significantly enough in the case of America, on a total Welsh basis not on a denominational one as in the case of the homeland. Finally, the movement was on for a great national annual gathering—a huge all-American Welsh Gymanfa Ganu with all the respective communities represented.[31]

In this way was founded the National Gymanfa Ganu Association of the United States and Canada, the largest and strongest association ever formed by the Welsh in America and the only successful attempt at forming an all-over national association of Welsh-Americans. The Association grew out of the efforts of the officers of the St. David's Society of Youngstown, Ohio, to plan an excursion for their fellow Welsh-Americans to Niagara Falls on Labor Day of 1929. A Gymanfa Ganu was to be a feature of the activities of the group after it had arrived at the popular vacation spot. When the day arrived (Sept. 1, 1929) some fourteen hundred men and women of the Western Reserve communities and about one thousand more from other scattered points gathered for the celebration. The event was a tremendous success and plans were set afoot to hold a similar and larger Gymanfa Ganu the following year. Through the efforts of *Y Drych, the Druid,* and other publications, sufficient publicity was obtained to make the following year's event on the same holiday at Niagara Falls an even greater success. The National Gymanfa Ganu Association was then formed to sponsor the annual event. Contacts were made with leading Welsh-Americans in virtually all the communities in an attempt to make the fete a truly national gathering of all Welsh Americans (the Canadian Welsh communities were also invited to participate). The next two sessions were also held at Niagara Falls, and then the various Welsh communities began to compete for the honor of playing host to the Association. The gathering has been held at key American centers each year thereafter on Labor Day.[32]

Today, the National Gymanfa Ganu Association is supported by most Welsh societies and clubs as well as by private individuals. It is governed by a board of officers elected annually in a special business meeting at the time of the fete. The officers and members decide a year in advance the place of the fete for the following year, and the former have the responsibility of arranging for the proper publicity and raising the necessary funds to make the fete a success. Organized originally specifically for the purpose of holding the national song fest, the Association has branched out to embark upon even more ambitious undertakings. It hopes to group all Welsh clubs and organizations into one great federation to sponsor interest in Welsh culture and institutions, and as one step in this direction has undertaken the ambitious project of establishing a National Welsh-American Library at the Brigham Young University at Provo, Utah. To what extent it will realize its larger aims remains to be seen. As of the moment it is unquestionably the strongest Welsh association in America.

The Gymanfa Ganus (*Cymanfaoedd Canu* in Welsh) sponsored by the Association attract each year enthusiastic Welsh-Americans to the number of five thousand and sometimes more who gather to enjoy and to partake in the singing of the old favorite Welsh hymns and anthems of their ancestors. The behavior of Welsh-Americans on such occasions, and the reaction of an American newspaper to such, has been revealed in an account written in the *Milwaukee Sentinel* of September 4, 1951 after the conclusion of the national fete held at Milwaukee:

> Countless conventions have ended on countless Sunday nights with festive people crowding the Schroeder Hotel lobby. If they reached the singing stage by mid-night, usually in the wee hours of Monday, they progress to the unprintable verses.
> It was different early Monday as about 2,000 Welshmen and their wives relaxed after their national "Gymanfa Ganu"—song festival.
> They jammed the Schroeder lobbies and sang and sang, massed in impromptu choruses. They sang with enough volume to bring stragglers in from the streets.

But where ordinary post-convention singers are fueled with fluids that help in ignoring one's own flat notes, these sang without artificial stimulation. They had no flat notes to ignore.

There was another difference. There wasn't a line of "I Want a Girl Just Like the Girl that Married Dear Old Dad" nor "You Tell Me Your Dream". The gay tunes were such hymns as "Count Your Blessings" and the sad ones were not schmaltz but prayer.

A drunk weaved in from the street, untangled himself from the revolving door, and stood listening intently.

" 'S' beautiful", he said.

"The Night is dark, and I am far from home—".

The drunk shivered and plunged into the revolving door again. "Too sad. I like barbershop myself."

Bellboys and night clerks stood listening happily. Not only good music; nobody was any trouble. The crowd started to thin a little. A Welshman said to another:

"It's late. We'd better get some sleep."

"We can't go now", his friend answered. "How could you leave when there's still singing?"[33]

The eisteddfod has practically died out in America and with it the attempt to establish a flourishing Gorsedd. Both were too intimately associated with the Welsh language to survive the Americanization of the Welsh-American communities. The Gymanfa Ganu remains strongly entrenched and is apt to remain so largely because it requires only a love of community singing. The time will come unquestionably when substitution of English for Welsh words will occur, but this is not apt to dampen the enthusiasm for mass singing, certainly not among Welsh-Americans. As a matter of fact, the Gymanfa Ganus have become popular with other Americans, too, who often attend and partake to the extent that they can. They will undoubtedly do so more enthusiastically in the future as and when the language of the fete becomes English. Indeed, it is this author's opinion that the Gymanfa Ganu, and it only, will be the institution the Welsh contribute to the American musical way of life.

FOOTNOTES ON CHAPTER VII

1. Tom Parry, *The Eisteddfod of Wales,* Denbigh, Wales (National Eisteddfod Council), n.d., pp. 25-38.

2. *Ibid.,* pp. 26-27.

3. *Ibid.,* pp. 27-33.

4. *Ibid.,* pp. 34-37.

5. *Ibid.,* p. 25.

6. *Ibid.,* pp. 38-39.

7. Williams, *A History of Modern Wales, op. cit.,* p. 271.

8. *Ibid.*

9. "Cynan," *The Council and Gorsedd of To-day,* Denbigh, Wales (National Eisteddfod Council), n.d., pp. 36-41.

10. *Ibid.,* p. 36.

11. *Ibid.,* pp. 37-38; D. E. Richards, "The Gorsedd," *The Royal Blue Book, Prize Productions of the Pittsburgh International Eisteddfod,* Pittsburgh, 1916, pp. 17-23.

12. "Cynan," *ibid.*, p. 36.

13. Richards, *op. cit.,* pp. 17-23; "Cynan," *op. cit.,* pp. 38-39.

14. "Cynan," *op. cit.,* p. 39.

15. See files of *Y Drych, the Cambrian, the Druid, passim.*

16. *Ibid.*

17. Henry M. Edwards, "Eisteddfod Reminiscences," *Druid,* III (Sept. 23, 30; Oct. 7, 21, 28; Nov. 4, 11, 18, 25; and Dec. 2, 1909).

18. Florence Jenkins Cope, "History of the Jackson Eisteddfod," unpublished M.A. thesis, Ohio State University, 1937; and Homer Mitchell, "The Eisteddfod in Ohio," unpublished M.A. thesis, Ohio State University, 1934.

19. Ben Hur Wilson, "The Iowa Eisteddfod," *Palimpsest,* XXII (Dec., 1941), pp. 357-73.

20. See "Bibliography" for programs of other American Eisteddfods.

21. *Ibid.*

22. Utica Eisteddfod, *Annual Programs.*

23. Edwardsville Cynonfardd Eisteddfod, *Annual Programs.*

24. Philadelphia Eisteddfod, *Annual Programs.*

25. Once renowned church eisteddfods of this sort were held by the Welsh Congregational Church of Hyde Park (Scranton) on New Year's Day, 1889-1930's; by Bethania Calvinistic-Methodist Church, Scranton, on Christmas Day, 1891-1924; and by Moriah Congregational Church, Nanticoke, Pa., 1900-1916. The Welsh Congregational Church of New York City also held annual eisteddfods in the 1920's and 1930's.

26. Ebenezer P. Thomas, *Glimpses of the Gorsedd, a Brief Sketch of the History and Progress of the American Gorsedd,* Pittsburgh, 1919, *passim.*

27. "Minutes of the American Gorsedd," manuscript, 1913-1941, *passim.* The "Minutes" were donated by David Nichols of Pittsburgh to the National Welsh-American Library, Brigham Young University, Provo, Utah.

28. *Ibid.*

29. *Ibid.*

30. J. Eiddon Jones, *Ieuan Gwyllt,* Treffynon, Wales (P. M. Evans & Son), 1881, pp. 52-59.

31. Wendell M. Jones, "The Gymanfa Ganu," unpublished M.A. thesis, Ohio State University, 1946, *passim.*

32. David O. Jenkins, "The Gymanfa Ganu," *Deuch, Canwn i'r Arglwydd, Favorite Welsh and English Hymns and Melodies,* Warren, Ohio (National Gymanfa Ganu Association of the United States and Canada), n.d., rear cover.

33. From the newspaper files of George Bundy for many years the secretary of the National Gymanfa Ganu Association of the United States and Canada.

CHAPTER VIII

WELSH-AMERICAN SOCIETIES AND CLUBS

Since religion played such an important part in the hearts of the Welsh immigrants, the various church organizations formed their strongest type of society or association. Love for the old homeland, strong consciousness of their kindred nationality, plus a number of social problems tended in time to cause them to organize societies or clubs of an all-Welsh makeup with representation from the Welsh of all denominations of a given locality. These Welsh societies or clubs tended to be of two varieties, cultural or benevolent. In some cases, however, the same society might sponsor both activities.

Most numerous were the cultural organizations. These were formed to sponsor good fellowship among the Welsh of a given locality, but in addition they sponsored programs on behalf of Welsh cultural interests such as Welsh Days at the parks in the summertime, gymanfa ganus and singing sessions, occasional concerts and readings, entertainment of distinguished guests from Wales, and like activities. Without a doubt, the most important feature of these societies was the proper observance of March first of each year, the anniversary of St. David, the patron saint of the Welsh. On this important occasion, all Welsh communities united in honoring the great saint and in remembering their Welsh heritage. Generally, an elaborate banquet would be held at which time toasts to St. David and to Wales would be offered, the glories of the Welsh past recollected, and the highlights of the locality's historic Welsh-American past recollected. Every effort was made to engage a distinguished speaker (usually a prominent Welsh-American) for the occasion. The banquet would end with the singing of the old Welsh favorite hymns. Usually, too, on the Sunday preceding St. David's Day, special services in honor of the Saint would be held in the various churches, often held jointly in one of the churches.

Because of the exhalted position which St. David holds among the Welsh, most of these Welsh cultural societies were named in his honor. Occasionally, the name Cambrian (from the Welsh word for Wales, *Cymru*) was preferred as was also the simple title, "Welsh" Society or Club. Virtually every Welsh-American settlement had its St. David's Society or the equivalent in the past and most of the larger centers still have such today. Over one hundred such societies existed at one time or another and many of them still exist today. In many cases the societies are well over fifty years old, in a few cases over one hundred years old. Generally these societies were organized on a male or female basis with the stronger Welsh settlements having separate societies of each sex. In many of the smaller communities, membership embraced both sexes. In the numerically strong Welsh settlements of the Wyoming Valley, Pennsylvania, separate societies on the basis of age also exist, thus there are Senior and Junior Cambrian Clubs for women in Wilkes-Barre, Plymouth, Nanticoke, and in neighboring Scranton.

As one might expect, the music-loving Welsh organized numerous glee clubs and singing societies. Practically every Welsh settlement had at least one of these and in the case of the numerically strong anthracite communities often several going strong at the same time. The various singing societies competed with each other at the various eisteddfods held annually as well as held concerts from time to time. Some of these choirs achieved national and international reputations. Among the better known in the late nineteenth century were the Cymrodorion Choral Society of Scranton led by the noted composer, Daniel Protheroe, the Scranton Choral Union under the leadership of Hadyn Evans, the Western Reserve Choral Union led by J. Powell Jones, and the Gwent Glee Society of Edwardsville (Wilkes-Barre) led by Evan Davis.

Two of the most famous Welsh-American singing societies were organized in the early part of the present century and are still in existence. The Orpheus Glee Club of Wilkes-Barre under the leadership of Gwilym Amos and later John Jones Owen won national reputation and innumerable prizes in competitions of various sorts from its date of foundation until the present. The Orpheus Male Chorus of Cleveland, organized and led by Dr. Charles D. Dawe, not only became perhaps America's best known male choir, but twice journeyed to Wales to compete with the best choirs of the homeland and returned to America with coveted honors. A third contemporary Welsh-American choir is the Poultney Welsh Male Chorus, organized in 1939, which, under the leadership of Evan G. Williams, has acquired a national reputation for the quality of its part-singing.

Less numerous than the cultural societies, but playing a very important part in the early days of the Welsh settlements, were the benevolent and charitable societies. The former were organized in the days before Social Security to provide sick and death benefits for members; the latter were organized to aid the newly arrived immigrants and other Welsh-Americans who were experiencing financial difficulties. Societies of both types were organized in most of the larger Welsh settlements. They passed out of existence for the most part with the cessation of immigration from Wales and because of the adoption of social legislation by the state and federal governments.

Taking precedence among the Welsh-American societies is the historic Welsh Society of Philadelphia, the oldest such organization in America and the oldest existing society of the Pennsylvania metropolis. The Society had its origins in the little group of Welshmen who met in Philadelphia on March 1, 1729, to honor St. David. The traditional banquet, toasts, and religious singing customary in the homeland followed. Each year thereafter down to the present, the Society has held such celebrations. In time, the little group of Welshmen banded together into a society with the goal of dispensing funds to destitute Welshmen and needy immigrants then arriving by way of Philadelphia. The Society was reorganized in 1798 when a formal constitution was adopted. The group was incorporated under its present name in 1802.[1]

Throughout the nineteenth century, the Society performed the valuable service of aiding Welsh immigrants, particularly those who had underestimated the cost of the journey to America and arrived without funds to continue on to their destinations. In such cases, the Society frequently furnished the funds to lodge the immigrant properly and to purchase the transportation to take him to his destination. Occasionally, the Welsh head of a family would die at sea leaving the widow and brood of youngsters to face an uncertain future upon arrival. In such cases, too, the Society stepped into the breach by providing funds and housing until the widow found employment or again providing the necessary transportation funds to allow the family to continue on to one of the Welsh settlements where they had friends. A special burial plot was purchased so that no needy Welsh-American would be buried in a pauper's grave.[2]

A glance at the roster of the Society's membership reveals the names of some of Philadelphia's most distinguished residents, all of Welsh extraction. Today, the Welsh Society of Philadelphia carries on the traditions of its distinguished historic past through the undertaking of benevolences and the sponsoring of interest in Welsh culture.[3]

Somewhat junior in age but equally ardent in influence is the numerically strong St. David's Society of the State of New York. This society had its origins in the little group of Welshmen who banded together to found the Ancient Britons Benefit Society of the city of New York in 1805. Provisions were made for the members to receive sick and death benefits. It was reorganized in 1835 when it was decided to honor the patron saint of Wales by assuming his name. At the same time, the group decided to inaugurate a program of benevolences to aid the Welsh immigrants and destitute of the city. From 1835 until 1841 it bore the name of the St. David's Benefit and Benevolent Society. In the latter year the two functions of the society were separated and two groups were formed, the St. David's Benevolent Society and the St. David's Benefit Society. The latter, a mutual benefit association, continued on until 1886 when its existence was terminated. The former had itself chartered the same year under its present name, the St. David's Society of the State of New York.[4]

Throughout its history, St. David's has carried on similar functions to those of the Welsh Society of Philadelphia. Situated as it was in New York City, the great entrepot for most of America's immigrants during the nineteenth and twentieth centuries, the Society did vaunted service on behalf of its newly arrived ethnic countrymen, a service which it is still performing today. It, too, has its own burial plot, as well as hospital beds, for the benefit of needy Welshmen. As in the case of its Philadelphia counterpart, proper homage to St. David in the form of an annual banquet has been a part of its program ever since its founding. A new feature which the Society has adopted recently consists of the awarding of a medal, donated by one of the members, each year to a Welshman who has distinguished himself in some outstanding field of endeavor.[5]

A similar benevolent society was organized in Utica, New York, in 1849, when several Welsh residents formed the Welsh Benevolent Society of Utica and Vicinity. It, too, rendered valuable assistance to immigrant and indigent Welsh. The Society was disbanded in 1948, its one hundredth year of existence, and its remaining funds were divided between the two Welsh churches of Utica to be used for charitable purposes.[6] A fourth society of this type, the Cambrian Benevolent Society of Chicago, was formed in 1854. It sought to meet similar problems besetting Welsh immigrants in the great western mecca for Welsh settlers. The Society is still in existence, now in its one hundred and thirteenth year.[7]

Welsh-American mutual benefit societies were organized in most of the larger settlements. Some had comparatively brief careers. Others, however, flourished for decades. In Utica, New York, such a society was organized in 1814 under the name of the Ancient Britons' Benefit Society. It survived until 1847. Another was active during the same years in Cincinnati. Out on the west coast, the Cambrian Mutual Aid Society of San Francisco, founded in 1869, flourished well into the twentieth century.[8]

Further organization of local Welsh-American mutual benefit societies tended to be minimized with the establishment of an American branch of the distinctly Welsh lodge, the Independent Order of True Ivorites. The Ivorites were founded in Wrexham, Wales, in 1836 by a little group of Welshmen of high ideals and patriotism whose love of the noble traditions of the Welsh nationality urged them to establish a benevolent order so that they might be of service to their fellows in times of sorrow and affliction. The American Order of True Ivorites was founded in Pittsburgh in 1848 by immigrant Welshmen who were familiar with what the order had been doing in the homeland. The Order is named after Ivor Hael (Ivor, the Liberal), a Welsh leader who was famous for his kind deeds and great hospitality and who lived at the beginning of the fourteenth century. The Order has a secret ritual and ceremonies which honor the great figures of Welsh history, such as St. David, Howell the Good, Llewellyn the Great, and Owen Glendower. Its constitution is based upon three ideals, love, friendship, and truth. Members pay annual dues and receive in return sick and death benefits as well as enjoy the cultural and social activities sponsored by the Order. Chapters were soon established in most of the Welsh-American settlements. At the height of its strength in the 1890's, the order numbered seventy-five chapters, each named after some leading figure or symbol associated with Welsh history.[9]

Although originally organized as a strictly male order, the Ivorites established special chapters for Welsh-American women in the late 1890's. A total of ten such female chapters came into existence. The business and ceremonies of the Order were conducted at first in the Welsh language, but as the Americanization of the Welsh proceeded, the wisdom of allowing certain chapters to use English instead was approved in 1881. The Order had its greatest membership in 1895 (2,285). The greatest value of its capital holdings was that of the year, 1925, ($76,774.28). As of 1965, its treasurer estimated that it had paid out some $805,761.69 in sick and death benefits and for charity since the year 1863.[10]

The effects of Americanization, the new Social Security programs, and a lack of interest in lodges generally all have had their influence on the Ivorites. Many of the older chapters have disbanded, the youngsters are no longer interested in joining, immigration from Wales has all but ceased. Today, there are only five active chapters and the membership as of 1965 numbered 159. The Order is making a strong bid, however, to keep its organization a living reality and faces the future optimistically.[11]

Of a benevolent nature also are the various Women's Welsh Clubs that are to be found throughout the Welsh-American settlements. Unlike the other organizations mentioned so far, however, these are all twentieth century creations. The movement which resulted in their organization started in 1912, when the Women's Auxiliary of the Welsh Society of Cleveland first began to discuss the possibilities of establishing a home for aged Welsh people. The idea became popular, similar Welsh Women's groups were organized in other localities, and, in 1914, the

Women's Welsh Clubs of America was formed for the definite purpose of establishing such a home for aged Welsh people. Within a decade some forty-five clubs with 2,500 members had been organized. A large private residence was purchased in Cleveland in 1919 and the Home officially opened on Thanksgiving Day of that year. The indebtedness of the Home was soon paid off. A new and larger Home was purchased in 1921 at Rocky River near Cleveland. Any aged man or woman of Welsh extraction or married to such a person is eligible for admission upon payment of a modest fee.[12]

The various Women's Welsh Clubs of America devote their efforts to raising funds in support of the Home. A convention with delegates from member clubs is held annually. This organization shares honors with the Ivorites in having organized successfully a Welsh-American body with branches throughout the various settlements.

Dissatisfaction with the far-away distance of the Cleveland Home led to the organization of another Welsh Home for the Aged in Scranton, Pa. The Women's Welsh Club of that community felt that it would be cruel to force their oldsters to go to far-away Cleveland to spend their declining days among strangers. Moreover, they argued that Scranton, as the center of the largest concentration of Welsh people in America, should be able to support a home of its own. Accordingly, the Scranton ladies sponsored the building of a second home. Property was purchased in that city in 1923 and the Home was officially opened. Unlike the Cleveland Home which is open to both male and female guests, the Scranton Home is for female guests only. Need for larger quarters resulted in the purchase of a larger residence in 1925 which has remained the site of the Home ever since. The Scranton Home for Aged Welsh Women is supported officially by the Lackawanna Welsh Women's Club and its affiliates, a junior women's club, and the male Cambrian Society of Scranton. It receives the support of the Welsh people of Lackawanna and Luzerne counties and their organizations.[13]

The other existing Welsh-American societies and clubs are chiefly of a cultural and social nature. Practically every area which received a quota of Welsh immigrants has a St. David's Society or some equivalent which conducts an annual banquet on March 1. In addition, such organizations frequently sponsor gymanfa ganus, outings, concerts, and other socials. They support the various appeals of the Women's Welsh Clubs for aid to the two homes and those of the Welsh churches upon occasion.[14]

Although certain of these societies date from the nineteenth century, most of the existing ones were organized in the twentieth, interestingly enough, at the very time when Americanization of the Welsh settlements and churches was in full swing. Pride in Welsh extraction, fond memories of the deceased parents and grandparents and their Welsh ways, and the wish to keep alive the link with the past unquestionably motivated their formation. In this respect, such societies are typically American in their cherishing of the past and in their attempt to bring all those of a common heritage together. It should be noted to the credit of the Welsh, however, that very little of the snobbishness exists in these societies that can be found ofttimes among similar groups. Mere proof of Welsh descent is all that is necessary to make one eligible even for such antiquarian groups as the 238 year old Welsh Society of Philadelphia and the 162 year old St. David's Society of the State of New York. In both groups, distinguished descendants of colonial Welsh settlers rub elbows with recent Welsh immigrants—all proud of their common Welsh heritage!

FOOTNOTES ON CHAPTER VIII

1. Welsh Society of Philadelphia, *The Charter and By-Laws of the Welsh Society With an Historical Sketch by Horatio Gates Jones and a List of Officers and Members from the Year 1798*, Philadelphia, 1947, pp. 3-15.

2. Welsh Society of Philadelphia, *Minutes, passim,* manuscript in Pennsylvania Historical Society Library, Philadelphia.

3. Edward George Hartmann, "The Welsh Society of Philadelphia," *Y Drych,* CII (Feb., 1953), pp. 12-13.

4. St. David's Society of the State of New York, *Saint David's Society of the State of New York, Our One Hundredth Year, 1835-1935,* New York, 1935, *passim.*

5. St. David's Society of the State of New York, *Annual Reports,* 1900-1966, *passim.*

6. John C. Roberts, *Hanes Cymdeithas Elusengar Utica a'r Cylchoedd o'r Sefydliad yn 1849 hyd Jonawr 1, 1882,* Utica, N. Y., 1882, pp. 63-78.

7. Cambrian Benevolent Society of Chicago, Inc., *Souvenir Program, 1853-1952, Celebrating the One Hundredth Annual St. David's Banquet and Concert, Saturday, March 1, 1952,* Chicago, 1952, *passim.*

8. David Hughes, *Welsh People of California, 1849-1906,* San Francisco, 1923, pp. 40-41.

9. American Order of True Ivorites, *American Order of True Ivorites, 75 Years of Active Benevolent Work,* 1943, *passim.*

10. American Order of True Ivorites, *Annual Reports, passim.*

11. Letter from Mrs. Blodwen G. Williams of Utica, New York, grand secretary of the Ivorites, to the author, March 17, 1965.

12. Mrs. David I. Jones, *Women's Welsh Clubs of America,* Cleveland, 1951, *passim.*

13. Welsh Women's Society of Lackawanna County, *Constitution and By-Laws,* n.d., *passim.*

14. See bibliography for data on other Welsh-American societies.

CHAPTER IX

CONCLUSION

The foregoing chapters have traced the story of Welsh immigrants in the United States. Statistics are lacking on the numbers that came during the colonial period and the first decades of the nineteenth century. But from 1820, when statistics began to be kept on immigrants by country of origin, until 1965, some 93,359 immigrants from Wales settled in America. Their descendants as well as the descendants of their predecessors have been estimated to number at least 500,000 Americans as of the present. The Welsh stock of America is therefore comparatively modest in relation to many other ethnic groups now present in the United States. Dispite paucity of numbers, however, the contribution of the Welsh stock to America has been considerable, and in the opinion of this author, taking numbers into consideration, has been excelled by few other ethnic groups if by any.

Thousands of Welsh immigrants and their descendants played modest roles pioneering and developing large sections of America's agricultural lands; thousands more played important roles as skilled workmen and supervisors in the key fields of steel production, coal mining, other extractive industries, and in slate production. Many others played various roles as workers in other economic activities, in politics and statecraft, in the professions, in the arts and sciences, in the field of entertainment, and in a variety of miscellaneous ways. These formed part of the solid core of American citizenry upon which our great civilization rests.

Many others of Welsh stock, however, rose from the ranks to acquire respected and even renowned fame in virtually every field of endeavor in the American environment. The contribution of the Welsh element in this respect during colonial and revolutionary times has already been treated. The fine example which they set was emulated by their nineteenth and twentieth century successors of Welsh stock. It would be impossible in a book of this sort to do justice to the success stories of prominent Welsh immigrants alone, let alone do the same for the great array of those of such stature who were of Welsh stock. Suffice it to say that scarcely a field of American enterprise existed which did not have at one time or another a prominent Welsh-American which it could count among its distinguished leaders.

Some statistics might prove helpful at this point to illustrate the Welsh contribution of distinguished Americans. The monumental scholarly study, the *Dictionary of American Biography,* restricted to biographical data concerning America's deceased outstanding leaders, includes 328 people of Welsh extraction and perhaps some others with Welsh names about whom ethnic origin is lacking but who may have been of Welsh blood. Of the 328 listed as being definitely Welsh, forty-eight were immigrants, twenty-six children of immigrants, twenty-nine grandchildren of immigrants, and the remaining two hundred and twenty-five of Welsh stock. Broken down these include four presidents of the United States, thirty governors, twenty-two United States Senators, nineteen leading jurists, twenty-seven other high public officials, thirty-nine ministers of the gospel, sixteen physicians, three composers, twenty engineers and inventors, seventeen scientists, seven educators, ten artists, five actors, twenty-one business and industrial leaders, fifteen scholars, thirty-seven military leaders, eleven authors, and twenty-two miscellaneous. Surely this is no mean record for an ethnic group of the size of the Welsh! In addition, many distinguished Americans of the contemporary period not included in the *Dictionary of American Biography* can be added to swell this list to even greater magnitude. If and when new supplements of the dictionary make their appearance they will include these people.

A full listing of these distinguished Americans as well as others, who in the opinion of the author have acquired prominence, will be found in the Appendix of this book. At this point, however, it might be helpful to list some of these well-known American figures. Presidents Thomas Jefferson, James Monroe, Abraham Lincoln, and Calvin Coolidge; chief justices, John Marshall and Charles Evans Hughes; secretaries of state Daniel Webster and William H. Seward; generals Winfield Scott Hancock, Jeb Stuart, George Catlett Marshall, and Daniel Morgan; Robert Morris, financier of the American Revolution; Jefferson Davis, president of the Confederacy; the explorers, Meriwether Lewis and Henry M. Stanley; the diplomats, Gouverneur Morris and Joseph E. Davies; labor leaders, John L. Lewis and William Green, the authors, William Dean Howells, Henry Demarest Lloyd, Jack London, Ben Ames Williams, and Edgar Lee Masters; the architect, Frank Lloyd Wright; the painter, Arthur Bowen Davies; frontiersman, Daniel Boone; inventors, David Rittenhouse and Oliver Evans; Francis Asbury, first Methodist Bishop of America; Nicholas Murray Butler, president of Columbia University; Norman Thomas, the Socialist leader; Lowell Thomas, the radio commentator; Edward Johnson, director of the Metropolitan opera; Alec Templeton, the blind pianist; Ray Milland,

Allen Jones, and Bob Hope, Hollywood actors; Thomas L. Thomas, the concert singer; Lawrence Langner, the playright; Arthur H. Hopkins, the dramatic producer; David Wark Griffith, pioneer photoplay producer; United States Senators, Walter F. George, James Duff, and Homer E. Capehart; and the leading business and industrial figures, John Pierpont Morgan, Benjamin Fairless, and Gwilym Alexander Price. These are merely the names of those who are familiar to most Americans, but in a sense they represent a cross-section of Welsh blood and talent in American leadership. A cursory examination of the Appendix will reveal to what a degree this list can be broadened in the various fields of human activity.

The Welsh because of their highly religious and highly musical interests naturally made their strongest impact culturally upon America in these fields. Wherever they appeared in numbers in the new American environment religion and music were strengthened. And to all extents and purposes, these were the only cultural fields in which the Welsh influence was considerable.

In respect to religion, the coming of Welshmen into any given area meant a strengthening of the church-minded population. In the case of many of the frontier regions wherein they settled, the Welsh were responsible for holding the first religious services of the area as well as the building of the first churches. In this respect, the Welsh contribution to the cause of law and order was overwhelmingly significant; particularly was this true of the California gold fields and the Rocky Mountain area. In respect to religion, too, the arrival of Welsh immigrants strengthened the cause of the Congregational, Baptist, and Presbyterian denominations. An examination of the history of the Baptists and Congregationalists of Pennsylvania and Ohio will reveal that Welsh immigrants renewed the strength of the two denominations and practically reestablished Congregationalism in Pennsylvania. Elsewhere in Wisconsin, Iowa, and the mid-west, Welsh churches were frequently the oldest established in all three denominations.

Significant in the Welsh contribution to the religious development of America was the fact that in the Pennsylvania mine fields and in certain other industrial areas, the Welsh were the only strong Protestant element among the thousands of immigrants who flocked into those areas. Whereas these others strengthened the Roman Catholic Church for the most part, the Welsh strengthened the cause of Protestantism in these same areas, and because of their ardent support of their creeds naturally tended to be in the forefront in the defense of Protestantism. Their ardent leadership of Protestantism in such areas tended to identify "Welsh" and "Protestant" to such an extent in the minds of many of the so-called newer nationalities that any Protestant church (such as a

German Lutheran) would be referred to as a "Welsh" church by many of the less discerning newer immigrants. It follows that the Welsh, with their highly puritanical and evangelical background and highly democratic control over the administration of their own churches, should hardly approve of the highly mystical, ceremonial, and authoritarian Roman Catholic faith of many of the newer nationalities that settled among them in the industrial regions. This contrast of background meant that most Welsh-Americans looked askance at Roman Catholicism. Many shared the anti-Catholic feeling of American Protestants generally during the nineteenth century. Balancing this, however, was the ingrained love of democracy of the Welsh and their fanatical devotion to the right of freedom of religion. They could be counted upon to spring to the defense of religion and remind their more zealous brethren that there should be no countenancing of interference with the rights of religious freedom.

It follows, too, that the Welsh because of the same evangelistic background would be in the forefront of the drives against slavery, for temperance and eventually prohibition in respect to the sale of alcoholic liquors, and in defense of strict observance of the Sabbath. They found the "continental Sunday" celebration ideas of their immigrant neighbors quite distasteful, and could be found, therefore, leading the drive against allowing Sunday movies, Sunday baseball, and horror of horrors, Sunday drinking, in the twentieth century. The fact that Pennsylvania for many years had none of these, and that this same Pennsylvania contains the largest Welsh population in America may be just coincidence, and although it would be an exaggeration to claim that the Welsh were responsible for this, it is certainly very true that they played a strong role in spearheading the drive to keep these desecrations of the Sabbath from materializing for a great many years.

In respect to music, the Welsh were likewise a strengthening factor wherever they settled in America. The arrival of Welsh in the area often introduced music in a serious way for the first time. The amazing gift of choral singing enjoyed by the Welsh soon made their little chapels missions of musical culture in the midst of an otherwise sterile environment from the musical standpoint, and when in time the inevitable eisteddfod made its appearance, some of these places became music-minded for the first time in their existence. It follows that the Welsh should find places quickly as teachers of music, choir directors, and as members of choirs in many of the larger non-Welsh congregations. Although few of these ever reached the stage of greatness as concert artists or musicians of national reputation, many were to be found teaching the fundamentals and rudiments of this art and rendering entertainment on a modest yet competent scale for their respective American communities.

Music was dear to the Welsh heart. Supporting it with a might, and propagandizing upon its behalf, became one of the chief influences of the Welsh people upon the American population among whom they settled. In the opinion of many music-minded Americans, it is to be regretted that Welsh immigration was not greater and its distribution more widespread. Had such been the case, America would have been the richer in its musical appreciation. As indicated in a previous chapter, the Welsh Gymanfa Ganu, or gathering for song, may prove to be the one Welsh cultural institution to find a permanent place in the life of America.

In time, the Welsh developed a keen interest in politics. As in the case of their Irish kinsmen who shared this interest, most of them were English speakers. For certain of the Welsh, the fields of politics offered an opportunity to advance oneself quickly. That they quickly became superb politicians is a matter of record. Many of the Welsh became the active political leaders of the Republican Party, particularly in the Pennsylvania mining communities. To the Welsh goes the credit of being the first to organize the so-called all-nationality slates of candidates for political office (a Welshman, a Pole, a Yankee, a Slovak, and say a German-American, all running for different posts). Presumably the Welsh did this to make up for their lack of numbers operating on the principle: better to share and win, rather than not win at all! From the standpoint of realistic politics it worked. The Welsh-supported slate usually won. Numerous Welsh-Americans held and still hold political office, not only on the modest local level, but on the state and national level as well. The honor roll of governors, United States senators, and federal and other important officials of Welsh extraction is a long and distinguished one, and the Welsh contribution to American political leadership an exceedingly important one. (See Appendix)

In respect to politics as in the case of their other interests, what the Welsh organized, they organized well. To the extent that what they organized fitted into the American pattern, they were successful. To the extent that certain of these, too intimately associated with their distinctive culture and traditions, did not, the Welsh failed in the long run in the face of the strong forces working for Americanization.

Nevertheless, today, some three centuries after the coming of John Myles and his party in 1663, Welsh culture and traditions continue to live on in twentieth century America. It is represented by the 116-year old *Y Drych,* the Welsh-American newspaper, and through Welsh services in churches in New York, Utica, Philadelphia, Detroit, Chicago, and Oakland. It is represented, too, by the twenty colonial Welsh churches (six Episcopalian, eight Baptist, two Presbyterian, and four Quaker meetings) which still carry on in the spirit of their Welsh founders, as well as by some seventy-six Congregational, sixty-eight Presbyterian, and thirty-four Baptist churches, all founded by post-Revolutionary War immigrants, and all cognizant of their Welsh origins. Cognizance of their Welsh origins still holds together the one hundred and twenty-seven year old Welsh Congregational Association of Ohio, and the one hundred and twelve year old Welsh Baptist Association of Northeastern Pennsylvania.

Consciousness of their Welsh heritage is reflected in the continued existence of the Welsh national fraternal order, the Order of American True Ivorites with its five lodges. In fact, the twentieth century has witnessed a type of renaissance of interest in their Welsh heritage upon the part of many Welsh-Americans. This is revealed in the organization of the large musical society, the National Gymanfa Ganu Association of the United States and Canada, and the national women's society, the Women's Welsh Clubs of America with its forty-eight branches. Some fourteen other women's organizations and some fifty men's societies, most organized in recent years, also reflect this trend. Pride in the achievements of their ancestors from the land of poetry and song thus still lingers on in the hearts of present-day Welsh-Americans.

And so the story of Americans from Wales comes to an end. Unless a new wave of immigration from Wales starts in anew (and this appears very unlikely), it is only a matter of time before the last of our present Welsh-American population disappears into the great body of the American people. The old Welsh churches have become Americanized; the Welsh language survives in only a few isolated places among the older generation of Welsh immigrants and soon it, too, will disappear.

When these things occur, the memory of cherished ancestors, their devotion to democracy, music, and the Christian faith, and the contributions of these people to every field of American activity will remain. The record is a noble one, the contribution of the people of one of Europe's smallest countries to the development of our own United States of America. It is part of the all-over pattern of the immigrant contribution to American civilization.

APPENDIX

COLONIAL CHURCHES FOUNDED BY WELSH IMMIGRANTS
(All extant as of 1967)

Baptist

Swansea, Mass., 1663
Pennepek, Pa., 1688
Iron Hill, Del., 1703
Brandywine, Pa., 1715
Tredyffrin, Great Valley, Pa., 1715
Montgomery, Pa., 1719
Tulpehoken, Pa., 1738 (now located in Reading, Pa.)
Welsh Neck, S. C., 1738
First Church, Philadelphia, Pa., 1746

Episcopal

St. David's, Radnor, Pa., 1700
Trinity, Oxford, Pa., 1711
St. James, Perkiomen, Pa., 1715
St. Peter's, Great Valley, Pa., 1720
Bangor, Churchtown, Pa., 1733
St. Thomas, Morgantown, Pa., 1756

Presbyterian

Pencader, Glascow, Del., 1710
Great Valley, Pa., 1714

Quaker Meetings

Haverford, Pa., 1682
Merion, Pa., 1682
Radnor, Pa., 1682
Gwynedd, Pa., 1700

CHURCHES FOUNDED BY THE WELSH IN THE
POST-COLONIAL PERIOD

Listed below by state and county are the respective churches or congregations founded by the Welsh immigrants or their children during the period 1776-1967. Churches still in existence are italicized as are the names of the places where they are located. The figures following the names of the states indicate the number of churches founded within those states and the number still existing. In most instances those listed as Welsh Presbyterian were founded as Welsh Calvinistic-Methodist churches. They changed their names after the merger of the Welsh Calvinistic-Methodist denomination with the Presbyterian Church in the United States in 1919.

Data on these churches was obtained from the respective denominational yearbooks, histories of the denominations and churches, the various association or gymanva records, Welsh-American periodicals, and from questionaires sent out by the author to the respective churches. In compiling this data, mistakes in respect to the dates can occur. The author hopes that he has been able to keep these to a minimum.

California (6 and 2)

> Brandy City, Sierra Co., Welsh Presbyterian (1857-1865?)
> Camptonville, Yuba Co., Welsh Presbyterian (1857-1865?)
> *Los Angeles, Welsh Presbyterian,* 1888
> *Oakland, Welsh Presbyterian,* 1889
> San Francisco, St. David's Presbyterian (1852-1961)
> Yorktown, Toulumne Co., Welsh Union Church (1849-1870?)

Colorado (4 and 0)

> Denver, Welsh Presbyterian (1886-1929)
> Erie, Weld Co., Welsh Presbyterian (1882-1900?)
> Lafayette, Boulder Co., Welsh Presbyterian (1909-1918?)
> Russell Gulch, Gilpin Co., Welsh Union Church (1885)

Idaho (1 and 0)

> Twin Falls, Welsh Presbyterian (fl. 1880's)

Illinois (13 and 1)

    Apple River, Jo Daviess Co., Welsh Presbyterian (1854-1860?)
    Big Rock, Kane Co., Welsh Congregational (1852-1880?)
    Braceville, Grundy Co.:
        Welsh Baptist (1850-1887)
        Welsh Congregational (1850?-1900?)
    Braidwood, Will Co., Welsh Baptist (1878-1886)

    Chicago:
        Bethany Wesleyan Methodist (1850?-1900)
        Hebron Welsh Presbyterian, 1845
        Humboldt Park Welsh Union Church (1888-1954)
        Sardis Welsh Congregational (1880-1902)
        Southside Welsh Congregational (1894-1920?)
        Southside Welsh Presbyterian (1894-1958)
            (merged with Hebron Welsh Presbyterian)
        West Pullman Welsh Presbyterian (1893-1910)
    Streator, La Salle Co., Welsh Congregational (1882-1900)

Indiana (1 and 0)

    Gas City, Grant Co., Welsh Presbyterian (1890?-1910?)

Iowa (28 and 8)

    Carroll County: Templeton, Welsh Congregational (1876-1914)
    Clay County: Linn Grove Vicinity
        Peniel Welsh Presbyterian (1891-1907)
        Welsh Baptist (1875?-1890?)
        Zion Welsh Presbyterian (1873-1901)
    Howard County:
        Foreston, Welsh Presbyterian (1867-1923)
        Lime Springs Welsh Presbyterian, 1876
        Proscairon, Welsh Presbyterian (1877-1882)
        Saratoga, Welsh Presbyterian (1887-1893)
    Iowa County:
        Welsh Prairie, Welsh Presbyterian (1868-1906)
        Williamsburg,
            Welsh Congregational, 1856
            Welsh Presbyterian, 1869
    Johnson County: *Iowa City, Welsh Congregational,* 1846
    Louisa County:
        Columbus Junction,
            Salem Presbyterian, 1859
            Welsh Congregational, 1845
        Cotter, Bethel Presbyterian, 1880?

Mahaska County:
 Beacon, Welsh Congregational (1865-1916)
 Carbonado, Welsh Presbyterian (1884-1901)
 Given,
  Welsh Congregational, 1875
  Welsh Presbyterian (1878-1900)
Monroe County:
 Georgetown, Welsh Congregational (1863-1884)
 Hiteman, Welsh Congregational (1895-1930)
 Postville, Welsh Presbyterian (1881-1925)
Montgomery County:
 Wales,
  Gomer Congregational (1872-1943)
  Welsh Baptist (1870?-1880)
  Welsh Presbyterian (1874-1921)
Polk County:
 Des Moines, Moriah Congregational (1878-1890?)
 Flint Creek, Welsh Congregational (1851-1889)
 Keb, Welsh Congregational (1895-1909)

Kansas (13 and 4)
Brown County: Hiawatha, Welsh Baptist (fl. 1880's)
Lyon County:
 Coal Creek, Peniel Congregational (1888-1920)
 Emporia,
  Salem Presbyterian (1869-1934)
  Sardis Congregational (1871-1900?)
  Second Congregational, 1868
  Second Presbyterian, 1871
  Welsh Baptist (1884-1900?)
 Reading, Welsh Congregational (1871-1889)
Osage County:
 Arvonia (vic. Barclay),
  Welsh Congregational (1869-1920?)
  Welsh Presbyterian, 1878
 Osage City,
  Welsh Congregational (1876-1922)
  Welsh Presbyterian (1877-1920?)
Riley County: *Bala, Welsh Presbyterian,* 1872

Maryland (2 and 2)
Frostburg, Allegany Co.,
  Welsh Congregational, 1873
  Welsh Memorial Baptist, 1868

Michigan (1 and 1)
  Detroit, Welsh Presbyterian, 1853; reorganized 1919

Minnesota (23 and 9)
  Blue Earth County:
    Butternut Valley,
        Bethel Presbyterian, 1867
        Carmel Presbyterian, 1867
        Goshen Congregational (1876-1891)
        Salem Congregational (1855-1882)
        Salem Presbyterian, 1869
    Cambria,
        First Presbyterian, 1920
        Horeb Presbyterian (1856-1942)
        Salem Congregational, 1853
    Custer,
        Bethel Congregational (1875-1927)
        Salem Congregational (1893-1895)
    Judson Township, Jerusalem Presbyterian, 1858
    Lake Crystal, Welsh Presbyterian, 1889
    Mankato, First Presbyterian, 1865
    South Bend:
        Welsh Congregational (1859-1901)
        Welsh Wesleyan-Methodist (1860?-1880?)
        Zion Presbyterian (1856-1937)
  Fillmore County: Bristol Grove, Welsh Presbyterian (1867-1935)
  LaSueur County:
    Big Woods Settlement,
        Elim Presbyterian (1860-1937)
        Sharon Presbyterian (1856-1923)
  Lyon County:
    Garvin, Welsh Congregational, 1891
    Tracy,
        Bethel Congregational (1872-1891)
        Salem Presbyterian (1893-1935)
  Minneapolis, Welsh Presbyterian (1881-1948)

Missouri (12 and 4)
  Carroll County: Plymouth (Low Gap) Welsh Presbyterian (1877-1900?)
  Johnson County: Valley, Welsh Congregational (1867-1880)
  Livingston County:
    Dawn,
        Welsh Congregational, 1865

Welsh Baptist (1870?-1950)
Welsh Presbyterian (1871-1910?)
Macon County:
Bevier,
Welsh Congregational, 1865
Welsh Baptist, 1865
New Cambria,
Welsh Baptist (1870-1941)
Welsh Congregational, 1866
Brush Creek Presbyterian (1878-1900?)
Marion County: Palmyra, Welsh Presbyterian (1878-1900?)
Randolph County: Huntsville, Welsh Presbyterian (1877-1900?)

Montana (1 and 0)
Butte, Welsh Presbyterian (1902-1947)

Nebraska (7 and 3)
Blue Springs, Gage Co., Welsh Presbyterian (1880-1900?)
Carroll, Wayne Co.,
Bethany Presbyterian, 1886
Zion Congregational, 1891
Norden, Keyapaha Co., Welsh Presbyterian (1885-1900?)
Omaha, Welsh Presbyterian (1881-1893)
Postville, Platte Co., Welsh Presbyterian (1881-1925)
Wymore, Gage Co., Welsh Presbyterian, 1909

New York (72 and 18)
Cattaraugus County:
Fairview, Welsh Congregational (1846-1900)
Freedom,
Ebenezer Baptist (1843-1919)
Bethel Baptist (1895-1919)
Merged to form
Freedom Baptist, 1919
Sandusky, Salem Presbyterian (1852-1920)
Chemung County: Elmira, Welsh Congregational (1874-1880)
Herkimer County:
Ilion, Welsh Presbyterian (1850-1935)
Newport, Salem Presbyterian (1842-1860)
Lewis County:
Collinsville, Welsh Presbyterian (1846-1900?)
Gomer Flats, Welsh Presbyterian (1842-1850)
Tug Hill,
Welsh Congregational (1843-1886)
Zion Presbyterian (1846-1881)

Turin, Welsh Congregational (1861-1886)
Valley, Welsh Presbyterian (1842-1849)
Madison County:
Farmersville, Siloam Congregational (1856-1900?)
Nelson,
Welsh Congregational, 1850
Welsh Presbyterian (1855-1932)
New York City:
Welsh Baptist (1807-1813)
Welsh Baptist Tabernacle (11th Street Church) (1833-1874)
Welsh Congregational, 1801 (inactive)
Welsh Presbyterian, 1826
Welsh Wesleyan Methodist (1850-1880?)
Oneida County:
Alder Creek, Bethel Congregational, 1839
Bridgewater, Bethel Presbyterian (1851-1900)
Bordwell, Baptist (1807-1927)
Deerfield,
Bryn Mawr Presbyterian (1841-1870)
Welsh Congregational (1831-1898)
East Steuben, Penymyndd Congregational (1831-1898)
Enlli near Remsen, Welsh Presbyterian, 1848
Floyd,
Camroden Presbyterian (originally Congre.), 1834
Welsh Congregational (1843-1920)
Welsh Presbyterian (1839-1900?)
Frankfurt Hill near Utica, Presbyterian (1849-1920)
French Road, Hebron Presbyterian (1828-1928)
Holland Patent,
Welsh Congregational, 1842
Welsh Presbyterian (1840-1905)
Jamesville, Welsh Congregational (1865-1875)
Marcy,
Bethany Congregational (1840-1913)
Rehoboth Presbyterian (1848-1920)
Nant near Remsen, Welsh Presbyterian (1928-1944)
New Hartford, Zion Presbyterian (no dates)
New York Mills, Welsh Congregational, 1847
Ninety-Six near Prospect, Congregational (1845-1889)
Oriskany, Welsh Presbyterian (1850-1900)
Prospect, Welsh Congregational (1856-1946)
Quaker Hill, Welsh Presbyterian (1846-1900?)

Remsen,
    First Baptist, 1831
    First Presbyterian, 1831
    Welsh Congregational (1838-1944)
    Welsh Wesleyan Methodist (1850?-1870?)
Rome,
    Welsh Congregational (1851-1927)
    Bethel Presbyterian, 1841
Salisbury, Welsh Presbyterian (1855-1865)
Sixty-Six, Welsh Presbyterian (1841-1900?)
Steuben,
    Penycaerau Presbyterian (1824-1907)
    Penygraig Presbyterian (1827-1935)
    Welsh Baptist (1880-1893)
    Welsh Congregational (1804-1946)
Trenton, Welsh Congregational (1854-1906)
Utica,
    Bethesda Congregational (now *Plymouth-Bethesda*), 1802
    Moriah Presbyterian, 1830
    Welsh Baptist (1801-1899)
    Welsh Wesleyan-Methodist (1850-1918)
Waterville, Welsh Congregational (1852-1910?)
Webster Hill, Welsh Presbyterian (1832-1920)
Otsego County:
Plainfield,
    Welsh Congregational (1861-1941)
    Welsh Presbyterian (1855-1900?)
St. Lawrence County: *Richville, Welsh Congregational,* 1853
Washington County:
Granville,
    Welsh Congregational, 1873
    Peniel Presbyterian, 1873
Middle Granville,
    Welsh Congregational (1860-1886)
    Welsh Presbyterian, 1853

Ohio (125 and 24)
  Allen County: *Gomer, Welsh Congregational,* 1835
  Athens County:
  Gloucester,
    Welsh Baptist (1870?-1937)
  Belmont County:
  Martin's Ferry, Etnaville Congregational (1876-1944)
  Maynard, Welsh Congregational (1884-1886)

Butler County:
    Fort Recovery, Pisgah Congregational (1870-1892)
    Shandon (Paddy's Run), Welsh Congregational, 1803
Carroll County:
    Dell Roy, Welsh Baptist (1885-1895)
    Sherodsville, Welsh Congregational (1887-1924)
Coshocton County: Coshocton, Welsh Presbyterian (1873-1900?)
Cuyahoga County:
    Cleveland,
        Jones Road Congregational, 1858
        Newburgh Welsh Presbyterian (1863-1906)
        St. Clair St. Presbyterian (1873-1910?)
        Westminster-Welsh Presbyterian (1903-1960)
        Westside Congregational (1871-1901)
Delaware County:
    Delaware, Welsh Congregational (1842-1888)
    Radnor,
        Welsh Congregational, 1853
        Welsh Presbyterian (1849-1900?)
    South Radnor, Troedrhiwdalar Congregational (1839-1918)
Franklin County:
    Brown Township (near Hilliard), Welsh Congregational (1850-1890)
    Columbus,
        Miami Avenue Presbyterian, 1849
        Washington Avenue Congregational (1837-1943)
Gallia County:
    Bethelem, Welsh Baptist (1870?-1883)
    Centerville,
        Ebenezer Baptist (1838-1885)
        Welsh Congregational (1859-1921)
        Welsh Presbyterian, 1840
    Justice, Welsh Baptist (1875-1913)
    Siloam, Welsh Congregational (1860-1946)
    Tynrhos, Welsh Congregational, 1841
    Wales,
        Ebenezer Baptist (no dates)
        Nebo Congregational, 1855
Hamilton County:
    Cincinnati,
        May Street Presbyterian, 1832
        Welsh Congregational (1840-1952)

Hocking County:
    New Straitsville,
        Welsh Baptist (1870-1900?)
        Welsh Congregational (1879-1903)
Jackson County:
    Brush Creek, Nebo Presbyterian (1867-1900?)
    Coalport, Welsh Presbyterian (1845-1900?)
    Coaltown, Welsh Presbyterian (1881-1910?)
    Glen Roy, Welsh Congregational (1885-1910)
    Jackson, Welsh Presbyterian (1880-1934)
    Jackson vicinity, Zoar Presbyterian, 1841
    Mount Carmel, Welsh Congregational (1848-1900?)
    Oak Hill,
        Welsh Baptist (1860?-1901)
        Welsh Congregational, 1841
        Welsh Presbyterian, 1850

    Oak Hill rural vicinity,
        Bethania Presbyterian (1846-1895)
        Beth'el Presbyterian, 1841
        Bethesda Presbyterian (1856-1880)
        Bryn Hyfryd Congregational, 1900
        Horeb Presbyterian, 1839
        Moriah Presbyterian, 1835
        Peniel Presbyterian, 1870
        Salem Presbyterian (1862-1880?)
        Sardis Presbyterian, 1843
        Tabor Presbyterian (1848-1866)
    Portland,
        Welsh Baptist (1860-1883)
        Welsh Congregational (1841-1879)
    Wellston, Welsh Congregational (1893-1897)
Lawrence County:
    Ironton,
        Welsh Congregational (1854-1891)
        Welsh Presbyterian (1853-1890?)
Licking County:
    Granville,
        Welsh Congregational (1841-1921)
        Welsh Presbyterian (1838-1902)
        Welsh Presbyterian (1876-1890)
    Lockport near Newark,
        First Congregational (1841-1918)
        Welsh Presbyterian (1838-1914)

Welsh Hills,
  Sharon Presbyterian (1835-1880?)
  Welsh Baptist, 1808
Mahoning County:
 Crabcreek, Welsh Congregational (1859-1895)
 Vienna, Welsh Baptist (fl. 1880's)
 West Austinville, Welsh Congregational (1873-1897)
 Youngstown,
  Elm Street Congregational, 1846
  Walnut Street Baptist (1846-1919)
  Welsh Presbyterian (1867-1917)
Meigs County:
 Carr's Run, Welsh Baptist (1860?-1879)
 Minersville,
  Welsh Congregationalist (1853-1900)
  Welsh Presbyterian (1864-1900?)
 Pomeroy,
  Welsh Baptist (1865?-1881)
  Welsh Congregational (1843-1892)
  Welsh Presbyterian (1872-1890?)
 Portland,
  Welsh Baptist (1860?-1883)
  Welsh Congregational (1841-1879)
Perry County:
 Shawnee,
  Welsh Congregational (1873-1918)
  Welsh Presbyterian (1877-1913)
Portage County:
 Palmyra,
  Welsh Baptist (1850?-1883)
  Welsh Congregational (1835-1914)
  Welsh Presbyterian (1835-1928)
 Wayland,
  Welsh Baptist, 1860?
  Welsh Congregational, 1850
Stark County:
 Alliance,
  Welsh Congregational (1867-1924)
  Welsh Presbyterian (1866-1920)
 East Greenville,
  Welsh Baptist (1870?-1920)
  Welsh Congregational (1893-1940)
 Pigeon Run, Welsh Baptist (1870?-1881)

Summit County:
 Akron, Welsh Congregational (1893-1946)
 Hametown (Sherman) Welsh Congregational (1881-1897)
 Tallmadge, Welsh Congregational (1847-1940)
 Thomaston, Welsh Baptist (1860?-1883)
Trumbull County:
 Brookfield (near Hubbard),
  Welsh Congregational, 1866
  Welsh Presbyterian (1872-1886)
 Coalburg,
  Welsh Baptist (1870?-1900)
  Welsh Congregational (1866-1897)
 Church Hill,
  Welsh Baptist (1870?-1900)
  Welsh Presbyterian (1869-1909)
 Girard,
  Welsh Baptist (1870?-1901)
  Welsh Congregational (1888-1918)
 Hubbard,
  Welsh Baptist (1860?-1898)
  Welsh Congregational (1856-1918)
 Mineral Ridge,
  Welsh Baptist (1870?-1920)
  Welsh Congregational (1865-1932)
 Niles,
  Second Welsh Presbyterian (? -1923)
  Welsh Baptist (1860?-1911)
  Welsh Congregational (1843-1903)
  Welsh Presbyterian (1870-1915)
 Weathersfield,
  Welsh Baptist (1860?-1882)
  Welsh Presbyterian (1856-1927)
 Wheatland,
  Welsh Baptist (1870-1883)
  Welsh Presbyterian (1872-1910?)
Tuscarawas County:
 Canal Dover, Welsh Congregational (1866-1924)
 Dennison, Welsh Baptist (1870?-1883)
 Sugar Creek,
  Welsh Congregational (1853-1893)
  Welsh Presbyterian (1858-1922)

Van Wert County:
    Jonesville, Zion Presbyterian, 1858
    Venedocia,
        Presbyterian, (1895-1918)
        Salem Presbyterian, 1848
    Vendocia Vic.:
        Bethel Presbyterian (1890-1903)
        Horeb Presbyterian (1864-1920)

Oregon (1 and 1)
  Clackamas County:
    Beaver Creek Welsh Congregational, 1884

Pennsylvania (190 and 79)
  Allegheny County:
    Homestead, Welsh Baptist, 1876
    Pittsburgh,
        Arlington Avenue Congregational, 1868
        Birmingham Presbyterian (1856-1865)
        Carmel Presbyterian, 1833
        Chatham Street Baptist (1831-1952)
        First Congregational (1824-1924)
        Puritan Congregational, 1892
  Armstrong County:
    Brady's Bend, Welsh Congregational (1841-1894)
    Sugar Creek, Welsh Presbyterian (1841-1860?)
  Bradford County: *Neath, Welsh Congregational,* 1833
  Cambria County:
    Beulah, *Welsh Baptist,* 1797 (now in Ebensburg)
    Ebensburg,
        Bethany Congregational, 1865
        North Congregational (1830-1912)
        Salem Presbyterian (1839-1923)
        Welsh Baptist, 1797
        Welsh Congregational, 1797
        Welsh Presbyterian (1841-1860?)
    Johnstown,
        Emmanuel Baptist, 1896
        First Congregational, 1854
        Memorial Baptist, 1920
        Welsh Baptist (1852-1920)
        Welsh Presbyterian (1854-1928)
        Welsh Wesleyan Methodist (1854-1873)
  Carbon County:
    Audenried,

Welsh Baptist (1867-1917)
Horeb Congregational, 1865
(now located in Hazle Village, Luzerne County)
Coleraine (Junedale), Welsh Congregational, 1837
Lansford,
First Baptist, 1872
First Congregational, 1850
Second Congregational, 1881
Summit Hill,
Welsh Baptist (1850-1918)
Welsh Congregational (1851-1864)
Clearfield County:
Brisbin,
Welsh Baptist (1876-1896)
Welsh Congregational (1876-1889)
Houtzdale,
Welsh Baptist (1870?-1883)
Welsh Congregational (1867-1891)
Welsh Presbyterian (1880-1890?)
Columbia County: Bloomsburg, Welsh Baptist (1853-1870)
Dauphin County: *Wiconisco, Welsh Baptist,* 1868
Indiana County: Green Township, Welsh Presbyterian (1840-1893)
Jefferson County:
Horatio,
Welsh Baptist (1892-1910)
Welsh Congregational (1889-1912)
Lindsey,
Clayville Baptist (1897-1910)
Welsh Congregational (1891-1924)
Lackawanna County:
Blakely, Welsh Presbyterian (1856-1923)
Carbondale,
Welsh Baptist (1830-1898)
Welsh Congregational (1831-1930)
Welsh Presbyterian (1832-1860)
Jermyn,
Welsh Baptist (1875-1895)
Welsh Congregational (1869-1920)
Welsh Presbyterian (1872-1877)
Mayfield, Welsh Baptist (1875-1910)
Moosic, Welsh Presbyterian (1873-1890)
Old Forge, Nebo Congregational, 1887
Olyphant,

Bethel Congregational, 1859
Welsh Baptist, 1859
Welsh Presbyterian, 1870
Scranton,
    Bethania Presbyterian, 1856
    First Welsh Baptist, 1849
    First Welsh Presbyterian (1849-1860)
    Ebenezer Presbyterian (now *Hyde Park Presbyterian*),
       1863
    Dr. Jones Memorial Congregational, 1855
    Memorial Welsh Baptist (1864-1931)
    Puritan Congregational, 1889
    Trinity Congregational, 1947
       (formed through the merger of:
         First Welsh Congregational, 1857
         Plymouth Congregational, 1882
         Tabernacle Congregational, 1886
         all Welsh churches)
    West Market Street Baptist, 1864
Spring Brook,
    Welsh Baptist (1886-1889)
    Welsh Congregational, 1839
    Welsh Presbyterian (1839-1869)
Taylor,
    Welsh Baptist, 1869
    Welsh Congregational, 1870
    Welsh Presbyterian (1875-1890)
Lawrence County:
Newcastle,
    Welsh Baptist (1900?-1914)
    Welsh Congregational, 1894
Lehigh County:
Catasauqua, Bethel Congregational (1882-1915)
Slatington,
    Bethel Congregational, 1886
    First Baptist, 1861
    Welsh Congregational (1852-1870?)
    Welsh Presbyterian, 1847
Luzerne County:
Beaver Meadows,
    Welsh Congregational (1844-1896)
    Welsh Presbyterian (1838-1840)
Drifton,
    Welsh Baptist (1878-1890)

Welsh Congregational (1870-1896)
Gowen, Welsh Baptist (1884-1895)
Hazle Village, Horeb Congregational, 1865
Jeansville,
 Welsh Congregational (1866-1894)
 Welsh Presbyterian (1847-1860)
Upper Lehigh, Welsh Baptist (1867-1889)
Wyoming Valley:
Alden,
 Welsh Baptist (1884-1888)
 Welsh Congregational (1884-1894)
Ashley, Welsh Presbyterian (1882-1946)
Duryea, Welsh Congregational (1895-1901)
Edwardsville,
 Bethesda Congregational, 1886
 Dr. Edwards Memorial Congregational, 1868
 Immanuel Baptist, 1886
 Welsh Baptist, 1873
 Welsh Presbyterian, 1889
Hanover Township,
 Buttonwood Congregational, 1903
 Lynnwood Congregational, 1932
Glen Lyon, Welsh Congregational (1884-1915)
Nanticoke,
 Bethel Congregational, 1874
 First Baptist, 1877
 Moriah Congregational (1883-1952)
 Nebo Baptist, 1870
 Welsh Presbyterian (1883-1943)
Pittston,
 Welsh Baptist (1851-1930)
 Welsh Congregational (1847-1946)
 Welsh Presbyterian (1856-1943)
Plymouth,
 Ebenezer Baptist, 1878
 Pilgrim Congregational, 1886
 Welsh Baptist, 1868
 Welsh Congregational, 1857
 Welsh Presbyterian, 1889
Sugar Notch, Welsh Presbyterian, 1885
Wanamie,
 Welsh Baptist (1869-1878)
 Welsh Congregational (1867-1912)

Warrior Run,
    Welsh Baptist, 1883
    Welsh Congregational (1888-1903)
    Welsh Presbyterian, 1874
West Pittston, Congregational, 1883
Wilkes-Barre,
    Bethel Baptist, 1884
    First Welsh Baptist, 1868
    First Welsh Congregational (1869-1955)
    First Welsh Presbyterian, 1864
    Miner Congregational, 1868
    Miners Mills Presbyterian (1885-1897)
    Parsons Welsh Baptist, 1870
    Parsons Welsh Congregational (1871-1908)
    Puritan Congregational, 1885
    Second Welsh Congregational, 1883
    Second Welsh Presbyterian, 1880
    Tabernacle Baptist, 1897
    Welsh Wesleyan-Methodist (1888-1902)
        (later St. Andrews M.E.)
Mercer County:
    Farrell Welsh Congregational, 1902, and
    Sharon Welsh Congregational, 1854, now
    United Congregational, Farrell, 1953
    Sharon Welsh Baptist, 1869
Montour County:
    Danville,
        Welsh Baptist (1845-1910)
        Welsh Congregational (1840-1903)
        Welsh Presbyterian (1842-1890)
Northampton County:
    Bangor,
        Peniel Presbyterian, 1873
        Welsh Congregational (1872-1945)
        Welsh Wesleyan-Methodist (fl. 1870's)
    Wind Gap,
        Welsh Congregational, 1891
        Welsh Presbyterian, 1889
Northumberland County:
    Mount Carmel,
        Welsh Baptist (1872-1888)
        Welsh Congregational, 1870

Shamokin,
  Mt. Zion Congregational, 1860
  Welsh Baptist (1883-1885)
  Welsh Presbyterian (1865-1870)
Philadelphia, Girard Avenue-Welsh Presbyterian, 1892
Schuylkill County:
  Ashland,
    Welsh Baptist, 1857
    Welsh Congregational (1855-1899)
  Belmont,
    Welsh Baptist (1853-1876)
    Welsh Congregational (1833-1846)
  Coaldale,
    First Congregational (1870-1930)
    Second Congregational (1892-1919)
  Mahanoy City,
    Welsh Congregational, 1863
    Welsh Baptist, 1865
  Minersville,
    Welsh Baptist (1835-1920)
    Welsh Congregational, 1833
    Welsh Presbyterian (1832-1890)
  Pottsville,
    Welsh Baptist (1832-1896)
    Welsh Congregational (1851-1912)
    Welsh Presbyterian (1832-1890)
  Saint Clair,
    Welsh Baptist (1853-1900)
    Welsh Congregational (1845-1889)
    Welsh Presbyterian (1845-1890)
  Shenandoah,
    Calvary Baptist, 1882
    Welsh Baptist, 1867
    Welsh Congregational, 1866
    Welsh Presbyterian (1865-1870)
  Tamaqua, Welsh Congregational (1842-1889)
Susquehanna County:
  Clifford Township near Dundaff, Welsh Hill Congregational,
    1835
  Forest City,
    Welsh Baptist (1888-1890)
    Welsh Congregational (1891-1928)

Tioga County:
    Antrim,
        Welsh Baptist (1873-1880?)
        Welsh Congregational (1879-1894)
    Arnot,
        Welsh Baptist (1874-1895)
        Welsh Congregational (1877-1885?)
    Blossburg,
        First Congregational (1841-1921)
        Second Congregational (1886-1950)
        Welsh Baptist (1853-1870?)
    Charlestown near Wellsboro, Congregational (1840-1927)
    Morris Run,
        Welsh Baptist (1864-1896)
        Welsh Congregational (1864-1895)
Westmoreland County:
    Irwin Station,
        Welsh Baptist (1870?-1905)
        Welsh Congregational (1873-1889)
York County:
    Delta,
        Rehoboth Presbyterian, 1854
        Welsh Congregational (1856-1915)
        Welsh Wesleyan-Methodist (fl. 1850's)

South Dakota (8 and 1)
    Canova, Miner Co., Welsh Presbyterian (1883-1892)
    Ipswich, Edmunds Co., Welsh Presbyterian (1886-1888)
    Plana, Brown Co., Welsh Presbyterian (1882-1895?)
    Plankinton, Aurora Co., Welsh Presbyterian (1883-1895)
    Powell, Edmunds Co.,
        Welsh Congregational (1883-1900)
        Welsh Presbyterian, 1885
    Spain, Marshall Co., Welsh Presbyterian (1886-1900?)
    Winfred, Lake Co., Welsh Presbyterian (1881-1903)

Tennessee (2 and 1)
    Knoxville, Welsh Congregational (1869-1895)
    Soddy, Hamilton Co., Welsh Congregational, 1873

Vermont (7 and 2)
    Rutland County:
        Fair Haven,
            Welsh Congregational (1857-1948)
            Welsh Presbyterian (1859-1951)

Farnamsville, Welsh Presbyterian (1871-1932)
Poultney, Welsh Presbyterian, 1870?
South Poultney, Welsh Presbyterian, 1870?
West Pawlet,
    Welsh Congregational (1881-1941)
    Welsh Presbyterian (1879-1943)

Washington (2 and 0)
    Seattle, St. David's Presbyterian (1892-1956)
    Spokane, Welsh Presbyterian (1890?-1938)

West Virginia (2 and 0)
    Mason County:
        Hartford City, Welsh Baptist (1870-1880)
        Mason City,
            Welsh Baptist (1860?-1898)
            Welsh Presbyterian (1856-1870)

Wisconsin (84 and 17)
    Columbia County:
        Caledonia Township, Welsh Presbyterian (1847-1900?)
        Cambria,
            Olivet Presbyterian, 1852
            Welsh Congregational (1889-1900)
        Columbus City, First Presbyterian, 1866
        Columbus City vicinity,
            Bethel Presbyterian (1845-1931)
            Moriah Presbyterian, 1878
        Portage Prairie, Berea Presbyterian (1849-1900?)
        Proscairon, Welsh Presbyterian (1850-1900?)
        Randolph,
            Bethania Presbyterian, 1868
            First Congregational, 1847
            Pen Llan Congregational (1848-1877)
        Welsh Prairie,
            Berw Congregational (1857-1877)
            Blaen-y-cae Presbyterian (1844-1900?)
            Carmel Presbyterian (1851-1900?)
            Zion Presbyterian (1848-1921)
        Wales, Jerusalem Presbyterian, 1855
    Dodge County:
        Lake Emily, Welsh Presbyterian (1845-1917)
    Fond du Lac County:
        Rosendale, Welsh Congregational (1848-1928)

Green Lake County:
  Rock Hill, Salem Presbyterian (1846-1900?)
  Berlin,
        Welsh Baptist (1860?-1900?)
        Welsh Presbyterian (1855-1900?)
Iowa County:
  Barneveld,
        Bethel Presbyterian (1850-1885)
        Goshen Presbyterian (1858-1931)
        Welsh Congregational, 1847
  Dodgeville,
        Caesgby (Holyhead) Congregational (1873-1906)
        Plymouth Congregational (1848-1900?)
        Salem Baptist (1860-1892)
        Salem Presbyterian (1858-1900?)
        Sardis Baptist, 1852
        Welsh Congregational (1845-1917)
        Welsh Presbyterian (1844-1923)
  Picatonica,
        Carmel Presbyterian, 1854
        and Peniel Presbyterian, 1850, now
        United Church of Picatonica, 1963
        Mt. Zion Congregational (1871-1923)
        Welsh Baptist (1864-1882)
  Ridgeway or Hyde,
        Welsh Baptist (1875-1900)
        Welsh Congregational (1853-1888)
Jefferson County:
  Ixonia,
        Bethel Presbyterian (1866-1952)
        Welsh Congregational (1852-1926)
  Watertown, Emmet Congregational, 1846
La Crosse County:
  Bangor,
        Welsh Congregational (1855-1904)
        Welsh Presbyterian (1854-1917)
  Rockland,
        Bethel Presbyterian (1854-1924)
        Blaendyffryn Presbyterian (1854-1930)
        Welsh Congregational (1859-1908)
Milwaukee,
        Bay View Congregational (1871-1903)

Tabernacle Congregational (1857-1903)
Welsh Presbyterian (1847-1954)
Monroe County:
Cataract, Welsh Presbyterian (1866-1890)
Racine County:
Mount Pleasant, Welsh Presbyterian (1847-1900?)
Pike Grove, Welsh Congregational (1842-1913)
Racine,
Church of the Covenant, 1843
(formerly Tabernacle Presbyterian)
Plymouth Congregational, 1847
Sauk County: Spring Green, Welsh Congregational (1850-1900)
Waukesha County:
Bark River,
Bethel Presbyterian (1859-1899)
Welsh Congregational (1860-1899)
Delafield, Welsh Congregational (1845-1900?)
Waukesha and vicinity,
Bethania Presbyterian (1849-1920?)
Bethesda Presbyterian, 1845
Bronyberllan Presbyterian (1842-1880?)
Lennon Presbyterian (1890-1920?)
Moriah Presbyterian (1860-1937)
Salem Presbyterian (1851-1878)
Tabernacle Congregational (1844-1923)
Zion Presbyterian (1868-1900?)
Zoar Presbyterian (1844-1897)
Waushara County:
Auroraville,
Berlin Coed Baptist (1850?-1892)
Berlin Coed Congregational (1849-1923)
Springwater Township,
Bethel Congregational (1857-1913)
Ebenezer Baptist (1872-1900?)
Tecca Presbyterian (1852-1860)
Wild Rose,
Horeb Presbyterian, 1907
Jerusalem Presbyterian (1859-1925)
Mt. Zion Presbyterian (1856-1860)
Nebo Congregational (1849-1900)
Zoar Presbyterian (1881-1908)

Winnebago County:
    Neenah,
        Sharon Presbyterian (1848-1900?)
        Welsh Congregational (1858-1902)
    Oshkosh,
        Plymouth Congregational, 1840
        Salem Baptist (1850?-1892)
        Salem Presbyterian (1855-1934)
    Pickett,
        El Dorado Township, *Peniel Presbyterian,* 1856
        Nekimi Township, *Bethesda Presbyterian,* 1848

SOME EXISTING WELSH SOCIETIES

National

> Order of American True Ivorites, 1848
> American Federation of Women's Welsh Clubs, 1912
> National Gymanfa Ganu Association, 1930

Men's Societies (open to both sexes in some cases)

> Welsh Society of Philadelphia, 1729
> St. David's Society of the State of New York, 1801
> St. David's Society of Utica, New York, 1849
> Cambrian Benevolent Society of Chicago, 1853
> St. David's Society of Cincinnati, 1865
> St. David's Society of Western New York, 1868
> St. David's Society of Racine and Vicinity, Wisconsin, 1887
> St. David's Society of Youngstown, 1890
> St. David's Society of Wyoming Valley (Wilkes-Barre), Pa., 1891
> Cambrian Association of Salt Lake City, 1892
> Cambrian Society of San Diego County, California, 1892
> Cymrodorian Associates of Boston, 1892
> Cymrodorian Society of California, 1894
> St. David's Society of Greater Kansas City, 1899
> Welsh American Society of Canton, Ohio, 1901
> St. David's Society of Milwaukee, 1904
> St. David's Society of Scranton, 1910
> St. David's Society of Baltimore, 1913
> Orpheus Choral Society, Wilkes-Barre, Pa., 1919
> St. David's Society of Oshkosh, Wisconsin, 1919
> Cambrian Society of Long Beach, California, 1921
> St. David's Society of Broome County, New York, 1921
> Welsh Cambrian Society of Rochester, New York, 1922
> St. David's Society of Washington, D.C., 1924
> Bangor Welsh Day Association, Bangor, Pa., 1930
> Beaver Valley Gymanfa Ganu Association, Aliquippa, Pa., 1931
> Heights St. David's Society, Wilkes-Barre, Pa., 1934
> Cambrian Society of Granville, Ohio, 1935
> Men's Welsh Society of Pittsburgh, 1937

Poultney Welsh Male Chorus, Poultney, Vermont, 1939
St. David's Society of Plymouth, Pa., 1941
St. David's Society of Albany, New York, 1942
Gymanfa Ganu Association of Steubenville, Ohio, 1945
St. David's Society of Schuylkill and Carbon Counties, Pa., 1946
St. David's Society of West Virginia, 1948
Welsh American Society of Southern California, 1948
Welsh Singing Society of Columbus, Ohio, 1948
Cambrian Society of New York City, 1950
Welsh Society of Knoxville, Tennessee, 1950
St. David's Society of Detroit
Gymanfa Ganu Association of Wisconsin
St. David's Society of Cleveland
Cambrian Society of Scranton
St. David's Society of Granite City, Illinois
St. David's Society of Lyon County, Kansas
St. David's Society of Pittston, Pa.
St. David's Society of Warrior Run, Pa.
St. David's Society of Schenectady, New York
St. David's Society of St. Petersburg, Florida
St. David's Society of Waukesha County, Wisconsin
St. David's Society of Allentown, Pa.
Cambrian Society of Palm Beach and Broward Counties, Fla.
St. David's Society of South Florida (Miami)
Welsh Singers Club of Buffalo, New York
Cambrian Society of Lake County, Indiana
Niagara Frontier Welsh Society, Niagara Falls, N. Y.
Summit Welsh Society, Akron, Ohio
Welsh Society of Greater Endicott, New York
Welsh Booster Club of Cleveland
Welsh Society of Cambria County, Pa.
Bethany Welsh Society, Bangor, Pa.
Cambrian Society of Delaware Valley, Pa.

Women's Societies

Welsh Women's Society of Lackawanna County (Scranton), Pa., 1920
Senior Cambrian Club, Plymouth, Pa., 1923
Senior Cambrian Club, Nanticoke, Pa., 1924
Senior Cambrian Club, Wilkes-Barre, Pa., 1924
Junior Cambrian Club, Wilkes-Barre, Pa., 1935
Junior Cambrian Club, Nanticoke, Pa., 1939

Druid Society of Oshkosh, Wisconsin
   (Daughters of Welsh Pioneers), 1939
Cambrian Club of West Pittston, Pa., 1949
Junior Cambrian Club, Plymouth, Pa.
Ladies Auxiliary, Welsh American Society, Canton, Ohio
Ladies Auxiliary, St. David's Society of Granite City, Ill.
Welsh Ladies Chorus, Cambria, Wisconsin
Welsh Ladies Aid Society, Spokane, Washington
Junior Welsh Women's Society of Lackawanna County (Scranton),
   Pa.
Cambrian Club of Allentown, Pa.
Cambrian Society of Phoenix, Arizona

Federation of Women's Welsh Clubs

Akron, Ohio, 1916
Akron (Bryn Mawr), Ohio, 1934
Aliquippa, Pa., 1931
Baltimore, 1925
Buffalo, 1923
Canton, Ohio, 1917
Carnegie, Pa.
Cleveland, 1911
Columbus, Ohio, 1917
Columbus (Cymry), Ohio, 1952
Deerfield, Ohio
Detroit, 1926
East Cleveland, Ohio, 1918
Farrell, Pa., 1919
Girard, Ohio, 1924
Harrisburg, Pa.
Homestead, Pa., 1919
Illinois (Chicago and vic.), 1955
Lakewood, Ohio
Loraine, Ohio, 1915
Mahanoy City, Pa., 1946
Martin's Ferry, W. Va., 1918
Massillon, Ohio, 1919
Massillon (Gwynette), Ohio, 1918
McKeesport, Pa.
Milwaukee, Wis.
Morgantown, W. Va., 1918
New Castle, Pa., 1918

New Kensington, Pa.
Newton Falls, Ohio, 1926
New York City, 1923
Niles, Ohio, 1916
Niles (Bronwyn), Ohio
Niles (Senior), Ohio, 1916
Niles (Cambria), Ohio, 1932
Philadelphia, 1923
Pittsburgh, 1919
Pottsville, Pa.
Radnor-Delaware, Ohio, 1946
Sharon, Pa.
Steubenville, Ohio
Utica, New York, 1953
Warren (Senior), Ohio, 1918
Warren (Metra Gwen), Ohio, 1933
Washington, D.C., 1926
Washington (Gwalia), D.C., 1945
West Cleveland, Ohio, 1922
Youngstown (Senior), Ohio, 1914
Youngstown (Glyn Dwr), 1932
Youngstown (Calon Lan), Ohio, 1950

Lodges of the Order of American True Ivorites

Madoc Lodge, Chicago, Ill. (male), 1892
Ceridwen Lodge, Rome, N. Y. (female), 1914
Eluned Lodge, Chicago, Ill. (female), 1914
Gwenfron Lodge, Utica, N. Y. (female), 1913
Martha Lodge, New Castle, Pa. (female), 1918

DISTINGUISHED WELSH AMERICANS

In compiling this list, the author has gone to great pains to include only those of definite Welsh extraction as indicated in his sources. There are hundreds of distinguished Americans with what are commonly accepted as Welsh surnames. Many of these may be of Welsh descent, but unless the source verified this, such persons were not included in his listings. In the case of the *Dictionary of American Biography* entries, the Welsh connection is usually mentioned in the biographical sketch. In some cases, where the Welsh connection is not mentioned, an ancestor, who is also listed in the *Dictionary* will provide the Welsh connection.

The author realizes that there are many other eminent Welsh-Americans that could be added to this list. He would gladly have added them if space permitted. With a few exceptions, he has limited his list to people whose biographical sketches appear in the standard reference works listed below.

Explanation of Abbreviations used in the listings

CAM   *The Cambrian* (the Welsh-American magazine)
CB   *Current Biography*
DAB   *Dictionary of American Biography*
DNB   *Dictionary of National Biography* (British)
DWB   *Dictionary of Welsh Biography*
NCAB   *National Cyclopedia of American Biography*
WWW   *Who Was Who in America,* 3 vols.
WWAm   *Who's Who in America*

Some Distinguished Immigrants

Beddoe, Daniel (1863-1937), concert tenor; teacher of music. *International Cyclopedia of Music and Musicians.*

Blackwell, Henry (1851-1928), bibliographer and printer of books in Welsh. DWB

Blythin, Edward (1884-   ), mayor of Cleveland, Ohio, 1941-43; judge, Cleveland Court of Common Pleas, 1949-

Bundy, George (1877-   ), Warren, Ohio, eisteddfod promoter; secretary of the National Gymanfa Ganu Association of the United States for over thirty-four years.

Chidlaw, Benjamin Williams (1811-1892), pioneer Welsh Congregational minister; missionary American Sunday School Union. CAM 1882, pp. 57-60; 1893, pp.1-6. DWB

Coke, Thomas (1747-1814), pioneer Methodist-Episcopal bishop. DAB

Courtney, William (ff. 1890's), concert tenor; pioneer Gilbert and Sullivan singer. CAM, 1895, pp. 193-95.

Davies, David (Dewi Emlyn) (1817-1888), Ohio Congregational minister; Welsh poet and historian. CAM, 1888, pp. 321-22. DWB

Davies, David Charles (1866-1928), naturalist; director, Field Museum of Natural History, Chicago, 1921-28. WWWI

Davies, David Lloyd (Dewi Glan Peryddon) (d. 1881), Welsh poet; baritone singer; and eisteddfod conductor. DWB

Davies, David Pryce (1870-1948), chief engineer, Allis-Chalmers Co.; honored for his application of science to the soil. NCAB, XXXVI, p. 89.

Davies, Edward (1827-1905), Congregational minister and editor of *Y Cenhadwr,* 1882-1901. CAM, 1905. DWB

Davies, Hywel (1858-1927), industrial mediator; mining engineer; U. S. Commissioner of Conciliation, Department of Labor, 1914-1919. WWWI

Davies, John Vipond (1826-1939), subaqueous engineer; builder of the Hudson River tunnels. NCAB XXIX, pp. 358-59.

Davies, Rachael Paynter (Rahel o Fon) (1851-1916), Baptist female preacher and one of America's first female evangelists. DWB

Davies, William J. (1848-19 ?), West Virginia coal operator. CAM, 1885, p. 198.

Davies, William Walter (1848-1922), Hebrew Scholar, Ohio Wesleyan University. CAM, 1898, pp. 521-23.

Davis, Daniel H. (1839-1914), Clay County, Indiana, coal operator and financier. NCAB, XVIII, pp. 402-3.

Davis, James J. (1873-1947), U. S. Secretary of Labor, 1921-30; U. S. Senator from Pennsylvania, 1930-45. WWWII

Easton, John (1625-1705), colonial Governor of Rhode Island, 1690-95; author, *A Narrative of the Causes Which Led to Philip's Indian War.* DAB

Easton, Nicholas (1593-1675), colonial Rhode Island leader; Governor of Rhode Island, 1672-73. DAB

Edwards, Daniel (1825-1901), Luzerne County, Pa. coal operator and mining engineer; Edwardsville, Pa. named in his honor. Harvey-Smith, *History of Wilkes-Barre,* V, p. 205.

Edwards, David (1816-1876), pioneer bishop, United Brethren in Christ. CAM, 1884, pp. 65-68.

Edwards, Henry Lee (1856-1947), Internationally known cotton broker of Dallas, Texas. NCAB, XXXVI, p. 313.

Edwards, Henry M. (1844-1925), Lackawanna County, Pa. jurist, 1893-1925; eisteddfod leader. CAM, 1889, pp. 129-30; 1894, p. 188.

Edwards, John (Eos Glan Twrch) (1806-1887), farmer and Welsh poet; cultural leader of Oneida County, N. Y. CAM, 1887, pp. 96-97. DWB

Edwards, Morgan (1722-1795), pioneer Baptist leader and one of the founders of Brown University. DAB

Edwards, Richard (1822-1908), Superintendent of Public Instruction of Illinois; professor at Wesleyan University of Illinois. WWWI

Edwards, Richard (Fl. 1840-1884), Baptist minister of Pottsville, Pa. and founder and editor of *Y Seren Orllewinol*, Welsh Baptist magazine. DWB

Edwards, Thomas Cynonfardd (1848-1927), Congregational minister; eisteddfod leader; dean of Welsh-American clergy. WWWI, DWB

Edwards, William Robert (1858-1921), Congregational minister; Welsh poet; and eisteddfod leader. DWB

Ellis, Morgan A. (1832-1901), Calvinistic-Methodist leader; editor of *Baner America*, Welsh-American newspaper. CAM, 1880, pp. 9-11. DWB

Ellis, Rowland (1650-1731), Pennsylvania Welsh Quaker leader and first settler of Bryn Mawr. DWB

Evans, Cadwallader (1664-1745), Quaker founder of Gwenedd, Pa. settlement; ancestor of Abraham Lincoln. DWB

Evans, Daniel (1866-1943), Congregational minister; professor of theology, Andover Newton Theological Seminary, 1931-43. WWWII

Evans, David (fl. early 18th century), pioneer Presbyterian leader in Pennsylvania and Delaware; author of religious works. Cooch, *Delaware Historic Events.*

Evans, Edward C. (1844-1912), Calvinistic-Methodist leader; editor of the *Cambrian*, Welsh-American magazine. CAM, 1912, pp. 13-14.

Evans, Evan (1671-1721), pioneer Anglican missionary to the Welsh in Pennsylvania; rector of Christ Church, Philadelphia. DAB, DWB

Evans, Evan William (1827-1874), mathematician; early Cornell University professor and leader. CAM, 1892, pp. 338-39. DWB

Evans, George S. (1841-1903), printer; Chief Postal Inspector for New England, 1897-1903. CAM, 1903, pp. 301-2.

Evans, Henry William (1840-1919), pioneer leader of mine workers; founded *Baner America*, Welsh-American newspaper. DWB

Evans, John (fl. 1703-1731), friend of William Penn; colonial Governor of Pennsylvania, 1703-07. DAB

Evans, John (1770-1799), explorer of the upper Missouri River basin 1795-97, prior to Lewis and Clark; seeker of the "Welsh Indians." DWB

Evans, Lewis (1700-1756), pioneer American geographer and map maker. *Columbia Encyclopedia.*

Evans, Llewellyn Ioan (1833-1892), Presbyterian Biblical scholar; professor of theology, Lane Seminary; associate editor of *Princeton Review.* CAM, 1892, p. 161. DWB

Evans, Thomas (1719-1742), pioneer Presbyterian minister; founder of first Presbyterian school in America at Pencader, Del. Cooch, *Delaware Historic Events.*

Evans, Thomas D. (1844-19 ?), leading Pittsburgh architect. CAM, 1903, pp. 344-45.

Evans, Thomas T. (1807-1895?), Calvinistic-Methodist preacher; private publisher of Welsh books. CAM, 1895, pp. 129-31.

Everett, Robert (1791-1875), Congregational minister; editor of *Y Cenhadwr Americanydd,* organ of the Welsh Congregationalists in America. DAB, DWB

Foxal, Henry (1758-1823), early American munitions manufacturer and iron-master. DAB

Gardiner, John Sylvester John (1765-1830), Episcopalian minister; rector of Trinity Church, Boston; classical scholar. DAB

Griffith, Benjamin (1688-1768), pioneer Baptist leader in Pennsylvania; compiler of Baptist historical records. DAB

Griffith, Griffith Jenkins (1850-1919), mining entrepreneur; Los Angeles philanthropist. NCAB, XXXII, p. 347-48.

Griffith, Owen (1832-1896) (Giraldus), Baptist leader; editor of *Y Wawr Americanaidd,* organ of the Welsh Baptists in America. CAM, 1896, pp. 193-95. DWB

Griffith, William (1832-1906) (Gwilyn Caledffrwd), Vermont slate manufacturer; composer of anthems. CAM, 1889, pp. 353-55; 1906, pp. 269-70.

Griffiths, David (1867-1935), botanist; specialist for the United States Department of Agriculture. *Columbia Encyclopedia.*

Griffiths, Edward Stephen (1872-1930), founder and president of Cleveland Machine and Manufacturing Company. NCAB, XXIII, p. 582.

Griffiths, James (1861-1943), Tacoma, Washington, operator of steamship lines. NCAB, XXXV, p. 475.

Griffiths, T. Solomon (1839-1914), Utica, New York, merchant tailor; editor of *Y Cyfaill,* organ of the Calvinistic-Methodists. CAM, 1915, pp. 14-15.

Griffiths, Thomas J. (fl. 1880), printer of books in Welsh; publisher of *Y Drych,* Welsh-American newspaper, for over fifty years.

Gwinnett, Button (1735-1777), wealthy planter; Revolutionary War patriot; Governor of Georgia, 1777. DAB

Harries, George Herbert (1860-1934), World War I general; associate editor, *Washington Evening Star.* WWWI

Harris, Albert Lewis (1869-1950), municipal architect for Washington, D.C., 1921-35; designer of the United States National Museum. NCAB, XXIV, p. 165.

Hathaway, Winifred Phillips (1870-1954), pioneer educator of the blind; director, National Society for Prevention of Blindness. *New York Times,* December 2, 1954.

Hope, Robert (Bob) (1903-   ), Hollywood and television star; born in England the son of Agnes Townes, Welsh concert singer. CB, 1953.

Howell, Daniel (1824-1895), pioneer railroad engineer of Union Pacific and other western railroads. CAM, 1896.

Howell, Llewelyn David (1812-1864), Congregational minister, author, and eisteddfod leader of Oneida County, N. Y. DWB

Howells, Anthony (1832-1910?), Massillon, Ohio, coal operator; state treasurer of Ohio, 1877-79. CAM, 1892, pp. 33-35.

Hughes, David Edward (1831-1900), inventor of telegraphic printing, the microphone, the induction balance, and other electrical inventions. DAB

Hughes, Ezekiel (1767-18 ?), Welsh pioneer in the Ohio country. CAM, 1882, pp. 109-12. DWB

Hughes, Griffith (early 18th century), Anglican missionary to the Welsh of Pennsylvania. Burr, "Welsh Episcopalians of Pennsylvania," p. 109.

Hughes, Hugh W. (1837-1890), Vermont slate manufacturer; known as the "slate king of America." CAM, 1890, pp. 129-30.

Hughes, John F. (1847-1910), Utica, New York, building contractor and community leader. CAM, 1903, pp. 215-17.

Hughes, Peter Davis (1855-1911), surgeon; professor of Medicine, University of Kansas. WWWI

Hughes, Price (d. 1715), Indian agent; defender of British interests against the French in the southwest. DAB

Hughes, Robert John (1931-   ), Foreign News Correspondent and Journalist, Winner of Pulitzer Prize for International Reporting, 1967. *N. Y. Times,* May 2, 1967, pp. 1, 44-45.

Jarrett, John (1843-1910?), early labor leader; secretary of the American Tin Plate Association. CAM, 1889, pp. 65-66.

Jenckes, Joseph (1632-1717), pioneer Rhode Island iron-master; founder of Pawtucket, R. I. DAB

Jenkins, Daniel Edwards (1866-1927), Presbyterian leader; theologian; president, University of Omaha, 1909-27. WWWI

Jenkins, David G. (1879-   ), lawyer and labor leader; Judge of the Court of Common Pleas, Mahoning County, Ohio, for over forty years, 1918-65. *Y Drych,* Oct., 1965, p. 5.

Jenks, Joseph (1602-1683), pioneer iron-master of Saugus, Massachusetts; minter of the famous Pine Tree Shilling. DAB

Job, Samuel (1842-19 ?), steelman; general superintendent, Pullman Iron & Steel Company, Chicago. CAM, 1890, pp. 193-94.

Jones, Captain Dan (?-1861), Mormon missionary; father of the Welsh Mormons. Evans, *A Century of Mormonism in Great Britain,* pp. 184-96.

Jones, David (1856-1937), leading Congregational minister; author of *Memorial Volume of Welsh Congregationalists in Pennsylvania,* pp. 281-85. *Scranton Times,* Mar. 31, 1937.

Jones, David I. (1818-1891), industrialist; co-founder of the Newburgh Rolling Mill Co., Newburgh, Ohio; Jones Road Welsh Congregational Church, Cleveland, Ohio, named in his honor.

Jones, David Richard (1832-1916), nineteenth century Chicago architect and Welsh poet. CAM, 1903, pp. 125-27. DWB

Jones, Edward (1814-189?), Lackawanna, Pa. coal operator and banker. CAM, 1891, pp. 354-55.

Jones, Edward (1818-189?), pioneer in the field of gas illumination; supervised installation of same in Boston, New York and other cities. *Welshmen as Factors,* p. 224.

Jones, Edward D. (1819?-19 ?), founder and head of the Detroit Dry Dock Engine Works. CAM, 1888, pp. 353-55.

Jones, Edwin C. (1867-1908), U. S. government printer; in charge of Federal printing office in Manila; editor of *Columbia,* Welsh-American newspaper. CAM, 1908, pp. 183-84.

Jones, Erasmus (1817-1909), Methodist Episcopal minister and historian of the Welsh settlements of Oneida County, N. Y. CAM, 1892, pp. 97-99. DWB

Jones, Evan William (1852-1908), mechanical engineer; inventor of the first power-driven mechanical underfeed stokers. DAB

Jones, Howel (1844-1928), lawyer; president, Burlington and Northwestern Railroad. NCAB, XXI, pp. 112-13.

Jones, Idwal (1890-1964), contemporary American novelist. CB, 1948; 1965.

Jones, James F. (1839-1908), Pennsylvania mining engineer; recognized as authority on the geology of coal mining. CAM, 1908, pp. 35-36.

Jones, James Milton (1827-19 ?), lawyer; justice of the Cleveland, Ohio, Court of Common Pleas, 1875-1886. NCAB, XXIII, pp. 106-7.

Jones, Jenkin Lloyd (1843-1918), Chicago Unitarian leader and peace advocate. DAB

Jones, John (1808-1870), industrialist; co-founder of the Newburgh Rolling Mill Co., Newburgh, Ohio.

Jones, John (January) (fl. mid-nineteenth century), Nevada gold mine operator and pioneer prospector. *The Druid,* Oct. 1, 1936, p. 8.

Jones, John Hughson, contemporary Welsh cultural leader of New York City; appointed by Queen Elizabeth II an Honourary Member of the Order of the British Empire for his efforts on behalf of Anglo-American friendship, 1963. *Y Drych,* Feb. 1963, p. 5.

Jones, John Percival (1829-1912), owner of silver mines; United States Senator from Nevada, 1873-1903. DAB

Jones, John Peter (1847-1916), Congregational missionary to India; author of various works. DAB

Jones, John Rice (fl. 1759-1824), leading frontier lawyer; judge of the Missouri Supreme Court, 1820-24. NCAB, XVI, p. 268. DWB

Jones, John T. (1836-1891), Iowa County, Wisconsin judge, 1877-91. CAM, 1893, pp. 321-22.

Jones, John Wynne (1845-1912), Baltimore Presbyterian minister; pioneer in adult education. CAM, 1895, pp. 161-63.

Jones, Joseph Addison (1873-1949), New York Reformed Church leader; president of the General Synod. WWWII

Jones, Malachi (16 ?-1729), pioneer Presbyterian leader; founder of churches in the Philadelphia area. Webster, *A History of the Presbyterian Church in America,* p. 346.

Jones, Morgan (fl. latter part of seventeenth century), Presbyterian minister; believer in "Welsh Indian" legend; credited with establishing the first Sabbath School in America at Newtown, Long Island. CAM, 1892, pp. 167-69.

Jones, Rhys Gwesyn (1826-1901), Congregational minister and Welsh author. CAM, 1892, pp. 97-99. DWB

Jones, Samuel Milton (1846-1904), oil entrepreneur; reform Mayor of Toledo, Ohio, 1897-1904; philanthropist. DAB

Jones, Thomas Jesse (1873-1949), sociologist; authority on the Negro in America. WWWII

Jones, William H. (1845-1916), president, Plano Manufacturing Company; vice-president, International Harvester Company. NCAB, XVIII, p. 391.

Langner, Lawrence (1890-1963), patent attorney; theatrical producer and dramatist. CB, 1944; 1963.

Leonard, James (fl. early seventeenth century), pioneer Massachusetts iron-master. (See DAB sketch of Daniel Leonard, his descendant.)

Lewis, Benjamin F. (1831-1897), Utica printer and editor of *Y Drych,* the Welsh-American newspaper from 1893-97. CAM, 1897, pp. 297-300.

Lewis, Claude Isaac (1880-1924), horticulturist; founder and editor, *American Fruit Grower*. NCAB, XX, pp. 339-40; WWWI.

Lewis, Edward Morgan (1872-1936), educator; president, University of New Hampshire, 1927-36. NCAB, XXX, pp. 362-63.

Lewis, Francis (1713-1802), colonial New York merchant; signer of the Declaration of Independence. DAB

Lewis, H. Edgar (1882-1948), industrialist; chairman, board of directors, Jones & Laughlin Steel Corporation.

Lewis, T. L. (fl. 1910), pioneer labor leader; president, United Mine Workers of America, 1908-10. CAM, 1909, p. 10.

Lewis, W. T. (1869-1909), pioneer labor leader; Commissioner of Labor for Ohio, 1882-86; 1908-09. CAM, 1909, p. 10.

Llewellyn, Silas James (1860-1920), steelman; president, Interstate Iron & Steel Company. WWWI

Lloyd, Abram (1845-1911), Soddy, Tennessee, coal operator; philanthropist. CAM, 1882, p. 20; 1911, p. 13.

Lloyd, David (1656-1731), leader of the liberal political party in Pennsylvania; chief justice of the province, 1717-31. DAB

Lloyd, Frederick Ebenezer John (1859-1933), Episcopalian minister; archbishop of the American Catholic Church. WWWI

Lloyd, Rees (1759-1862), Congregational minister; founder of the Ebensburg, Pa. Welsh settlement. CAM, 1889, pp. 228-29.

Lloyd, Thomas (1640-1694), leader of the liberal political party in Pennsylvania; Governor of Pennsylvania, 1691-93. DAB

Mason, D. J. J. (fl. 1880's), composer of songs, oratorios, and piano music. CAM, 1890, pp. 321-23.

Matthews, G. T. (1847-19 ?), New York City tea merchant and importer. CAM, 1891, pp. 33-35.

Matthews, Robert David (1886-1943), businessman; president, Pacific States Oil Company of Los Angeles. WWWII

Meredith, Robert R. (1823-1893), printer of Welsh books in Rome, New York; later in Racine, Wis. CAM, 1894, pp. 158-59.

Miles, William (1812-1902), New York City merchant and banker; philanthropist; owner of Cypress Hills Cemetery; donated plot to St. David's Society of New York. CAM, 1891, pp. 65-69; 1892, pp. 374-75.

Milland, Ray (Reginald Trescott Jones) (1907-   ), Hollywood motion picture star. CB, 1946.

Mitchell, George (fl. 1900), copper mining entrepreneur; Arizona banker. CAM, 1906, pp. 225-27.

Morgan, Abel (1673-1722), pioneer Baptist leader; author of a Welsh concordance to the *Bible*. DAB

Morgan, D. Parker (1843-19 ?), New York Episcopal leader; rector, Church of the Heavenly Rest. CAM, 1894, pp. 65-67.

Morgan, Morgan (1688-1766), pioneer frontiersman; first settler of West Virginia, 1730. Ambler, *West Virginia Stories and Biographies,* 1942.

Morgan, Taliesen (1858-1941), contemporary composer and choir leader. Pratt, *New Encyclopedia of Music and Musicians.*

Morgan, Thomas Rees (1834-1897), steelman; Pittsburgh manufacturer of heavy machinery. CAM, 1891, pp. 289-93. DWB

Morris, J. Hayden (fl. 1890's), organist; composer; director of leading boy choirs. CAM, 1900, pp. 279-80; 1906, 39-40.

Morris, Robert (1734-1806), financier of the American Revolution; United States Superintendent of Finance, 1781-84; United States Senator from Pennsylvania, 1789-95. (Born Liverpool of Welsh parents.) DAB

Moxham, Arthur James (1854-1931), pioneer steelman; founder of Johnson Steel Co.; partner, E. I. du Pont de Nemours Powder Company. DAB

Myles, John (c. 1621-1683), pioneer Baptist leader; founder of the Swansea, Massachusetts, Welsh Colony. DAB. DWB

Nicholson, John (?-1800), financier; Comptroller-General of Pennsylvania, 1782-94. DAB

Owen, David Dale (1807-1860), pioneer geologist of the northwestern states. DAB

Owen, Goronwy (1723-1769), Virginia Anglican minister; one of Wales' great poets. DNB

Owen, Griffith (c. 1647-1717), Philadelphia Quaker preacher and physician. DAB

Owen, Joshua T. (1821-1887), lawyer; Union general; founder of the *New York Daily Register,* a legal publication. CAM, 1888, pp. 2-5.

Owen, Robert Dale (1801-1877), free-thinker; abolitionist; social reformer. DAB

Owen, William Florence (1844-1906), post-Civil War Shakespearian actor. (Born, Ireland of Welsh stock.) DAB

Owens, John Edmond (1823-1886), character actor; comedian; theatre manager. DAB

Parry, Joseph (1841-1903), Wales' greatest composer; discovered by fellow Welsh iron workers at Danville, Pa., who underwrote costs of his musical education. DNB, Sup. III. DWB

Phillips, D. T. (?-1905), Baptist clergyman; Chicago Republican leader; United States Consul to Cardiff. CAM, 1897, p. 382; 1905, p. 84.

Phillips, D. W. (1809-1890), Baptist missionary to the Negroes; founder and first president, Roger Williams University, Nashville, Tenn., 1864-90. CAM, 1882, pp. 112-14; 1890, pp. 353-56.

Phillips, F. R. (fl. 1900), tin-plate industrialist; organizer of the Welsh-American Tin Plate Co. of Philadelphia. CAM, 1891, pp. 257-59.

Phillips, Llewellyn (1869-1923), educator; Dean of Bucknell University, Lewisburg, Pa. WWWI

Plumbe, John (1809-1857), railroad builder; pioneer photographer; trans-continental railroad advocate. DAB

Powell, Charles Stuart (ff. 1790's), pioneer Boston theatre manager. DAB (See sketch of Snelling Powell.)

Powell, Snelling (1758-1821), pioneer Boston actor and theatre manager. DAB

Powell, Thomas Watkins (1797-1882), lawyer; probate judge, Delaware County, Ohio, 1863-70; author of *A History of the Ancient Britons and Their Descendants.* CAM, 1880, pp. 14-15; 1883, pp. 5-7.

Powell, William H. (1825-1904), pioneer iron-master; Union general in Civil War. CAM, 1882, pp. 114-17.

Price, J. W. Parson (fl. 1880's), operatic tenor; composer of songs and sacred music; actor. CAM, 1900, pp. 185-86.

Price, Thomas (1835-1912), California chemist; authority on toxicology. CAM, 1912, p. 11.

Protheroe, Daniel (1866-1934), composer of religious music; internationally renowned choir-leader. CAM, 1891, pp. 161-62; XX, 1900, pp. 377-79; Howard, *Our American Music,* p. 555. DWB

Pugh, Ellis (1656-1718), Philadelphia Quaker preacher; author of *Amnerch i'r Cymru,* first book to be published in the Welsh language in America. DAB, DWB

Pughe, John Samuel (1870-1909), artist; pioneer political cartoonist for various New York newspapers. CAM, 1911, pp. 14-15.

Rees, James (1821-1889), pioneer iron-master; steamboat manufacturer and inventor. DAB

Reese, Abram (1829-1908), Pennsylvania iron-master and inventor. DAB

Reese, Isaac (1821-1908), Pennsylvania brick manufacturer and inventor. DAB

Reese, Jacob (1825-1907), Pennsylvania metallurgist; inventor; pioneer in the iron industry. DAB

Rhees, Morgan John (1760-1804), Baptist leader; humanitarian; founder of the Beulah, Pennsylvania, Welsh colony. DAB, DWB

Rhys-Herbert, William (fl. 1880's), composer of operettas, songs and contatas. Howard, *Our American Music.*

Richards, David (1824-1906), pioneer iron-master of the South; founder of Knoxville Iron Works, Tennessee. CAM, 1906, pp. 181-82.

Richards, David (fl. 1855-1900), leading nineteenth century sculptor. CAM, 1894, pp. 361-63.

Roberts, George (1769-1862), Congregational minister; Cambria County, Pennsylvania, jurist. Jones, *Welsh Congregationalists in Pennsylvania,* p. 316.

Roberts, Hugh (1644?-1702), Quaker leader of the Pennsylvania Welsh Tract settlement. DWB

Roberts, John C. (1840-1911), Utica journalist; editor of *Y Drych,* Welsh-American newspaper. CAM, 1905, pp. 312-13.

Roberts, Peter (1859-1932), sociologist; authority on immigrants; YMCA leader. WWWI

Roberts, William (1809-1887), Utica cultural leader; editor of *Y Cyfaill,* the organ of the Calvinistic-Methodists of America. DWB

Roberts, William Charles (1832-1903), Presbyterian leader; president, Lake Forest College, 1886-98. DAB, DWB

Roberts, William Henry (1844-1920), Presbyterian leader; stated clerk, Presbyterian General Assembly. WWWI, DWB

Rowlands, William (1807-1866), Calvinistic-Methodist leader; founder and editor of *Y Cyfaill,* denominational magazine. DAB, DWB

Shelby, Evan (1719-1794), Revolutionary patriot; frontiersman; general in command of the Virginia frontier. DAB

Smith, William Henry (1806-1872), Shakespearian actor and theatre manager. DAB

Stanley, Henry M. (1841-1905), African explorer and journalist. DAB

Stephens, Evan (1854-19 ?), Mormon composer; organist; director of noted Tabernacle Choir. *Latter Day Saints Encyclopedia,* I, pp. 740-46.

Templeton, Alec (1910-1963), contemporary concert pianist and modern composer. CB, 1940; 1963.

Thomas, Benjamin (fl. 1870's), Baptist missionary: founder and president, Judson University, Arkansas. *Welshmen as Factors,* p. 312.

Thomas, David (1794-1882), iron-master of America; father of the Pennsylvania anthracite iron industry. DAB, DWB

Thomas, David Owen (1852-1925), Minneapolis surgeon; professor of Dermatology and Genital-Urinary diseases, Hamline University, Minneapolis. NCAB, XX, p. 91.

Thomas, Evan (1863-1947), mathematician; University of New Hampshire professor. NCAB, XXXVI, p. 226.

Thomas, J. Griff (fl. 1880's), authority on harmony, counterpoint, and orchestration; author of the hymn, *Rock of Ages.* CAM, 1907, p. 228.

Thomas, John Rogers (1829-1896), composer of popular songs, operettas, and church music. Baker, *Biographical Dictionary of Musicians.*

Thomas, Richard (1829-1906), Birmingham, Alabama, pioneer coal operator and industrialist; inventor of Thomas Coke Oven. CAM, 1906, pp. 180-81; 1909, p. 13.

Thomas, Robert D. (1817-1889), *(Iorthryn Gwynedd)*, Congregational minister; writer on the Welsh in America. CAM, 1889, pp. 225-28. DWB

Thomas, Thomas L. (contemporary), concert baritone and radio and television favorite.

Thompson, David (1770-1857), pioneer fur-trader; explorer of the Oregon Country. DAB

Treharne, Bryceson (1879-194?), contemporary composer; song writer; teacher of music. Baker, *Biographical Dictionary of Musicians;* Pratt, *New Encyclopedia of Music and Musicians.*

Watts, Evan (1824-1908), pioneer San Francisco building contractor and civic leader. CAM, 1908, pp. 84-86.

Watts, Frederick (1719-1795), Revolutionary War patriot; general in command of the Pennsylvania frontier. (See DAB sketch of grand-son, Frederick Watts), Appleton, *Cyclopedia of American Biography,* VI, p. 395.

Williams, John (1768-1825), Baptist liberal minister refugee; first preacher in Welsh in New York City; pastor of Oliver Street Baptist Church, 1798-1825. DWB

Williams, John (1865-192?), pioneer labor leader; New York State Commissioner of Labor, 1907-09. CAM, 1907, pp. 472-73.

Williams, John Charles (1876-1936), tin-plate industrialist; president, Weirton Steel Company. NCAB, XXVII, p. 169.

Williams, John Elias (1853-1919), pioneer union leader; industrial mediator. DAB

Williams, Lewis H. (1845-1887), leading building contractor in New York City in post-Civil War period. CAM, 1887, pp. 129-30.

Williams, Morgan B. (1831-1903), Wilkes-Barre, Pa. coal operator and Congressman. CAM, 1888, pp. 161-63; 1896, p. 372. Harvey-Smith, *History of Wilkes-Barre,* V, p. 232.

Williams, Rhys (1897-   ), character actor and Hollywood motion picture star.

Williams, Robert Einion (1856-1940), leader of the Calvinistic-Methodists in America. WWWI

Williams, William Aubrey (Gwilyn Gwent) (1844-1895), composer of songs, anthems, and hymns; known as the "Mozart of the coal mines." CAM, 1895, pp. 353-57. DWB

Williams, William C. (1837-19 ?), pioneer Detroit drug manufacturer. CAM, 1889, pp. 161-62.

Williams, William Nugent (1851-1927), Salt Lake City business entrepreneur and Utah political leader. NCAB, XXI, p. 457.

Worthington, John (fl. 1890-1915), oil geologist and mining engineer. *Pittsburgh Blue Book.*

Wynne, Thomas (? -1692), Quaker physician; first speaker of the Pennsylvania Provincial Assembly. CAM, 1896, p. 212.

Some Distinguished Children of Welsh Immigrants

Bebb, William (1802-1873), lawyer; Whig leader; Governor of Ohio, 1846-48.

Boone, Daniel (1734-1820), American frontiersman and Kentucky pioneer. (Mother, a Welsh Quaker.) Jenkins, *Historical Collections Relating to Gwynedd,* pp. 325-26.

Cadwallader, Thomas (1707-1799), pioneer Philadelphia physician; founder of Philadelphia Hospital. DAB

Daniels, Charles (1825-1897), New York Supreme Court judge, 1863-91; Congressman from Buffalo, 1892-96; dean, University of Buffalo Law School. NCAB, XXII, p. 126.

Davies, Arthur Bowen (1862-1928), leading painter; sponsor of modern art. DAB

Davies, Harriet (1872-1952), Calvinistic-Methodist physician-missionary to India; one of the first female physician-missionaries. CAM, 1906, p. 363.

Davies, John Pugh (1853-1908), Racine, Wisconsin, steel industrialist. NCAB, XVIII, pp. 114-15.

Davies, Joseph Edward (1876-   ), leading corporation lawyer; federal official; Ambassador to the Soviet Union, 1936-45. CB, 1942.

Davies, Samuel (1723-1761), Presbyterian divine; president of Princeton University, 1759-61. DAB

Davis, Milton Fennimore (1864-1938), explorer of the Grand Canyon; brigadier-general, U.S. Air Corps; superintendent, New York Military Academy. NCAB, XXVII, p. 453.

Ellis, Griffith Ogden (1869-1948), founder and editor of *American Boy Magazine;* one of the founders of the Boy Scouts of America. NCAB, XXXVI, p. 155.

Evans, Alice Catherine (1881-   ), bacteriologist; discoverer of the bang bacillus in milk. CB, 1943.

Evans, Edward Payson (1831-1917), animal psychologist; man of letters. DAB

Evans, Evan Alfred (1876-1948), judge of the United States Circuit Court of Appeals, Wisconsin, 1916-48. WWWII

Evans, William Davis (1852-1934), chief justice, Iowa Supreme Court, 1908-34. NCAB, XVIII, pp. 91-92.

Fairless, Benjamin F. (Williams) (1890-1962), industrialist; chairman, board of directors, United States Steel Corporation. CB, 1957; 1963.

Francis, John M. (1823-1897), editor and owner of Troy, N. Y. *Times;*

minister to Austria-Hungary, 1882-85. CAM, 1894, pp. 257-60; 1897, pp. 343-44.

Gaines, Samuel Richards (1869-1945), musical composer of oratorios and choral compositions. Howard, *Our American Music,* pp. 555-56.

George, Thomas John (1873-1947), twentieth century New York architect. NCAB, XXXV, pp. 84-85.

Green, William (1873-1952), union leader; president, American Federation of Labor. CB, 1942.

Griffith, David (1742-1789), Anglican missionary and physician; chaplain in Revolutionary Army; first Episcopal Bishop of Virginia, 1786-89. *P. E. Church Historical Magazine,* IX, (Sept., 1940), pp. 194-230.

Griffiths, Charles W. (1871-1954), owner and publisher of *Y Drych,* the Welsh-American Newspaper for fifty years.

Griffiths, John (1846-1937), leading Chicago building contractor; built Union Station, Marshall Field & Co., and Atlanta Federal Prison. NCAB, XXVII, pp. 318-19.

Griffiths, John Willis (1809-1882), naval architect and ship builder; inventor of lifeboats. CAM, 1892, pp. 353-55.

Gwin, William McKendree (1805-1885), lawyer; United States Senator from California, 1850-61. DAB

Hopkins, Arthur Melancthon (1878-   ), Broadway theatrical producer and playwright. CB, 1947.

Howells, William Dean (1837-1920), leading nineteenth century novelist. DAB. CAM, 1882, p. 93; 1894, p. 318.

Hughes, Charles Evans (1862-1948), Chief Justice of the United States, 1930-41; Governor of New York, 1908-10. CB, 1941; WWWII.

Huntington, Margaret Jane Evans (1842-1926), leader of the Women's Clubs movement. DAB

James, Arthur H. (1883-   ), lawyer; Luzerne County district attorney; Governor of Pennsylvania, 1938-42. CB, 1940.

Jenckes, Joseph (1656-1740), colonial Governor of Rhode Island, 1727-31. DAB

Jenkins, Elwyn V. (1917-   ), Youngstown, Ohio, civic leader; Judge of the Court of Common Pleas, Mahoning County, Ohio, 1966-   . *Martindale-Hubbell Law Directory,* 1967.

Johnson, Edward (1880-1953), operatic tenor; general manager of the Metropolitan Opera, New York City. CB, 1943, 1953.

Jones, Allen (contemporary), concert tenor and Hollywood motion picture actor. (Son of Daniel Jones of Cwmbach, Wales.)

Jones, Benjamin R. (1869-1942), district attorney; judge of the Court of Common Pleas, Luzerne County, Pa., 1921-42.

Jones, Daniel I. (1841-1899), Congregational leader; founder and publisher of the *Cambrian,* Welsh-American magazine. CAM, 1899, pp. 377-78.

Jones, David (1736-1820), Baptist minister; Revolutionary War patriot and army chaplain. DAB

Jones, Gabriel (1724-1806), King's Attorney for Virginia; Federalist leader. DAB

Jones, Gaius J. (1843-19 ?), Ohio physician; founder and president, Cleveland Medical College. CAM, 1894, pp. 321-24.

Jones, George (1811-1891), publisher of the *New York Times;* exposer of the notorious Tweed Ring. DAB

Jones, George Wallace (1804-1896), pioneer lawyer; United States Senator from Iowa, 1848-54; Minister to Colombia, 1859-61. DAB

Jones, Rebecca (1739-1817), Quaker humanitarian and hospital founder. Rees, *History of the Quakers in Wales,* pp. 208-9.

Jones, Thomas D. (1811-1881), Ohio sculptor during the post-Civil War period. CAM, 1882, pp. 161-64; 1908, pp. 505-6.

Jones, William Richard (1839-1889), mechanical genius; steelman; consulting engineer for the Carnegie Steel interests. DAB

Kinloch, Robert Alexander (1826-1891), Confederate Army surgeon; South Carolina medical educator. DAB

Lewis, John Llewellyn (1880-   ), union leader; president, United Mine Workers of America; founder of the CIO. CB, 1942.

Lewis, Morgan (1754-1844), Revolutionary soldier; Chief Justice of the Supreme Court of New York, 1801-04; Governor of New York, 1804-08. DAB. CAM, 1895, pp. 289-91.

Lewis, Thomas Morgan (1891-   ), district attorney; judge of the Court of Common Pleas, Luzerne County, Pa., 1947-66. Harvey-Smith, *History of Wilkes-Barre,* V, pp. 187-88.

Lewis, William David (1792-1881), Philadelphia financier and patron of the arts. DAB

Llewellyn, Morgan (1846-1920), Tennessee coal operator and industrialist of Chattanooga. NCAB, XXVI, pp. 239-40.

London, Jack Griffith (1876-1916), one of America's leading novelists. *Twentieth Century Authors.*

Meredith, Samuel (1741-1817), Philadelphia financier; first Treasurer of the United States, 1789-91. CAM, 1895, pp. 43-45.

Morgan, George (1743-1810), land speculator; Indian agent; gentleman farmer. DAB

Morgan, John (1735-1789), physician-in-chief, Revolutionary Army; founder of University of Pennsylvania Medical School. DAB

Morris, Edward Dafydd (1825-1915), Presbyterian theologian; moderator, Presbyterian General Assembly. DAB

Morris, Lewis (1671-1746), wealthy landholder; Chief Justice of New York, 1715-38; Governor of New Jersey, 1738-46. DAB

Morris, William Thomas (1884-1946), industrialist; president, American Chain and Cable Company. WWWII

Nash, Abner (1740-1786); lawyer; Revolutionary War patriot; Governor of North Carolina, 1780-81. DAB

Nash, Francis (1742-1777), Revolutionary War general; mortally wounded in battle. DAB

Price, Gwilym Alexander (1895-   ), lawyer; president, Westinghouse Electric Corporation. CB, 1949.

Price, Ira Maurice (1856-1939), linguist and scholar; professor of Semitic languages, University of Chicago, 1900-25. WWWII

Richards, John Evans (1856-1932), Judge of the Supreme Court of California, 1924-32. NCAB, XXIII, p. 77.

Rittenhouse, David (1732-1796), colonial scientist, astronomer, and mathematician. DAB

Roberts, David Evan (1854-1918), district attorney; judge of the Douglas County, Wisconsin Court, 1889-1903. NCAB, XVI, p. 327.

Roberts, Edward David (1864-1920), Los Angeles Banker; State Treasurer of California, 1911-14. NCAB, XIX, pp. 145-46.

Roberts, Edward Howell (1895-1954), Presbyterian theologian; dean, Princeton Theological Seminary, 1945-54. WWWIII

Roberts, Ellis Henry (1827-1918), editor, Utica, N. Y. *Morning-Herald;* Treasurer of the United States, 1897-1905. CAM, 1890, pp. 65-67. DAB

Roberts, Marshall Owen (1814-1880), New York financier; operator of coastal shipping lines. DAB

Shelby, Isaac (1750-1826), Revolutionary War patriot; first Governor of Kentucky, 1792-96; again Governor, 1812-16. DAB

Thomas, Arthur L. (1851-19 ?), federal official; Governor of Utah Territory, 1889-96. CAM, 1893, pp. 33-34.

Thomas, Lewelyn R. (1859-1925), pioneer union leader; Commissioner of Conciliation, United States Department of Labor, 1917-21. *American Labor Who's Who.*

Williams, Daniel Jenkins (1874-   ), leading Presbyterian minister; author of *100 Years of Welsh Calvinistic Methodism in America. Alumni Catalogue of Union Theological Seminary.*

Williams, Daniel Webster (1862-19 ?), editor, Jackson, Ohio, *Standard Journal;* United States Consul to Cardiff. CAM, 1905, pp. 136-37.

Williams, Harry Evan (1867-1918), concert tenor. WWWI

Williams, John Elias (1871-1927), Presbyterian missionary to China; founder of Nanking University. DAB

Williams, Otho Holland (1749-1794), Revolutionary War general; active in the southern campaigns. DAB

Williams, William R. (1804-1885), Baptist minister, theologian, and scholar. DAB

Yale, Elihu (1649-1721), wealthy merchant; head of the British East India Company; benefactor of Yale University. DAB

Some Distinguished Grandchildren of Welsh Immigrants

Adams, James Hopkins (1812-1861), wealthy planter; Governor of South Carolina, 1854-58. DAB

Bibb, William Wyatt (1781-1820), physician; United States Senator from Georgia, 1813-16; first Governor of Alabama, 1817-20. DAB

Cadwallader, John (1742-1786), wealthy Philadelphia merchant; Revolutionary War general. DAB

Cadwallader, Lambert (1743-1823), wealthy Philadelphia merchant; Revolutionary War patriot; Congressman from New Jersey, 1789-95. DAB

Cross, Edward (1798-1887), pioneer Arkansas political leader; judge, Superior Court of Arkansas, 1832-36. DAB

Davis, Jefferson (1808-1889), United States Senator from Mississippi, 1847,1851-61; Secretary of War, 1853-57; President, Confederate States of America, 1861-65. DAB. CAM, 1896, p. 77.

DeWolfe, Billy (William A. Jones), contemporary actor, television and Hollywood motion picture star. *World Almanac,* 1966.

Evans, Lawrence Boyd (1870-1928), legal scholar and authority on international law. DAB

Evans, Oliver (1755-1819), mechanical genius; builder of America's first steam-engine. DAB

Howell, Richard (1754-1802), Revolutionary War soldier; Federalist leader; Governor of New Jersey, 1793-1801. DAB

Humphries, Joshua (1751-1838), shipbuilder and naval architect. DAB

James, Thomas Lemuel (1831-1916), publisher, Hamilton, N. Y. *Democratic-Republican;* Postmaster General of the United States, 1881-82; exposer of the "Star Route" frauds. DAB

Jones, Benjamin Rowland (1906-   ), lawyer; president judge of Orphans Court, Luzerne County, Pa., 1952-57; Associate Justice of the Supreme Court of Pennsylvania, 1957-. WWAm, 1966.

Jones, Frank (1832-1902), wealthy brewer; railroad executive; Congressman from New Hampshire, 1875-79. DAB

Jones, Horatio Gates (1777-1853), Baptist minister; historian of the Philadelphia Baptist Association. CAM, 1893, pp. 97-98.

Jones, John (1729-1791), pioneer New York surgeon; author of the first American surgical textbook. DAB

Jones, William (1753-1822), Revolutionary War soldier; Federalist leader; Governor of Rhode Island, 1811-17. DAB

Jones, William (1760-1831), naval officer; Secretary of the Navy, 1812-14. DAB

Lewis, Kathryn (1911-   ), labor leader; executive official, United Mine Workers of America. WWAm, 1966.

Mastin, Claudius Henry (1826-1898), surgeon in the Confederate army; leading Southern specialist in genito-urinary diseases. DAB

Maxey, George W. (1878-   ), leading Pennsylvania state jurist. Murphy, *History of Lackawanna County*, Pa., pp. 791-92.

Meredith, William Morris (1799-1873), Pennsylvania Whig and Republican leader; Secretary of the Treasury, 1849. DAB

Morgan, Daniel (1736-1802), Revolutionary War general; victor at the Battle of Cowpens. DAB

Morris, Gouverneur (1752-1816), statesman; United States Senator from New York, 1800-03; Minister to France, 1792-94. DAB

Morris, Lewis (1726-1798), wealthy New York landholder; signer of the Declaration of Independence. DAB

Morris, Richard (1730-1810), lawyer; Chief Justice of the Supreme Court of New York, 1779-90. DAB

Morris, Robert Hunter (1700-1764), wealthy New Jersey landholder; Governor of Pennsylvania, 1754-56; Chief Justice of New Jersey, 1738-54; 1756-64. DAB

Morris, Thomas Armstrong (1811-1904), Union general; builder of midwestern railroads. DAB

Moses, Harry Morgan (1896-   ), industrialist; president, United States Coal and Coke Company. CB, 1949.

Rhees, William Jones (1830-1907), bibliographer; secretary, Smithsonian Institution of Washington. DAB

Rice, Fenelon Bird (1841-1901), organist; director of Oberlin Conservatory of Music, 1871-1901. DAB

Roberts, Owen J. (1875-1955), Philadelphia lawyer; Associate Justice of the United States Supreme Court, 1930-45. CB, 1941; WWWIII

Thomas, Francis (1799-1876), lawyer; Governor of Maryland, 1841-45; Minister to Peru, 1872-75. DAB

Thomas, George Clifford (1839-1909), banker and philanthropist; partner of Jay Cooke and Company. DAB

Thomas, Norman (1884-   ), distinguished Socialist leader and writer. CB, 1962.

Thomas, Robert Bailey (1766-1846), founder, editor, and publisher of the *Old Farmers' Almanac*. DAB

Watts, Frederick (1801-1889), pioneer agriculturalist; Pennsylvania jurist; Federal Commissioner of Agriculture, 1871-77. DAB

Williams, Ben Ames (1889-1953), contemporary novelist. (Son of Daniel Webster Williams q.v.) *Twentieth Century Authors.*

Williams, David Rogerson (1776-1830), pioneer southern manufacturer; Governor of South Carolina, 1814-16. DAB

Wright, Frank Lloyd (1869-1959), contemporary architect; one of the founders of modern architecture. CB, 1952; WWWIII

Vaughan, Victor Clarence (1851-1929), pioneer bacteriologist and authority on epidemics. DAB

Some Distinguished Americans of Welsh Stock

Anderson, Richard Clough (1750-1826), Revolutionary soldier and Kentucky pioneer. DAB

Anderson, Richard Clough (1788-1826), Congressman from Kentucky; United States Minister to Colombia. DAB

Anderson, Robert (1805-1871), Union General; gained national renown as Major Anderson, defender of Fort Sumter. DAB

Asbury, Francis (1754-1816), pioneer Methodist Episcopal bishop. DAB

Bowen, Henry Chandler (1813-1896), wealthy merchant and abolitionist. DAB

Bowen, Herbert Wolcott (1856-1927), career diplomat; United States Minister to Venezuela. DAB

Brickwell, Robert Coman (1824-1900), chief justice, Alabama Supreme Court, 1874-84. DAB

Broadus, John Albert (1827-1895), Baptist leader; president of Louisville Theological Seminary. DAB

Brooks, Maria Gowen (c. 1794-1845), early nineteenth century poet. DAB

Buell, Don Carlos (1818-1871), Union General. DAB

Burdette, Robert Jones (1844-1914), Baptist clergyman; humorist writer. DAB

Burt, Maxwell Struthers (1882-), contemporary novelist. *Twentieth Century Authors.*

Butler, Nicholas Murray (1862-1947), statesman; president of Columbia University. (Direct descendant of Morgan John Rhees.) WWII

Cadwallader, John (1805-1879), United States District Judge, Pennsylvania. DAB

Calkins, Mary Whiton (1863-1930), philosopher; psychologist; Wellesley College professor. DAB

Calkins, Phineas Wolcott (1831-1924), Congregational leader and author. DAB

Capehart, Homer Earl (1897-), United States Senator from Indiana, 1945-63. CB, 1947; WWAm, 1966.

Clay, Cassius Marcellus (1810-1903), leader in the abolitionist movement. DAB

Clay, Green (1757-1826), Kentucky pioneer; Major-General, War of 1812. DAB

Clough, John Everett (1836-1910), Baptist missionary to India; founder of Teluga Theological Institute, India. DAB

Coffin, Levi (1789-1877), abolitionist and organizer of the famous "Underground Railroad." DAB

Coit, Henry Augustus (1830-1895), Episcopal minister; founder of St. Paul's School, New Hampshire. DAB

Condit, John (1775-1834), United States Senator from New Jersey, 1803-17. DAB

Coolidge, Calvin (1872-1933), President of the United States. (Mother of Welsh descent.) DAB

Crittenden, George Bibb (1812-1880), Confederate General. DAB

Crittenden, John Jordan (1787-1863), early United States Senator from Kentucky. DAB

Crittenden, Thomas Leonidas (1819-1893), Union general. DAB

Crittenden, Thomas Theodore (1832-1909), Governor of Missouri, 1880-84. DAB

Crittenton, Charles Nelson (1833-1909), wealthy merchant evangelist; founder of the Florence Crittenton missions. DAB

Curry, Jabez Lamar Monroe (1825-1903), president, Howard College, Alabama; Minister to Spain, 1885-88. DAB

Davis, David (1815-1886), Associate Justice, United States Supreme Court, at time of the Hayes-Tilden dispute; United States Senator from Illinois. DAB

Davis, David William (1873-   ), Governor of Idaho, 1919-23. WWWI

Davis, Harold Lenoir (1896-   ), Pulitzer prize poet and novelist. *Twentieth Century Authors.*

Davis, Henry Winter (1817-1865), Maryland Congressman; co-author of the Wade-Davis Bill. DAB

Davis, Joseph Robert (1802-1852), Confederate general. DAB

Davis, Noah (1818-1902), Associate Justice, Supreme Court of New York, 1873-86; presided at Tweed Ring trials. CAM, 1896, pp. 65-67. DAB

Davis, Raymond Cazallis (1836-1919), pioneer in library service. DAB

Dodge, David Low (1774-1852), wealthy merchant; founder of the New York Peace Society. DAB

Duff, James Henderson (1883-   ), Governor of Pennsylvania, 1947-51; Senator from Pennsylvania, 1951-57. WWAm, 1966.

Duke, Benjamin Newton (1855-1929), tobacco industrialist and philanthropist. DAB

Edwards, Bela Bates (1802-1852), religious scholar and founder of *Bibliotheca Sacra,* religious periodical. DAB

Edwards, Clarence Ransom (1860-1931), World War I general. DAB

Edwards, Justin (1787-1853), Congregational leader and temperance reformer. DAB

Ellis, John Willis (1820-1861), Governor of North Carolina, 1858-64. DAB

Enright, Elizabeth (1909-   ), contemporary author of children's books. CB, 1947.

Evans, Clement Anselm (1833-1911), Confederate general. DAB

Evans, Evan Alfred (1876-1948), United States Circuit Judge, Wisconsin. DAB

Evans, George Alfred (1850-1925), pioneer specialist in the treatment of tuberculosis. DAB

Evans, Hugh Davey (1792-1868), legal scholar and religious writer. DAB

Evans, Luther Harris (1902-   ), Librarian of Congress, 1945-53; General Director, UNESCO, 1953-58. WWAm, 1966-67.

Evans, Thomas Wiltberger (1823-1897), distinguished Parisian dentist. DAB

Fargo, William George (1818-1881), founder of Wells, Fargo Express Company. DAB

Flint, Charles Rawlett (1850-1934), industrialist; called the "Rubber King of America." DAB

Floyd, William (1734-1821), wealthy New York landowner; Revolutionary War general; signer of the Declaration of Independence. DAB

Force, Manning Ferguson (1824-1899), Union general. DAB

Foulke, William Dudley (1848-1935), lawyer; municipal reformer; author. DAB

Fuller, George (1822-1884), nineteenth century romantic painter. DAB

George, Walter Franklin (1878-1957), United States Senator from Georgia, 1922-57. CB, 1943; WWWIII.

Gideon, Peter Miller (1820-1899), pioneer pomologist of the upper Mississippi Valley. DAB

Gilman, Daniel Coit (1831-1908), president, Johns Hopkins University. DAB

Griffes, Charles Tomlinson (1884-1920), composer of symphonic poems and other musical compositions. DAB

Griffin, Solomon Buckley (1852-1925), journalist; editor, Springfield, Mass. *Daily Republican.* DAB

Griffis, William Elliot (1843-1928), Congregationalist leader and authority on Japan. DAB

Griffith, David Lewelyn Wark (1880-1948), pioneer motion picture producer and director. WWWII.

Hackley, Charles Henry (1837-1905), pioneer Michigan lumberman. DAB

Hancock, Winfield Scott (1824-1886), Union general (descendant of Gwenedd, Pa. Welsh settlers.) DAB. Jenkins, *Historical Collections Relating to Gwynedd,* p. 396.

Hardee, William Joseph (1815-1874), Confederate general. DAB

Harris, John (1726-1791), founder of Harrisburg, Pa. DAB

Hopper, Edward (1882-   ), contemporary artist. CB, 1950.

Houston, George Smith (1811-1879), Governor of Alabama, 1874; Senator from Alabama, 1878-79. DAB

Howell, Thomas Jefferson (1842-1912), botanist and authority on the flora of the Pacific northwest. DAB

Hughes, Rupert (1872-   ), contemporary novelist. NCAB, C, p. 314.

Humphreys, Andrew Atkinson (1810-1883), Union general. DAB

Humphreys, Harry Elmer, Jr. (1900-   ), president, United States Rubber Company. CB, 1949.

Humphreys, West Hughes (1806-1882), United States District Judge, Tennessee; editor of legal reports. DAB

James, Thomas Chalkley (1766-1835), specialist on obstetrics; editor of *Eclectic Repertory.* DAB

James, Thomas Potts (1803-1882), botanist; authority on the flora of the United States. DAB

Jarvis, William (1770-1859), federal official in the consular service; specialist in animal husbandry. DAB

Jefferson, Thomas (1743-1826), author of the Declaration of Independence and President of the United States. DAB

Jenckes, Thomas Allen (1818-1875), Congressman from Rhode Island; father of Civil Service reform. DAB

Jenkins, Albert Gallatin (1830-1864), Confederate general. DAB

Jenkins, Howard Malcolm (1842-1902), newspaper editor; Quaker leader; Pennsylvania historian. DAB

Jenkins, Micah (1835-1864), Confederate general. DAB

Jenks, Jeremiah Whipple (1856-1929), economist; authority on immigration. DAB

Jenks, Tudor Storrs (1857-1922), author of children's books. DAB

Jenks, William (1778-1866), Congregationalist leader; humanitarian; antiquarian. DAB

Jones, Allen (1739-1807), Revolutionary War general and North Carolina statesman. DAB

Jones, Amanda Theodosia (1835-1914), late nineteenth century poet; inventor of food preservative containers. DAB

Jones, Benjamin Franklin (1824-1903), industrialist; co-founder of Jones & Laughlin Steel Company. DAB

Jones, Calvin (1775-1846), pioneer North Carolina Physician. DAB

Jones, Catesby ap Roger (1821-1877), Confederate naval officer; in charge of the Merrimac. DAB

Jones, Charles Alvin (1887-   ), jurist, U. S. Circuit Court of Appeals, 1939-45; Supreme Court of Pennsylvania, 1945-56, Chief Justice, 1956-   . WWAm, 1965.

Jones, George Heber (1867-1919), Methodist missionary to Korea; authority on Korea. DAB

Jones, Herschell Vespasian (1861-1928), mid-western journalist; owner, *Minneapolis Journal.* DAB

Jones, Horatio Gates (1822-19 ?), Philadelphia civic leader; writer of local Pennsylvania history. CAM, 1893, pp. 161-64.

Jones, Jacob (1768-1850), naval officer; in command of the Wasp during the War of 1812. DAB

Jones, James Kimbrough (1829-1908), United States Senator from Arkansas, 1885-19 ? DAB

Jones, Jehu Glancy (1811-1878), Pennsylvania Congressman; Minister to Austria-Hungary, 1858-61. DAB

Jones, Joseph (1727-1805), Virginia Revolutionary War statesman and patriot. DAB

Jones, Lewis Webster (1899-   ), economist and educator; president, Bennington College, 1941-47; University of Arkansas, 1947-51, **Rutgers University, 1951-**   . CB, 1958.

Jones, Thomas ap Catesby (1790-1858), naval officer; in command of Pacific fleet during War with Mexico. DAB

Jones, Thomas Chalkley (1766-1835), pioneer obstetrician and Philadelphia medical leader. DAB

Jones, William Palmer (1819-1897), pioneer psychiatrist; president, Nashville Medical College. DAB

Jones, Willie (1741-1801), early North Carolina statesman and patriot. DAB

Kenton, Simon (1755-1836), pioneer frontiersman and Indian fighter. DAB

Knight, Edward Henry (1824-1883), mechanical expert; author of numerous works on the subject. DAB

Langley, Samuel Pierpont (1834-1906), pioneer in aviation. DAB

Leonard, Daniel (1740-1829), loyalist lawyer; Chief Justice of Bermuda. DAB

Leonard, Harry Ward (1861-1915), electrical engineer; inventor of numerous electrical appliances. DAB

Letcher, Robert Perkins (1788-1861), Governor of Kentucky, 1841-45; Minister to Mexico, 1849-52. DAB

Lewelling, Lorenzo Dow (1846-1900), Governor of Kansas, 1893-96. DAB

Lewis, Charlton Thomas (1834-1904), Methodist leader; classical scholar; authority on Germany. DAB

Lewis, Diocletian (1823-1886), pioneer in the field of physical education. DAB

Lewis, Dixon Hall (1802-1848), United States Senator from Alabama, 1844-48. DAB

Lewis, Edmund Darch (1835-1910), noted landscape artist of Philadelphia. DAB

Lewis, Ellis (1798-1871), Chief Justice of Pennsylvania, 1854-57. DAB

Lewis, Enoch (1776-1856), abolitionist leader; educator; Quaker journalist. DAB

Lewis, Fielding (1725-1782), Virginia Revolutionary War patriot. DAB

Lewis, Meriwether (1774-1809), explorer; leader of the Lewis and Clark expedition; Governor of Louisiana Territory. DAB

Lewis, Mumford (1854-1929), noted mechanical engineer. DAB

Lewis, Orlando Faulkland (1873-1922), pioneer social worker; penologist. DAB

Lewis, Sinclair (1885-1951), contemporary novelist. *Twentieth Century Authors.*

Lewis, Wilfred (1854-1929), mechanical engineer; expert on the mechanics of gears. DAB

Lincoln, Abraham (1809-1865), President of the United States (descendant of Cadwallader Evans of Gwenedd, Pa. Welsh settlement through his mother). DAB. Jenkins, *Historical Collections Relating to Gwynedd,* p. 325-26.

Lloyd, Edward (1779-1834), Governor of Maryland, 1809-11. DAB

Lloyd, Henry Damerest (1849-1903), social reformer and author of *Wealth Versus Commonwealth.* DAB. NCAB, XXVIII, p. 191.

Lowndes, Lloyd (1845-1905), Governor of Maryland, 1895-99. DAB

Luelling, Henderson (1809-1878), pioneer Oregon nurseryman. DAB

Malcom, Howard (1799-1879), Baptist missionary; president, Bucknell University, 1851-57. DAB

Marshall, George Catlett (1880-1959), general of the armies, World War II; Secretary of State. CB, 1947, 1959.

Marshall, John (1755-1835), Chief Justice of the United States. DAB

Marshall, Louis (1773-1866), educator; president, Transylvania University, Kentucky. DAB

Marshall, Thomas Alexander (1794-1871), chief justice, Kentucky Court of Appeals, 1866-67. DAB

Marshall, William Louis (1846-1920), Army general; civil engineer. DAB

Martin, Elizabeth Price (1864-1932), Philadelphia civic leader. DAB

Masters, Edgar Lee (1869-1950), well-known contemporary poet. NCAB, A, p. 387. CB, 1959.

Matthews, Stanley (1824-1889), United States Senator from Ohio; Associate Justice, United States Supreme Court, 1881-89. DAB. CAM, 1882, p. 99.

Meeker, Ezra (1830-1928), Oregon-country pioneer. DAB

Meredith, Edwin Thomas (1876-1928), editor of farming journals; Secretary of Agriculture, 1920-21. DAB

Merrick, Edwin Thomas (1808-1897), chief justice of Louisiana, 1856-64. DAB

Merrick, Frederick (1810-1894), Methodist leader; president, Ohio Wesleyan University, 1860-73. DAB

Miles, Nelson Appleton (1839-1925), Spanish-American War general. DAB

Monroe, James (1758-1831), President of the United States (Welsh descent through his mother, Eliza Jones). DAB

Morehead, John Motley (1796-1866), Governor of North Carolina, 1840-44. DAB

Morgan, Anne (1873-1936), woman's rights advocate; philanthropist. *Columbia Encyclopedia.*

Morgan, Charles (1795-1878), coastal shipper; railroad entrepreneur. DAB

Morgan, Daniel Nash (1844-1931), Treasurer of the United States, 1893-97. NCAB, XXVIII, p. 21.

Morgan, Edwin Barber (1806-1881), founder of United States Express Company, 1854; enemy of the Tweed Ring; philanthropist. DAB

Morgan, Edwin Denison (1811-1883), Governor of New York, 1858-62; United States Senator from New York, 1863-70. DAB

Morgan, Edwin Vernon (1856-1934), career diplomat; Ambassador to Brazil. DAB

Morgan, George Washington (1820-1893), Union general; Congressman from Ohio; foe of the Radical Republicans. DAB

Morgan, James Dade (1810-1896), Union general. DAB

Morgan, James Morris (1845-1928), author of sea stories; soldier of fortune. DAB

Morgan, John Pierpont (1837-1913), internationally known banker and financier. DAB

Morgan, John Pierpont (the Younger) (1867-1943), internationally known banker and financier. *Columbia Encyclopedia.*

Morgan, John T. (1824-1907), Confederate general; United States Senator from Alabama, 1877-1907. DAB

Morgan, Junius Spencer (1813-1890), pioneer banker and financier; founder of the House of Morgan. DAB

Morgan, Lewis Henry (1818-1881), ethnologist; authority on the Iroquois Indians. DAB

Morgan, Morris Hickey (1859-1910), classical scholar; Harvard professor. DAB

Morgan, Philip Hickey (1825-1900), diplomat; associate justice, Louisiana Supreme Court, 1873-76; judge, International Court, Egypt, 1877-80. DAB

Morris, Lewis Richard (1760-1825), early Vermont political leader. DAB

Morris, Newbold (1902-1966), New York City civic leader and municipal official. CB, 1952.

Morris, Richard Valentine (1768-1815), naval commander in the fight against the Tripoli pirates. DAB

Morris, Robert (1745-1815), Chief Justice of New Jersey, 1777-79; Federal Judge of New Jersey district, 1789-1815. DAB

Morris, Thomas (1776-1844), abolitionist leader; United States Senator from Ohio, 1833-39. DAB

Nichols, Clarina Irene Howard (1810-1885), pioneer leader in the women's rights movement. DAB

Oakes, Thomas Fletcher (1843-1919), pioneer railroad entrepreneur; president, Northern Pacific Railroad, 1888-93. DAB

Oates, William Calvin (1835-1910), Governor of Alabama, 1895-97. DAB

Owen, Edward Thomas (1850-1931), grammarian; University of Wisconsin professor. DAB

Owen, Thomas McAdory (1866-1920), Alabama lawyer and historian. DAB

Powell, Dawn (1897-   ), contemporary novelist. *Twentieth Century Authors.*

Powell, John Wesley (1834-1902), explorer of the Colorado River and the Grand Canyon. DAB

Powell, Lucien Whiting (1846-1930), landscape artist. DAB

Price, Bruce (1845-1903), late nineteenth century architect; builder of hotels, churches, and civic buildings. DAB

Price, Eli Kirk (1797-1884), legal scholar and reformer. DAB

Price, Eli Kirk (1860-1933), Philadelphia civic leader; father of Fairmount Parkway. DAB

Price, Hiram (1814-1901), Congressman from Iowa; United States Commissioner for Indian Affairs, 1881-85. DAB

Price, Ira Maurice (1856-1939), noted orientalist. DAB

Price, Sterling (1809-1867), Governor of Missouri, 1852; Confederate general. DAB

Pritchard, Jeter Connelly (1857-1921), United States Senator from North Carolina, 1894-1904. DAB

Pugh, Evan (1828-1864), chemist; authority on plant life; president, Pennsylvania State College. DAB

Randolph, George Whyte (1818-1867), Confederate general; Confederate Secretary of War. DAB

Randolph, Thomas Jefferson (1792-1875), authority on Thomas Jefferson. DAB

Reese, Lizette Woodworth (1856-1935), lyric poet. DAB

Rhodes, James Allen (1909-   ), Mayor of Columbus, Ohio, 1944-53; State Auditor, 1953-63; Gov. of Ohio, 1963-   . CB, 1949; WWAm, 1967.

Rice, David (1733-1816), father of Presbyterianism in Kentucky. DAB

Richards, John Kelvey (1856-1909), Soliciter General of the United States, 1897-1903; United States Circuit Judge, 1903-09. DAB

Ringgold, Cadwalader (1802-1867), naval officer in command of the Union blockade. DAB

Roberts, Benjamin Stone (1810-1875), Union general. DAB

Roberts, George Brooks (1833-1897), pioneer railroad entrepreneur; president, Pennsylvania Railroad. DAB; CAM, 1896, pp. 1-4.

Roberts, Howard (1843-1900), late nineteenth century sculptor. DAB

Roberts, Job (1756-1851), pioneer agriculturalist and experimenter. DAB

Roberts, Jonathan (1771-1854), United States Senator from Pennsylvania, 1814-21. DAB

Roberts, Oran Milo (1815-1898), chief justice of Texas, 1864-68; Governor of Texas, 1878-83. DAB

Roberts, Robert Richford (1778-1843), pioneer Methodist preacher and bishop. DAB

Roberts, William Milner (1810-1881), civil engineer; pioneer railroad builder. DAB

Rogers, Robert William (1864-1930), orientalist; Old Testament scholar. DAB

Rotch, Thomas Morgan (1849-1914), pioneer in the field of pediatrics. DAB

Runcie, Constance Faunt LeRoy (1836-1911), pianist and composer of poetry and songs. DAB

Russell, Joseph (1719-1804), early New Bedford, Massachusetts, merchant and ship-owner. DAB

Rutherford, Lewis Morris (1816-1892), astrophysicist and experimenter in the field of spectroscopy. DAB

Saulsbury, Eli (1817-1893), United States Senator from Delaware, 1871-88. DAB

Saulsbury, Gove (1815-1881), Governor of Delaware, 1865-72. DAB

Saulsbury, Williard (1820-1892), United States Senator from Delaware, 1860-72; Chancellor of Delaware, 1873-92. DAB

Saulsbury, Williard (1861-1927), (son of above), United States Senator from Delaware, 1913-19. DAB

Savery, William (1750-1804), Quaker preacher and missionary to the Seneca Indians. DAB

Shelby, Joseph Orville (1830-1897), Confederate general. DAB

Simpson, Edward (1824-1888), Rear Admiral, United States Navy. DAB

Snethen, Nicholas (1769-1845), founder of the Methodist Protestant Church. DAB

Stephens, Alice Barber (1858-1932), noted illustrator and engraver. DAB

Stuart, James Ewell Brown (Jeb) (1833-1864), Confederate general. (Mother of Welsh Descent.) DAB

Thomas, Amos Russell (1826-1895), leading homeopathic physician; dean, Hahnemann Medical College. DAB

Thomas, Edith Matilda (1854-1925), poet and writer of children's books. DAB

Thomas, Frederick William (1806-1866), newspaper editor and novelist. DAB

Thomas, George Henry (1816-1870), Union general. DAB

Thomas, Isaiah (1749-1831), Revolutionary War patriot; pioneer printer; historian of the press. DAB

Thomas, Jerome B. (1814-1866), landscape and portrait artist. DAB

Thomas, Jess (1927-   ), leading Wagnerian tenor and Metropolitan Opera singer. CB, 1964.

Thomas, John Jacobs (1810-1895), pioneer pomologist; editor, agricultural journals. DAB

Thomas, Joseph (1811-1891), lexicographer; compiler of scholarly reference books. DAB

Thomas, Lowell Jackson (1892-   ), nationally known commentator; explorer and writer. CB, 1952.

Thomas, Martha Carey (1857-1935), suffragist; president, Bryn Mawr College, 1894-1924. DAB

Thomas, Richard Henry (1854-1904), Baltimore physician; poet and novelist. DAB

Thompson, Cephas Giovanni (1809-1888), nineteenth century portrait painter. DAB

Thompson, Zadock (1796-1856), Vermont historian; naturalist; mathematician. DAB

Van Rensselaer, Martha (1864-1932), pioneer in the field of home economics. DAB

Walker, Robert Franklin (1850-1930), associate justice, Missouri Supreme Court, 1913-30. DAB

Webster, Daniel (1782-1852), Secretary of State, 1841-43; United States Senator from Massachusetts, 1827-41, 1845-50. (Welsh through his mother, Abigail Eastman.) DAB

Wheaton, Henry (1785-1848), historian of international law. DAB

Wilkins, William (1779-1865), United States Senator from Pennsylvania, 1831-34; Minister to Russia, 1834-36; Secretary of War, 1844-45. DAB

Williams, Edwin (1797-1854), journalist and compiler. DAB

Williams, Elkanah (1822-1888), Cincinnati physician and pioneer in the field of opthalmology. DAB

Williams, G. Mennon (1911-   ), Governor of Michigan, 1948-61; Assistant Secretary of State for African Affairs, 1961. CB, 1961.

Williams, George Henry (1820-1910), United States Senator from Oregon, 1865-72; Attorney General of the United States, 1871-75. DAB

Williams, Henry Shaler (1847-1918), paleontologist and Cornell University professor. DAB

Williams, John James (1904-   ), prominent businessman; United States Senator from Delaware, 1947-   . CB, 1952.

Williams, Reuel (1783-1862), United States Senator from Maine, 1837-43. DAB

Wines, Frederick Howard (1838-1912), prison reformer and social worker. DAB

Wright, George Grover (1820-1896), United States Senator from Iowa, 1871-77; chief justice, Supreme Court of Iowa, 1856-60. DAB

Wright, Joseph Albert (1810-1867), Governor of Indiana, 1849-57; Minister to Prussia, 1857; United States Senator from Indiana, 1862-63. DAB

Yale, Caroline Ardelia (1848-1933), pioneer educator of the deaf. DAB

Yale, Linus (1821-1868), inventor and manufacturer of the well-known Yale locks. DAB

Yoakum, Henderson (1810-1856), lawyer; Texas historian. DAB

CLASSIFIED BIBLIOGRAPHY OF WRITINGS
ON THE WELSH IN AMERICA

Bibliographies

Blackwell, Henry, "A Bibliography of Welsh Americana," *National Library of Wales Journal, Supplement Series,* III, No. 1, 1942.
———— "Bibliography of What Has Been Published in the United States Relating to Wales and the Welsh from the Earliest to the Present Time Together with the Productions of Welsh Authors on Miscellaneous Subjects Chronologically Arranged," Feb. 25, 1886. Manuscript in Yale University Library, New Haven, Connecticut.
Lewis, Idwal, "A Bibliography of Welsh Americana," *National Library of Wales Journal,* XI, No. 4 (Winter), 1960, pp. 371-81.
Library of Congress, *Y Cymry yn America, the Welsh in America. References to Literature Available in the Library of Congress,* mimeographed, 1933.

General Items on the Welsh in America

Berthoff, Rowland Tappan, *British Immigrants in Industrial America,* Cambridge, Mass., (Harvard University Press), 1953, 296pp.
Casson, Herbert N., "The Welsh in America," *Munsey's Magazine,* XXV, (Sept., 1906), pp. 749-54.
Conway, Alan, edit., *The Welsh in America, Letters from the Immigrants,* Minneapolis, (University of Minnesota Press), 1961.
Davenport, F. M., "The Spirit of the Welsh Race," *Cambrian,* XXXI, (Apr. 1, 1911), pp. 4-5.
Davies, David, "The Important Part Taken by Welshmen in Forming American History," *Cambrian,* IX, (Jan., 1889), pp. 9-11.
Davis, David, "Early Welshmen as Peace Factors," *Cambrian,* XXXI, (Apr. 1, 1911), pp. 4-5.
Darlington, Thomas, "The Welsh in the United States," *Wales,* I, pp. 349-52.
Dodd, A. H., *The Character of Early Welsh Emigration to the United States,* Cardiff, (University of Wales Press), 1953; 36 page pamphlet.
Edwards, Ebenezer (William Penn, pseud.), *Facts about Welsh Factors, Welshmen as Factors in the Foundation and Development of the U.S. Republic,* Utica, N. Y., (T. J. Griffiths), 1899, 429pp.

Edwards, Glen, "Welsh Americans," *Cambrian,* XXI, (June, 1901), pp. 254-57.

Evans, Albert, "The Welshmen in Early American History," *Cambrian,* IX, (Oct., 1889), pp. 290-92.

Evans, E. C., "Census Reports of the Welsh Population in the United States from 1850-1890," *Cambrian,* XIII, (May, 1893), pp. 131-39.

———— "The Welsh People in America," *Cambrian,* XXXI, (March 15, 1911), pp. 4-7.

Griffiths, Samuel, "The Influence of the Cymry on English and American Institutions," *Cambrian,* IX, (Aug., 1889), pp. 231-33.

Harries, Frederick James, *Welshmen and the United States,* Pontypridd, (Glamorgan County *Times*), 1927, 27pp.

Haskin, Frederic J., "The Foreign Elements in America," *Cambrian,* XXVII, (June, 1907), pp. 267-70.

James, Thomas L., "The Welsh in America, Additional Facts," *Cambrian,* XIII, (Mar., 1893), pp. 68-77.

———— "The Welsh in the United States," *Cosmopolitan,* X, (Feb., 1891), pp. 466-76; also reprinted in *Cambrian,* XII, (Jan., 1892), pp. 4-7; (Mar., 1892), pp. 74-77.

———— "The Welshman's Contribution to the Development of the United States and Canada," *Royal Blue Book, Prize Productions of the Pittsburgh International Eisteddfod,* Pittsburgh, 1913, pp. 127-211.

Jenkins, Ann M., "What the Welsh Have Done for the World," *Cambrian,* XXV, (Sept., 1905), pp. 379-82.

Jones, Alexander, *The Cymry of '76; or, Welshmen and Their Descendants of the American Revolution,* New York, (Sheldon, Lamport & Co.), 1855.

Jones, Erasmus W., "The Welsh in America," *Atlantic Monthly,* XXXVII, (Mar., 1876), pp. 305-13.

Jones, Howell, "The Welsh," *Cambrian,* XXVI, (Apr., 1906), pp. 156-58.

Jones, W. B., "What America Owes to Welshmen," *Cambrian,* VII, (Dec., 1887), pp. 355-60.

Morgan, W. P., "The Welsh in the United States," *Wales,* III, (1896), pp. 17-24.

Owens, J. E., "The Welsh in Politics," *North American Review,* CLVII, (Nov., 1893), pp. 635-36.

Peters, Madison C., "America's Debt to the Welsh," *Cambrian,* XXXIV, (Aug. 15, 1914), pp. 5-6.

Powell, Thomas Watkins, *The History of the Ancient Britons and Their Descendants,* Delaware, Ohio, 1882, 481pp.

Prosser, William, "The Influence of the Welsh in America," *Cambrian,* XXVIII, (Apr., 1908), pp. 151-61.

Thomas, H. E., "The Welsh in the United States," *Chautauquan*, VIII, (Jan., 1888), pp. 238-40; also reprinted in *Cambrian*, X, (Feb., 1890), pp. 35-37; (Mar., 1890), pp. 67-69.

Thomas, Robert D., *Hanes Cymry America*, Utica, N. Y., (T. J. Griffiths), 1872, 527pp.

Williams, David, "The Contribution of Wales to the Development of the United States," *The National Library of Wales Journal*, II, (Summer, 1942), pp. 97-108.

——— *Cymru ac America, Wales and America*, Cardiff, (Univ. of Wales Press Board), 1946.

——— "Some Figures Relating to Emigration from Wales," *Bulletin of The Board of Celtic Studies*, VII, (1935), pp. 396-415.

Wilson, E. S., "The Welsh People as American Citizens," *Cambrian*, XVII, (May, 1897), pp. 222-23.

WELSH INDIAN LEGEND

Blackwell, Henry, "Madoc and His Discovery of America," *Cambrian,* X, (Nov., 1890), pp. 324-26.

Boland, Charles Michael, *They All Discovered America,* New York, (Doubleday & Co.), 1961, Chapter 16. (Also in a Permabook edition, 1963.)

Bowen, Benjamin Franklin, *America Discovered by the Welsh in 1170 A.D.,* Philadelphia, 1876, 184pp.

Burder, George, *The Welsh Indians: or a Collection of Papers Respecting a People Whose Ancestors Emigrated from Wales to America in the Year 1170, with Prince Madoc, and Who Are Said Now to Inhabit a Beautiful Country on the West Side of the Mississippi,* London, 1797.

Catlin, George, *North American Indians, Being Letters and Notes on Their Manners, Customs, and Conditions, Written During Eight Years' Travel amongst the Wildest Tribes of Indians of North America, 1832, 1839,* 2 vols., Edinburgh, (John Grant), 1926, Vol. I, p. 231; Vol. II, pp. 295-98.

Coburn, Margaret Thomas, "A Chapter of American Antiquities," *Cambrian,* XXVIII, (Mar., 1908), pp. 124-28.

Davies, W. D., "David Samwell's Poem—'The Padouca Hunt'," *National Library of Wales Journal,* II, (Summer, 1942), pp. 120-23.

De Costa, Benjamin Franklin, *Myvyrian Archaiology: the Pre-Columbian Voyages of the Welsh to America,* Albany, N. Y., 1891; also reprinted in *New England Historical and Genealogical Register,* XLV, (Jan., 1891), pp. 15-23.

De Voto, Bernard, *The Course of Empire,* Boston, (Houghton-Mifflin), 1952, pp. 68-73; 373-79.

Evans, E., "Madog ab Owain," *Cambrian,* III, (Sept.-Oct., 1883), pp. 232-34.

Greenwood, Isaac J., "The Rev. Morgan Jones and the Welsh Indians of Virginia," *New England Historical and Genealogical Register,* LII, (Jan., 1898), pp. 28-36.

Jones, Anewin, "Alleged Discoveries of America" (The Madogian Tradition Refuted), *Cambrian,* XX, pp. 241-43, 292-95, 336-59, 388-91, 448-54, 492-97.

Jones, J. J., "The Legend of Madoc," *National Library of Wales Journal,* II, (Summer, 1942), pp. 120-23.

Lewis, Benjamin F., "The Madog Tradition. The Search for the Madogians and Other Incidents in the Welsh History of Utica, Past and Present," *Transactions of the Oneida Historical Society,* No. 6, 1892-94, pp. 117-35, Utica, N. Y., 1894; also in *Cambrian,* XIV, (June, 1894), pp. 163-67; (July, 1894), pp. 193-97; (Aug., 1894), pp. 231-34.

Leyshon, Lewis, "Among Welsh Indians," *Cambrian,* XVIII, (Jan., 1898), pp. 11-14.

Morrison, Alfred T., "The Mabinogion of the West," *William and Mary Quarterly,* XIX, (Jan., 1911), pp. 163-65.

Nasatir, A. F., "John Evans, Explorer and Surveyor," *Missouri Historical Review,* XXV, (Jan., 1931), pp. 219-39; (Apr., 1931), pp. 432-60; (July, 1931), pp. 585-608.

Roberts, Joseph, "A Welsh Tribe of Indians," *Cambrian,* XI, (July, 1891), pp. 205-6.

Skinner, Hubert M., "Centennial Reproduction of the Departure of Prince Madoc. By the Laureate Robert Southey, 1805," *Cambrian,* XXV, (Oct., 1905), pp. 434-39.

———— "Welsh Indians," *Cambrian,* XXV, (Nov., 1905), pp. 302-3.

Southey, Robert, "Madoc, an Epic Poem," *Poems,* I, 1854, pp. 3-364.

Williams, David, "John Evans' Strange Journey," *American Historical Review,* LIV, (Jan., 1949), pp. 277-95; (Apr., 1949), pp. 508-29.

————"John Evans' Strange Journey," Honourable Society of the Cymmrodorion, *Transactions,* 1948, pp. 105-46.

Williams, John, *An Enquiry into the Truth of the Tradition, Concerning the Discovery of America by Prince Madog ab Owen Gwynedd, about the Year 1170,* London, 1791, 82pp.

————*Farther Observations on the Discovery of America by Prince Madog ab Owen Gwynedd, about the Year 1170. Containing the Account Given by Gen. Bowles, the Creek or Cherokee Indian, Lately in London, and by Several Others, of a Welsh Tribe of Indians, Now Living in the Western Parts of North America,* London, (J. Brown), 1792, 51pp.

Wolff, Geoffrey A., "Case Built for Welsh Columbus," *Boston Sunday Globe,* Feb. 5, 1967, p. 2.

COLONIAL PERIOD

DELAWARE SETTLEMENT

Cooch, Edward W., "The Folks of Welsh Tract," in his *Delaware Historic Events, a Compilation of Articles and Addresses,* Cooch's Bridge, Del., 1946, pp. 71-78.

Cooch, Frances A., *Little Known History of Newark, Delaware and Its Environs,* Newark, Del., 1936, pp. 257-65.

(see also Colonial Period: Welsh Anglicans, Baptists, and Presbyterians)

MASSACHUSETTS SETTLEMENT

Wright, Otis Olney, *History of Swansea, Massachusetts, 1667-1917,* Swansea, Mass., 1917.

(see also Colonial Period: Welsh Baptists)

PENNSYLVANIA SETTLEMENTS

Dunaway, Wayland E., "Early Welsh Settlements of Pennsylvania," *Pennsylvania History,* XII, (Oct., 1945), pp. 251-69.

Eschelman, H. Frank, "Two Centuries of Caernarvon History," Lancaster County Historical Society, Proceedings, XXVI, (June, 1922), pp. 145-51.

Evans, Allen, "Our Welsh Heritage," *Y Drych,* C, (Mar. 15, 1951), pp. 3, 15-16.

Fisher, Sydney G., "The Welsh Element in Pennsylvania," *Cambrian,* XVII, (Mar., 1897), pp. 115-17.

Jones, Horatio Gates, "Where and When Was the First Colony of Welsh Established in the United States," *Cambrian,* IV, (Jan., 1884), pp. 43-45.

Jones, W. B., "The Early Welsh Settlers in America," *Cambrian,* VII, (Aug., 1887), pp. 227-29.

McKenna, John J., "Early Welsh in Berks Co.," *Historical Review of Berks County,* XV, (Jan., 1950), pp. 179-86.

Owen, Benjamin F., "Tradition vs. Fact—Bangor Church," Lancaster County Historical Society, *Papers,* VII, No. 4.

———— *The Welsh of Cumru Township, an Address Delivered before the Historical Society of Berks County, Pa., September 12, 1899,* Reading, Pa., 1899. 6 page pamphlet.

"Welsh Worthies of Pennsylvania," *Cambrian*, XV, (Nov., 1895), pp. 325-26.

Williams, J. Ambler, "The Influence of the Welsh on the History of Pennsylvania," *Pennsylvania History*, X, (Apr., 1943), pp. 118-23.

(see also Colonial Period: Welsh Anglicans, Baptists, Quakers, and Presbyterians)

SOUTH CAROLINA SETTLEMENT

Gregg, Alexander, *History of the Old Cheraws*, New York, (Richardson & Co.), 1867, pp. 45-102.

McMaster, Louise, "The Welsh Settlement of South Carolina," Columbia, S. Car., *The State Magazine*, (Jan. 18, 1953), p. 6.

Meriwether, Robert L., *The Expansion of South Carolina*, Kingsport, Tenn., (Southern Publishers), 1940, pp. 90-96.

(see also Colonial Period: Welsh Baptists)

WELSH ANGLICANS OR EPISCOPALIANS

Barrow, A. J., "St. James's Perkiomen," *Pennsylvania Magazine of History and Biography*, XIX, (Apr., 1895), pp. 87-95.

Bryden, G. MacLaren, "David Griffith, 1742-1789," *Protestant Episcopal Church Historical Magazine*, IX, (Sept., 1940), pp. 194-230.

Burr, Nelson R., "The Welsh Episcopalians of Colonial Pennsylvania and Delaware," *Historical Magazine of the Protestant Episcopal Church*, VIII, (June, 1939), pp. 101-22.

Clement, John, "Clergymen Licensed Overseas by the Bishops of London, 1696-1710 and 1715-1716," *Protestant Episcopal Church Historical Magazine*, XVI, (Dec., 1947), pp. 318-49.

——— "Griffith Hughes: S.P.G. Missionary to Pennsylvania and Famous 18th Century Naturalist," *Protestant Episcopal Church Historical Magazine*, XVII, (June, 1948), pp. 151-63.

Clement, Mary, "Henry Nichols, the First Residential S.P.G. Missionary to Pennsylvania," *Protestant Episcopal Church Historical Magazine*, XII, (Sept., 1943), pp. 242-45.

Everlain, Harold, *The Church of St. Peters' in the Great Valley*, 1700-1940.

Groton, Nathaniel, *250th Anniversary, 1700-1950, St. James Episcopal Church, Perkiomen, R.D. 2, Collegeville, Pa.*, 1950; 6 page pamphlet.

Jones, David, "Christ Church and the Old Welsh Settlers of Philadelphia, Pa.," *Cambrian*, X, (Sept., 1887), pp. 260-64.

Owen, Benjamin F., "Letters of the Rev. Griffith Hughes of St. David's Church, Radnor, Penna., 1733-1736," *Pennsylvania Magazine of History and Biography*, XXIV, (July, 1900), pp. 139-48.

Rightmyer, Nelson Waite, "List of Anglican Clergymen Receiving a

Bounty for Overseas Service, 1680-1688," *Protestant Episcopal Church Historical Magazine,* XVII, (June, 1948), pp. 174-82.

Scofield, Charles F., "Supplementary History of St. James Church, Perkiomen," Historical Society of Montgomery County, Pa., *Historical Sketches,* V, 1925.

Williams, Archdeacon, "St. David's Church," *Cambrian,* (Jan., 1901), pp. 15-17.

Williams, I. C., "St. James Church, Perkiomen, Evansburg," Historical Society of Montgomery County, Pa., *Historical Sketches,* V, 1925.

WELSH BAPTISTS

General

Armitage, Thomas, *A History of the Baptists Traced by Their Vital Principles from the Time of Our Lord and Savior Jesus Christ to the Year 1886,* New York, (Bryan, Taylor & Co.), 1887, pp. 598-616, 678-81, and 712-13.

Davis, J., *History of the Welsh Baptists from the Year Sixty-Three to the Year One Thousand Seven Hundred and Seventy,* Pittsburgh, (D. M. Hogan), 1835.

Edwards, Morgan, *Materials towards a History of the American Baptists,* I, Philadelphia, 1770.

Delaware Settlement

"An Ancient Welsh Baptist Church," (Iron Hill, Delaware), *Cambrian,* XII, (Oct., 1892), pp. 292-93.

Cooch, Edward W., "Welsh Tract Baptist Meeting House," in his *Delaware Historic Events, a Compilation of Articles and Addresses,* Cooch's Bridge, Del., 1946, pp. 71-78.

Cook, Richard B., *The Early and Later Delaware Baptists,* Philadelphia, (American Baptist Publication Society), 1880, pp. 13-20.

Edwards, Morgan, *Materials towards a History of the Baptists in Delaware State,* Philadelphia, (Lippincott), 1885.

"Pencader Hundred, New Castle Co., Del. Welsh Tract Meeting. Records of the Welsh Tract Baptist Meeting, Pencader Hundred, New Castle County, Delaware, 1701-1828 . . . Copied from the Original Records in the Possession of the Meeting Officials," *Papers of the Historical Society of Delaware,* XLIII, 2 vols., Wilmington, Del., 1904.

Massachusetts Swansea Settlement

Boone, Ilsley, edit., *Elements in Baptist Development,* Boston, (Backus Historical Society), 1913, 250pp.

Rowe, Henry K., "The Welsh Element in American Baptist Development" in Boone's *Elements in Baptist Development,* pp. 129-48.

Smith, Arthur Warren, "The Early History of Swansea Church," in Boone's *Elements in Baptist Development,* pp. 71-84.

Wright, Otis Olney, *History of Swansea, Massachusetts, 1667-1917,* Swansea, Mass., 1917, pp. 101-7.

Pennsylvania Settlements

Gillette, A. D., edit., *Minutes of the Philadelphia Baptist Association from A.D. 1707 to A.D. 1807; Being the First One Hundred Years of Its Existence,* Philadelphia, (American Baptist Publication Society), 1851, pp. 3-21.

Griffith, John T., "The Relationship of the Early Baptists of Pennsylvania to the Welsh Baptists of Wales," in his *Reminiscences: Forty-Three Years in America from April, 1865 to April, 1908,* Morristown, Wales, (Jones & Son), 1913, pp. 148-64.

Jones, David, "The Early Welsh Baptist Churches of Pennsylvania," *Cambrian,* XIII, (Feb., 1893), pp. 40-41.

Jones, Horatio Gates, "The Baptist Church in the Great Valley, Tredyffrin Township, Chester County, Pa.," *Cambrian,* IV, (Jan., 1884), pp. 8-14; (Feb., 1884), pp. 33-39.

———— *Historical Sketch of the Lower Dublin (or Pennepek) Baptist Church,* Morrisania, N. Y., 1869; 30 page pamphlet.

———— "The Lower Dublin or Pennepek Baptist Church, Philadelphia, Pa.," *Cambrian,* III, (Jan.-Feb., 1883), pp. 19-25.

———— "Welsh Pastors of the Pennepek Baptist Church, Philadelphia," *Cambrian,* III, (Mar.-Apr., 1883), pp. 54-73.

Keen, William Williams, edit., *The Bi-Centennial Celebration of the Founding of the First Baptist Church of the City of Philadelphia, 1898,* Philadelphia, (American Baptist Publication Society), 1899, 511pp.

Tumbelston, Robert T., edit., "History of Old Pennepack," *250th Anniversary, Old Pennepack Baptist Church, 1688-1938,* Philadelphia, 1938; 24 page pamphlet.

South Carolina Welsh Neck Settlement

Gregg, Alexander, *History of the Old Cheraws,* New York, (Richardson & Co.), 1867, pp. 45-102.

McMaster, Louise, "The Welsh Settlement of South Carolina," Columbia, S. C., *The State Magazine,* (Jan. 18, 1953), p. 6.

Meriwether, Robert L., *The Expansion of South Carolina, 1729-1765,* Kingsport, Tenn., (Southern Publishers), 1940, pp. 90-96.

WELSH FRIENDS OR QUAKERS

Browning, Charles H., *Welsh Settlement of Pennsylvania (sic),* Philadelphia, (W. J. Campbell), 1912, 631pp.

Bunting, Samuel J., *Merion Meeting House, 1695-1945,* Merion, Pa., 1945; 16 page pamphlet.

Centennial Supplement to the Meeting, Haverford, Pa., 12th month, 1934; 12 page pamphlet with miscellaneous data on the Welsh Friends of Haverford.

Chitlaw, Benjamin Williams, "Revisiting the Home of Childhood. Bala and Dolgelly and the Quakers of the Time of William Penn," *Cambrian,* IX, (Nov., 1889), pp. 333-34.

Corbit, W. F., "Welsh Emigration to Pennsylvania," *Pennsylvania Magazine of History and Biography,* I, No. 3, (1877), pp. 330-32.

Glenn, Thomas A., *Merion in the Welsh Tract,* Norristown, Pa. (Herald Press), 1896, 394pp.

———— *Welsh Founders of Pennsylvania,* Oxford, Eng., (Jones), 2 vols., 1911-13.

———— "Welsh Settlers in Chester County and Their Descendants," Chester County Historical Society, *Bulletin,* 1898, 7pp.

———— "The Welsh Tract," *Pennsylvania Magazine of History and Biography,* XVII, (Oct., 1893), pp. 372-74.

Hibbard, Ruth, *Our Town, How We Began, How We Are Governed, Bryn Mawr and Lower Merion Township,* Bryn Mawr, Pa., 1920, 47pp.

Jenkins, Howard M., *Historical Collections Relating to Gwynedd, a Township of Montgomery County, Pennsylvania, Settled 1689 by Welsh Immigrants, with Some Data Referring to the Adjoining Township of Montgomery, also a Welsh Settlement,* Philadelphia, (Ferris Brothers), 1884, 465pp.

———— "The Name Gwynedd in Welsh History," *Pennsylvania Magazine of History and Biography,* VII, (Apr., 1883), pp. 35-44.

———— "The Welsh Settlement at Gwynedd," *Pennsylvania Magazine of History and Biography,* VIII, (1884), pp. 174-83.

———— "The Welsh Tract," *Pennsylvania Magazine of History and Biography,* XVII, (Apr., 1893), p. 117.

———— "The Welsh Tract Purchases," *Pennsylvania Magazine of History and Biography,* XVI, (Jan., 1893), pp. 457-58.

Levick, James J., *The Early History of Merion,* Philadelphia, (Collins), 1880, 41pp.

———— "The Early Welsh Quakers and their Emigration to Pennsylvania," *Pennsylvania Magazine of History and Biography,* XVII, (Jan., 1894), pp. 385-413.

———— "John ap Thomas and His Friends. A Contribution to the Early History of Merion, Near Philadelphia," *Pennsylvania Magazine of History and Biography,* IV, No. 3, (1880), pp. 301-28.

———— "An Old Welsh Pedigree. A Sequel to John ap Thomas and His

Friends," *Pennsylvania Magazine of History and Biography,* IV, No. 4, (1880), pp. 471-83.

Rees, T. Mardy, *A History of the Quakers in Wales and Their Emigration to North America,* Carmarthen, Wales, (W. Spurrell), 1925, 292pp.

"Welsh Emigration to Pennsylvania, an Old Charter Party, 1697-1698," *Pennsylvania Magazine of History and Biography,* I, No. 3, (1887), pp. 330-32.

"The Welsh Tract," *Pennsylvania Magazine of History and Biography,* XVII, (Apr., 1893), p. 117.

"The Welsh Tract Purchases," *Pennsylvania Magazine of History and Biography,* XVI, (Jan., 1893), pp. 457-58.

WELSH PRESBYTERIANS

(Not to be confused with the Calvinistic Methodists of the Nineteenth Century)

Delaware Pencader Settlement

Cooch, Edward W., "The Human Side of Pencader's History," in his *Delaware Historic Events, A Compilation of Articles and Addresses,* Cooch's Bridge, Del., 1946, pp. 71-78.

———— "Pencader—Chief Chair of Presbyterianism," in his *Delaware Historic Events, op. cit.,* pp. 85-88.

Evans, Rees C., "Welsh Settlers of Pencader, Delaware," *Pennsylvania Magazine of History and Biography,* II, No. 3, pp. 343-45.

Skinner, W. T., "History of Pencader Presbyterian Church of Glasgow, Delaware, in *History of Pencader Presbyterian Church, Historical Addresses,* Wilmington, Del. (John M. Rogers Press), 1899, pp. 31-51.

Welbon, Henry G., *A History of Pencader Presbyterian Church, (Welsh in Origin) of Glasgow, Delaware,* Newark, Del., 1936. 63 pages.

Pennsylvania Settlements

An Historic Church. "The Great Valley Presbyterian Church Torn Down and Rebuilt," *Cambrian,* X, (March, 1890), pp. 91-92.

Davies, Hezekiah, "History of the United Congregations of Great Valley, Charleston, and West Chester," *Journal of the Presbyterian Historical Society,* II, (Dec., 1904), pp. 332-39.

Historical Booklet, Abington Presbyterian Church, Pennsylvania, Founded 1714, 225th Anniversary, 1939; 20 page pamphlet.

Patterson, Robert M., *History of the Presbyterian Church of the Great Chester Valley,* Philadelphia (Alfred Martien, printer), 1869; 52 page pamphlet.

Early Welsh Books

"Early Printing in Welsh in America," *Pennsylvania Magazine of History and Biography,* XVI, (July, 1892), p. 254.
Gibbins, Frederick J., "An Early American Welsh Book," *Cambrian,* XXIII, (June, 1903), pp. 228-32.
Jones, Horatio Gates, "The First Welsh Book in America," *Cambrian,* IV, (Oct., 1884), pp. 286-87.
Williams, William, "The First Three Welsh Books Printed in America," *National Library of Wales Journal,* II, (Summer, 1942), pp. 109-20.
———— "More about the First Three Books Printed in America," *National Library of Wales Journal,* III, (Summer, 1943), pp. 19-22.

POST-COLONIAL PERIOD
CULTURAL ACTIVITIES

General

Berthoff, Rowland Tappan, *British Immigrants in Industrial America,* Cambridge, Mass., (Harvard University Press), 1953, *passim.* An excellent analysis and account of the cultural activities of the Welsh in America.

Welsh Baptists

Davies, W. E., "Brief Historical Sketch of the Welsh Baptist Association of Northeastern Pennsylvania," *Fiftieth Anniversary of the Welsh Baptist Association of Northeastern Pennsylvania,* Scranton, Pa., 1905; 10 page pamphlet.

Griffith, John Thomas, "The Baptists of Wyoming Valley," *Cambrian,* XXVI, (Jan., 1906), pp. 20-22.

——— *Brief Biographical Sketches of Deceased Welsh Baptist Ministers Who Have Labored in Northeastern Pennsylvania from 1832 to 1904,* Wilkes-Barre, Pa., 1904; 88 page pamphlet.

——— "Brief Biographical Sketches of the Pastors of the First Welsh Baptist Church of Wilkes-Barre, Pa.," *Cambrian,* XXVII, (Jan., 1908), pp. 67-69.

——— "The Early Baptists of the Wyoming Valley and Edwardsville," *Cambrian,* XXIV, (Mar., 1904), pp. 103-6; (Apr., 1904), pp. 147-49.

——— "The Welsh Baptists in Their Relation to the Beginning of the Baptist Cause in Baltimore," *Cambrian,* XXI, (Sept., 1901), pp. 404-7.

Hartmann, Edward George, edit., *Welsh Baptist Association of Northeastern Pennsylvania, 1855-1955,* Plymouth, Pa., (Payne Printery), 1955; 31 page pamphlet.

——— "The Welsh Baptists in America," *The Chronicle,* XIX, (Apr., 1956), pp. 90-96.

——— "The Welsh Baptists in America—An Evaluation," in his *Welsh Baptist Association of Northeastern Pennsylvania, 1855-1955,* pp. 25-31.

Lewis, James V., "A Brief Historical Sketch of the Welsh Baptist Association of Northeastern Pennsylvania for the Past Twenty-Five Years,

1905-1930," *Seventy-Fifth Anniversary of the Welsh Baptist Association of Northeastern Pennsylvania, 1855-1930,* Wilkes-Barre, Pa., 1930, pp. 7-10.

Newman, A. H., edit., *A Century of Baptist Achievement,* Philadelphia, (Am. Bapt. Publication Society), 1901, chapter IV.

Seventy-Fifth Anniversary of the Welsh Baptist Association of Northeastern Pennsylvania, 1855-1930, Wilkes-Barre, Pa., 1930; 16 page pamphlet.

Welsh Baptist Association of Northeastern Pennsylvania, *Annual Reports,* 1885-1966.

Welsh Baptist Association of Ohio and Western Pennsylvania, *Annual Reports,* 1895-1922.

(See also *Post-Colonial Period: Geographical Settlements* for histories of local Welsh Baptist churches.)

Welsh Calvinistic-Methodists or Presbyterians

Calvinistic Methodist Church in the United States, "Minutes of the General Assembly of the Calvinistic Methodist Church in the United States, 1869-1920," (translation of original documents from the Welsh by the Rev. E. Edwin Jones, D.D., Sept. 1, 1934), 224 page *ms.* in Presbyterian Historical Society, Philadelphia.

Davies, Hugh, *Hanes Cymanfa Dwyreinbarth Pennsylvania, 1845-1896,* Utica, N. Y., (T. J. Griffiths), 1898, 470pp.

Jones, E. Edwin, and Jones, T. W., *Brief History of the Calvinistic Methodist Missionary Society (Welsh Board of Missions), 1869-1936, and Final Accounting of Its Funds, September, 1936,* Columbus, Ohio, (Welsh Board of Missions), c. 1936; 36 page pamphlet.

Griffiths, T. Solomon, *Hanes y Methodistiaid Calfinaidd yn Utica, N. Y.,* Utica, (T. J. Griffiths), 1896.

Presbyterian Church, U.S.A., *Minutes of the General Assembly of the Presbyterian Church in the United States of America,* New Series, XX, August, 1920, *passim.,* (for data on merger of Welsh Calvinistic Methodists).

———— *Minutes of the Synod of Minnesota, (Welsh),* 1921-1933.

———— *Minutes of the Synod of New York and Vermont, (Welsh),* 1921-36.

———— *Minutes of the Synod of Ohio, (Welsh),* 1921-33.

———— *Minutes of the Synod of Pennsylvania, (Welsh),* 1921-36.

———— *Minutes of the Synod of Wisconsin, (Welsh),* 1921-44.

Rowlands, W., *The Welsh Calvinistic Methodists: a Sketch of Their History, Constitution, and Present Standing,* Rome, N. Y., (R. R. Meredith), 1854; 54 page pamphlet.

Williams, Daniel Jenkins, *One Hundred Years of Welsh Calvinistic*

Methodism in America, Philadelphia, (Westminster Press), 1937, 448pp.

(See also *Post-Colonial Period: Geographical Settlements* for histories of local Welsh Calvinistic Methodist or Presbyterian churches.)

Welsh Congregationalists

Congregational Association of Iowa, *Annual Minutes.*
Congregational Association of Kansas, *Annual Minutes.*
Congregational Association of New York, *Annual Minutes.*
Congregational Association of Ohio, *Annual Minutes.*
Congregational Association of Pennsylvania, *Annual Minutes.*
Congregational Association of Wisconsin, *Annual Minutes.*
Davis, Howell D., "The Welsh Congregational Churches of Wisconsin," in Frank N. Dexter's *A Hundred Years of Congregational History in Wisconsin,* Fond du Lac, Wis., 1933, pp. 103-8.
Douglas, Truman O., *The Pilgrims of Iowa,* Boston, (Pilgrim Press), 1911, chapter XVI.
Johnson, P. Adelstein, *The First Century of Congregationalism in Iowa, 1840-1940,* Cedar Rapids, Ia., (Congregational-Christian Conference of Iowa), 1945, pp. 158 and 241.
Jones, David, *Memorial Volume of the Welsh Congregationalists of Pennsylvania, U.S.A.,* Utica, N. Y., (Utica Printing Co.), 1934, 362pp.
Jones, J. Vincent, "A Saga of Ohio Welsh Settlements," *Y Drych,* CIV, (Nov. 15, 1955), p. 2.
Leonard, Delaven L., *A Century of Congregationalism in Ohio,* Oberlin, Ohio, (Pearce & Randolph), 1896, Chapter XII.
One Hundredth Anniversary of the Welsh Gymanfa of Ohio, Radnor, Ohio, 1930; 4 page pamphlet.
(See also *Post-Colonial Period: Settlements* for histories of local Welsh Congregational churches.)

Welsh Mormons

(See *Post-Colonial Settlements: Utah*)

Welsh Preaching

Morgan, Vyrywy, *The Cambro-American Pulpit,* New York, (Funk & Wagnalls), 1898, 595pp. (Sermons of the leading Welsh-American ministers.)

Hymns and Hymnals

Crocker, Bertram, "Welsh Hymnody in the United States," *Crozier Quarterly,* XVI, (1939), pp. 26-31.

Edwards, T. C., et al., *The Congregational Hymnal,* 2nd ed., Kingston, Pa., (E. Humphrey Owen), 1937, 224pp. (Hymns in Welsh and English.)

Jones, John P., and Samuel, Evan, editors, *Telyn yr Undeb,* Racine, Wis., (Advocate Press), 1873.

Protheroe, Daniel, edit., *Can a Mawl, Song and Praise, Llyfr Hymnau a Thonau Methodistiaid Calfinaidd, Unol Dalaethau yr America, The Hymnal of the Calvinistic Methodist Church of the United States of America,* Chicago, (Wagner and Hanson Co.), c. 1918, 405pp.

Newspapers and Magazines

Blackwell, Henry, "Bibliography of What Has Been Published in the United States on the Welsh from the Earliest to the Present Time Together with the Productions of Welsh Authors on Miscellaneous Subjects Chronologically Arranged," Feb. 25, 1886. *Ms.* in Yale University Library, *passim.*

———— "Printers of Books in Welsh in the United States," *Cambrian Gleanings,* I, (May, 1914), pp. 65-69.

Costa, Richard H., "Utica Is Home of Only Welsh Language Paper," *Y Drych,* CV, (Dec. 15, 1956), pp. 9 and 15.

Lewis, Idwal, "Welsh Newspapers and Journals in the United States," *The National Library of Wales Journal,* II, (Summer, 1942), pp. 124-30.

Owen, Bob, "Welsh American Newspapers and Periodicals," *The National Library of Wales Journal,* VI, (Winter, 1950), pp. 373-84.

Williams, Daniel J., *The Welsh of Columbus, Ohio; a Study in Adaptation and Assimilation,* Oshkosh, Wis., 1913, pp. 143-44.

Eisteddfodau

ApMadoc, W., "The Chicago International Eisteddfod," *Cambrian,* XIII, (Oct., 1893), pp. 312-16.

———— "The Columbian International Eisteddfod of 1893 at Chicago," *Cambrian,* XI, (July, 1891), pp. 257-63.

———— "The Grand International Eisteddfod of the World's Fair," *Cambrian,* XIII, (Sept., 1893), pp. 257-63.

———— "The World's Fair Eisteddfod," *Cambrian,* XI, (Aug., 1891), pp. 245-47.

Alaska Yukon Pacific Eisteddfod, *Souvenir Program of the Alaska Yukon Pacific Eisteddfod to Be Held at the Exposition Auditorium, Seattle, Washington, August 27 and 28, 1909,* Seattle, 1909.

Blackwell, Henry, "In the Good Old Days, When the Eisteddfod Was the Genuine Article and Full of Cymric Hwyl," *Druid,* III, No. 48, (Dec. 2, 1909), p. 7.

Columbus, Ohio, Eisteddfod Association, *Official Program, Jan. 1, 1913,* Columbus, O., 1913; 32 page pamphlet.

Cope, Florence Jenkins, "History of the Jackson Eisteddfod," unpublished M.A. thesis, Ohio State University, 1937.

Edwards, Ebenezer (William Penn, pseud.), *Facts about Welsh Factors. The Successful Prize Essay at the International Eisteddfod of the World's Columbian Exposition, Chicago, 1893,* Utica, (T. J. Griffiths), 1889, 429pp.

Edwards, Henry M., "Eisteddfodic Reminiscences," *Druid,* III, No. 38, (Sept. 23, 1909), p. 1; No. 39, (Sept. 30, 1909), p. 1; No. 40, (Oct. 7, 1909), p. 1; No. 42, (Oct. 21, 1909), p. 1; No. 43, (Oct. 28, 1909), p. 1; No. 44, (Nov. 4, 1909), p. 1; No. 45, (Nov. 11, 1909), p. 1; No. 46, (Nov. 18, 1909), p. 1; No. 47, (Nov. 25, 1909), p. 1; No. 48, (Dec. 2, 1909), p. 1.

Edwards Memorial Congregational Church, Edwardsville, Pa., *Cynonfardd Eisteddfod, Annual Programs,* 1920-67.

Evans, Harry F., "The Eisteddfod in Utah," *Cambrian,* XXII, (Oct., 1902), pp. 445-48.

Girard Avenue-Welsh Presbyterian Church, Philadelphia, *Eisteddfod, Annual Programs,* 1910-1966.

Golden Gate International Exposition Eisteddfod, 1939, *Awards in Music, Prose and Poetry,* San Francisco, (David Hughes), 1944; 58 page pamphlet.

"Grand Musical Eisteddfod," (Wilkes-Barre), *Cambrian,* VIII, (Aug., 1888), pp. 227-29.

Hughes, David, *Welsh People of California, 1849-1906,* San Francisco, 1923, 120pp. (Prize essay of the San Francisco Eisteddfod, 1906).

Jones, David E., "Music in Lackawanna County," in Murphy's *History of Lackawanna County,* I, pp. 338-47. (Treats of early Eisteddfodau of Scranton.)

Mitchell, Homer, "The Eisteddfod in Ohio," unpublished M.A. thesis, Ohio State University, 1934.

Moriah Congregational Church, Nanticoke, Pa., *Annual Eisteddfod, Programs,* 1900-16.

Pittsburgh International Eisteddfod, 1913, *The Royal Blue Book. Prize Productions of the Pittsburgh International Eisteddfod, July 2, 3, 4, and 5, 1913.* Pittsburgh, c. 1916, 464pp.

Roberts, Ellis J., "100th Anniversary of Utica Eisteddfod to be Observed on April 20-21," *Y Drych,* CV, (Feb. 15, 1956), p. 9.

San Francisco International Exposition Eisteddfod, *The International Exposition Eisteddfod, San Francisco, July 27, 28, 29, and 30, 1915,* San Francisco, 1915.

Stark County, Ohio, Eisteddfod, *The Second Annual Musical Eisteddfod, Official Program, Canton, O., July 4, 1906,* Canton, 1906; 64 page pamphlet.

Trumbull County, Ohio, Eisteddfod Association, Inc., *Official Program. Warren-National Eisteddfod, Friday and Saturday, June 24th and 25th, 1938,* Warren, O., 1938; 32 page pamphlet.

Utica, New York, Eisteddfod, *Annual Programs,* 1858-1966.

Welsh Eisteddfod Society of Los Angeles, *Official Programs,* 1911-36.

Wilkes-Barre National Eisteddfod, 1928, *The National Eisteddfod of America of 1928, November 8-9-10, at 9th Regiment Armory,* Wilkes-Barre, Pa., Wilkes-Barre, 1928; 32 page pamphlet.

Wilson, Ben Hur, "The Iowa Eisteddfod," *Palimpsest,* XXII, (Dec., 1941), pp. 357-73.

The Gorsedd in America

(See Societies, National: American Gorsedd)

The Gymanfa Ganu

Jones, Wendell M., "The Gymanfa Ganu," unpublished M.A. thesis, Ohio State University, 1946.

National Gymanfa Ganu Association of the United States and Canada, Inc., *Annual Programs,* 1929-66.

———— *Constitution and By-Laws,* n.d.

———— *Favorite Welsh and English Hymns and Melodies,* Warren, Ohio, n.d. Pamphlet.

Welsh Churches of Lackawanna County, *Gymanfa Ganu, Scranton, Pa., Sunday, June 13, 1926, under the Auspices of the Welsh Churches of Lackawanna County, Pa.,* Scranton, 1926; 31 page pamphlet.

Welsh Congregational Churches of Wyoming Valley, *Gymanfa Ganu, Sacred Song Festival of the Welsh Congregational Churches, Wyoming Valley, Pa., Nov. 27, 1924 at Edwardsville,* Wilkes-Barre, Pa., 1924; 28 page pamphlet.

Societies, National

AMERICAN GORSEDD

American Gorsedd, "Minutes of the American Gorsedd," 1913-1941, *ms.* in Welsh National Library, Brigham Young University, Provo, Utah.

"The Gorsedd for America," *Cambrian,* XXXII, (Oct. 1, 1912), p. 7.

Richards, D. E., "The Gorsedd" in *The Royal Blue Book. Prize Productions of the Pittsburgh International Eisteddfod,* 1916, pp. 17-23.

Thomas, Ebenezer Pugh, *Glimpses of the Gorsedd, a Brief Sketch of the*

History and Progress of the American Gorsedd, Pittsburgh, 1919; 16 page pamphlet.

AMERICAN ORDER OF TRUE IVORITES

American Order of True Ivorites, *American Order of True Ivorites, 75 Years of Active Benevolent Work,* 1943; 18 page pamphlet.
———— *Annual Reports,* 1900-1966.
Morris, John Courier, *Ivorism,* Utica, N. Y., (Utica Printing Co.), 1914; 12 page pamphlet.
Thomas, John O., *Yr Urdd Iforaidd Americanaidd, Ei Hanes Am Haner Can Mlynedd,* Utica, N. Y., 1917. Pamphlet.

GYMANFA GANU ASSOCIATION

National Gymanfa Ganu Association of the United States and Canada, Inc., *Annual Programs,* 1929-1966.
———— *Constitution and By-Laws,* n.d. Pamphlet.
———— *Favorite Welsh and English Hymns and Melodies,* Warren, Ohio, n.d. Pamphlet.

WOMEN'S WELSH CLUBS OF AMERICA

Jones, Mrs. David I., *Women's Welsh Clubs of America,* Cleveland, 1951; 20 page pamphlet.

Societies, Local

BOSTON

Cymrodorion Welsh Associates, *Constitution and By-Laws of the Cymrodorion Welsh Associates of Boston and Vicinity, Organized March 31, 1892,* Boston, 1915, 19 page pamphlet.

CHICAGO

Cambrian Benevolent Society of Chicago, Inc., *Revised Constitution and By-Laws Adopted 1906;* 11 page pamphlet.
———— *Revised Constitution and By-Laws, Adopted 1942;* 11 page pamphlet.
———— *Souvenir Program, 1853-1952, Celebrating the One Hundredth Annual St. David's Day Banquet and Concert, Saturday, March 1, 1952;* 6 page pamphlet with history of the Society.
Pritchard, R. G., "A Short History of the Cambrian Benevolent Society of Chicago, Ill.," in latter's *Souvenir Program, 1853-1952 . . . ,* pp. 3-4.

CLEVELAND

Orpheus Male Chorus, *The Orpheus Male Chorus of Cleveland,* n.d.; 6 page pamphlet.

EDWARDSVILLE, PA.

"History of the Gwents," *Druid,* II, No. 1, (Jan. 2, 1908), p. 1 (Gwent Singing Society)

NEW YORK CITY

Miles, William, "St. David's Society of New York," *Cambrian,* XVII, (May, 1897), pp. 203-7; (June, 1897), pp. 307-12; (Aug., 1897), pp. 355-60; (Sept., 1897), pp. 405-8; (Oct., 1897), pp. 457-59; (Dec., 1897), pp. 555-58; XVIII, (Feb., 1898), pp. 72-75; (May, 1898), pp. 206-8; (June, 1898), pp. 261-64; XIX, (Apr., 1899), pp. 155-58; (May, 1899), pp. 204-7.

St. David's Society of the State of New York, *Annual Reports,* 1900-1966.

—————— *Constitution and By-Laws of the St. David's Society of the State of New York, Organized January 18, 1841,* New York, (Peck Press), 1930.

—————— *Saint David's Society of the State of New York, Our One Hundredth Year, 1835-1935,* New York, 1935; 4 page pamphlet.

Williams, J. Newton, "Charity and St. David's Society of New York City," *Cambrian,* VIII, (Nov., 1888), pp. 325-29.

PHILADELPHIA

Hartmann, Edward George, "The Welsh Society of Philadelphia," *Drych,* CII, (Feb. 15, 1953), pp. 12-13.

Jones, David, "History of the Welsh Society of Philadelphia, Pa.," *Cambrian,* X, (May, 1880), pp. 130-33.

Jones, Horatio Gates, "Historical Sketch," in Welsh Society of Philadelphia's *The Charter and By-Laws . . . ,* Philadelphia, c. 1947, pp. 3-15.

Lewis, Howard Benton, *The Welsh Society of Philadelphia, an Account of the Early Settlement of the Welsh in Philadelphia and its Vicinity, and the Formation and Organization of the Welsh Society,* Philadelphia, 1926; 13 page pamphlet.

Welsh Society of Philadelphia, *The Charter and By-Laws of the Welsh Society with an Historical Sketch by Horatio Gates Jones and a List of Officers and Members from the year 1798,* Philadelphia, c. 1947, 96pp.

POULTNEY, VT.

Poultney Welsh Male Chorus, *Poultney Welsh Male Chorus,* Poultney, Vt., 1948; 4 page pamphlet.

SAN FRANCISCO

Cambrian Mutual Aid Society of San Francisco, *Constitution, By-Laws and Rules of Order of the Cambrian Mutual Aid Society of San Fran-*

cisco, California, San Francisco, (Joseph Winterburn & Co.), 1879, 60 pp.

SCRANTON, PA.

Welsh Women's Society of Lackawanna County, *Constitution and By-Laws of the Welsh Women's Society of Lackawanna County,* n.d.

UTICA, N.Y.

Jones, Griffith, "The Utica Philharmonic Society," *Cambrian,* XXIX, (Jan. 1, 1909), pp. 6-7, 14.

Musicus, "The Hadyn Male Chorus, Utica, N.Y.," *Cambrian,* XXIX, (Jan. 15, 1909), pp. 7-8.

Roberts, John C., *Hanes Cymdeithas Elusengar Utica a'r Cylchoedd o'r Sefydliad yn 1849 hyd Jonawr 1, 1882,* Utica, 1882, 100pp. (History of the Welsh Benevolent Society in Welsh and English.)

WEST PITTSTON, PA.

Cambrian Club of West Pittston, *Charter and By-Laws of the Cambrian Club of West Pittston, Pennsylvania,* 1950; 19 page pamphlet.

WILKES-BARRE, PA.

"The Cambro-American Society of Wilkes-Barre," *Cambrian,* XI, (Mar., 1891), p. 93.

Junior Cambrian Club, *Constitution and By-Laws of the Junior Cambrian Club, Wilkes-Barre, Pa.,* 1950.

Senior Cambrian Club, *Constitution and By-Laws of the Senior Cambrian Club, Wilkes-Barre, Pa.,* 1947.

Industry

Berthoff, Rowland Tappan, *British Immigrants in Industrial America,* Cambridge, Mass., (Harvard University Press), 1953, *passim.* (Contains excellent account of the Welsh contribution to America's industrial development.)

Edwards, Ebenezer (William Penn, pseud.), *Facts About Welsh Factors, Welshmen as Factors in the Foundation and Development of the U.S. Republic,* Utica, N.Y., (T. J. Griffiths), 1899, *passim.*

Ellis, E. G., "The Slate Production of the United States for 1881," *Cambrian,* X, (Nov., 1890), pp. 336-37.

Jefferson Iron Company, *Celebration of the Ninety-Second Anniversary of the Founding of Jefferson Furnace Held on the Furnace Grounds Labor Day, Monday, September 2, 1946;* 28 page pamphlet.

Jones, J. Vincent, "Newburg—Flashbacks to Yesteryears," *Y Drych,* CV, (Oct. 15, 1956), Supplement B., (Welsh Iron Works).

Keeler, Vernon David, "Economic History of Jackson County Iron Industry," *Ohio Archaeological and Historical Quarterly*, XVII, (Apr., 1933), pp. 132-244.

Prosser, William, "The Influence of the Welsh in America," *Cambrian*, XXVIII, (Apr., 1908), pp. 151-61.

Roy, Andrew, *A History of the Coal Miners of the United States*," Columbus, Ohio, 1907.

Rutherford, Roy, *Romancing in Tin Plate*, Warren, Ohio, (Wean Engineering Co.), 1951, pp. 55-60, (Welsh in Tin-Plate industry).

POST-COLONIAL SETTLEMENTS

General

Thomas, Robert D., *Hanes Cymry America,* Utica, N. Y., (T. J. Griffiths), 1872, 527 pp. A thorough survey of the history and development of the various Welsh settlements prior to 1870.

Williams, Daniel Jenkins, *One Hundred Years of Welsh Calvinistic Methodism in America,* Philadelphia, (Westminster Press), 1937. Although dealing primarily with the Welsh Calvinistic Methodists, contains much data of importance on most of the Welsh settlements in America.

California

GENERAL

Hughes, David, *Welsh People of California, 1849-1906,* San Francisco, 1923, 120pp.

SAN FRANCISCO

Cambrian Mutual Aid Society of San Francisco, *Constitution, By-Laws and Rules of Order of the Cambrian Mutual Aid Society of San Francisco, California,* San Francisco, (Joseph Winterburn & Co.), 1879, 60pp.

Smith, Ronald C., *History of St. David's Presbyterian Church, San Francisco, California, One Hundredth Anniversary, 1853-1953,* San Francisco, 1953.

Colorado

GENERAL

Williams, Evan, *Traethawd ar Hanes Cymry Colorado, o'i Seifydliad Boreauaf hyd yn Awr. Testyn Eisteddod Gwyl Dewi Sant,* Denver, Colorado, 1889, 69pp.

Georgia

ROCK MART

Hughes, John, "The Welsh at Rock Mart, Georgia," *Cambrian,* VIII, (May, 1888), pp. 151-52.

Illinois

CHICAGO

Cambrian Benevolent Society of Chicago, Inc., *Revised Constitution and By-Laws, Adopted 1906,* Chicago, 1906; 11 page pamphlet.
────── *Revised Constitution and By-Laws, Adopted 1942,* Chicago, 1942; 11 page pamphlet.
────── *Souvenir Program, 1853-1952, Celebrating the One Hundredth Annual St. David's Day Banquet and Concert, Saturday, March 1, 1952,* Chicago, 1952; 6 page pamphlet with history of the society.
Fiftieth Anniversary, 1888-1938, Humboldt Park Welsh Union Church, Chicago, Chicago, 1938; 12 page pamphlet.
Griffith, William J., edit., *Our Hundredth Anniversary, 1848-1948, Hebron Welsh Presbyterian Church, Chicago, Illinois,* Chicago, 1948; 44 page pamphlet.
Jones, John C., edit., *A Brief History of Hebron Presbyterian Church, Chicago, Illinois, 1844-1909,* Chicago, 1909; 32 page pamphlet.
Monaghan, Jay, "The Welsh People in Chicago," *Illinois State Historical Society Journal,* XXXII, (Dec., 1939), pp. 498-516.
Pritchard, H. G., "A Short History of the Cambrian Benevolent Society of Chicago, Ill.," in latter's *Souvenir Program, 1853-1952 . . .* , pp. 3-4.

Iowa

COLUMBUS JUNCTION

Chord, R. N., edit., *Centennial Program of the Welsh Congregational Church, Columbus Junction, Iowa, 1846-1946,* Columbus Junction, Iowa, 1946; 8 page pamphlet with history of the church.

GOMER

Thomas, T. D., "Gomer, Iowa," *Cambrian,* II, (May-June, 1882), pp. 120-21.

IOWA CITY

Reichard, George, *The History of the Welsh Congregational Church Known as "Old Man's Creek," Iowa City, Iowa,* West Branch, Iowa, 1946; 16 page pamphlet.

LIME SPRINGS

Williams, Daniel, "The Welsh Settlement of Lime Springs, Iowa," in Thomas E. Hughes', *Hanes Cymru Minnesota, Foreston a Lime Springs, Iowa,* Mankato, Minn., 1895, pp. 138-58.

Kansas

EMPORIA

A Brief History of the Sardis Congregational Church, 1871-1949, Emporia, Kansas, Emporia, Kan., 1949; 47 page pamphlet.

Carpenter, Paul L., edit., *Memorial Pipe Organ Dedication, Second Presbyterian Church, Emporia, Kansas, December 12, 1948,* Emporia, Kan., 1948; 12 page pamphlet with history of the church.

Massachusetts

BOSTON

Constitution and By-Laws of the Cymrodorion Welsh Associates of Boston and Vicinity, Organized, March 31, 1892, Boston, 1915.

Michigan

DETROIT

Hughes, Daniel, edit., "The History of the Welsh Church of Detroit," *Directory and Telephone Register, 1945, Welsh Presbyterian Church, Detroit, Michigan,* Detroit, 1945, pp. 13, 15, and 17; 32 page pamphlet.

Minnesota

BLUE EARTH COUNTY AND VICINITY

Hughes, Owen S., edit., *Souvenir Program of the Dedicatory Service, First Presbyterian Church, Lake Crystal, Minnesota, December 19, 1937,* Lake Crystal, Minn., 1937; 16 page pamphlet with history of the church.

Hughes, Thomas E., "History of the Welsh in Minnesota," in his *Hanes Cymry Minnesota, Foreston a Lime Springs, Iowa,* pp. 1-110.

———— "History of the Welsh Settlements in the Minnesota Valley," *Cambrian,* IV, (Oct., 1884), pp. 277-80; (Nov., 1884), pp. 304-8; (Dec., 1884), pp. 333-38.

———— "Mankato, Minnesota," *Cambrian,* III, (Sept.-Oct., 1883), pp. 237-38.

Hughes, Thomas E., *et al., Hanes Cymry Minnesota, Foreston a Lime Springs, Iowa,* Mankato, Minn., 1895.

Williams, J. T., "The Welsh of Blue Earth and La Sueur Counties, Minn., Their Interest in Politics," in Hughes, Thomas E., *et al., Hanes Cymry Minnesota . . . ,* pp. 113-16.

LYON COUNTY

Thomas, Edward, "The Welsh Settlers of Lyon County, Minn.," in Hughes, Thomas E., *et al., Hanes Cymry Minnesota* . . . , pp. 121-37.

MINNEAPOLIS

Evans, Joshua T., "The Welsh of Minneapolis," in Hughes, Thomas E., *et al., Hanes Cymry Minnesota* . . . , pp. 112-16.

Missouri

MACON COUNTY

Edwards, Ohla Edsall, "The Welsh in Macon County, Missouri," *Y Drych*, CII, (Sept. 15, 1953), pp. 14-15.
White, Edgar, "A Noted Welsh Colony," *Cambrian*, XXXI, (Aug. 15, 1911), pp. 4-5.

Montana

BUTTE

Williams, E. R., "Butte, Its Welsh People and Welsh Church," *Cambrian*, XXIX, (June 1, 1909), pp. 13-14.

Nebraska

CARROLL

Bethany Presbyterian Church, Carroll, Nebraska, Carroll, Neb., 1949; 4 page pamphlet with history of the church.
Morris, Lot, edit., *History of Zion Congregational Church, Carroll, Nebraska,* Carroll, Neb., 1948; 2 page mimeo.

PRAIRIE UNION

"Welsh Pioneers of Nebraska," *Druid,* III, No. 6, (Nov. 18, 1909), p. 7.

New York

CATTARAUGUS COUNTY

Adams, William, *Historical Gazeteer and Biographical Memorial of Cattaraugus County,* Syracuse, N.Y., (Lyman, Horton & Co.), 1892, pp. 609-10, 676-80.

LEWIS COUNTY

Williams, Lewis, "Lewis County, New York," *Cambrian,* XXV, (Sept., 1905), pp. 272-78.

MADISON COUNTY

Jones, Benjamin L., "History of Peniel Church, Nelson, N.Y.," *Y Drych,* Nov. 6, 1902.

NEW YORK CITY

Blackwell, Henry, "The Welsh in America," *Cambrian Gleanings,* I, (June, 1914), pp. 84-96.

Hartmann, Edward George, "The History of the Welsh Congregational Church of the City of New York," unpublished mss., 1966.

Jones, William R., *Welsh Presbyterian Church, New York, N.Y., 1828-1953, One Hundred and Twenty-fifth Anniversary,* New York, 1953; 24 page pamphlet.

Myles, William, "St. David's Society of New York," *Cambrian,* XVII, (May, 1897), pp. 203-7; (June, 1897), pp. 307-12; (Aug., 1897), pp. 355-60; (Sept., 1897), pp. 405-8; (Oct., 1897), pp. 457-59; (Dec., 1897), pp. 555-58; XVIII, (Feb., 1898), pp. 72-75; (May, 1898), pp. 206-8; (June, 1898), pp. 261-64; XIX, (Apr., 1899), pp. 155-58; (May, 1899), pp. 204-7.

Savage, Theodore Fiske, *The Presbyterian Church in New York City,* New York, 1949, pp. 219-20.

St. David's Society of the State of New York, *Annual Reports,* 1900-1966.

———— *Constitution and By-Laws of the St. David's Society of the State of New York, Organized January 18, 1841,* New York, (Peck Press), 1930.

———— *Saint David's Society of the State of New York, Our One Hundredth Year, 1835-1935,* New York, 1935; 4 page pamphlet.

Williams, J. Newton, "Charity and St. David's Society of New York City," *Cambrian,* VIII, (Nov., 1888), pp. 325-29.

UTICA AND ONEIDA COUNTY

"The Bethesda Centennial," (Congregational Church, Utica), *Cambrian,* XXII, (Feb., 1902), pp. 372-78.

Costa, Richard H., "Utica Is Home of Only Welsh Language Paper," *Y Drych,* CV, (Dec. 15, 1956), pp. 9 and 15.

Davies, Edward, "Nineteenth Anniversary of the Welsh Congregational Church of Utica, N.Y.," *Cambrian,* XII, (Feb., 1892), pp. 44-47; (Mar., 1892), pp. 81-83; (Apr., 1892), pp. 99-102.

Davies, Llewellyn, "The First Welsh in America," *Cambrian,* XXXIII, (Dec. 1, 1912), pp. 10-11.

Ellis, Sam, "Background," (coming of the Welsh to Oneida County) in Llewellyn Jones' *Moriah Presbyterian Church,* 1830-1930, pp. 38-39.

Evans, Paul DeMund, "The Welsh in Oneida County," unpublished master's thesis, Cornell University, 1914.

Everett, Mary H., "An Historical Sketch of the First Welsh Congregational Church of Steuben, N.Y. (Capel Ucha)," *Cambrian*, XXXIII, (Sept. 15, 1913), pp. 14-15.

Griffiths, T. Solomon, *Hanes y Methodistiaid Calfinaidd yn Utica, N.Y.*, Utica, (T. J. Griffiths Press), 1896.

Jones, Emrys, "Some Aspects of Cultural Change in an American Welsh Community" (Utica), Honourable Society of the Cymmrodorion, *Transactions, 1952*, London, 1954, pp. 15-41.

Jones, Erasmus W., "The Early Welsh Settlers of Oneida County, N.Y.," *Cambrian*, IX, (Feb., 1899), pp. 38-40; (Mar., 1889), pp. 78-80; also printed in *Transactions of the Oneida Historical Society*, No. 5, (1889-92), pp. 60-67.

Jones, Griffith, "The Utica Philharmonic Society," *Cambrian*, XXIX, (Jan. 1, 1909), pp. 6-7, 14.

Jones, Llewelyn, edit., *Moriah Presbyterian Church, 1830-1930*, Utica, 1930, 72pp.

Jones, Pomeroy, *Annals and Recollections of Oneida County*, Rome, 1851, *passim*.

Lewis, Benjamin, "The Madog Tradition," *Cambrian*, XIV, (June, 1894), pp. 163-67; (July, 1894), pp. 193-97; (Aug., 1894), pp. 231-34.

"The M. C. Church of Utica, a Record of Sixty Years," *Cambrian*, X, (May, 1890), pp. 140-42.

"Memorial Services at Penycaerau Church," *Cambrian*, XXXIII, (Sept. 15, 1913), pp. 14-15.

Musicus, "The Hadyn Male Chorus, Utica, N.Y.," *Cambrian*, XXIX, (Jan. 15, 1909), pp. 7-8.

Owain, Iago ap, "The Early Welsh Settlers of Steuben and Vicinity," *Cambrian*, VII, (Nov., 1887), pp. 334-35.

Roberts, John C., *Hanes Cymdeithas Elusengar Utica a'r Cylchoedd o'r Sefydliad yn 1849 hyd Jonawr 1, 1882*, Utica, 1882, 100 pp. (A history of the Welsh Benevolent Society of Utica in Welsh and English.)

Thomas, Howard, "The Welsh Came to Remsen," *New York History*, XXX, (Jan., 1949), pp. 33-42.

"Utica. The Capital of the Valley of the Mohawk," *Cambrian*, XXV, (Sept., 1905), pp. 372-78.

Utica Eisteddfod, *Annual Programs*, 1838-1966.

Ohio

GENERAL

Chidlaw, Benjamin W., "The Early Welsh Settlers of Ohio," *Cambrian*, VIII, (May, 1888), pp. 132-35.

———— *Yr American, yr Hwn Sydd yn Cyanwys Nodau ar Daith o Ddyffryn Ohio i Gymru, Colweg ar Dalaeth Ohio; Hanes Sefydliadau Cymreig yn America; Cyfarwyddiadau i Ymofynwry Cyn y Daith ar a Daith, ac yn y Wlad . . . yr Ail Argraffiad*, Llanrwst, Wales, (J. Jones), 1840, 48pp.

———— "Translation of *Yr American*, a Welsh pamphlet," *Quarterly Publications of the Historical and Philosophical Society of Ohio*, VI, (Jan.-Mar., 1911), pp. 1-41.

Jones, William Harvey, "Our Welsh Forefathers," *Cambrian*, XXV, (Dec., 1905), pp. 514-18; XXVI, (Jan., 1906), pp. 6-10.

———— "Welsh Settlements in Ohio," *Ohio Archaeological and Historical Quarterly*, XVI, (Apr., 1907), pp. 194-227. Also, *Cambrian*, XXVII, (July, 1907), pp. 311-17; (Aug., 1907), pp. 344-50; (Sept., 1907), pp. 395-99.

BROOKFIELD

"The Welsh Settlements, Brookfield, Trumbull County, Ohio," *Cambrian*, XXIX, (Jan. 15, 1909), pp. 13-14; (Feb. 15, 1909), pp. 11-12.

CINCINNATI

Jones, Vincent, edit., *The Saga of the Welsh Congregational Church, Lawrence Street, Cincinnati, Ohio, 1840-1952*, Cincinnati, 1952; 35 page pamphlet.

CLEVELAND

Jones, J. Vincent, "Newburg—Flashbacks to Yesteryears," *Y Drych*, CV, (Oct. 15, 1956), Supplement B.

Jones, T. Henry, edit., *Centennial Congregational Church*, Cleveland, 1896; 25 page pamphlet.

COLUMBUS

"The New Welsh Presbyterian Church, Columbus, O.," *Cambrian*, VIII, (Sept., 1888), pp. 257-58.

Williams, Daniel Jenkins, *The Welsh of Columbus, Ohio; a Study in Adaptation and Assimilation*, Oshkosh, Wis., 1913, 144pp.

GALLIA AND JACKSON COUNTIES

Davis, Dan T., *A Condensed History of the Sunday School Conference of the Presbyterian Churches of Jackson and Gallia Counties for the Century Beginning in 1844*, Jackson, O., 1944; 18 page pamphlet.

Davis, Dan T., edit., *Early History of Horeb Church As Compiled and Edited for Its Centennial, August 12, 13, 14, 1938*, Jackson, Ohio, 1938; 42 page pamphlet.

Davis, David, "How Welsh People Settled Ohio," *Druid*, XV, No. 11, (June 15, 1923), p. 2; No. 12, (July 1, 1923), p. 5. (The Story of the Tyn Rhos Settlement.)

———— "Nebo Church," *Report of the Directors and Officers of the Tyn Rhos Cemetery Association*, pp. 54-55.

———— "Siloam Church," *Report of the Directors of the Tyn Rhos Cemetery Association*, pp. 55-57.

Evans, A. V., "A History of the First Welsh Settlers in Gallia and Jackson Counties, Ohio," *Cambrian*, VIII, (Nov.-Dec., 1888), pp. 322-25.

Evans, J. W., "The Founders of the Welsh Settlement in Gallia and Jackson Counties, Ohio," *Cambrian*, III, (Nov.-Dec., 1883), pp. 286-87.

Evans, R. H., "The Contribution of Gallia and Jackson Counties, Ohio, to the Gospel Ministry," *Cambrian*, IX, (Nov., 1889), pp. 326-28.

Evans, William R., *Hanes Sefydliadau Cymreig Siroedd Jackson a Gallia, O.*, Utica, N.Y., (Thomas J. Griffiths), 1896, 160pp.

Jefferson Iron Company, *Celebration of the Ninety-Second Anniversary of the Founding of Jefferson Furnace Held on the Furnace Grounds, Labor Day Monday, September 2, 1946*, Jackson, Ohio; 28 page pamphlet.

Jenkins, Estelle Jones, *Centennial, Oak Hill Presbyterian Church, 1850-1950*, 1950; 42 page pamphlet.

Jones, D. I., "Historical Address," *Report of the Directors and Officers of the Tyn Rhos Cemetery Association*, pp. 28-39.

Jones, Daniel M., "History of Jefferson Furnace" in *Celebration of the Ninety-Second Anniversary of the Founding of Jefferson Furnace*, pp. 8-13.

Jones, E. I., "The Early Churches of Jackson and Gallia Counties, Ohio," *Cambrian*, XXIII, (Feb., 1903), pp. 53-60.

Keeler, Vernon David, "Economic History of Jackson County Iron Industry," *Ohio Archaeological and Historical Quarterly*, XVII, (Apr., 1933), pp. 132-244.

Lloyd, David A., "The Moriah Calvinistic Methodist Church, Jackson County, O.," *Cambrian*, IV, (Apr., 1884), pp. 108-11.

Tyn Rhos Cemetery Association, *Report of the Directors and Officers of the Tyn Rhos Cemetery*, 1930, 66 page pamphlet.

Vigilax, "The Accidental Settlement of the Welsh in Gallia and Jackson Counties, O.," *Cambrian*, pp. 120-31.

GIRARD

"The First Baptist Church, Girard," *The Ohio Baptist Annual, 1904*, pp. 101-2.

GOMER

Bradbury, Clarence J., *Centennial Anniversary, 1839-1939, Gomer Congregational Church, Gomer, Ohio,* Gomer, Ohio, 1939; 28 page pamphlet.

Chidlaw, Benjamin W., "The First Funeral in Gomer, O., *Cambrian,* II, (Sept.-Oct., 1884), pp. 271-72.

Jones, Josiah, "Beginning and Growth of the Welsh Congregational Church, Gomer, O.," *Cambrian,* III, (July-Aug., 1883), pp. 183-85; (Sept.-Oct., 1883), pp. 234-36.

———— "The First Church in the Village of Gomer," *Cambrian,* XXVIII, (Oct., 1908), pp. 439-44.

"Reminiscences of the Welsh Settlement of Gomer and Vicinity, Allen County, O.," *Cambrian,* III, (Mar.-Apr., 1883), pp. 71-72.

LICKING COUNTY AND WELSH HILLS

Jones, Thomas H., "Pioneer Days at Elida, Ohio," *Cambrian,* XXXI, (Oct. 1, 1911), p. 10.

"Pioneer Days at Elida, O., *Cambrian,* XXX, (Sept. 1, 1910), pp. 5-6.

Price, Ira M., *Historical Sketch of One Hundred Years of the Welsh Hills Baptist Church,* Granville, Ohio, 1908; 7 page pamphlet.

Smucker, Isaac, *History of the Welsh Settlements in Licking County, Ohio; the Characteristics of our Welsh Pioneers—Their Church History, with Biographical Sketches of our Leading Welshmen, Read at the Licking County Pioneer Meeting, April 7, 1869,* Newark, Ohio, (Wilson & Clark), 1869; 22 page pamphlet.

———— "The Welsh Pioneers of Licking County, Ohio," *Cambrian,* III, (Jan.-Feb., 1883), p. 14.

Thomas, John, and Thomas, Anna, "An Old Letter—a Relic of the Olden Time," *Cambrian,* II, (Mar.-Apr., 1882), p. 79.

RADNOR

Chidlaw, Benjamin W., "Old Welsh Preachers in Radnor, O.," *Cambrian,* III, (Mar.-Apr., 1883), pp. 57-58.

Crocker, Bertram, edit., *Bethel Congregational Church, Radnor, Ohio, Services in Connection with Dedication of Renovated Edifice,* Radnor, Ohio, 1950; 8 page pamphlet with history of the church.

Harris, B., edit., *One Hundredth Anniversary of the Congregational Church, Radnor, Ohio,* Radnor, Ohio, 1920; 4 page pamphlet with history of the church.

SHANDON OR PADDY'S RUN

Chidlaw, Benjamin W., "Paddy's Run Congregational Church," *Cambrian,* II, (Sept.-Oct., 1882), pp. 265-68.

———— "The Welsh Pioneers in the Miami Valley," *Cambrian*, (Sept., 1884), pp. 248-51.

Gleason, Charles A., "History of Paddy's Run Congregational Church," *Papers of the Ohio Church History Society*, X, (1899), pp. 80-100.

Williams, Stephen Riggs, *The Saga of Paddy's Run*.

VAN WERT COUNTY

Johnson, Gerald B., edit., *Centenary History of the Salem Presbyterian Church, Venedocia, Ohio, September 3, 4, and 5, 1948,* Venedocia, Ohio, 1948; 58 page pamphlet.

Morgan, J. P., "Early History of the Welsh Settlement in Van Wert County, Ohio," *Cambrian*, II, (Jan.-Feb., 1882), pp. 1-5.

Roberts, Edward, edit., *Adroddiad Pwyllgor Adeiladu Capel Newydd, Salem, Venedocia, Swydd, Van Wert, Ohio, Agorwyd Hydref 15-16, 1898,* Van Wert, Ohio, 1898; 44 page pamphlet.

YOUNGSTOWN

Aubrey, Joseph, "A Brief Historical Sketch of the Walnut Street Baptist Church, Youngstown, Ohio," *Minutes of the Sixty-Fourth Anniversary of the Welsh Baptist Association of Ohio and Western Pennsylvania, 1903,* pp. 13-18.

Oregon

BEAVER CREEK

"Among the Raspberries and Strawberries, Festivities at Beaver Creek," *Yr Enfys*, No. 16, (Summer, 1952), p. 15.

Pennsylvania

GENERAL

Jones, David, *Memorial Volume of the Welsh Congregationalists of Pennsylvania, U.S.A.*, Utica, (Utica Printing Co.), 1934. (Although featuring the Welsh Congregationalists, contains a wealth of data on the Pennsylvania settlements generally.)

ALLEGHENY COUNTY

PITTSBURGH

Davies, D. D., "The Welsh Baptist Church of Pittsburgh, Pa.," *Cambrian*, II, (Nov.-Dec., 1882), pp. 268-71.

Edwards, T., "Reminiscences of the Welsh Congregational Church, Birmingham, Pa.," *Cambrian*, III, (May-June, 1883), pp. 131-32.

Gomerian, "Lingering Echoes of Carmel's Centenary," *Druid*, XXV, No. 1, (Jan. 1, 1933), p. 5; No. 2, (Jan. 15, 1933), p. 5; No. 3, Feb.

1, 1933), p. 5; No. 4, (Feb. 15, 1933), p. 5. (Story of the CM Church.)

Jones, E. Mona, "Brief Historical Sketch of the Chatham St. Welsh Baptist Church, Pittsburgh, Pa.," *Minutes of the 65th and 66th Anniversaries of the Welsh Baptist Association of Ohio and Western Pennsylvania,* 1904-05, pp. 14-18.

BRADFORD COUNTY

NEATH

Bradsby, H. C., *History of Bradford County, Pennsylvania,* Philadelphia, (S. B. Nelson & Co.), 1891, p. 481.

Craft, David, *History of Bradford County, Pennsylvania,* Philadelphia, (L. H. Everts Co.), 1878, pp. 143, 342-43.

CAMBRIA COUNTY

BEULAH AND EBENSBURG

Barnes, J. F., "History of the City of Beulah; Also of the Beulah Church," in John T. Griffith's *Rev. Morgan John Rhys, the Welsh Baptist Hero . . . of the 18th Century,* Lansford, Pa., 1899, pp. 59-73.

Brinkman, Charles W., "Once Thriving Village Lost Cambria County Seat to Ebensburg," *Pittsburgh Press,* Apr. 8, 1934.

Francis, Marian, *A History of the First Congregational Church of Ebensburg, Penna., 1797-1947, One Hundred and Fifty Years of Service,* Ebensburg, 1947, 47pp.

Griffith, John T., "A Few Facts Respecting the Founders of Ebensburg and Beulah, Pa.," *Cambrian,* XXII, (May, 1902), pp. 217-18.

———— "The Last Enterprise of Morgan John Rhees," *Cambrian,* XXI, (Dec., 1901), pp. 545-48.

———— *Rev. Morgan John Rhys: the Welsh Baptist Hero of Civil and Religious Liberty of the Eighteenth Century,* Carmarthen, Wales, (W. M. Evans & Son), 1910.

———— *Rev. Morgan John Rhys, the Welsh Baptist Hero of Civil and Religious Liberty of the 18th Century,* Lansford, Pa., (Leader Job Press), 1899.

Jones, William Harvey, "Welsh Settlements in Ohio," *Cambrian,* XXVII, (July, 1907), pp. 196-98.

"Rev. Rees Lloyd, Early Minister at Ebensburg," *Cambrian,* IX, (Aug., 1889), pp. 228-29.

JOHNSTOWN

Jones, Evan W., "Our Welsh Churches," *Johnstown Democrat,* (in eight parts), Apr. 3, 10, 17, 24, May 1, 8, 15, 23, 1897.

We Return Thanks, a Memorial Booklet Dedicated to Our Parishioners and Friends, the Memorial Baptist Church, Johnstown, Pennsylvania, Johnstown, 1951.

Whalen, Henry J., edit., *Dedication, Memorial Baptist Church, Johnstown, Pennsylvania, May 8-15, 1927,* Johnstown, Pa., 1927; 12 page pamphlet.

CARBON COUNTY

Brenckman, Fred, *History of Carbon County, Pennsylvania,* Harrisburg, Pa., (James J. Nungesser), 1913.

———— *Audenried,* pp. 178-79.

———— *Beaver Meadows,* pp. 177-78.

———— *Coleraine,* p. 180.

———— *Lansford,* pp. 211-12; 217-18.

King, John H., "75th Anniversary Service at Audenried Congregational Church," *Hazleton Standard Sentinel,* Nov. 28, 1941.

Griffith, John T., "A Brief Sketch of the History of Summit Hill, Pa. Baptist Church and its Branches," *Cambrian,* XXIII, (Aug., 1903), pp. 323-26; (Sept., 1903), pp. 361-64.

———— "Historical Reminiscences of the Lansford Baptist Church," *Cambrian,* XXV, (May, 1905), pp. 191-94.

DAUPHIN COUNTY - WICONISCO

Gatskill, George Evan, *1870-1920, Golden Jubilee, First Baptist Church, February 1st-4th, 1920;* 8 page pamphlet.

SCRANTON AND LACKAWANNA COUNTY
GENERAL

Murphy, Thomas, *Jubilee History, Commemorative of the Fiftieth Anniversary of the Creation of Lackawanna County, Pennsylvania,* 2 vols., Topeka-Indianapolis, (Historical Pub. Co.), 1928. (Volume 1, *passim,* has much on the various Welsh settlements.)

CARBONDALE

"Early Settlers of Carbondale," *Druid,* II, No. 50, (Dec. 17, 1908), p. 12.

OLYPHANT

Jones, Elias, edit., *Eighty-Fifth Anniversary, Olyphant Welsh Baptist Church, 1839-1944,* Olyphant, Pa., 1944; 8 page pamphlet.

SCRANTON

"The First Welsh Baptist Church of Scranton, Pa.," *Cambrian,* X, (Sept., 1890), pp. 257-60.

Golden Anniversary of Puritan Congregational Church, Scranton, Pennsylvania, 1889-1939, Scranton, 1939; 12 page pamphlet.

Golden Anniversary, Plymouth Congregational Church, Scranton, Pennsylvania, April 3-4-5-6, 1932, Scranton, 1932; 24 page pamphlet.

Golden Anniversary of Tabernacle Congregational Church, Scranton, Pennsylvania, 1886-1936, Scranton, 1936; 16 page pamphlet.

Griffith, John T., *History of the First Baptist Church of Wilkes-Barre and the First Welsh Baptist Church of Scranton, Penna.,* Wilkes-Barre, Pa., 1905; 52 page pamphlet.

Jones, David E., "Hyde Park (Scranton) as Welsh 'Athens' Feted Musicana's Leaders," *Scrantonian,* July 24, 1938.

———— "Music in Lackawanna County," in Thomas Murphy's *Jubilee History . . . Lackawanna County,*" I, pp. 338-47.

———— "Music Just Natural When Cymry Meet," *Scrantonian,* July 24, 1938.

Jones, Davy Edgar, edit., *One-Half Century of Work, History of the Providence Welsh Congregational Church of Scranton, Pennsylvania,* New York, 1903; 56 page pamphlet.

One Hundredth Anniversary of the Founding of the First Welsh Baptist Church on October 1, 1850, Scranton, 1950; 20 page pamphlet.

Seventieth Anniversary, Ebenezer Welsh Presbyterian Church, Scranton, Penna., 1864-1934, Scranton, 1934; 12 page pamphlet.

Seventy-Fifth Anniversary of the First Welsh Baptist Church, Scranton, Pa., 1850-1925, Scranton, 1925; 20 page pamphlet.

Seventy-Fifth Anniversary, First Welsh Congregational Church, Scranton, Pennsylvania, Scranton, 1939; 12 page pamphlet.

Welsh Women's Society of Lackawanna County, *Constitution and By-Laws of the Welsh Women's Society of Lackawanna County,* n.d. Pamphlet.

SPRINGBROOK

Pearce, Stewart, *Annals of Luzerne County,* Philadelphia, 1860, p. 223.

LEHIGH COUNTY - SLATINGTON

Kell, W. B., edit., *First Baptist Church, Slatington, Penna., Twenty-Fifth Anniversary, Present Church Building Dedicated June 17th, 1900, Souvenir,* Slatington, Pa., 1925; 16 page pamphlet.

Lawrence, Thomas G., edit., *Historical Sketch and Reminder of the First Baptist Church, Slatington, Pa.,* Slatington, 1932; 12 page pamphlet.

Roberts, Charles Rhodes et al., *History of Lehigh County, Penna.,* Allenton, Pa., (Lehigh Valley Publishing Co.), 1914, Vol. I, pp. 593-94, 615, 692-93.

LUZERNE COUNTY

WILKES-BARRE AND WYOMING VALLEY

GENERAL

Griffith, John Thomas, "The Baptists of Wyoming Valley," *Cambrian,* XXVI, (Jan., 1906), pp. 20-22.
―――― "The Early Baptists of the Wyoming Valley and Edwardsville," *Cambrian,* XXIV, (Mar., 1904), pp. 103-06; (Apr., 1904), pp. 147-49.
Monroe, W. S., "Welsh Poets and Poetry of the Wyoming Valley, Pa.," *Cambrian,* VIII, (July, 1888), pp. 201-04.
"Wyoming Valley Keeps Welsh Traditions Alive," *Y Drych,* CVI, (May 15, 1957), p. 9.

ASHLEY

"Ashley Welsh Church to Disband," *Wilkes-Barre Record,* Dec. 5, 1946. (Welsh Presbyterian)
"Welsh Parish is Dissolved," *Wilkes-Barre Record,* Dec. 16, 1948. (Welsh Presbyterian)

EDWARDSVILLE

"Church Plans Anniversary; Welsh Baptist Congregation Founded 75 Years Ago," *Wilkes-Barre Record,* Oct. 30, 1948.
"Baptists Will Mark Jubilee, Special Program Arranged for Immanuel Church," *Wilkes-Barre Record,* Sept. 26, 1936.
Edwards, Thomas Cynonfardd, *The Jubilee Memorial, 1868-1918, Welsh Congregational Church, Edwardsville,* Wilkes-Barre, Pa., (Caxton Press), 1918.
Edwards Memorial Congregational Church, *Cynonfardd Eisteddfod, Annual Programs,* 1920-67.
"Edwardsville Church to Be 60 October 13; Bethesda Congregational withdrew in 1885 from Parent Body because of Use of Welsh," *Wilkes-Barre Record,* Oct. 2, 1946.
"History of the Gwents," *Druid,* II, No. 1, (Jan. 2, 1908), p. 1 (Gwent Singing Society of Edwardsville).
Hughes, Thomas W., edit., *75th Anniversary Celebration of the Welsh Baptist Church, Edwardsville, Penna., Sunday, October 31, 1948;* 6 page mimeograph.
Lewis, Victor E., *Anniversary Poem, November 28, 1948, the Edwards Memorial Congregational Church on the Occasion of Its 80th Birthday Anniversary,* Wilkes-Barre, Pa., 1948.
―――― *A Brief Account of the Outstanding Events of the Welsh Congre-*

gational Church, Edwardsville, Pa., for the Past Ten Years, 1918-1928, Wilkes-Barre, Pa., (Caxton Press), 1928.

Wilson, Mrs. Thomas P., "History of the First Welsh Baptist Church, Edwardsville, Penna. from 1872 to 1948;" 12 page typed mss.

HANOVER TOWNSHIP

"New Church is Dedicated," *Wilkes-Barre* Record, June 19, 1937. (Lynwood Congregational)

NANTICOKE

"Bethel Church Opens Jubilee," *Wilkes-Barre Record,* June 31, 1937. (Bethel Congregational)

"Historical Sketch of the Welsh Baptist Church, Nanticoke, Pa.," *Sixty-First Annual Session of the Welsh Baptist Association of Northeastern Pennsylvania,* 1916, pp. 18-19.

Jones, David J., edit., *75th Anniversary, 1870-1945, Nebo Baptist Church, Nanticoke, Penna.,* Nanticoke, Pa., 1945; 8 page pamphlet.

PITTSTON

"Old Landmark Being Razed," *Wilkes-Barre Record,* Aug. 13, 1946. (Welsh Congregational Church)

PLYMOUTH

Fiftieth Anniversary of the Pilgrim Congregational Church, Plymouth, Pennsylvania, April 26, 27, 28 and 29, 1936, Wilkes-Barre, Pa., 1936; 20 page pamphlet.

First Welsh Congregational Church, Plymouth, Pa., Jubilee Services, September 25th to 29th, Wilkes-Barre, Pa., 1924; 21 page pamphlet.

First Welsh Congregational Church, Plymouth, Pennsylvania, *100th Anniversary, 1864-1964,* Plymouth, Pa., 1964; 16 page pamphlet.

Jones, Mona, edit., *Souvenir, Fiftieth Anniversary, First Welsh Baptist Church,* Plymouth, Pa., 1918; 12 page pamphlet.

Pilgrim Congregational Church, *Service of Rededication, October 20, 1940,* Plymouth, Pa., 1940; 8 page pamphlet.

Straw, W. Russell, edit., *Dedication of Organ, Welsh Presbyterian Church, Plymouth, Pennsylvania, October 12th and 13th, 1946,* Plymouth, Pa., 1946, 8 page pamphlet.

Williams, Henry G., "The Welsh Calvinistic Methodist Church of Plymouth, Pa.," *Cambrian,* IV, (June-July, 1884), pp. 167-70.

Williams, W. Glyn, "A Brief Historical Sketch of Welsh Preaching and Singing in Plymouth," *100th Anniversary Celebration, 1853-1953,* Plymouth, Pa., (Gymanfa Ganu Assn.), 1953; 28 page pamphlet.

Williams, W. Glyn, edit., *100th Anniversary Celebration, 1853-1953,* Plymouth, Pa., (Gymanfa Ganu Assn.), 1953; 28 page pamphlet.

SUGAR NOTCH

"Sugar Notch Welsh Presbyterian Church to Mark 50th Anniversary," *Wilkes-Barre Record,* March 19-20, 1937.

WARRIOR RUN

Robinson, Norman A., edit., *Seventy-Fifth Anniversary of the Welsh Presbyterian Church, Warrior Run, Penna., November 27, 1949,* Wilkes-Barre, Pa., 1949; 20 page pamphlet.

WEST PITTSTON

Cambrian Club of West Pittston, *Charter and By-Laws of the Cambrian Club of West Pittston, Pennsylvania,* 1950; 19 page pamphlet.

WILKES-BARRE

"Bethel Baptist Church to Observe Jubilee," *Wilkes-Barre Record,* Nov. 9, 1934.
"The Cambro-American Society of Wilkes-Barre," *Cambrian,* XI, (Mar., 1891), p. 93.
Davies, Hugh, "The Second Welsh Presbyterian Church of Wilkes-Barre," *Cambrian,* XXIX, (Aug. 15, 1909), pp. 11-12.
Davies, R. R., edit., *First Welsh Presbyterian Church, Wilkes-Barre, Pa., 1864-1914,* Wilkes-Barre, Pa., 1914; 54 page pamphlet.
Edmunds, Willard F., edit., *The Parsons Welsh Baptist Church, 85th Anniversary,* Wilkes-Barre, Pa., 1954; 8 page pamphlet.
Golden Jubilee, Second Presbyterian Church (Welsh), Wilkes-Barre, Pa., 1874-1924, Wilkes-Barre, Pa., 1924; 16 page pamphlet.
Griffith, John T., "Brief Biographical Sketches of the Pastors of the First Welsh Baptist Church of Wilkes-Barre, Pa.," *Cambrian,* XXVII, (Jan., 1908), pp. 67-69.
——— *History of the First Baptist Church of Wilkes-Barre and the First Welsh Baptist Church of Scranton, Penna.,* Wilkes-Barre, Pa., 1905; 52 page pamphlet.
Junior Cambrian Club of Wilkes-Barre, *Constitution and By-Laws of the Junior Cambrian Club, Wilkes-Barre, Pa.,* Wilkes-Barre, Pa., 1950. Pamphlet.
Lewis, James V., edit., *Directory, Bethel Parrish Street Baptist Church, Wilkes-Barre, Pa.,* Wilkes-Barre, Pa., 1919; 32 page pamphlet with history of the church.
Miner Congregational Church, *50th Anniversary of the Edifice and the Rededication Services, November 7th, 8th, 11th, 1945.* Mimeographed pamphlet.
One Hundred Years, 1864-1964, A History of the First Welsh Presby-

terian Church, Wilkes-Barre, Pennsylvania, West Pittston, Pa., (La Barre Printing Co.), 1964.

Our Fiftieth Anniversary, the Puritan Congregational Church, Wilkes-Barre, Pa., 1885-1935, Wilkes-Barre, Pa., 1935; 8 page pamphlet.

"Parsons Church 75 Years Old," *Wilkes-Barre Record,* Sept. 27, 1944. (Parsons Welsh Baptist)

Puritan Congregational Church, Wilkes-Barre, Pennsylvania, Seventy-Fifth Anniversary, October 22nd and 23rd, 1960, Wilkes-Barre, Pa., 1960; 12 page pamphlet.

Puritan Congregational Church, Wilkes-Barre, Pennsylvania, Re-dedication Services, October 20th and 21st, 1957, Wilkes-Barre, Pa., 1957; 24 page pamphlet.

Roberts, R. T., "First Welsh Presbyterian Church, Wilkes-Barre," *Cambrian,* XXVIII, (Dec., 1908), pp. 524-26.

"St. Andrews' 45 Years Old," *Wilkes-Barre Record,* March 18, 1933. (1st Welsh Methodist Episcopal Church of Wilkes-Barre.)

Second Welsh Presbyterian Church, Wilkes-Barre, Penna., Diamond Jubilee, October 14, 15, 16, 1949, Wilkes-Barre, Pa., 1949; 32 page pamphlet.

Senior Cambrian Club of Wilkes-Barre, *Constitution and By-Laws of the Senior Cambrian Club, Wilkes-Barre, Pa.,* Wilkes-Barre, Pa., 1947. Pamphlet.

Williams, W. Owen, edit., *Seventy-Fifth Anniversary of the First Welsh Presbyterian Church, Wilkes-Barre, Pennsylvania, September 14th to 17th, 1939,* Wilkes-Barre, Pa., 1939; 8 page pamphlet.

NORTHAMPTON COUNTY

Heller, William J., *History of Northampton County and the Great Valley of the Lehigh,* Boston, (Am. History Society), 1920, Vol. II.
———— *Bangor,* pp. 519-21.
———— *Pen Argyl,* pp. 522-23.
———— *Wind Gap,* pp. 524-25.

Bangor Welsh Day Association, *Sixth Annual Welsh Day Program, Lutheran Grove, Bangor, Pa., September 5, 1936,* Bangor, Pa., 1936; 42 page pamphlet containing history of the settlement.

Williams, William, edit., *Welsh Presbyterian Church, Bangor, Pa., Fiftieth Anniversary Souvenir, 1873-1923,* Bangor, Pa., 1923; 31 page pamphlet.

NORTHUMBERLAND COUNTY—SHAMOKIN

Seventy-Fifth Anniversary of Mt. Zion Congregational Church of Shamokin, Pa., 1860-1935, Shamokin, Pa., 1935; 10 page pamphlet.

PHILADELPHIA

Girard Avenue-Welsh Presbyterian Church, Eisteddfod, *Annual Programs,* 1910-1966.

Hartmann, Edward George, "The Welsh Society of Philadelphia," *Y Drych,* CII, (Feb. 15, 1953), pp. 12-13.

Jones, David, "History of the Welsh Society of Philadelphia, Pa.," *Cambrian,* X, (May, 1880), pp. 130-33.

Jones, Horatio Gates, "Historical Sketch," in *The Charter and By-Laws of the Welsh Society,* Philadelphia, 1947, pp. 3-15.

Lewis, Howard Benton, *The Welsh Society of Philadelphia, an Account of the Early Settlement of the Welsh in Philadelphia and Its Vicinity, and the Formation and Organization of the Welsh Society,* Philadelphia, 1926; 13 page pamphlet.

Welsh Society of Philadelphia, *The Charter and By-Laws of the Welsh Society with an Historical Sketch by Horatio Gates Jones and a List of Officers and Members from the Year 1798,* Philadelphia, c. 1947; 96 page pamphlet.

SCHUYLKILL COUNTY

Calvary Baptist Church, Shenandoah, Pa., Service of Dedication, December 4—December 9, 1927; 4 page pamphlet with history of the church.

Schalck, Adolf W., and Henning, D. C., edits., *History of Schuylkill County, Pennsylvania,* (State Historical Association), Vol. I.

———— *Ashland,* p. 200.

———— *Mahanoy City,* pp. 233-34.

———— *Minersville,* pp. 190-92.

———— *Pottsville,* p. 281.

———— *Shenandoah,* pp. 242-43.

Zimmerman, Theron A., edit., *One Hundredth Anniversary of Our House of Worship, One Hundred Fifteenth Anniversary of Our Church, 1832-1847-1947, the First Congregational Church, Minersville, Pennsylvania,* Minersville, Pa., 1947; 12 page pamphlet.

SUSQUEHANNA COUNTY—WELSH HILL, CLIFFORD TOWNSHIP (often referred to as Dundaff)

Blackman, Emily C., *History of Susquehanna County, Pennsylvania,* Philadelphia, (Claxton, Remsen, & Haffelfinger), 1873, pp. 397-99.

Stocker, Rhamanthus M., *Centennial History of Susquehanna County, Pennsylvania,* 1887, pp. 806-7.

"Welsh Hill Church Marks 122nd Jubilee," *Y Drych,* CV, (July 15, 1956), p. 18.

Williams, Garford F., "The Welsh Hill Church," *Looking Back Souvenir Book of the Susquehanna County Sesquicentennial Celebration, 1810-1860, passim.*

YORK COUNTY—DELTA (once known as Bangor, West)

Evans, W. Fleming, "Delta, Pa. Observes Its Centennial with Week's Celebration, June 27-July 4," *Y Drych*, CII, (Aug. 15, 1953), p. 7.

Hartmann, Edward G., "Background Notes on the Delta, Pa. Welsh Community," *Y Drych*, CII, (Aug. 15, 1953), p. 7.

Prowell, George R., *History of York County, Pennsylvania*, Chicago, (J. H. Beers & Co.), 1907, Vol. I, pp. 1050-51.

South Dakota

POWELL

"History of the Powell Presbyterian Church; 70th Anniversary of Christian Witness in Powell Township, Edmunds County, South Dakota," mss. 1953.

Llewellyn, John T., "The Welsh Colony of Powell, Edmunds County, South Dakota," *Cambrian*, XIV, (Apr., 1894), pp. 103-6.

Tennessee

Jones, D. I., "A Visit to Soddy and Chattanooga, Tennessee," *Cambrian*, II, (Jan.-Feb., 1882), pp. 5-10.

Shepperson, Wilbur S., *Samuel Roberts: A Welsh Colonizer in Civil War Tennessee*, Knoxville, (University of Tenn. Press), 1961.

Utah

THE WELSH MORMONS

Bennett, Archibald F., "The Record Harvest in Wales," *Improvement Era*, LI (July, 1948), pp. 432-33, 467-69.

Carter, Kate B., *The Welsh in Utah*, Salt Lake City, Utah (Daughters of Utah Pioneers, Central Company, Lesson for 1949), 1949.

Evans, Richard L., *A Century of "Mormonism" in Great Britain*, Salt Lake City, (Deseret News Press), 1937, pp. 184-96.

Jensen, Andrew, edit., *Encyclopedic History of the Church of Jesus Christ of Latter Day Saints*, Salt Lake City, (Deseret News Press), 1941, pp. 463, 751, 918, 936-37.

Webb, Ina T., "Congregational Singing in the Church of Jesus Christ of Latter Day Saints," unpublished M.A. thesis, Brigham Young University, 1931, pp. 75-79.

"The Welsh Mission," *mss.* in Historical Library of the Church of Latter Day Saints, Salt Lake City, Utah.

"Welsh Mormons in Utah," *Herald of Wales,* Aug. 27, 1949.

Vermont

RUTLAND COUNTY

Gardner, Clara M., "Upon This Sod," *Vermont Quarterly,* XV, (July, 1947), pp. 188-90. (Dissolution of the Fair Haven Welsh Congregational Church.)

Poultney Welsh Male Chorus, *Poultney Welsh Male Chorus,* Poultney, Vt., 1948; 4 page pamphlet.

Smith, H. P., and Rann, W. S., *History of Rutland County, Vermont,* Syracuse, N. Y., 1886, p. 602.

"Wales in Vermont," *Coronet,* XXVI, (Oct., 1949), p. 22.

"The Welsh in Vermont," *Cambrian,* II, (Mar.-Apr., 1882), pp. 76-78.

Wisconsin

COLUMBIA COUNTY
CAMBRIA

Evans, Richard W., edit., *Our Ninety-fifth Anniversary, 1853-1948, Olivet Welsh Presbyterian Church, Cambria, Wisconsin,* 1948; 20 page pamphlet.

Rowlands, M. J., "Welsh Prairie, Cambria, Wisconsin," *Cambrian,* XXXII, (Aug. 15, 1912), pp. 11-12.

COLUMBUS

Jones, John R., "The Bethel Welsh C. M. Church near Columbus, Wis.," *Cambrian,* XXVIII, (Nov., 1908), pp. 477-82.

——— *Hanes yr Eglwysi Cymreig yn Columbus, Wisconsin,* Utica, (T. J. Griffiths), 1898, 204 pp.

WALES

Roberts, E. S., edit., *Centennial Souvenir Program, Y Capel Log, the Present Jerusalem Church Society, Wales, Wisconsin, June 1842-June 1942,* Wales, Wis., 1942; 20 page pamphlet.

IOWA COUNTY
BARNEVELD

Vanderwerp, Donald W., *Plymouth's Centennial, 1847-1947, Plymouth Congregational Church, Barneveld, Wisconsin,* Barneveld, Wis., 1947; 20 page pamphlet.

PICATONICA

Peniel Church Centennial, 1847-1947; 9 page pamphlet.

JEFFERSON COUNTY—IXONIA

Jones, Chester Lloyd, *Youngest Son,* Madison, Wis., (Democrat Printing Co.), 1938, 111 pp.

RACINE COUNTY—RACINE

Davies, John, edit., *The Welsh Calvinistic Methodist Church of Racine, Wisconsin, a Brief History and an Account of the Building of the New Tabernacle,* Racine, Wis., 1908; 47 page pamphlet.

Pugh, Mary E., and Roberts, John D., *More Than a Century with the Welsh in Racine, 1840-1948,* Racine, Wis., 1948; 8 page pamphlet.

"Racine Presbyterian Church Observes Its 90th Birthday," *Druid,* XXV, No. 23, (Dec. 1, 1933), p. 2.

Roberts, D. Kendrick, edit., *Looking Backward, Historical Sketches Presented at the Celebration of the Ninetieth Anniversary of the Founding in October, 1843, of the Welsh Calvinistic Methodist (Now Known as the Tabernacle Presbyterian) Church of Racine, Wisconsin, November, 19, 1933,* Racine, Wis., 1933; 13 page mimeographed pamphlet.

Williams, Mrs. T. L., "The First Welsh Settlers of Racine, Wis.," *Cambrian,* XI, (Oct., 1891), pp. 294-95.

Wilson, D. D., edit., *Plymouth Congregational Church, One Hundredth Anniversary,* Racine, Wis., 1948; 48 page pamphlet.

WAUKESHA COUNTY

Price, Sadie Rowlands, "Welsh of Waukesha County," *Wisconsin Magazine of History,* XXVI, (Mar., 1943), pp. 323-32.

Rice, George, "Welsh Pioneers of Waukesha County," *Cambrian,* XXXII, (Sept. 1, 1912), pp. 11-12.

Williams, Daniel Jenkins, *The Welsh Community of Waukesha County,* Columbus, Ohio, 1926, 334pp.

WINNEBAGO COUNTY

Davies, David, edit., *Oshkosh, Wisconsin, Welsh Centennial, 1847-1947,* Oshkosh, Wis., 1947.

Davies, Howell D., *History of the Oshkosh Welsh Settlement,* Amarillo, 1947.

GENERAL INDEX

INDEX OF DISTINGUISHED WELSH AMERICANS